Legal Framework of Digital Economy and Digital Trade Under the Belt and Road Initiative

Jamil Afzal · Yongmei Chen

Legal Framework of Digital Economy and Digital Trade Under the Belt and Road Initiative

A Path to Digital Silk Road

Springer

Jamil Afzal
School of International Law
Southwest University of Political Science
and Law
Chongqing, Chong Qing, China

Yongmei Chen
School of International Law
Southwest University of Political Science
and Law
Chongqing, Chong Qing, China

ISBN 978-981-92-4443-0 ISBN 978-981-92-4444-7 (eBook)
https://doi.org/10.1007/978-981-92-4444-7

This Springer imprint is published by the registered company Springer Nature Singapore Pte Ltd.
The registered company address is: 152 Beach Road, #21-01/04 Gateway East, Singapore 189721, Singapore

We owe a debt of gratitude to Southwest University of Political Science and China-ASEAN Legal Research Center, Chongqing, China. Our most sincere thanks go to Lydia Wang and her team, including Naomi Portnoy, Rathika Ramkumar, and the dedicated editorial staff at Springer.

Foreword by Yasir Munir

This book is a significant scholarly achievement. It offers a comprehensive, well-structured, and thought-provoking analysis of the digital transformation of global economic and legal systems under the BRI framework. It will undoubtedly serve as an essential reference for academics, policymakers, and practitioners interested in digital trade, international law, and global governance. The authors are to be commended for producing a work that is both intellectually rigorous and practically relevant. Drawing on a carefully structured and logically sequenced set of chapters, the book offers readers a holistic exploration of the digital economy as it is being shaped by China's initiatives and their global implications. One of the most commendable aspects of this book is its strong legal focus. The authors skillfully navigate complex areas such as data sovereignty, cybersecurity, cross-border data flows, and regulatory harmonization. These discussions are not only academically rigorous but also highly relevant for policymakers, practitioners, and scholars seeking to understand the emerging legal order of the digital age. The chapters devoted to fintech innovation, digital financial inclusion, and green digital economy further broaden the scope of the work. They underscore the multidimensional nature of the Digital Silk Road, demonstrating how digital transformation intersects with sustainability, financial access, and inclusive growth. This interdisciplinary approach enhances the book's value, making it relevant to a wide audience beyond legal scholars. Moreover, the book critically examines issues such as technological dependence, digital sovereignty, and the potential export of governance models, encouraging readers to engage with these questions in a nuanced and balanced manner.

Dr. Yasir Munir
Head of Department
MY School of Law
MY University
Islamabad, Pakistan

Foreword by Tanzeela Urooj

The emergence of the Digital Silk Road as a central pillar of the Belt and Road Initiative marks a profound shift in the dynamics of global connectivity and cooperation. This book provides an in-depth and critical examination of that transformation, offering readers a nuanced understanding of the legal, economic, and geopolitical dimensions of digital integration across regions. What distinguishes this work is its clarity of vision and coherence of structure. Each chapter builds upon the previous one, guiding the reader from foundational concepts to complex analytical discussions. The early chapters establish a strong conceptual framework, explaining the evolution and scope of the Digital Silk Road, while subsequent chapters delve into its practical implications, including infrastructure development, trade facilitation, and technological innovation. The authors demonstrate a deep understanding of the legal challenges associated with digitalization. Issues such as jurisdictional conflicts, regulatory divergence, and the absence of comprehensive global frameworks are addressed with precision and insight. The discussion of emerging mechanisms, including international ODR platforms and specialized digital courts, highlights the innovative approaches being developed to address the complexities of digital trade and transactions. These insights are invaluable for legal practitioners and policymakers seeking effective solutions in an increasingly digitalized world.

Dr. Tanzeela Urooj
Faculty of Arts and Education Research
Deakin University
Melbourne, VIC, Australia

Preface

The rapid expansion of the digital economy has transformed the foundations of global trade, governance, communication, finance, and development. In the twenty-first century, digital connectivity is no longer a supplementary feature of economic progress; rather, it has become one of the principal drivers of international cooperation and strategic competition. Against this evolving global landscape, China's Digital Silk Road (DSR), introduced as a component of the Belt and Road Initiative (BRI), has emerged as one of the most influential frameworks for promoting digital infrastructure, technological integration, and cross-border digital governance. The DSR has reshaped discussions surrounding digital trade, cybersecurity, data governance, fintech innovation, artificial intelligence, and international legal harmonization.

This book begins by exploring the evolution of China's digital economy and the regulatory foundations of the Digital Silk Road. Early chapters examine the conceptual foundations of digitalization, the strategic objectives of the DSR, and its relationship with the broader Belt and Road Initiative. Particular attention is given to the legal and institutional mechanisms through which China promotes digital cooperation, infrastructure connectivity, and digital governance frameworks. Subsequent chapters analyze the economic and legal implications of digital trade, ICT connectivity, payment systems, and cross-border digital commerce. The discussion highlights the importance of international legal instruments, including WTO frameworks, UNCITRAL model laws, and emerging international standards governing electronic commerce and digital transactions. The book also addresses the increasing significance of legal harmonization and regulatory cooperation in facilitating a secure and efficient digital economy. Recognizing that digital transformation creates substantial regulatory and geopolitical challenges, several chapters critically assess issues related to cybersecurity, data localization, intellectual property protection, jurisdictional conflicts, sovereign risk, technological rivalry, and regulatory fragmentation. The volume evaluates how geopolitical tensions, technological competition, and concerns regarding surveillance and digital sovereignty are shaping contemporary debates on global digital governance.

An important contribution of this book lies in its examination of digital dispute resolution mechanisms and online legal systems. With the rapid expansion of digital transactions and cross-border operations, traditional dispute resolution methods often prove inadequate for addressing the speed and complexity of digital commerce. This volume therefore investigates emerging models of Online Dispute Resolution (ODR), blockchain-enabled dispute systems, smart contracts, and digital judicial platforms developed in various jurisdictions, including China's innovative internet courts and international arbitration initiatives. The book also dedicates substantial attention to financial technology and digital financial inclusion under the Digital Silk Road. Fintech innovations, mobile payment systems, AI-driven financial services, blockchain applications, and digital currencies are profoundly reshaping the global financial architecture. By examining both opportunities and regulatory risks, the volume highlights how digital financial inclusion can contribute to sustainable development while also requiring robust legal safeguards and regulatory oversight.

Another distinctive feature of this work is its focus on sustainability and the green digital economy. The intersection of digitalization and sustainable development has become increasingly important in international policymaking. Through discussions on green finance, smart technologies, sustainable infrastructure, and environmental governance, the book demonstrates how digital transformation can support global sustainability objectives when accompanied by effective legal and policy frameworks. The book argues that the future of the Digital Silk Road will significantly influence not only economic integration but also the broader balance of geopolitical power and the evolution of international law. By integrating legal analysis with economic and geopolitical perspectives, the book seeks to contribute to scholarly debates and policy discussions surrounding the future of the digital economy and transnational digital governance.

Chongqing, China

Jamil Afzal
Yongmei Chen

Acknowledgments Our sincere appreciation goes to the following fellows, whose guidance and expertise were instrumental in shaping the research direction of this book.

- Mian Muhammad Afzal Advocate, Lahore High Court, Lahore, Pakistan
- Professor Yang Guohua, Tsinghua University, School of Law, Beijing, China
- Mst. Almas Bibi, from Government College University, Faisalabad, Pakistan
- Dr. Afef Dhaffouli, from the University of Monastir, Tunisia
- Muhammad Adeel Afzal, School of Economics & Management Science, China Three Gorges University, Yichang, China
- Asmat Ullah Khan, Director Appeals/ Deputy Prosecutor General, Public Prosecution Department, Government of the Punjab, Pakistan
- Muhammad Nawaz Shahid, Director (Legal/Prosecution) Anti-Corruption Establishment, Punjab, Pakistan
- Mian Muhammad Aslam, Public Prosecution Department, Government of the Punjab, Pakistan

Competing Interests The authors have no competing interests to declare that are relevant to the content of this manuscript.

Contents

Abbreviations

ADR	Alternative Dispute Resolution
AI	Artificial Intelligence
AIIB	Asian Infrastructure Investment Bank
AML	Anti-Money Laundering
APEC	Asia-Pacific Economic Cooperation
B2B	Business-to-Business
BDS	BeiDou Navigation Satellite System
BITs	Bilateral Investment Treaties
BRI	Belt and Road Initiative
BRICS	Brazil, Russia, India, China, and South Africa
BRIGC	BRI International Green Development Coalition
CAC	Cyberspace Administration of China
CAFTA	China-ASEAN Free Trade Agreement
CAIH	China-ASEAN Information Harbor
CBDCs	Central Bank Digital Currencies
CCPA	California Consumer Privacy Act
CERAT	Climate and Environment Risk Assessment Toolbox
CICC	China International Commercial Courts
CIETAC	China International Economic and Trade Arbitration Commission
CMS	Case Management System
CPEC	China-Pakistan Economic Corridor
CPTPP	Comprehensive and Progressive Agreement for Trans-Pacific Partnership
CSL	Cybersecurity Law
CTF	Counter-Terrorism Financing
CToD	Contemporary Theory of Digitalization
DDoS	Distributed Denial-of-Service
DDRM	Digital Dispute Resolution Mechanism
DFS	Digital Financial Services
DFTZ	Digital Free Trade Zone
DISC	Digital Innovation and Sustainable Economy Centre

DMCC	Digital Markets, Competition, and Consumer
DODR	Digital Online Dispute Resolution
DPI	Digital Public Infrastructure
DPO	Data Protection Officer
DSA	Digital Services Act
DSL	Data Security Law
DSR	Digital Silk Road
DTD	Debt-Trap Diplomacy
eBLs	Electronic Bills of Lading
eBRAM	International Online Dispute Resolution Centre
e-CNY	Digital Yuan
EDDRS	Efficient Digital Dispute Resolution System
EGDC	European Green Digital Coalition
EIA	Environmental Impact Assessment
ERIA	Economic Research Institute of ASEAN and East Asia
ERST	Environmental Risk Screening Tool
ESG	Environmental, Social, and Governance
EVs	Electric Vehicles
G2B	Government-to-Business
GATS	General Agreement on Trade in Services
GATT	General Agreement on Tariffs and Trade
GBA	Greater Bay Area
GDA	Hub Green Digital Action Hub
GDP	Gross Domestic Product
GDPR	General Data Protection Regulation
GGGI	Global Green Growth Institute
GHG	Greenhouse Gas
GIP	Green Investment Principle
ICADRP	International Centre for Appropriate Dispute Resolution and Prevention
ICBC	Industrial and Commercial Bank of China
ICT	Information and Communication Technology
IEEE	Institute of Electrical and Electronics Engineers
IoT	Internet of Things
IP	Intellectual Property
IPR	Intellectual Property Rights
ISO	International Organization of Standardization
ITA	Information Technology Agreement
ITU	International Telecommunication Union
JSI	Joint Statement Initiative
KYC	Know Your Customer
mCBDC	multi-currency Central Bank Digital Currency
MDEC	Malaysia Digital Economy Corporation
MEAs	Multilateral Environmental Agreements
MEE	Ministry of Ecology and Environment

MENA	Middle East and North Africa
ML	Machine Learning
MLETR	Model Law on Electronic Transferable Records
MNCs	Multinational Corporations
MoUs	Memoranda of Understanding
MSMEs	Micro, Small, and Medium Enterprises
NFRA	National Financial Regulatory Administration
NGOs	Non-Governmental Organizations
NLP	Natural Language Processing
ODR	Online Dispute Resolution
OECD	Organization for Economic Cooperation and Development
PBOC	People's Bank of China
PEACE	Pakistan and East Africa Connecting Europe
PGII	Partnership for Global Infrastructure and Investment
PIPL	Personal Information Protection Law, China
POPIA	Protection of Personal Information Act
PPPs	Public-Private Partnerships
PUAN	Pakistan-U.S. Alumni Network
QRIS	Quick Response Code Indonesian Standard
RCEP	Regional Comprehensive Economic Partnership
RegTech	Regulatory Technology
SDGs	Sustainable Development Goals
SHIAC	Shanghai International Arbitration Center
SIA	Social Impact Assessment
SMEs	Small and Medium Enterprises
SOEs	State-Owned Enterprises
SWIFT	Society for Worldwide Interbank Financial Telecommunication
TCFD	Task Force on Climate-related Financial Disclosures
TRIPS	Trade-Related Aspects of Intellectual Property Rights
UNCITRAL	UN Commission of International Trade Law
UNODC	United Nations Office on Drugs and Crime
UPI	Unified Payments Interface
USMCA	United States-Mexico-Canada Agreement
WEF	World Economic Forum
WTO	World Trade Organization

Chapter 1
Chinese Digital Economy Initiatives and Regulatory Framework of the Digital Silk Road

Abstract The digital economy of China emerged as one of the most effective force in the modern economic growth and globalization. With the development of digital infrastructure, China has successfully implemented digital technologies in its domestic business and in foreign economic activity. Over the last few years, the Belt and Road Initiative (BRI) has developed an ever-increasing digital economy aspect, as the model of cooperation is technology-enabled and knowledge-intensive. This chapter focuses on the history of the Chinese digital economy and how the digital economy is becoming central to the BRI. It examines the role of digital infrastructure, e-commerce, fintech, and new technologies in cross-border connectivity and economic integration between the involved countries. The chapter also assesses the possible economic, social, and technological effects of the digital rise in China on BRI partner states. Specific focus is put on legal and regulatory factors, such as data governance, cybersecurity, and regulatory coordination. With its accessible and comprehensive discussion, this chapter makes a contribution to the understanding of the strategic role of the Chinese digital economy in the formation of the path to the BRI.

Keywords Belt and Road Initiative · Digital economy · Digital Law · Digital Silk Road · Digital economy of China

1 Introduction

The world economy has been transformed radically by digital technologies, redesigning the process of creating, exchanging, and regulating values.[1] Digitalization in modern economies is not a problem of communication or information processing; it has already turned into the principle of organization on a large scale,

[1] Barbara Brenner, "Transformative Sustainable Business Models in the Light of the Digital Imperative—A Global Business Economics Perspective," *Sustainability* 10, no. 12 (2018): 4428.

J. Afzal and Y. Chen, *Legal Framework of Digital Economy and Digital Trade Under the Belt and Road Initiative*, https://doi.org/10.1007/978-981-92-4444-7_1

determining production, finance, trade, governance, and even social interaction.[2] The use of platforms, data flows, cloud computing, and smart technologies is gaining popularity in the economic system. It is transforming the character of relationships between firms, consumers, and the government.[3] Forms that are digitally negotiated enable coordination in real time, predictive decision-making, and scalable innovation. It has taken the place of physical structures and labor, making it the major arbiter of economic activity. Digitalization is no longer a part of economic development; it is a driver of economic emergence, competitiveness, and reorganization.[4] China is not the exception, as it is one of the big and powerful players in the digital transformation among the countries that have been at the forefront of digital transformation.[5,6] The two previous decades may be characterized by the boom of the digital economy in the country. China is not an information and communication technology consumer but has already positioned itself as a multi-level ecosystem.[7] The domestic economy of China has undergone a revolution due to the new technologies; these technologies have allowed the creation of new industries, business organizations, and even patterns of consumption. Meanwhile, it allowed China to become a large force in the digital markets of the world, able to export technologies. The Chinese state has a direct correlation with the national Chinese digital transformation since the policies are directed at strategic investment, planned growth, and development based on innovations.[8] The government programs have proved useful for the development of infrastructure, research and development, and the development of the integrated digital ecosystem. The huge incentives to adopt mobile technologies, the wide proliferation of broadband facilities, and the building of service platforms have facilitated the rapid adoption by the business and household sectors. They rejuvenated the economic activity in the domestic economy and also introduced the technological and institutional competence to respond to the international markets. China has demonstrated that national development and modernization of technologies can be mutually reinforcing.[9]

---

[2] Jamil Afzal, *Exploring the New Horizons of International Law Concerning Globalization of Economy* (Springer Nature, 2026).

[3] Alexander Benlian et al., "The Transformative Value of Cloud Computing: A Decoupling, Platformization, and Recombination Theoretical Framework," *Journal of Management Information Systems* 35, no. 3 (2018): 719–39.

[4] Tatyana Boikova et al., "The Determinants and Effects of Competitiveness: The Role of Digitalization in the European Economies," *Sustainability* 13, no. 21 (2021): 11689.

[5] Hong Jiang and Johann Peter Murmann, "The Rise of China's Digital Economy: An Overview," *Management and Organization Review* 18, no. 4 (2022): 790–802.

[6] Quan Ma, "Leadership and Innovation in the Digital Economy," *Academic Journal of Business & Management* 5, no. 10 (2023): 146–50.

[7] Yijia Jing and Danyao Li, "Private Roles in Enhancing Multi-Level Governance: China's 'Internet+' National Strategy," *Public Policy and Administration* 34, no. 2 (2019): 144–64.

[8] Lijun Zhu, "The Influence of Digital Transformation on Chinese Firms' Outward Foreign Direct Investment," *Finance Research Letters* 72 (2025): 106567.

[9] Xinxiang Chen et al., "ICT in China: A Strong Force to Boost Economic and Social Development," in *Perspectives and Policies on ICT in Society: An IFIP TC9 (Computers and Society) Handbook* (Springer, 2005).

Now China is playing key role in international economic connectivity, trade, and regional cooperation.[10] The Belt and Road Initiative (BRI), which was initiated as a grandiose program of developing infrastructure and trade networks across the world, first emphasized physical connectivity, in terms of transport corridors, energy, and logistics hubs.[11] With the increased digitalization of global economic activity, it has become evident that the traditional infrastructure cannot be fully relied upon to ensure sustainable development or economic integration over the long term.[12] So, the BRI over time developed to include a digital aspect with a major focus on the evolution of telecommunications networks, data infrastructure, cross-border e-commerce platforms, and technology-facilitated services.[13] This transformation reiterates the realization that digital connectivity, data flows, and intelligent systems have become as important as traditional infrastructure in enhancing regional integration and economic development.

The overlapping of the digital economy and the BRI is a strategic merger between national power and global aspiration.[14] With the expansion of digital technologies, platforms, and infrastructure across national borders, China attempts to increase the extent of economic connections, trade, and offer new ways of cooperating. This vision is commonly summarized in terms of the Digital Silk Road (DSR), which focuses on the importance of digital technologies in minimizing the connectivity distances, enhancing performance, and bringing BRI economies into global digital value chains.[15] The main elements of this strategy are the creation of digital infrastructure like fiber-optic networks and data centers, the advancement of e-commerce across borders to increase the number of customers, the introduction of smart logistics to streamline the supply chains, and the technology cooperation programs to enhance the local digital capabilities.[16] All these efforts are evidence of the fact that digital tools are important facilitators of economic and social development.

The availability of digital technologies has the potential to impact labor markets, skills development, education, the quality of health services, and the efficiency of

[10] Rafael Leal-Arcas, "China and the Regional Comprehensive Economic Partnership," *Journal of Global Policy and Governance* 2, no. 2 (2013): 287–304.

[11] Zhao Xu et al., "China-Pakistan Cultural Exchanges and Cooperation under Belt & Road Initiative," *Siazga Research Journal* 2, no. 3 (2023): 186–91.

[12] Pramila Paudel, "Divergent Digital Paths: A Comparative Study of Regulatory Frameworks and Participation in the Digital Silk Road between China and Nepal," *International Journal of Law and Legal Advancement* 1, no. 2 (2025).

[13] Guo Huadong, "Steps to the Digital Silk Road," *Nature* 554, no. 7690 (2018): 25–27.

[14] Yujia He, "Chinese Digital Platform Companies' Expansion in the Belt and Road Countries," in *China's Digital Expansion in the Global South* (Routledge, 2024).

[15] Fakhar Hussain et al., "Infrastructure Development for the Digital Silk Road (DSR) and Its Implications for China under the Belt and Road Initiative," *Asia–Pacific Social Science Review* 23, no. 4 (2023): 7.

[16] Tim Winter, "Geocultural Power and the Digital Silk Roads," *Environment and Planning D: Society and Space* 40, no. 5 (2022): 923–40.

administration.[17,18] Those who can utilize these tools well may benefit from faster innovation, greater productivity, and better social services. Conversely, infrastructural, institutional, or skills vulnerabilities may increase inequalities or bring in new vulnerabilities. This chapter gives a comprehensive view of one of the most significant changes in modern economic governance in the world by considering the intersection of domestic Chinese digital dynamics and internationalization orientation via the BRI.

2 Evolution of Chinese Digital Economy

China's digital economy has developed through a state-coordinated model that combines large-scale public investment, regulatory guidance, and rapid private-sector innovation.[19] In the last 20 years, digital technologies started to occupy not a peripheral but a core position in administrative and industrial processes, becoming the major source of economic growth, productive efforts, and structural changes. Today, the digital economy is a broad field of activities that touch upon digital infrastructure development, platform-based business models, online financial services, data-driven industries, and new technologies.[20] All these elements contribute to the economic performance of China and the technical and institutional background to China's participation in projects like the Belt and Road Initiative. Digital transformation of China in the early years was directly associated with the modernization of communication systems, the slow penetration of information technologies into the administrations and industries.[21] At the beginning, digitalization served as the main product to enhance efficiency in government institutions and giant enterprises in the form of support. In the same period, computers and network technologies were put into use to process data, enterprise resource management, and administrative coordination, but not yet to change the structure of the economy or business models. However, these initial investments preconditioned the expansion of their usage by increasing the level of digital literacy, introducing the institutions to the technological possibilities, and establishing the ability to process more complex information streams.[22]

---

[17] Roman Chinoracký and Tatiana Čorejová, "Impact of Digital Technologies on Labor Market and the Transport Sector," *Transportation Research Procedia* 40 (2019): 994–1001.

[18] Anahit Melkumyan and Maria Sahakyan, "Digital Technologies and Labour Market Development in the Republic of Armenia," *Management Research and Practice* 14, no. 2 (2022): 37–45.

[19] Mengmeng Ni, *Policy Approaches and Entrepreneurial Responses in Strategic Industries: Comparing Innovation Ecosystems in China and the United States*, 2025.

[20] Rashmi Malhotra and DK Malhotra, "The Impact of Technology, Big Data, and Analytics: The Evolving Data-Driven Model of Innovation in the Finance Industry," *Journal of Financial Data Science* 5, no. 3 (2023).

[21] Christine Zhen-Wei Qiang, *China's Information Revolution: Managing the Economic and Social Transformation* (World Bank Publications, 2007).

[22] Tlou Maggie Masenya, "Digital Literacy Skills as Prerequisite for Teaching and Learning in Higher Education Institutions," *Mousaion* 39, no. 2 (2021).

One of the most crucial points that made China digital was the fast development of mobile connections.[23] Contrary to several developed economies, which followed a fixed-line internet path, China adopted a mobile-first model by capitalizing on the high concentrations of cheap smartphones and fast-growing mobile networks. Mobile technology has assisted millions of individuals who live in rural and underserved regions in accessing the internet as well as communication, doing business, and exchanging information.[24] This mobile first channel allowed digital services to spread rapidly, enter the everyday life, and form new consumption, work, and interaction patterns.[25] It also increased the spread of the digital channel which enabled businesses to reach the customers without necessarily using the traditional middlemen and also collect real-time databases to enhance the products and services.

The central area of rapid development of the digital economy is the digital infrastructure.[26] High-speed connection and bulk processing of data has been the result of massive investment in broadband, data centres, and cloud computing systems. These infrastructures not only make the successful implementation of digital services possible, but also enable the creation of more sophisticated applications, such as cloud computing, artificial intelligence, smart logistics, and digital manufacturing. By a well-thought-out expansion of digital infrastructure, China reduce the internal connectivity gaps, integrate more distant regions into the nationwide economic contacts, and spread of digital literacy and engagement practices in various geographic and demographic locations.[27] This hub is not only supportive of the local digital services but also turning China into a country where infrastructure experience and platform solutions could be exported to other countries based on international cooperation systems.

The transfer of information in the chain of supply chain, in smart cities, and automated use in industry requires continuous transfer of information as enabled by large capacity networks.[28] The computing resources that are offered by the cloud computing solutions can be scaled and therefore any business, whether large or small, can use the advanced tools without necessarily investing heavily in them. The infrastructure-based implementation is capable of scaling the digital services with greater speed and introduces further resiliency and flexibility. Combined with mobile

---

[23] Becky PY Loo and Yu Loong Ngan, "Developing Mobile Telecommunications to Narrow Digital Divide in Developing Countries? Some Lessons from China," *Telecommunications Policy* 36, nos. 10–11 (2012): 888–900.

[24] Lorna Philip and Fiona Williams, "Remote Rural Home Based Businesses and Digital Inequalities: Understanding Needs and Expectations in a Digitally Underserved Community," *Journal of Rural Studies* 68 (2019): 306–18.

[25] Winston Ma, *China's Mobile Economy: Opportunities in the Largest and Fastest Information Consumption Boom* (John Wiley & Sons, 2016).

[26] Xiaolong Li et al., "Digital Infrastructure," in *Development Practice of Digital Business Environment in China* (Springer, 2022).

[27] Tian Yang Luo and Yu Qin Zhu, "Pathways for the Digital Economy to Drive Urban–Rural Integration in Guangxi, China," *GAS J. Econ. Bus. Manag* 1 (2024): 162–74.

[28] Christina Öberg and Gary Graham, "How Smart Cities Will Change Supply Chain Management: A Technical Viewpoint," *Production Planning & Control* 27, no. 6 (2016): 529–38.

connectivity, it can allow a seamless combination of a host of digital applications to create a cogent ecosystem in which production, logistics, finance, and consumption are increasingly interdependent. The popularity of platform-based business models could be taken as one of the most unusual characteristics of the digital economy of China.[29]

Digital platforms do not exist as independent service providers; they are an integrated ecosystem and combine online marketplaces, payment platforms, logistics coordination, and data analytics. These platforms employ network effects to improve efficiency and convenience, which can bring more users and provide rich data that can be used to innovate constantly. By having bigger user bases, platforms are able to improve services based on the data-driven feedback, which brings in more users and business partners.[30] The popular platforms offer a spectrum of services, including e-commerce and ride-hailing to financial transactions and cloud computing, showing the breadth and diversity of the Chinese platform economy.[31] The platform economy has changed consumption and production trends. To consumers, it gives them more choices, reduces the costs of transactions, and increases the speed of access to goods and services. To the businesses, it opens up access to domestic and international markets, offers valuable information on consumer behaviour, and reduces the traditional barriers to entry, e.g., distribution network or financial limitations. The smaller and medium-level businesses, especially, have enjoyed the lowered friction in market access to be able to get involved in e-commerce and grow outside the local markets.[32] This digital participation democratization facilitated entrepreneurship, diversification of the economic activity in regions, and new business models have emerged.

3 Role of China's Digital Economy in the DSR

The Belt and Road Initiative (BRI) has been largely seen as a model to increase physical connectivity in Eurasia and other areas, with the focus on transport infrastructure, energy corridors, and networks of logistic routes.[33] These projects were

---

[29] Xiaolan Fu et al., "Platform-Based Business Model and Entrepreneurs from Base of the Pyramid," *Technovation* 119 (2023): 102451.

[30] Mark Anthony Camilleri, "The Use of Data-Driven Technologies for Customer-Centric Marketing," *International Journal of Big Data Management* 1, no. 1 (2020): 50–63.

[31] Жун Ли and Екатерина Геннадьевна Господарик, "Platform Economy Development in SCO Countries: Current Status, Regional Differences, and Key Drivers," *Веснік Брэсцкага Ўніверсітэта. Серыя 2. Гісторыя. Эканоміка. Права*, no. 2 (2025): 90–96.

[32] Wei Ma et al., "Inhibit or Promote: Assessing the Impact of Digital Economy on Poverty Reduction in the Belt and Road Initiative Countries," *Applied Spatial Analysis and Policy* 18, no. 4 (2025): 132.

[33] Abdulgaffar Muhammad et al., "The Belt and Road Initiative: Implications for Infrastructure Development and Economic Integration in Eurasia," *J Environ Sci Econ* 2, no. 2 (2023).

conceptualized as being the basis of economic growth, trade, investment, and movement. However, the last few years of practice have proved that physical infrastructure is not enough to maintain the long-term integration of the digital global economy. Digital connectivity has become an indisputable fact as trade, production, finance, and governance processes are increasingly mediated by digital technologies. The digital economy of China has become a fundamental element of the BRI that supplements the traditional infrastructure with advanced information and communication technologies, platform-based services, and technology-enabled collaboration.[34,35] This development is indicative of a larger perspective in that sustainable development, regional integration, and economic competitiveness rely more and more on the free flow of digital systems and physical networks.

Using decades of experience at home, Chinese platforms offer avenues through which companies in the participating countries can tap regional and global markets.[36] These platforms make transactions easier, informational asymmetries lower, logistics and payment services merge, and marketing and customer engagement tools are provided. SMEs that are usually characterized by steep entry barriers into foreign markets are given the rarest of chances to engage in cross-border business without making huge investments or physical location.[37] This trade democratization is especially pronounced in the case of the developing economies, as it enables the participation of local firms in global value chains and also promotes entrepreneurship.

Under the BRI, digital infrastructure operates as a cross-border coordination mechanism, enabling real-time integration of logistics, payments, and regulatory processes.[38] Not only do these investments facilitate and improve the capacity of communication, but they also lead to the minimization of information barriers and real-time cross-border coordination. In less digitalized countries, this infrastructure forms the basis of further digital transformation, making economic modernization and participation in global value chains possible. Enhanced internet connectivity enables companies, governments, and citizens to use services more effectively, leading to increased trade, money laundering, and administrative activities.[39] Closing

---

[34] Chuanman You and Qingxiu Bu, "Transformative Digital Economy, Responsive Regulatory Innovation and Contingent Network Effects: The Anatomy of E-Commerce Law in China," *European Business Law Review* 31, no. 4 (2020).

[35] Siyabonga Mhlongo et al., "Challenges, Opportunities, and Prospects of Adopting and Using Smart Digital Technologies in Learning Environments: An Iterative Review," *Heliyon* 9, no. 6 (2023).

[36] Yujia He, "Chinese Digital Platform Companies' Expansion in the Belt and Road Countries," in *China's Digital Expansion in the Global South* (Routledge, 2024).

[37] Mahfuzur Rahman et al., "Barriers to Enter in Foreign Markets: Evidence from SMEs in Emerging Market," *International Marketing Review* 34, no. 1 (2017): 68–86.

[38] Michael Wang et al., "Global Logistics and Supply Chain Integration in the Digital Era: A Focus on China's Belt and Road Initiative," *Journal of International Logistics and Trade* 22, no. 2 (2024): 58–79.

[39] Abdulaziz Al-khawatreh and Ahmad Imad Yusuf Mefleh Al-Ghoiwari, "Modern Technologies in Enhancing the Oversight of Money Laundering Crimes and Their Social Impact," in *Artificial Intelligence for Sustainable Innovation Management and Risk Management: A Systems (and Network) Perspective* (Springer, 2026).

the technological divide, digital infrastructure under the BRI establishes the environment of sustainable economic development and preconditions the long-term cooperation between China and other countries.[40] The efficiency and effectiveness of projects in physical infrastructure are also strengthened by the integration of digital infrastructure. Ports, railways, and transport corridors can act more accurately with the help of smart logistics systems, sensor networks, and digital monitoring platforms, minimize delays, distribute resources much better, and become more resilient in the face of disruptions. As an example, predictive maintenance systems, cargo monitoring systems, and transportation route optimization may be introduced using data-driven management tools to develop the stability of the operations of the main trade routes. This convergence between the digital and physical infrastructure not only lowers the cost of doing business but also makes it easy to cross borders in the movement of goods and services in accordance with the overall goals of the BRI, which is to improve connectivity to and reduce trade frictions.[41]

The other major mandate of the digital economy in the BRI is the support of digital trade and e-commerce. The other area of China involved in digital activities is the smart supply chains and data-driven logistics networks.[42] The benefits of inventory management, demand forecasting, and shipment tracking can be achieved by means of advanced algorithms and combined digital systems since the firms are able to respond very fast to the changes in the market and to unforeseen events. Due to the immature physical logistics of the area, digital technology can be applied to address the structural limitations, which would become the foundation of the intensified movement of goods and the heightened competitiveness.[43] These technologies promoted through adoption will promote transparency in application, reduce the likelihood of bottleneck and promote responsive just-in-time supply chains to dynamic global markets. Infrastructures and platforms are not the only means to enhance human capital and institutional capabilities; China is considering training programs and technical support.[44] They contribute to the attainment of skills in the area of digital governance, data management, platform operation, cybersecurity, and emerging technologies. These actions facilitate sustainable and locally based digital ecosystems since they augment the technical and institutional readiness of the partner countries. Capacity-building programs also develop skills in designing policies,

---

[40] Sainan Zhao et al., "Dynamic Influence of Digital and Technological Advancement on Sustainable Economic Growth in Belt and Road Initiative (BRI) Countries," *Sustainability* 14, no. 23 (2022): 15782.

[41] Wei Chen et al., "Assessing the Structural Connectivity of International Trade Networks along the 'Belt and Road,'" *Plos One* 18, no. 3 (2023): e0282596.

[42] Yuxia Guo et al., "Data-Driven Coordinated Development of the Digital Economy and Logistics Industry," *Sustainability* 14, no. 14 (2022): 8963.

[43] Carl Dahlman, "Technology, Globalization, and International Competitiveness: Challenges for Developing Countries," *Industrial Development for the 21st Century: Sustainable Development Perspectives*, 2007, 29–83.

[44] Yinghui Fan et al., "Overview and Developmental Analysis of China's Technical and Vocational Education and Training," *International Journal of Innovative Research and Scientific Studies* 7, no. 1 (2024): 251–60.

implementing regulations, and managing innovation, which form a body of knowledge that can be used over time to realize development outcomes even after the initial investment in infrastructure. Cross-border trade activities are made possible by digital payment systems.[45] The digital finance solutions are integrated to enable fast, secure, and cost-efficient transactions, avoiding the use of cash and conventional banking intermediaries. They facilitate trade payments, remittance and consumer payments, which increase the financial inclusivity of the countries involved. These services reduce the cost of transactions, increase the level of trust, and the predictability of cross-border exchange by integrating payment systems into digital platforms. Digital finance, thus, not just serves as an intermediary of business, but also serves as a tool of wider economic inclusion and integration.[46]

Exporting of digital business models forms another aspect of the strategic engagement of China.[47] China propagates integrated digital ecosystems that unite infrastructure, platforms, and services into unified models instead of transferring individual technologies.[48] These ecosystems are based on the domestic experience and supplemented by the experience of the Chinese fast digitalization and tailored to the local economic, social, and institutional environment. By doing so, the participating countries will be able to implement the best practices of digital organization and tailor the solutions to their local requirements, whether it is the optimization of logistics, digital governance, or the growth of e-commerce. By encouraging systemic, not isolated technology, China supports scalable, flexible, and sustainable digitalization throughout the BRI. Besides an economic and technical aspect, the digitalization of the BRI also cuts across the area of governance and policy alignment. Digital systems also shape the controls of the market, data management, and providing services to the population, and it is necessary to pay close attention to the corresponding alignment of regulatory frameworks across the boundaries. The experience of China in the functioning of large-scale digital networks can be described as the point of reference when the regulations are designed, including the cybersecurity, data protection, and platform governance standards.[49] However, the disparity in the legal tradition, the institutional strength, and the policy priorities of the BRI countries demand adaptable approaches without interference with sovereignty but enabling coordination. Partnered coordinated standards, capacity-building, and policy structures are therefore necessary in an attempt to get the maximum benefits of digital integration, as well as minimizing the risk of regulatory divergence manifestations.

---

[45] Dong He, "Digitalization of Cross-Border Payments," *China Economic Journal* 14, no. 1 (2021): 26–38.

[46] Atina Shofawati, "The Role of Digital Finance to Strengthen Financial Inclusion and the Growth of SME in Indonesia," *KnE Social Sciences*, 2019, 389–407.

[47] Bo Hu et al., "A Digital Business Model for Accelerating Distributed Renewable Energy Expansion in Rural China," *Applied Energy* 316 (2022): 119084.

[48] Weidi Zheng, "Digital Vines: Mapping China's Network of Global Platform Ecosystems," *Information, Communication & Society* 28, no. 14 (2025): 2563–79.

[49] Bo Zhao and Yang Feng, "Mapping the Development of China's Data Protection Law: Major Actors, Core Values, and Shifting Power Relations," *Computer Law & Security Review* 40 (2021): 105498.

The main outcome of the increased digital aspect of the BRI is also regional connectivity, not only in economic flows but also in the digital one, sharing of knowledge, research, and innovation collaboration.[50] Digital networks offer channels of international contact to add to conventional trade and investment. As digital collaboration is incorporated into a larger economic and social system, the BRI makes a more embedded and stronger regional network, which can enable sustainable development in the digital age.[51] The social and developmental impacts of digital cooperation are gaining relevance. The e-government systems enhance accountability, administration performance, and provision by the citizens, and the learning opportunities of the students who could be geographically or socioeconomically underprivileged increase as a result of using digital education. Digital health and telemedicine enhance access to good care, and digital agriculture programs draw the attention of small-scale farmers to real-time market records, weather forecasts, and resource management apps.[52] These examples demonstrate the way in which digital cooperation opportunities might be implemented to augment traditional infrastructure projects with medium-term social positive effects, as one of the outcomes of general inclusive growth and development. However, the Chinese digital economy is not just coming with both opportunities and gains, but threats as well when it becomes part of the BRI. Technological dependence, information sovereignty, and cybersecurity questions are having an impact on policy discussions and the perception of citizens of their respective countries. The presence of a few providers having the majority of the digital capabilities can lead to structural dependencies, which can influence long-term autonomy and power. Such challenges require well-constituted governance machineries, well-structured contracts, and equitable systems of benefits sharing in order to make sure that the process of digital integration will not only boost but also hurt national development goals. The BRI countries do not have equal digital-readiness, and it influences the results. In addition to the fact of connection gaps, technical expertise, and institutional potential, the counterparts of other countries can afford to boast of an established digital ecosystem, strong infrastructures, and talented personnel. Such disparities affect the sharing of benefits and risks that may be related to digital becoming.[53] To make sure that the development of digital projects leads to the creation of balanced, inclusive, and sustainable development throughout

[50] Sainan Zhao et al., "Dynamic Influence of Digital and Technological Advancement on Sustainable Economic Growth in Belt and Road Initiative (BRI) Countries," *Sustainability* 14, no. 23 (2022): 15782.

[51] Sainan Zhao et al., "Dynamic Influence of Digital and Technological Advancement on Sustainable Economic Growth in Belt and Road Initiative (BRI) Countries," *Sustainability* 14, no. 23 (2022): 15782.

[52] Mostafa Kamal and Tarek Aziz Bablu, "Mobile Applications Empowering Smallholder Farmers: A Review of the Impact on Agricultural Development," *International Journal of Social Analytics* 8 (2023): 36–50.

[53] Allison Goh, "Digital Readiness Index for Arbitration Institutions: Challenges and Implications for Dispute Resolution under the Belt and Road Initiative," *Journal of International Arbitration* 38, no. 2 (2021).

the BRI network, certain support, adaptive deployment, and policy direction are consequently needed.

The digital economy of China is strategically positioned in the BRI as a result of global trends and geopolitical factors. Information technologies have an impact on the sphere of economic competitiveness, national security, and strategic influence. Consequently, there is a geopolitical role of digital infrastructure, platforms, and standards, which meets a wider understanding of economic regulation and international collaboration. Through facilitating digital projects, China aims to install digital connectivity in a multilateralized system of mutual growth by making digital development a shared goal rather than a divisive one.[54] One of the main penetrations of this strategic positioning is the fact that the digital dimension is an essential part of BRI that may support physical infrastructure and trade initiatives, and long-term connectivity, including regional and global.

4 Potential Impact on BRI Participating Countries

With the Belt and Road Initiative, the growth of the digital economy in China can transform the economic, social, and institutional environment of the member countries to a great extent.[55] China opens up new avenues of development that transcend the boundaries of its traditional trade and investment by expanding digital infrastructure, platforms, and tech-based services. The effects of this digital interaction are two-dimensional, which include productivity, market access, governance, and social inclusion. Meanwhile, the results differ considerably due to the conditions on the ground, institutional capabilities, and policy decisions, and it is important to evaluate both opportunities and challenges in a moderate way. The economic effects of enhanced digital connectivity differ significantly across BRI countries, depending on institutional capacity, infrastructure readiness, and regulatory quality. Improved telecommunications, broadband, and data infrastructure can help the participating countries to become more smoothly integrated in regional and global economic systems. The enhanced relationship is minimizing information asymmetry, decreasing transaction costs, and enhancing effective coordination between firms and institutions. In nations with a low level of digital infrastructure, they can enhance the digital transformation process and contribute to the general economic modernization.[56]

54 Maaike Okano-Heijmans and Wilhelm Vosse, "Promoting Open and Inclusive Connectivity: The Case for Digital Development Cooperation," *Research in Globalization* 3 (2021): 100061.

55 Sainan Zhao et al., "Dynamic Influence of Digital and Technological Advancement on Sustainable Economic Growth in Belt and Road Initiative (BRI) Countries," *Sustainability* 14, no. 23 (2022): 15782.

56 Tatiana V. Kokuytseva et al., "Preconditions for the Transition of Developed and Developing Countries to the Cyber Economy through the Process of Digital Modernization," in *The Cyber Economy: Opportunities and Challenges for Artificial Intelligence in the Digital Workplace* (Springer, 2019).

The growth of digital connectivity also improves the performance of the trade. Digital platforms help companies to enter new markets, engage in e-commerce across borders, and diversify the structure of exports. Small and Medium Enterprises (SMEs) are especially beneficiaries of fewer entry barriers and better entry to digital markets. Digital platforms ease the process of complex trade by combining logistics, payments, and customer interaction, thus facilitating international trade.[57] This may help in increasing exports, income, and the creation of employment, particularly in areas that were formerly self-inhibiting in terms of structure. The industry development trends in BRI countries also depend on the digital economy of China.[58] The technologies based on data enable boosting productivity in the manufacturing, agricultural, and services sectors by assisting in managing resources more effectively, managing quality, and streamlining processes. The impact of intelligent production systems and digital supply chains is to make the firms more efficient and resistant to fluctuations in the market. These capabilities have the capacity of maintaining the modernization and diversification of industries and mining, and end-to-end the reliance on low-value-added operations and competitiveness of the process in the long term.

The other important area of influence is financial inclusion. The digital financial services make payment, credit, and insurance accessible, particularly to people and small businesses who lack access to traditional banking systems. Credit evaluation applications based on data and payment systems lower the cost of financial inclusion, which may expand the scope of economic participation. Access to financial services is improved and enables entrepreneurship, household consumption, and business growth, resulting in more inclusive growth. In addition to the economic impact, the digital connection of China in the BRI has social implications.[59] Digital government sites can make the administration more efficient and transparent, which increases the quality of the delivery of publicly available services and increases interactions between citizens and the state.[60] Another way digital technologies impact labor markets and skill development is through digital technologies. Although automation and the use of data-driven systems can lead to a decrease in the number of people seeking the majority of routine work, it is also opening up new prospects in the digital services sphere, technology administration, and creative fields. Digital ecosystem participation promotes skill upgrading and the transfer of knowledge, especially

---

[57] Mansi Trivedi and Jitendra Kumar Gautam, "Transforming Cross Border Trade with the Advancement of Digital Platform: An Analysis," *Journal of International Economics* 16, no. 1 (2025): 33–44.

[58] Sainan Zhao et al., "Dynamic Influence of Digital and Technological Advancement on Sustainable Economic Growth in Belt and Road Initiative (BRI) Countries," *Sustainability* 14, no. 23 (2022): 15782.

[59] Jean-Marc F. Blanchard and Bas Hooijmaaijers, "Connecting into the Social Sustainability Effects of Infrastructure through China's Digital Silk Road: Issues, Indices, and Indications," *Sustainability* 13, no. 22 (2021): 12739.

[60] Jamil Afzal, *Implementation of Digital Law as a Legal Tool in the Current Digital Era* (Springer, 2024).

through training and capacity-building efforts.[61] The effects on employment are long-term and will require changes in the system of education and labor policies in response to the changes in the skills requirements.[62] At the organisational level, the introduction of digital systems changes the governance framework and policymaking. Planning, monitoring and service delivery is also more responsive and evidence based through the use of data-driven decision-making. The internet tools help in transparency, reduced workloads on the administration and better co-ordination of the agencies. These can be used to enhance the capacity of the state and the trust of the people by offering them institutional benefits, which consequently result in the greater achievement of development.

Yet even the Chinese implications of the involvement (digitally) are problematic. One of the problems is the reliance on technology because of the restriction of local control and future independence by the use of international digital infrastructure and platforms.[63] The concentration of the players in concentrating on the digital capabilities which is controlled by a few players, can be a weakness and decrease the bargaining power of the countries involved. The three strategies would deal with these risks and they would involve capacity building, diversification and local-level transfer of knowledge. Others are data governance, and digital sovereignty. The issue of the ownership of data, data privacy protection, and transnational data flows has become increasingly significant. The various inequality in the regulations system and institutional capacity affect how the issues are resolved. The fast-growing digital systems can be perceived as a security endangerment of the countries and decrease the confidence of the people to digital technologies without appropriate governance frameworks.[64] The other potential challenge is digital inequality. Although the digital interaction can minimize the connectivity gap in the event of its uneven distribution, it can generate uneven advantage in some places and socioeconomic groups due to the lack of appropriate infrastructure, skills, and digital literacy. Megacities and big corporations are more likely to recuperate faster in digital integration, and settlements and small corporations in rural areas may find it hard to enter the market. Inclusive results should be attained with the help of some policies that encompass the areas of gaps that influence the development of infrastructures, skills, and affordability.

The effect of the digital economy on the local innovation systems is also complicated in China.[65] Contact with developed digital technologies and business models

---

[61] Satya Subrahmanyam, "Capacity Building and Skill Development in Rural Manufacturing," in *Rural Social Entrepreneurship Development: Network-Based Manufacturing System Model* (IGI Global Scientific Publishing, 2025).

[62] Yidan Wang and Yidan Wang, *Education in a Changing World: Flexibility, Skills, and Employability*, vol. 69104 (World Bank Washington, 2012).

[63] Lizhi Liu, "The Rise of Data Politics: Digital China and the World," *Studies in Comparative International Development* 56, no. 1 (2021): 45–67.

[64] Igor Linkov et al., "Governance Strategies for a Sustainable Digital World," *Sustainability* 10, no. 2 (2018): 440.

[65] Lin Liang and Yan Li, "How Does Government Support Promote Digital Economy Development in China? The Mediating Role of Regional Innovation Ecosystem Resilience," *Technological Forecasting and Social Change* 188 (2023): 122328.

can, on the one hand, cause innovation and entrepreneurship. Conversely, high risks of competition due to the established platforms might constrain the development of the local digital companies when the barriers of market entry are high. The challenge of openness and support of domestic innovation is thus a significant policy concern to participating countries. The digital impact is further influenced by environmental and sustainability factors. Digital technologies are capable of ensuring the efficiency of resources, environmental surveillance, and intelligent energy control, playing roles in sustainable development goals.[66] Simultaneously, digital infrastructure and data centers are energy and resource consumers, and some have concerns regarding environmental footprints. Sustainability principles are necessary to be incorporated into digital development strategies so that the benefits can be reaped in the long term. Nations that are well digital and have well-developed institutions are in a better place to exploit digital opportunities, whilst those with low capacity may experience more challenges. Specific solutions based on the priorities of local development, institutional environment, and social backgrounds are thus essential in ensuring that the best is achieved. International policy coordination and collaboration are also crucial in the determination of the digital impacts.[67] This can be done by harmonizing standards, sharing best practices, and capacity building to minimize risks and maximize benefits. Cybersecurity and digital trade would create a more predictable and stable place of digital integration with the collaborative approaches of data governance. Such coordination, as provided by the digital cooperation under the BRI, enhances trust and long-term sustainability.

5 Legal and Regulatory Considerations

Data governance has become one of the key regulatory issues in the digital aspect of the BRI, specifically with respect to cross-border data flows, privacy protection, and national sovereignty. The enormous growth of data generated by digital platforms, smart infrastructure, financial mechanisms, and cross-border services provides gigantic opportunities for economic growth, innovation, and efficiency. It also raises certain fundamental issues regarding ownership of data, access, control, and accountability of the same.[68] There are significant differences in the approaches to data governance practiced by the BRI countries: some of them focus on the national control and localization of data to protect the independence and sovereignty of the economy and politics, while others are more liberal in their approaches and base their policies on the freedom of data flow to facilitate its inclusion into the global digital

---

[66] Zhencheng Fan et al., "Deep Learning and Artificial Intelligence in Sustainability: A Review of SDGs, Renewable Energy, and Environmental Health," *Sustainability* 15, no. 18 (2023): 13493.

[67] TechComp Innovations, "Managing Digital Economic Corridors: International Cooperation and Regional Integration in the Digital Age," *TechComp Innovations: Journal of Computer Science and Technology*, 2025.

[68] Martin Fadler and Christine Legner, "Data Ownership Revisited: Clarifying Data Accountabilities in Times of Big Data and Analytics," *Journal of Business Analytics* 5, no. 1 (2022): 123–39.

markets. These differences may cause regulatory ambiguity, interfere with cross-border cooperation, and restrict the potential of digital integration. Therefore, it is necessary to have specifically complex and coordinated data governance structures that would allow treating data as a strategic asset, but at the same time, pursue national interests and the rights of individuals. These structures must define the designations of the data collection, storage, sharing, and processing, to offer the best economic utility as compared to security and privacy.

The concept of privacy protection is closely related to data governance and has become a significant regulatory concern as a result of the penetration of digital services into the finance, healthcare, e-government, and social services. Collecting, processing personal and sensitive data in large volumes must be supported by a strong legal protection, institutional regulation, and technical standards according to the social norms and legal traditions. The problem of privacy is particularly complex in a cross-border context involving the likelihood of differences between the different regulatory frameworks, and therefore would introduce ambiguity concerning the consent, storage, transmission, and use of information. Weak or low privacy will ruin the trust of the citizens, demoralize them from utilizing the digital services, and expose them and organizations to online exploitation.[69] The capacity to harmonize privacy guidelines in various jurisdictions, impose effective accountability arrangements, and attain transparency in data activities is therefore regarded as the key towards building trust, protecting users, and effective engagement in the cross-border digital networks. The other area of regulatory complexity that is critical is cybersecurity. As digital networks continue to expand and penetrate the core services of banking, logistics, and smart infrastructure, the interface of the cyber menace, such as hacking and data breaches, system disruption, and unauthorized access, grows exponentially. Cross-border platforms, cloud resources, and smart networks in the logistics operation are digital projects under the BRI and are to be supported with a comprehensive cybersecurity infrastructure that encompasses risk evaluation, incident response, round-the-clock monitoring, and resilience-building support.[70] The regulation of cybersecurity is especially difficult due to the combination of national security, sovereignty, and international relations issues.[71] The cooperation, as well as protective measures, have to be balanced by designing legal tools, such as bilateral or multilateral information sharing agreements, joint training, or coordinated threat mitigation approaches. The joint cybersecurity projects, without jeopardizing national interests, may increase the overall resilience and minimize the vulnerability to cyberattacks and ensure that the cross-border digital operations are safe.

---

[69] Maurice E. Stucke and Ariel Ezrachi, "How Digital Assistants Can Harm Our Economy, Privacy, and Democracy," *Berkeley Technology Law Journal* 32, no. 3 (2017): 1239–300.

[70] Vasant C. Joshi, "Changing Dimensions of Financial Services and Banking Regulation," *Springer Books*, 2025.

[71] Fabio Ramazzini Bechara and Samara Bueno Schuch, "Cybersecurity and Global Regulatory Challenges," *Journal of Financial Crime* 28, no. 2 (2021): 359–74.

The legal environment of digital interaction in China, as a part of the BRI, is also influenced considerably by the policy of competition and market regulation.[72] The characteristics of the digital market are that they are vulnerable to the network effects and economies of scale, which often create market concentration of the market and the emergence of dominant platforms. On the one hand, large platforms can offer effectiveness, innovation, and extensive reach, yet on the other side, excessive concentration may result in the absence of rivalry, the absence of choices to the consumer, and the assemblage of the entry of local firms. The BRI countries' regulatory agencies are faced with a highly difficult task of striking a balance between scale benefits and innovative benefits, and the need to introduce and provide competitive markets.[73] In order to have an effective competition structure, one must consider dominance of platforms, mergers and acquisitions, pricing, interoperability, and access to valuable digital infrastructure. The digital technologies depend on the quality of software, algorithm and data-driven innovation, and hence the existence of sound intellectual property regimes is significant to further investment, innovation, and the transfer of technologies.[74] Nonetheless, overprotective regimes of IPR may inhibit the flow of technology and the localization process, and limit the innovativeness of local activity, especially in developing economies. It would be the responsibility of the concerned countries to strike a balance on this fine line by coming up with legal frameworks that would safeguard the rights of creators and, in the process, allow the transfer of knowledge, learning, and realization of local potential. One can also ease the cross-border collaborations, minimize tensions, and build confidence among the stakeholders involved in digital cross-border operations using simple and clear IPR regimes. Regulatory ability is one of the determining factors of the efficacy of legal structures. The outcome of enhancing the regulatory capacity is concentrated investments in human capital, regulatory special agencies, and technical infrastructure. It requires programs such as knowledge sharing, regional collaboration strategy, and capacity building seminars to enhance institutional preparedness, effective implementation, and regulatory frameworks to stay in line with the technological revolution.

Without standardization of the regulatory standards, or at least harmonization, the businesses can be subjected to different and contrasting obligations, which make compliance costly and market entry difficult.[75] It is important to develop a system to harmonize digital trade protocols, ease the process of resolving disputes, and to enable the convergence of regulations to ensure sustainable cross-border trade in the BRI. The existence of such frameworks will provide certain predictability, lessen

[72] Yujia He, "Chinese Digital Platform Companies' Expansion in the Belt and Road Countries," in *China's Digital Expansion in the Global South* (Routledge, 2024).

[73] Jingxia Shi and Fenghua Li, "Aligning the BRI with Sustainable Development: A Regulatory Framework and Its Implementation," *Journal of World Trade* 57, no. 6 (2023).

[74] Chunling Zhang and Yumei Xu, "Institutional Innovation Essence and Knowledge Innovation Goal of Intellectual Property Law in the Big Data Era," *Journal of Innovation & Knowledge* 8, no. 4 (2023): 100417.

[75] Surendra Challapalli, "Benefits and Constraints Associated with the Harmonization of Financial Regulations: An Overview," *Asian Journal of Economics, Business and Accounting* 23, no. 15 (2023): 49–56.

obstacles to entry, and share the advantages of digital integration among countries involved on equal footing. One of the key issues regarding digital governance is national sovereignty.[76] Digital infrastructure, cross-border information flows, and platform activities are also considered strategic assets, which are strongly associated with economic self-reliance and political self-sufficiency.[77] The countries involved should have an option to control their digital resources, regulatory policies, and make decisions relating to the interests of the countries to protect their national interests. It demands clear governing structures, good contractual arrangements, and oversight systems to prevent excessive dependency, independence in policymaking, and increase domestic legitimacy. The sovereignty matter is another factor to manage, which can boost the population with confidence, and it is very important in the ubiquity of digital services and infrastructure.

The aspect of the trust of the population is very tight with the points of law and regulation, and it is among the most important aspects of digital initiatives' functioning and sustainability.[78] These digital platforms, services, and infrastructure should be effective in that the businesses, consumers, and governments should trust the systems to be safe, transparent, and accountable. The deficiency of trust is particularly crucial in the virtual realm when real things and services are substituted with virtual ones, such as information and algorithms, and the incompetence in information handling or market monopoly can have much more extensive consequences. It is not possible to build trust without good legal frameworks, meaningful regulations, independent controls, and inclusive processes of policymaking. The latter two can be viewed as the establishment of a regulatory framework that will allow the digital initiatives to be maintained and thrive as both parties are involved in it, and accountability is promoted through the avenues of public consultation and transparency. Technology is dynamic and is always changing, and therefore, the law and regulations system should be dynamic and adaptable. High-speed innovation, changing market dynamics, and new geopolitical risks necessitate that regulators look ahead to the unknown aspect of new challenges, balance between the economic potential and social safety, and integrate jurisdictional management. The policymakers need to come up with dynamic, adaptive, and integrative regulation strategies that will keep up with the changes in technology but will protect both the ethical, economic, and social goals.[79]

---

[76] Lin Li, "Data Sovereignty and National Security: Governance Challenges and Pathways in the Digital Age," *Global Review of Humanities, Arts, and Society* 1, no. 1 (2025): 49–58.

[77] Melody Musoni et al., "Global Approaches to Digital Sovereignty: Competing Definitions and Contrasting Policy," *Maastricht: ECDPM*, 2023.

[78] Jiaqi Xu et al., "Role of Digitalization in Environment, Social and Governance, and Sustainability: Review-Based Study for Implications," *Frontiers in Psychology* 13 (2022): 961057.

[79] Lyytinen Lescrauwaet et al., *Law and Economics*, 2022.

6 Policy Frameworks of Digital Silk Road

6.1 Key "Soft Law"

6.1.1 Information Silk Road Initiative (2015)

The base layer of inter-border digital connectivity is developed by the Information Silk Road Initiative (2015) with a priority in developing optical fiber networks, satellite networks, and digital transmission routes.[80,81] Information flow across borders, storage, and accessibility is determined by the management of these communication channels. The connectivity introduced by such an infrastructure is not only a matter of connectivity, but it also introduces structural pathways of how digital interaction takes place, defining how data practices and security architecture of the involved states are governed. Such a project, based on the physical grounding of the physical hardware of the internet, implies that the stream of international data is always reliant on specific technological dimensions.

6.1.2 China Standards 2035 & Made in China 2025

The policy agenda is still changing to a technological standardization of China Standards 2035 and Made in China 2025 in the main sectors, such as 5G, artificial intelligence, and smart cities.[82,83] The export of these norms to the partners becomes a natural match with Chinese technologies and has an effect on the tendencies of technological evolution. Use of standards influences the procurement decisions, system architecture, and innovation direction, which may eventually entrench local digital ecosystems into a specific technological platform. It is interoperable, market competitive, and technology independent in the long-term because it has introduced some form of logic and protocols into the digital heart of emerging nations.

---

[80] Hong Shen, "Building a Digital Silk Road? Situating the Internet in China's Belt and Road Initiative," *International Journal of Communication* 12 (2018): 19–19.

[81] Jean-Marc F. Blanchard and Colin Flint, "The Geopolitics of China's Maritime Silk Road Initiative," *Geopolitics* 22, no. 2 (2017): 223–45.

[82] Max J. Zenglein and Anna Holzmann, "Evolving Made in China 2025," *MERICS Papers on China* 8 (2019): 78.

[83] Bonnie S. Glaser, *Made in China 2025 and the Future of American Industry* (Center for Strategic and International Studies (CSIS), 2022).

6.1.3 Green Investment Principles for the Belt and Road

By incorporating the intensity of digital infrastructure resources, the Green Investment Principles in the Belt and Road add environmental aspects to the digital expansion process.[84] The digital policy also requires sustainability in the data centers, network systems, and digital devices due to the high amounts of energy and material resources required to power these systems.[85] These values lead to efficiency, good stewardship of resources, and observation of the international global environmental requirements, and also boost the sufficiency of the legitimacy of massive digital investment in global environments. This framework attempts to minimize the ecological footprint of rapid digitalization by focusing on low-carbon and resource-efficient development.

6.1.4 China-Arab States Digital Cooperation Forum

China-Arab States Digital Cooperation Forum is a systematic method of collaboration in such aspects as digital finance, e-commerce, and cybersecurity.[86,87] Through the technical contacts and coordination activities, countries in question obtain access to the model of operation and regulation strategies that determine the management of digital systems. The interaction also facilitates building institutional capacity and taking an influence on the regulation and implementation of digital services at the national level. These forums are diplomatic avenues that convert the higher-level policy ambitions into state-level online legislation.

6.1.5 E-Commerce Cooperation Dialogues

The E-Commerce Cooperation Dialogues appear with the Central Asian countries, offering the organization of the online trade without applying binding documents.[88] Such models take into consideration such practical factors as payment integration, the execution of logistics, operations, and customs of the platform. Their

---

[84] Tian Huifang, "Green Investment Principles for the Belt and Road," in *The Routledge Handbook of the Belt and Road* (Routledge, 2022).

[85] Dlzar Al Kez et al., "Exploring the Sustainability Challenges Facing Digitalization and Internet Data Centers," *Journal of Cleaner Production* 371 (2022): 133633.

[86] Karim Mohamed Aboul-Dahab, "The Virtual Silk Road between China and the Arab States," *Asian Journal of Middle Eastern and Islamic Studies* 15, no. 1 (2021): 51–65.

[87] WANG Xiaoyu, "High-Quality Development in China-Arab Digital Economy Cooperation: Opportunities, Challenges and Prospect," *International Relations* 12, no. 4 (2024): 147–55.

[88] Jane Kelsey, *Opportunities and Challenges for ASEAN and East Asia from the Regional Comprehensive Economic Partnership on E-Commerce* (Economic Research Institute for ASEAN and East Asia, 2022).

adaptive constituency makes them adjust the digital trade behaviors step by step, and the operation frictions are reduced, and the cross-border transactions become smooth. This continued coordination helps in the development of a networked e-commerce space that facilitates the growth of digital markets in different geographic locations.

6.2 *Operational Mechanisms*

6.2.1 DSR Special Cooperation Program for Spatial Information

The BRI Special Cooperation Program on Spatial Information is a key pillar on which the transformation of the Belt and Road Initiative to a Digital Silk Road is based.[89] Such an operational mechanism is the technological foundation of digital connectivity and changes the emphasis of the BRI on physical infrastructure that is now covered with high-tech services. The core aspect of this growth is the worldwide implementation of the BeiDou Navigation Satellite System (BDS), which can deliver the high-precision positioning and timing needed by the modern 5G networks and autonomous logistics.[90] Creating a network of ground stations and earth observation satellites, China provides the involved countries with real-time information to use in disaster mitigation and urban planning. Such infrastructure (space-based) enables BRI partner countries to circumvent the old systems and develop what can be termed a Smart City infrastructure, which would serve to establish a smooth information channel that will limit the dependence on Western satellite congregations.[91] Adding to this technical growth, there is the Corporate Integrity and Compliance Evaluation System, a vital framework that is employed to control the Chinese tech corporations that serve in various international legal practices. With the world becoming increasingly globalized, as major actors in the online sphere, Alibaba, Tencent, and Huawei are increasing their presence in the global arena, this system offers a systematic roadmap that allows the company to adapt its operations to international standards and national digital self-determination. The model puts risk management at the center of the focus of anti-bribery zones, data security, and legal red lines to avoid business interruption and sanctions imposed at international levels. Through the formulation of these compliance standards, the Chinese government tries to professionalize its

[89] Hong Shen, "Building a Digital Silk Road? Situating the Internet in China's Belt and Road Initiative," *International Journal of Communication* 12 (2018): 19–19.

[90] Rui Li et al., "Advances in BeiDou Navigation Satellite System (BDS) and Satellite Navigation Augmentation Technologies," *Satellite Navigation* 1, no. 1 (2020): 12.

[91] Ajey Lele and Kritika Roy, *Analysing China's Digital and Space Belt and Road Initiative* (Institute for Defence Studies and Analysis, 2019).

tech export model, and it creates an image of reliability that allows these companies to become more integrated into the domestic economy of BRI partners.

6.2.2 Corporate Integrity and Compliance Evaluation System

The collaboration between the mechanisms and the overall efforts of the Chinese to develop a digital economy is a game-changer in the Belt and Road environment.[92] The accuracy information of the spatial programs is maximizing the Smart Ports and Digital Customs, reducing the friction of the cross-border trade and logistics across Southeast Asia, Africa, and Europe. At the same time, the compliance systems also help to introduce Chinese technical frameworks in the new markets, since companies working within such frameworks could be considered as reputable corporate citizens. Collectively, these efforts will enable the BRI countries to jump over the old developmental phases and use the hard technology of the satellites and the soft infrastructure of the laws to create a strong, digital-based economy.[93] Such mechanisms of operation are ultimately indicative of a strategic change in the BRI, where the project was based on physical connectivity to a project based on the global digital value chain.

7 Conclusion

The digital economy has taken a leading role in transforming the economy of China, as well as the economic activities of the country in the global arena, through the Belt and Road Initiative. Through spreading digital infrastructure, platforms, and technology-facilitated services across its borders, China has changed the very definition of connectivity, moving it toward being more of a digitally integrated construct rather than a largely physical concept. The chapter has demonstrated that digital cooperation within the framework of the BRI presents an important opportunity to the countries that are participating in it, such as better market access, industrial modernization, and better service delivery. Simultaneously, the advantages of digital integration are skewed and rely on the national institutional capacity, regulatory frameworks, and digital preparedness. Legal and regulatory factors, especially data governance, cybersecurity, competition, and digital sovereignty, appear as defining factors in whether digital engagement can contribute to inclusive and sustainable

[92] Cheng Guo, "China's Digital Silk Road in the Age of the Digital Economy: Political Analysis," *Вестник Российского Университета Дружбы Народов. Серия: Международные Отношения* 22, no. 2 (2022): 271–87.

[93] Sisay Tadesse Arzo et al., "Essential Technologies and Concepts for Massive Space Exploration: Challenges and Opportunities," *IEEE Transactions on Aerospace and Electronic Systems* 59, no. 1 (2022): 3–29.

development. Risk mitigation and prevention of dependency in the long run requires effectiveness in governance, policy coordination, and capacity building. In a world where digital technologies keep transforming the global economic ties, the digital aspect of the BRI will gain more significant weight. Its success in the long term will be based on the capacity of the countries that participated in it to make technological cooperation consistent with the larger development objectives in order to make digital integration a part of common growth, strength, and sustenance.

Chapter 2
Leveraging Digital Silk Road Within the Belt and Road Initiative

Abstract Digital Silk Road has become one of the pillars of the Belt and Road Initiative, reflecting the growing significance of digital technology in modern economic and social development. This chapter dwells on the Digital Silk Road and its changes, the ways it has evolved, the extent of its scope, and its importance in enhancing digital infrastructure, such as broadband internet, fiber-optic network, mobile communication, data center, and other technologies, including artificial intelligence, cloud computing, e-commerce, and smart city solutions. It sheds light on the economic effects of the Digital Silk Road, especially in facilitating trade efficiency, investment inflow, small and medium businesses, entrepreneurship, and financial inclusion using digital financial services. Moreover, the chapter addresses legal and regulatory issues related to the Digital Silk Road, including cybersecurity, data protection, privacy, intellectual property rights, digital governance, and cross-border data flows. It also presents opportunities and challenges in the future, including technological innovation, 5G growth, sustainable development of digital, and the necessity of international coordination of policy. The findings of this chapter reveal that the Digital Silk Road is a revolutionary system that ensures increased global digital connectivity, benefits economic modernization, and sustainable and inclusive development in the larger BRI context.

Keywords Digital Silk Road projects · Growth in Trade · Infrastructure development · Industrial transformation · Data sovereignty and surveillance

1 Introduction

Digital systems enable governments to manage information and provide services at a more efficient location.[1] The development of digital technologies has become one of the major aspects of economic development and social

[1] Will Serrano, "Digital Systems in Smart City and Infrastructure: Digital as a Service," *Smart Cities* 1, no. 1 (2018): 134–54.

J. Afzal and Y. Chen, *Legal Framework of Digital Economy and Digital Trade Under the Belt and Road Initiative*, https://doi.org/10.1007/978-981-92-4444-7_2

advancement.[2] Digital development in all countries is not the same; poor internet access, lack of digital skills, and poor communication networks are still affecting many developing countries in a serious way.[3] In some areas, online services are not easily accessible to people due to the limited or prohibitive digital infrastructure. This scenario leaves a digital divide between the developed and developing nations.[4] This means that the digital economy cannot be fully enjoyed by many countries. It is possible to narrow this gap only through the collaboration of nations, investing in technology, and planning development in the long run. The Belt and Road Initiative (BRI) is a project that China has introduced to facilitate economic collaboration and growth between various parts of the world.[5] The international economy has turned digital, and digital relationships are no longer less significant than their real ones.[6] Due to this shift, development strategies had to involve the use of digital infrastructure and technology collaboration.

In order to react to these changes in the globe, China introduced the Digital Silk Road within the Belt and Road Initiative. Digital Silk Road is concerned with enhancing digital connectivity among nations that are members of the BRI.[7] The aim is to assist in digital growth and assist nations to participate in the digital economy on a global level. Digital Silk Road encompasses numerous kinds of digital initiatives. It also keeps up with the new digital spaces like e-commerce, online payments, smart cities, and digital innovation. Among the advantages of the Digital Silk Road, one should mention that it facilitates economic development. Business activities with the aid of digital technologies become quicker and cheaper. To the developing countries, digital infrastructure would assist in the generation of new employment and economic diversification. The Digital Silk Road promotes collaboration between nations.[8] By collaborating, nations can gain experience and upgrade their digital capabilities and infrastructure.[9] This partnership will help strengthen the ties as well as establish trust between the involved nations.

---

[2] Elena G. Popkova et al., "A Theory of Digital Technology Advancement to Address the Grand Challenges of Sustainable Development," *Technology in Society* 68 (2022): 101831.

[3] Jeffrey James, "Confronting the Scarcity of Digital Skills among the Poor in Developing Countries," *Development Policy Review* 39, no. 2 (2021): 324–39.

[4] Judith Mariscal, "Digital Divide in a Developing Country," *Telecommunications Policy* 29, nos. 5–6 (2005): 409–28.

[5] Muhammad Khalil Khan et al., "China's Belt and Road Initiative: A Global Model for an Evolving Approach to Sustainable Regional Development," *Sustainability* 10, no. 11 (2018): 4234.

[6] Ikrom Ahmedov, "The Impact of Digital Economy on International Trade," *European Journal of Business and Management Research* 5, no. 4 (2020).

[7] Hong Shen, "Building a Digital Silk Road? Situating the Internet in China's Belt and Road Initiative," *International Journal of Communication* 12 (2018): 19–19.

[8] Yebin Wang et al., "The Digital Silk Road and Trade Growth–A Quasi-Natural Experiment Based on Silk Road E-Commerce," *Research in International Business and Finance* 67 (2024): 102140.

[9] Gong Sen and Li Bingqin, *The Digital Silk Road and the Sustainable Development Goals*, 2019.

This chapter sets out to describe the Digital Silk Road in a simple and straightforward manner. The chapter demonstrates how digital infrastructure interacts with physical infrastructure to facilitate the current development and economic integration. It also presents significant digital projects, economic gains, legal issues, and future challenges.

2 The Concept and Scope of the Digital Silk Road

The concept of the Digital Silk Road is based on the same principles as the Silk Road of the past. The ancient Silk Road was a route that linked countries and people in terms of trading, knowledge, and culture.[10] The Digital Silk Road is similarly supposed to bring nations together by the use of digital networks, online platforms, and the transfer of information.[11] Through enhancing online connectivity, nations are able to exchange information, communicate at a higher speed, and carry out business more effectively. To address the increasing role of digital technology in the development of the world, the Digital Silk Road was proposed as a part of the BRI. The Digital Silk Road aims at establishing digital infrastructure in the respective countries, which is among the primary objectives. This will involve the construction of fiber-optic networks, the development of the mobile communication infrastructure, and the formation of data centers. DSR is targeted at enhancing e-commerce and online trade. It lowers the entry barriers of companies in the developing countries and provides new trade opportunities.

Besides infrastructure and trade, other advanced technologies that are covered by the Digital Silk Road include artificial intelligence (AI), big data, cloud computing, and smart cities.[12] The Digital Silk Road encourages innovation and modernization in the countries in which it supports these technologies. Digital governance and cybersecurity are also considered to be digital cooperation under the DSR.[13] The DSR pushes nations to come up with policies and standards of data protection, privacy, and cybersecurity. It facilitates international collaboration in solving digital risks and challenges. The DSR facilitates training, workshops, and knowledge-sharing programs to develop human capacity in information technology, digital management, and innovations. Digital Silk Road does not just cover Asia and the immediate neighbors of China. It also encompasses Africa,

---

[10] Xinru Liu, *The Silk Road in World History* (Oxford University Press, 2010).

[11] Ovigwe Eguegu, "The Digital Silk Road: Connecting Africa with New Norms of Digital Development," *Asia Policy* 17, no. 3 (2022): 30–39.

[12] Nariman Aliyev, "Artificial Intelligence in Digital Silk Road: Driving Innovation and Economic Transformation," *Euroasia Journal of Social Sciences & Humanities* 12, no. 1 (2025): 95–102.

[13] Bilal Khan et al., *Global Digital Risk Governance and Cyber Sovereignty: Implications for Coordinated Infrastructure Defense*, 2024.

Europe, and countries that comprise the BRI network. The DSR supports the international partnership and global connectivity by enabling countries to enhance economic growth, social development, and technological capacity through supporting the digital development.

3 Digital Silk Road Projects

3.1 Southeast Asia

The Digital Silk Road has gained center stage in Southeast Asia because it has emerged as a key location in the application of the digital economy, technologically diversified areas, and a strategic location between East Asia and South Asia.[14] The heterogeneity of digital preparedness and infrastructure in the region is a challenge and an opportunity for the implementation of integrated technologies. The projects of the DSR in Southeast Asia are built upon physical connectivity, as well as the establishment of interoperable digital ecosystems, with the idea of collaboration between governments, local businesses, and global suppliers of technology. The China-Laos railway is a perfect example of the merging of conventional and digital infrastructure.[15] The COVID-19 pandemic has seen the implementation of smart railway technologies by the companies Huawei and ZTE, providing real-time monitoring, automated control, and predictive maintenance, which has increased efficiency, passenger security, and service reliability.[16] The application of built-in sensors, artificial intelligence-based traffic control, and communication networks allows the railway to respond dynamically to the state of operations, which is a more general tendency in the DSR that entails the integration of digital intelligence into the development of large-scale infrastructure.

The 5G technology in Thailand diffuses the digital revolution to the health sector and to other areas. The collaboration between Huawei and Siriraj Hospital confirms that high-speed networks matter to provide an opportunity to use telemedicine, remote diagnostics, and rapid exchange of medical data.[17] Thailand is currently undergoing technological experimentation, which is also highlighted by the development of the first 5G testbed in the country. The testbed will provide a

---

[14] Huong Ha and CK Peter Chuah, "Digital Economy in Southeast Asia: Challenges, Opportunities and Future Development," *Southeast Asia: A Multidisciplinary Journal* 23, no. 1 (2023): 19–35.

[15] Ziying Cheng, *China's Influence on Laos' Infrastructure Investment and Lao People's Views on It-the Case Study of China-Laos Railway*, 2022.

[16] Xiaoyin Zhao et al., "Advancing Railway Systems with Next-Generation 5G Connectivity," 2024, 357–62.

[17] Pengfei Sun, "Media, Education, and Healthcare," in *Unleashing the Power of 5GtoB in Industries* (Springer, 2021).

controlled platform to develop and test new applications in such sectors as healthcare, manufacturing, and smart city management so that the stakeholders can experiment with new development without disrupting the existing system. The concentration in data infrastructure supporting local and global digital activity is underlined by the 3AZ data centers of Indonesia and multiple deals with 5G.[18] Such projects also enable local enterprises to take full advantage of e-business, financial technology, and service delivery at a global level due to the enhanced capacity in cloud computing, storage reliability, and network resiliency. The data management infrastructure also assists in supporting cross-border collaboration, regarding information exchange that is performed in real time, and in strengthening the incorporation of Indonesia in the digital trading systems across the world. The desire to establish a special center on cybersecurity indicates that it is very conscious of the threat of fast digitalization. Under DSR projects, Malaysia will protect the key digital networks, assets, and data against cyber threats by establishing advanced monitoring, threat detection, and response systems.[19] These campaigns play a pivotal role in maintaining trust in the Internet environment, compliance with the regulatory framework of development, and an investment in the development of the economy and technology in the long term.

In 2016, a regional digital cooperation center was opened in the China-ASEAN Information Harbor (CAIH).[20] Linking southern China and the ASEAN nations to each other by means of the combined big data, cloud computing, and cross-border information exchange systems, CAIH enhances the interoperability and aligned technological progress.[21] The project also enhances the connectivity within the region and enables member countries to share resources, common standards, and technological strategies, which aid the general digital ecosystem. These DSR projects in Southeast Asia are suggestive of a bigger strategy of combining infrastructure, technology, and governance to create integrated and data-based economic and urban systems. They demonstrate that the digital transformation might extend beyond the physical network to other sector-specific innovations, regulatory alignment, and regional interlocking. All the projects will focus on enhancing technological skills and the digitalization of the economy, as well as making Southeast Asia a strategically important location in the international Digital Silk Road system.

---

[18] Liza Mahavianti Syamsuri and Whildan Pakartipangi, "Challenges and Opportunities in Implementing Green Data Centers in Indonesia Toward Sustainable Digital Infrastructure," *Jurnal Penelitian Pendidikan IPA* 11, no. 6 (2025): 104–18.

[19] Barr-Kumarakulasinghe Cheryl and Boon-Kwee Ng, "Protecting the Unprotected Consumer Data in Internet of Things: Current Scenario of Data Governance in Malaysia," *Sustainability* 14, no. 16 (2022): 9893.

[20] Liang Cao et al., "Artificial Intelligence Empowering the Construction of the China–Cambodia Community of Shared Future: Mechanisms and Collaborative Pathways," *Advances in Social Behavior Research* 17, no. 1 (2026): 105–22.

[21] Yue Yang, *Digital Economy and the Sustainable Development of ASEAN and China*, vol. 9 (World Scientific, 2022).

3.2 *Middle East & North Africa*

The Middle East and North Africa (MENA) region represents an example of the Digital Silk Road implementation, whereby digital infrastructure is planned to be in line with the overall economic diversification objectives and the urban modernization efforts.[22] The projects in this region are concentrated on high-value sectors like smart cities, advanced telecommunications, digital logistics, and data-driven governance, thus, a clear transition to knowledge-based, digitally enabled economies. The NEOM Smart City in Saudi Arabia represents the most successful example of the implementation of cloud computing, big data analytics, and IoT technologies in the management of the city.[23] The participation of Alibaba Cloud allows implementing centralized platforms that will be able to process large amounts of urban data, and fulfill the functions of energy optimization, traffic management, and the provision of services to the population.[24] The project proves to be a move towards an algorithm-based planning of the city in which predictive analytics and data monitoring in real-time would inform the operational decision-making of the infrastructure, utilities, and municipal services.

The development of 5G networks in the United Arab Emirates by Huawei is a DSR project with a high-speed and low-latency network structure.[25] The infrastructure supports the smart services, industrialization, and digital-intensive applications in towns and businesses. The use of digital integration goes to the logistical front via the iMile Delivery platform, based in the UAE, backed by ByteDance.[26,27] The platform will exploit real-time tracking, the optimization of routes, and the automatic coordination to simplify the processes of e-commerce delivery. It helps to facilitate the increasing cross-border trade, especially transactions between Chinese suppliers, and increase the overall trustworthiness of digital supply chains by minimizing operational inefficiencies and increasing the speed of goods delivery across borders.

---

[22] Andrew Mazen Dahdal and Adel Abdel Ghafar, "The Digital Silk Road: 'Tech-Diplomacy' as a Paradigm for Understanding Technological Adoption and Emerging Digital Regulations in MENA," *Asian Journal of Law and Society* 12, no. 2 (2025): 163–88.

[23] Tanweer Alam et al., "Big Data for Smart Cities: A Case Study of NEOM City, Saudi Arabia," in *Smart Cities: A Data Analytics Perspective* (Springer, 2020).

[24] Gongtao Zhang and MN Ravishankar, "Exploring Vendor Capabilities in the Cloud Environment: A Case Study of Alibaba Cloud Computing," *Information & Management* 56, no. 3 (2019): 343–55.

[25] Sultan Ahmed Albalooshia et al., "Deployment of 5G Technology in the United Arab Emirates: Perspectives and Insights," *Kamu Yönetimi ve Politikaları Dergisi* 2, no. 1 (2021): 35–53.

[26] Robert Mogielnicki, "The Intersection of Digital Development Trajectories," *Routledge Handbook on China–Middle East Relations*, 2021.

[27] Jian Lin et al., *Chinese Platforms: A Critical Introduction* (John Wiley & Sons, 2025).

The 2Africa submarine cable project is an unprecedented shift in digital infrastructure in the region.[28] The project will link African nations to Europe and the Middle East and provide vast bandwidth capacity, lower the latency, and enhance the redundancy of international data networks.[29] The cable enables cloud computing, electronic trade, and cross-border information sharing, which supports MENA to integrate into the wider Digital Silk Road. Using these projects, the DSR of the Middle East and North Africa (MENA) region brings together urban digitalization and telecommunications modernization with cross-border connectivity. The region is making the infrastructure and the provision of services to people more advanced, with the integration of new, sophisticated digital systems, which makes the region a smart city and a digitally enabled economic growth.

3.3 Asia & Eastern Europe

Digital Silk Road projects in Asia are paying much attention to consolidating strategic data corridors and providing high-capacity connectivity to facilitate economic integration at the regional level.[30] The Pakistan China Fiber optic cable serves as a key backbone of connecting Xinjiang to Pakistan and offers secure and high speed in data transmission.[31] The project connects this land-based network to the wider submarine cable networks, thereby increasing digital divides across borders and helping to facilitate the regional economic pathways; thus, facilitating effective communication across the industrial, business, and governmental spheres. Redundancy, reliability, and resilience of the national telecommunications infrastructure are also enhanced by the availability of this network. Pakistan and East Africa Connecting Europe (PEACE) Fiber Optic Network is an extension of the connectivity system, and it connects China with Europe via Pakistan to form a long-distance digital path where information flows.[32,33] This network has played a

---

[31] Jamil Afzal et al., "Completion of the Ten Years of the China-Pakistan Economic Corridor (CPEC) and Its Economical Goals," *Inverge Journal of Social Sciences* 2, no. 4 (2023): 23–29.

[28] Ovigwe Eguegu, "The Digital Silk Road: Connecting Africa with New Norms of Digital Development," *Asia Policy* 17, no. 3 (2022): 30–39.

[29] Chinese Academy of Cyberspace Studies, "Development of the World's Information Infrastructure," in *World Internet Development Report 2017: Translated by Peng Ping* (Springer, 2018).

[30] Anita Prakash, "Connecting the Connectivity Plans in Asia and beyond: International Cooperation for Expanded Supply Chains and Resilient Growth," *The Comprehensive Asia Development Plan 3.0 (CADP 3.0): Towards an Integrated, Innovative, Inclusive, and Sustainable Economy*, 2022, 100.

[32] Xin Yue Shen, *Chinese ICT on the Digital Silk Road: A Case Study of Infrastructure Building in Pakistan*, 2020.

[33] Nowmay Opalinski et al., "The Quest for a Resilient Internet Access in a Constrained Geopolitical Environment," 2024, 55–66.

significant role in ensuring that bandwidth becomes highly available, the latency is lowered, and cross-border data flows become smoother. This kind of infrastructure allows communication over the world, cloud-based services, and also improves business access to international markets by businesses and government agencies operating along the route.

In Eastern Europe, the focus is on the city administration and intelligent cities technologies.[34] The Safe City project of Serbia, in cooperation with Huawei, presents advanced surveillance systems, which are characterized by a mixture of high-resolution surveillance, facial recognition, and centralized data management.[35] This project will be aimed at enhancing the safety of the population, increasing the response capacity in the event of an emergency, and giving municipal governments viable data to make relevant decisions. Constant data gathering and analysis of cities, as well as assistance in solving traffic jams, law enforcement, and resource distribution, exemplify how digital infrastructure can make the administration efficient. The Kyrgyzstan and Tajikistan countries in Central Asia are adopting smart city models that would enhance urban management with digital applications.[36] Duisburg exhibits a unique trend of DSR engagement where there is cross-over between the smart city planning and the logistics and trade infrastructure.[37] In this case, the digital systems are merged with transport networks, warehouses, and supply chain operations to enhance data sharing and coordination in operations. These technologies contribute to the optimization of cargo flow, real-time monitoring, and the allocation of resources, which makes Duisburg a key station in Eurasian digital and economic interconnectedness.

4 Implications of the Initiatives Under the Digital Silk Road

The DSR brings together both physical and digital connectivity, which opens possibilities in economic growth, social development, and regional collaboration. While many of the countries involved in the BRI do not have a well-developed digital infrastructure means that they cannot be fully involved in the digital

---

[34] Stefan Vladisavljev, *China's' Digital Silk Road'Enters the Western Balkans* (Association for International Affairs, 2021).

[35] Bartosz Kowalski, "V. Serbia-China Relations: The Security Dimension," *Publishing Series IEŚ Policy Papers Number 6/2022*, n.d., 59.

[36] Irina Turgel et al., "'Smart City'concept in Digital Economics: Practice of Russia and Kazakhstan," *International Journal of Economic Policy in Emerging Economies* 16, nos. 2–4 (2022): 139–57.

[37] John Manners-Bell et al., *Logistics and Supply Chains in Emerging Markets* (Kogan Page Publishers, 2014).

economy of the world.[38] The DSR assists individuals, companies, and governments in being digitally connected, even where connectivity to communication services was shaky in the past, by enhancing the mobile networks.[39] The enhanced connectivity also helps in supporting applications such as telemedicine, online education, and digital financial services, which are paramount to social and economic development.

A large number of BRI countries lack adequate data storage and management capabilities, thus restricting their capacity to exploit digital technologies. The DSR facilitates the process of building and running data centers to offer dependable digital services and make sure the information is safe, reachable, and under effective management.[40] The DSR allows countries to trade goods digitally to export their products, find new customers, and lessen the barriers to international trade. There are efforts such as the creation of online markets, cross-border payment systems, and digital logistics networks, which enhance the efficiency of trade. Most of the BRI countries have poor access to conventional banking services, particularly in rural regions. FinTech initiatives help individuals to gain access to digital financial services by using mobile phones, applications, and the internet.

5 The Economic Impact of the Digital Silk Road

5.1 Growth in Trade and E-Commerce

Digital Silk Road essentially changes the face of global trade by integrating digital processes in international trade to overcome structural inefficiencies that have in the past restricted the flow of trade.[41] Combining digital solutions with customs, regulatory bodies, and logistics providers will allow automating documentation, electronically clearing, and improving compliance reporting transparency.[42]

---

[38] Cheng Guo, "China's Digital Silk Road in the Age of the Digital Economy: Political Analysis," *Вестник Российского Университета Дружбы Народов. Серия: Международные Отношения* 22, no. 2 (2022): 271–87.

[39] Fakhar Hussain et al., "Infrastructure Development for the Digital Silk Road (DSR) and Its Implications for China under the Belt and Road Initiative," *Asia–Pacific Social Science Review* 23, no. 4 (2023): 7.

[40] Anahit Parzyan, "China's Digital Silk Road: Empowering Capabilities for Digital Leadership in Eurasia," in *China and Eurasian Powers in a Multipolar World Order 2.0* (Routledge, 2023).

[41] Maseeh Ullah et al., "Towards a Digital Silk Road: The Role of China's Digital Trade Provisions in Shaping Global Economic Corridor," *Journal for Current Sign* 3, no. 2 (2025): 365–78.

[42] Mykola Denysenko, "Management Technologies for Enhancing Integrated Processes in the Customs and Logistics Services Sector," *Вісник Київського Національного Університету Технологій Та Дизайну. Серія Економічні Науки*, 2020.

These steps will reduce administrative bottlenecks, reduce transaction costs, and the time span of delivery, which is a major benefit to small and medium-sized business enterprises that had earlier barriers to entry into global markets due to their structure. Increased levels of digital connectivity have the benefit of increasing the efficiency of the trade through stabilization of supply chains and real-time coordination between producers, distributors, and retailers. Being able to access accurate and timely data enables businesses to predict demand changes, manage inventory, change production schedules, and increase responsiveness to changes in the market. This leads to increased levels of trade, greater dependability in imports and exports, as well as their resistance to any interference caused by geopolitical, logistical, or environmental factors.

The phenomenon of the Silk Road E-Commerce is an illustrative attempt to institutionalize the digital trade cooperation.[43] China has developed e-commerce frameworks, digital payment frameworks, and integrated logistics, and these have been developed through bilateral and multilateral agreements.[44] Such arrangements promote cross-border compatibility of national systems, internationalization of regulatory standards, and the practice of best digital trade. Participation of countries in the DSR will enable the countries to enjoy better market access, organization of trade procedures, and better coordination of customs, taxation, and exchange of data.

DSR digital platforms enable companies to establish direct contact with consumers abroad without the intermediaries and less reliance on the traditional distribution channels.[45] This transformation of the market enhances competition, widens consumer preference, and boosts the transportation of goods between the regional and international markets. Agricultural, manufacturing, and technological producers have an opportunity to use the e-commerce platforms to tap into the new markets, and the growth of digital payment systems and the incorporation of fintech can streamline transactions and make money available to more people.

Digital cross-border trade also helps in the development of the related companies, such as logistics and warehousing, fintech, and IT services.[46] The companies that are involved in the last-mile delivery, digital tracking of logistics, and optimization of the supply chain receive higher demand due to higher volumes of trade. Simultaneously, data analytics and AI-based forecasting enhance the efficiency of

---

[43] Xin wei Chen, "The Legal Protection of" Silk Road E-Commerce": Challenges, Approaches, and Solutions," *International Journal of Law and Politics Studies* 7, no. 3 (2025): 01–14.

[44] Yue Hongfei, "National Report on E-Commerce Development in China," *Inclusive and Sustainable Industrial Development Working Paper Series WP17* 6 (2017).

[45] Elisa Oreglia et al., "The Puzzle of the Digital Silk Road," *Digital Silk Road in Central Asia: Present and Future* 1 (2021).

[46] Mansi Trivedi and Jitendra Kumar Gautam, "Transforming Cross Border Trade with the Advancement of Digital Platform: An Analysis," *Journal of International Economics* 16, no. 1 (2025): 33–44.

operations and strategic decision-making in any sector.[47] All these developments reinforce economic interconnections and integration of regional trade and development of an ecosystem that is digitally enabled with trade efficiency, market access, and technological innovation.

5.2 *Infrastructure Development and Investment*

Digital Silk Road investment is devoted to developing a strong digital infrastructure to promote long-term economic growth and technological modernization.[48] The central part of such work is the creation of telecommunications infrastructure, such as the implementation of 5G networks, large-scale fiber-optic infrastructures, and satellite communications networks. The Chinese technology companies like Huawei and ZTE offer essential expertise, equipment, and management of project thus implementing these networks in the areas where the current communication systems are inadequate to meet the needs faster.[49] Fast and low-latency connectivity increases the ability to implement sophisticated applications like cloud computing, e-commerce, AI, and IoT solutions. Ensuring digital infrastructure gaps are one of the main goals targeted, especially in developing nations in Africa, Southeast Asia, and some areas of Central Asia. Inadequate ICT systems in the areas have, in the past, limited access to online services, effective communication, and digital economic activities. DSR investment projects increase broadband access, enhance network reliability, and improve cross-border connectivity. Improved digital infrastructure enables expanded access to online services in education, health, government services, and business processes to enable socioeconomic inclusion and make regions competitive.

A key area of concentration in the development initiatives of infrastructure is urban digitalization.[50] Through the development of safe and high-capacity facilities, the involved countries will have the capacity to store, process, and handle a high amount of data generated by both government and individuals in digital activities. These centers are backup facilities, support for cloud services, and

[47] Abdulrahman Al-Surmi et al., "AI Based Decision Making: Combining Strategies to Improve Operational Performance," *International Journal of Production Research* 60, no. 14 (2022): 4464–86.

[48] Vitaly Ambalov and Irina Heim, "Investments in the Digital Silk Road," in *Kazakhstan's Diversification from the Natural Resources Sector: Strategic and Economic Opportunities* (Springer, 2020).

[49] Frasminggi Kamasa and Riva'atul Adaniah Wahab, "China Technological Transformation: A Case Study of Telecommunications Equipment Industry," *Buletin Pos Dan Telekomunikasi*, 2021, 59–80.

[50] Fakhar Hussain et al., "Infrastructure Development for the Digital Silk Road (DSR) and Its Implications for China under the Belt and Road Initiative," *Asia–Pacific Social Science Review* 23, no. 4 (2023): 7.

digital platforms without jeopardizing the stability of the system, its reliability, and cybersecurity. The merger of data infrastructure and telecommunication infrastructures and intelligent cities is a holistic ecosystem that supports industrial innovation, the development of financial technologies, and the development of e-commerce.

The fiber-optic cables, 5G networks, and connected data systems connect two or more countries, allowing digital trade, cross-border communication, and information to be shared without any obstacles.[51] These networks minimize the technical obstacles, cut down operational expenses, and lay the foundation for the new digital industries. The investments in physical and digital infrastructure reinforce capacities on the national and regional levels, facilitate modernization of the industries, and form the principles of sustainable involvement in the global digital economy.

5.3 Industrial Transformation and Innovation

Digital Silk Road creates structural change in various sectors as it inserts high-technological digital technology in vintage production and service systems.[52] Artificial intelligence, analytics based on big data, and the Internet of Things are being gradually implemented in manufacturing, agriculture, logistics, and service industries, and allow monitoring operations in real time, maintaining machinery predictively, and making decisions based on data. Smart factories and precision agriculture, as well as automated logistics systems, are on the rise, which leads to an increase in the efficiency of operations, a decrease in the amount of wasted material, minimization of downtimes, and a general increase in productivity.

In the production sector, AI-based quality checks, robotization, and smart supply chain management can enable a company to respond to the demands of the market rapidly and to decrease the use of human labor. Sensors and IoT networks help agricultural sectors to track the health of soil, climate, and crops, and maximize resource management and yield. Likewise, the logistics and transportation networks also make use of digital tracking, smart inventory management, and route optimization to lower costs, enhance delivery times, and enhance the effectiveness of cross-border trade. The project encourages technological leapfrogging, which enables the partner nations to skip the middle steps towards industrialization. Availability to Chinese platforms, infrastructure, and technical know-how hastens modernization and, through this, the economic systems are able to merge

[51] Bilal Ahmed, "Cross-Border Connectivity: Strengthening Economic Ties and Regional Integration," *Journal of Regional Connectivity and Development* 3, no. 1 (2024): 70–84.

[52] Arturo Guillén and Ivan Cortés Torres, "Changes in the World Geopolitical Order and the Reconfiguration of Productive Systems: The Mexican Case," *Agrarian South: Journal of Political Economy* 14, no. 1 (2025): 26–59.

the sophisticated production systems without necessarily going through the conventional industrialization of long periods.[53] This promotes the knowledge transfer, innovation-based development, and enables countries to shift to the high-value production and service-defined sectors. The local companies are also able to implement the latest technological advances and engage in the regional and global digital supply chains.

The digital financial innovation supplements the transformation in the industrial sphere as it offers the means of increased economic involvement.[54] The growth of mobile payment systems and digital wallets, online banking, and fintech platforms enhances efficient and secure money transfers, particularly in areas with a low level of traditional banking facilities.[55] This exposes small and medium enterprises to credit, tracking of transactions, and digital marketplaces, which help in the growth of entrepreneurship and expansion of markets. Greater financial inclusion will intensify consumer engagement in the digital economy and business resilience and allow new business models to be developed based on digital platforms and cross-border trade.[56] The DSR promotes the industrial data ecosystems, where production, distribution, and consumer data can be gathered, analyzed, and shared on the networks.[57] Such integrated systems will allow predictive analytics, scenario planning, and resource optimization to be more resilient and adaptive industrial landscape. The extensive industrial change brought about by technological modernization, automation of processes, and digitalization of finances increases productivity levels, competitiveness, and innovation potential among the countries involved.

5.4 Regional and Strategic Economic Effects

The Digital Silk Road strengthens economic relations between China and its partners through the establishment of a China-centric digital ecosystem that is

---

[53] Jiangang Zhang, "The Development Strategy and Practice Path of Chinese Industrial Modernization from the Perspective of Technological Revolution," *China Political Economy* 8, no. 1 (2025): 45–62.

[54] Mikhail Yakovlevich Veselovsky et al., "Financial and Economic Mechanisms of Promoting Innovative Activity in the Context of the Digital Economy Formation," *Entrepreneurship and Sustainability Issues* 5, no. 3 (2018): 672–81.

[55] Mohamed Cherif El Amri et al., "Enhancing Financial Inclusion Using FinTech-Based Payment System," in *Islamic FinTech: Insights and Solutions* (Springer, 2021).

[56] Engidaw Abriham Ebabu et al., "Navigating Sustainable Digital Transformation in South-South Cross-Border E-Commerce: Insights on Cultural Adaptation, Green Marketing Strategy, and Inclusive Business Model Innovation," *International Review of Economics & Finance*, 2026, 104907.

[57] Matthew S. Erie and Thomas Streinz, "The Beijing Effect: China's Digital Silk Road as Transnational Data Governance," *NYUJ Int'l L. & Pol.* 54 (2021): 1.

China-centric.[58] Conformity to the Chinese technical standards, provision of compatible digital infrastructure, and integration and use of interconnected platforms ensure a smooth cross-border communication, data exchange, and commercial dealings.[59] This union allows the involved countries to coordinate digital functions, decrease the technical strain on trade, and boost collaboration in the business and government sectors. The incorporation into the DSR framework also helps countries to upgrade their place in the global value chains. This revolution enables economies to no longer rely on cheap, work-intensive sectors, which makes them more competitive in the world markets and also enables the growth of their economies to become more innovation-oriented.

The program helps the Chinese technology firms in global growth.[60] Corporations like Alibaba, Tencent, Baidu, and Huawei enjoy chances of implementing digital platforms, infrastructure, and services in participating countries.[61] Such investments help to create regional digital ecosystems, encourage the usage of Chinese technical standards, and enhance the spread of technological innovation. The modern technologies, experience in deploying digital infrastructure, and cooperation in such spheres as e-commerce, smart cities, and fintech lead partner countries to the creation of a self-enhancing network of digital development.

Under the DSR, strategic economic centers are the points of regional connectivity. An example is the Guangxi province in China, which serves as a critical digital and logistical hub between China and ASEAN markets.[62] Infrastructure projects, such as fiber-optic systems, smart ports, and connected data centers, allow the effective flow of information, goods, and services. Other hubs in Pakistan, Southeast Asia, and Eastern Europe enable local economic integration, connecting the local economies to the rest of the digital world. They are not only trade and logistics hubs, but they also act as knowledge transfer, innovation centers, and collaboration in digital governance, establishing long-term strategic value to the participating countries.

---

[58] Fakhar Hussain et al., "The Digital Rise and Its Economic Implications for China through the Digital Silk Road under the Belt and Road Initiative," *Asian Journal of Comparative Politics* 9, no. 2 (2024): 238–53.

[59] Meng Chen, "Developing China's Approaches to Regulate Cross-Border Data Transfer: Relaxation and Integration," *Computer Law & Security Review* 54 (2024): 105997.

[60] Peter Nolan and Jin Zhang, "The Challenge of Globalization for Large Chinese Firms," *World Development* 30, no. 12 (2002): 2089–107.

[61] Yujia He, "Chinese Digital Platform Companies' Expansion in the Belt and Road Countries," in *China's Digital Expansion in the Global South* (Routledge, 2024).

[62] Chunyang Wei and Qinjie Shen, "Strengthening ASEAN-Guangxi Trade Relations: Enhancing Regional Integration and Industrial Collaboration," *American Journal of Business Science Philosophy*, 2025, 150–68.

6 Legal Implications of the Digital Silk Road

6.1 Data Sovereignty and Surveillance

The Digital Silk Road development introduces multiple legal and operational implications of data sovereignty and national security. Combining overseas-constructed digital infrastructure, perhaps 5G networks, cloud infrastructure, and massive data centers, partner nations may be vulnerable to foreign interference in terms of the collection, storage, and transportation of valuable data. The involvement of Chinese technology firms in the design, building, and regulation of such systems appears to cast doubt on the suitability of home-based legislation on contractual or regulating law provisions that were developed in China, particularly on the chances of obtaining sensitive information. Some of the information passing through such networks is likely to be the communications of the state, banking operations, industrial operations, and personal information of citizens. Whatever the foreign parties do with this information will present undesired areas of weakness, and it can lead to the exposure of state secrets, business secrets, and individual privacy. This exposure is particularly valuable in such areas of national defense, health care, financial, and telecommunication sectors where the factors of operational security and confidentiality are the most important. There is also surveillance in relation to DSR-related projects. The availability of real-time data collection and analytics is provided through smart city efforts and other applications of the advanced monitoring systems. On one hand, these systems help in terms of efficiency and service delivery; on the other hand, it fosters the prospect of foreign access, surveillance, or control by foreign providers that could undermine the legal frameworks and the current oversight systems.

The partner countries must embrace holistic governance policies to deal with these risks, such as legal, technical, and organizational policies. The law safeguards may be the boundary of the possession and the access to the data, the elaboration of the control institutions, and the organization of the terms of the contract that may limit foreign intrusion to the sector of sensitive activities.[63] Technical controls involve encryption, network segmentation, secure storage of data, and checking system integrity at any given time. The methods used by organizations include capacity building, training of the staff on how to manage the digital infrastructure, and regular check-ups of compliance with the national standards of cybersecurity.[64] The balance between the positive elements of the connectivity,

[63] Martina Francesca Ferracane, "Data Flows and National Security: A Conceptual Framework to Assess Restrictions on Data Flows under GATS Security Exception," *Digital Policy, Regulation and Governance* 21, no. 1 (2019): 44–70.

[64] Milad Aslaner, *Cybersecurity Strategies and Best Practices: A Comprehensive Guide to Mastering Enterprise Cyber Defense Tactics and Techniques* (Packt Publishing Ltd, 2024).

economic modernization, and digital innovation on the one hand and the security of the critical assets, privacy of the citizens, and the ability of the state to regulate the flow of information on the other; are the main aspect that the countries involved in the initiative are taking into consideration.

6.2 Data Localization and Content Control

Digital Silk Road projects often demand partner nations to adopt Chinese-style regulations that focus on the localization of data. According to these policies, any data created within the field of jurisdiction of any country has to be stored in local servers or a specific regional hub. Such a structure has operational controls, adherence to technical and contractual requirements, and centralized control over vital infrastructure, i.e., 5G networks, data centers, and government information systems. These policies are designed to improve security, ensure system reliability, and control the cross-border flow of data according to the operational needs of the project by controlling the place of data storage. Digital service deployment and management are other areas that are affected by the adoption of data localization standards.[65] Firms involved in DSR programs must have infrastructure that is consistent with these storage and transfer needs, such as safe backup measures, backup servers, and access control measures. In order to make sure that data handling follows the recommended guidelines, the compliance measures typically involve encryption, monitoring systems, and frequent audits.

Besides the storage needs, content management and regulatory tools typically form part of Digital Silk Road platforms on Chinese standards.[66] Such systems are able to put filtering, monitoring, and restriction mechanisms on online information based on predetermined rules. The measures of content control also affect the access to information on both the public and the private network, impacting the social media, e-commerce, online services, and the communication channels used publicly. The combination of these systems alters the operation of digital services, their algorithms, and permissions of access, as well as the way of delivery of services by service providers. These measures also influence the operations of the government and business practices. These regulatory norms of e-government services, digital health systems, and smart city projects can be transferred to public institutions, and the companies in the sphere of the market have to synchronize their data processing, cloud storage, and manage the data of customers with the requirements of localization. Users of the platforms are influenced by limited or censored access to material, a distorted flow of information, and the presence of certain regulations that govern online communication.

---

[65] Richard D. Taylor, "'Data Localization': The Internet in the Balance," *Telecommunications Policy* 44, no. 8 (2020): 102003.

[66] Paul Triolo et al., "The Digital Silk Road: Expanding China's Digital Footprint," *Eurasia Group* 8 (2020): 1–13.

6.3 Regulatory Harmonization

The Digital Silk Road invites nations that establish a digital policy to meet the technical regulations and standards applied in China.[67] This harmonization covers various elements of digital infrastructure, such as network design, 5G deployment guidelines, cloud computing models, data storage, and cybersecurity. The implementation of these standards by countries will facilitate the union of the technology platforms, digital services, and smart infrastructure systems being offered by Chinese companies. The involved developing countries, considering the DSR, can align their legal frameworks with the laws regarding privacy, data protection, and the digital government to guarantee consistency with Chinese laws.[68] Such changes usually entail a re-evaluation of the domestic laws to support data management methods, encryption guidelines, and cybersecurity requirements in line with the Chinese demands. The procedure can also involve setting up certification processes, technical audits, and compliance verification systems for the digital service providers within these jurisdictions.

The common protocols permit digital systems produced in one country to interact with those produced in another country effectively, promote the unrestricted flow of data, and minimize the obstacles to the implementation of e-commerce systems, telecommunication infrastructures, and online payment systems.[69] This has caused a change in the legal and operational practice in partner countries due to the change towards standardized regulations. It establishes policies on how to govern the movement of information across borders, the management of cloud resources, and the tracking of cybersecurity threats. The technical and legal requirements that must be adhered to by the private enterprises are the localization of the data storage, reporting policy, and audit of the operations. These standards can be incorporated into the national digital infrastructure, smart cities, and e-government strategies of public institutions. The harmonization process tends to be conducted with technical assistance, knowledge-sharing programs, and co-training to enhance local capacity in network management, computer security, and enforcement of digital policies. The government regulators, technology providers, and industry stakeholders coordinate so that the implementation of technical standards is effective, and yet, operational continuity and system interoperability are maintained.

[67] David Gordon and Meia Nouwens, *The Digital Silk Road: China's Technological Rise and the Geopolitics of Cyberspace* (Taylor & Francis, 2022).

[68] Pramila Paudel, "Divergent Digital Paths: A Comparative Study of Regulatory Frameworks and Participation in the Digital Silk Road between China and Nepal," *International Journal of Law and Legal Advancement* 1, no. 2 (2025).

[69] Subhajit Basu, "E-government and Developing Countries: An Overview," *International Review of Law, Computers & Technology* 18, no. 1 (2004): 109–32.

6.4 Arbitration and Technical Standards

Digital Silk Road projects are catalyzing the development of jurisdiction-oriented models of cross-border digital trade, which include legal, technical, and operational aspects. These frameworks provide guidelines for the implementation and sustenance of the digital infrastructure, provide standards for e-commerce and online transactions, and provide mechanisms for resolving conflicts that might arise among the participating entities. The frameworks will be structured to capture local regulatory landscapes, technological capacity, and local economic priorities of DSR partner nations that may lead to standards that are inconsistent with current international standards or global standards that are commonly used by the world.

The introduction of new arbitration mechanisms in these models defines the procedures of resolving conflicts in such areas as performance of contracts, copyright, software licensing, and service-level agreements in digital projects. Controversy resolution can be based on arbitration committees, technical committees, or both legal and technical skills. Differences in technical requirements, network interoperability needs, and compliance regulations affect the process of drafting, enforcement, and interpretation of agreements across borders. These frameworks need to be developed with the assistance of the government agencies, technology providers, and other partners in the private sector. The regulatory and arbitration protocols contain guidelines for technical evaluation, certification of digital systems, and compliance monitoring. This is an ecosystem that includes training programs of legal and technical professionals, knowledge-sharing programs, and cross-border technical cooperation.

6.5 Cybersecurity Risks

The use of Chinese technology to provide hardware, software, and digital infrastructure under the Digital Silk Road exposes the participating nations to numerous cybersecurity threats.[70] Introduction of foreign systems into the critical networks provides a potential vulnerability that may be used by malicious actors. Such vulnerabilities can be characterized by vulnerabilities of hardware, software, network settings, or inadequate security measures. The finance, healthcare, transportation, and public administration sectors are critical and more and more rely on the digital infrastructure, but they are at risk of data breaches, ransomware attacks, and unauthorized access. These can also target industrial networks, manufacturing control systems, and smart city platforms and interfere with essential

[70] Bora Ly, "Challenge and Perspective for Digital Silk Road," *Cogent Business & Management* 7, no. 1 (2020): 1804180.

services, supply chains, or urban management processes. Depending on outsourcing partners to update their technology, maintain, and provide security patches may present further vulnerability. System integrity may be affected by a supply chain attack, manipulation of the firmware, or embedded software vulnerabilities on imported technology. There is also the fear of strategic or political risk, whereby exposure to sensitive governmental, commercial, or personal data may lead to external influence to make decisions or control operations. Through coordinated cyber activities, communication networks and information channels can be observed or distorted, and industrial or logistical systems can be impaired.

7 Digital Silk Road Legal Agreements

7.1 Digital Economy & Investment Agreements (MOUs)

In 2023, an MOU was signed between China and Turkmenistan dedicated to collaboration in the digital economy.[71] The contract also involves the formation of online trading platforms, the use of data centers, and the development of communication infrastructures. It identifies the technology transfer mechanisms, joint research programmes, and knowledge exchange in the area of emerging digital technology like cloud computing, artificial intelligence, and big data analytics.

In 2017, China and Malaysia signed an MOU of the Digital Free Trade Zone (DFTZ), containing Alibaba Group and Malaysia Digital Economy Corporation (MDEC).[72,73] The collaboration includes e-commerce across borders, online logistics networks, and e-payment systems. The agreement provides the procedures of the SMEs to engage in international digital trade, guidance in the development of infrastructure, including fulfillment centers, as well as coordination of ICT-enabled services.

China has also signed more MOUs with nations in Asia, Africa, and Latin America,[74,75] Such deals concern the deployment of land-based and subsea fiber-optic cables, building smart city platforms, and the adoption of secure data centers. Among the agreements, technical cooperation, digital operations standardization, and network interoperability are outlined. The provisions of the MOUs

---

[71] Agha Bayramov and Fabio Indeo, "Uzbekistan, and Turkmenistan," *European Union Governance in Central Asia: A Sectoral Approach*, 2024.

[72] Evelyn S. Devadason, "Rethinking Trade Policy in Malaysia," *Post-Pandemic Economic and Social Development: Recovery, Challenges, and Policy in Malaysia*, 2024.

[73] Tham Siew Yean, "Development of E-Commerce in Malaysia," *E-Commerce, Competition & ASEAN Economic Integration*, 2019, 169–92.

[74] Kevin P. Gallagher, *The China Triangle: Latin America's China Boom and the Fate of the Washington Consensus* (Oxford University Press, 2016).

[75] Thomas Lum, *China's Assistance and Government-Sponsored Investment Activities in Africa, Latin America, and Southeast Asia* (2009).

also concern digital governance, data protection, cybersecurity standards, and cross-border information management. Some of these agreements also detail training regimes, capacity-building initiatives, and joint ventures to enhance human resources in information technology, digital management, and innovations.

7.2 Digital Infrastructure & Technology Agreements

China-ASEAN Information Harbor (CAIH) is one of the initiatives linking southern China and ASEAN nations.[76] The project will entail laying down the terrestrial fiber-optic network, integration of cloud computing systems, and the deployment of regional data hubs. CAIH aids in the mass exchange of data, increases the effectiveness of communication in the region, and facilitates cross-border e-trade and e-commerce. Growth of other services like cloud storage, big data analytics, and digital financial systems is also possible through the infrastructure.

In Serbia, contractual deals signed in 2022–2023 allowed the projects of Safe City to be made.[77] Some of the projects under these systems are innovative surveillance, live tracking of urban settings, intelligent traffic control systems, and unified community security platforms by Huawei. The program is aimed at enhancing city services, managing the city better, and coordinating the response system to emergencies.

The construction of 5G networks and the creation of modern data centers became the central topics of agreements between China and the UAE that were signed in 2023–2024.[78] The projects enable quick connectivity, manage large-scale cloud computing and e-government services, and deploy the next-generation digital applications, such as smart healthcare, online education systems, and online logistics systems.

The same cooperative model has been used to implement submarine cable projects in Latin America and the Caribbean, like PEACE cable. These projects promote international connectivity, network coverage, and digital infrastructure in the region. The smart city projects in these areas involve the creation of integrated traffic systems, urban IoT networks, and centralized data platforms for municipal management.

[76] Bahareh Sazmand, "China and Global South: BRI in Southeast Asia," in *Implications, Prospects, and Challenges in China's Global South Strategy* (IGI Global Scientific Publishing, 2025).

[77] Mladen Grgić, *Chinese Infrastructure Diplomacy in the Balkans: Beijing 'Sponsored' Consensus* (Taylor & Francis, 2025).

[78] Mona Omar Ali Massalha, *China's Digital Silk Road Impact on the Gulf Cooperation Council's Information and Communication Technology Sector Growth Amid Sino American Competition* 2025 ,رسالة دكتوراة.

7.3 *Trade Agreements with DSR Provisions*

The Nicaragua–China Free Trade Agreement (2024) contains special provisions to facilitate the development of digital trade so that e-commerce, mobile and online payment systems, as well as integrated digital logistics networks, could be conducted in a cross-border manner.[79] These clauses are meant to ensure that the internal borders of the businesses are opened to allow international markets entry and enhance their trade transactions.

Ecuador-China Free Trade Agreement (2024) is based on close collaboration in the digital economy.[80] It promotes the use of online platforms to trade, the application of data-driven procedures to streamline the supply chain, and the integration of the technological system to be more competitive. This framework helps both the government and the business in Ecuador to streamline trade activities and engage effectively in the global marketplace in the digital world.

The 2024 agreements between China and Belarus are aimed at investment and service trade, with the introduction of technology transfer and sharing of knowledge.[81] Such agreements can help Belarus to use Chinese experience in information and communication technology (ICT), the development of the digital infrastructure, and innovation-based solutions to offer the means to empower domestic businesses and improve economic diversification.

7.4 *Digital Standards & Technical Cooperation*

The Digital Silk Road places a lot of stress on the creation of common technical standards and regulatory frameworks to guarantee interoperability, security, and work efficiency across the countries involved.[82] The standardization plays a key role in facilitating the smooth integration of networks, platforms, and digital services, especially when different countries with diverse technological capabilities are engaged. Standardized technical requirements will minimize the problem of compatibility, ease inter-country transactions in digital form, and contribute to the scalability of infrastructure development plans in the long term of the DSR. The online Silk Road is based on China's 3rd Five-Year Plan of National

---

[79] Yanji Lu and Li Sun, "Research on the Economic Effects of China-Nicaragua FTA Under the Background of 'The Belt and Road' _based on GTAP-Dyn Model," 2024, 192–98.

[80] Eddy S. Astudillo Aguilar, "Waking the Sleeping Lion: The China-Ecuador FTA and Its Implications," *Global Trade and Customs Journal* 19, no. 11/12 (2024).

[81] Huirong Zhao, "China and Belarus' High-Quality Collaboration in the Belt and Road Initiative: Achievements, Challenges, and Prospects," *Chinese Journal of Slavic Studies*, 2025.

[82] Alex He, *The Digital Silk Road and China's Influence on Standard Setting* (CIGI Papers, 2022).

Informatization (March 2016).[83] It offers comprehensive principles to the digital infrastructure, e-governments, cloud computing, and cross-border connectivity development. The plan stimulates the adoption of the newest technologies, such as big data, artificial intelligence, and smart city solutions, to stimulate the coordinated digital development and the improvement of economic and social integration throughout the network.

The Five-Year Action Plan of Highway Technical Cooperation,[84] under CPEC in Pakistan in 2023–2027, shows how physical infrastructure work within the framework of the DSR can integrate digital technologies. The plan consists of digital traffic management systems, alignment of technical standards, and transport network monitoring based on data. The latter integration emphasizes the prospect of hybrid infrastructural solutions, in which the digital solutions are used to enhance the physical constructions, enhance functionality, and promote sustainable urban and intercity development.

Another significant tool of technical cooperation is the Global Initiative on Data Security, provided with the help of several signatory countries.[85] This project will establish standardized data protection and cybersecurity, together with transnational information transfers. The initiative can be used to reduce the risks of data breaches, cyberattacks, and unauthorized access, as well as to make sure that digital infrastructure throughout the DSR network works safely and reliably by encouraging compliance with these standards.

8 Future Prospects and Challenges

Managing the Digital Silk Road (DSR) has provided a new avenue to the countries that are part of the Belt and Road Initiative (BRI). It has contributed to the enhancement of trade, investment, and social development by concentrating on digital infrastructure, technology, and connectivity. Countries comprehend the future opportunities but also the challenges that might arise in order to reap the maximum benefits of digital development. The Digital Silk Road has one of its primary opportunities in the form of the expanded digital infrastructure. Greater infrastructure development will also enable the developing countries to engage in global trade more actively, have access to digital education, and utilize digital healthcare services. Infrastructure developments will experience new opportunities

---

[83] Scott Kennedy and Christopher K. Johnson, *Perfecting China, Inc.: China's 13th Five-Year Plan* (Bloomsbury Publishing USA, 2016).

[84] Houkai Wei et al., "China's Strategies and Policies for Regional Development during the Period of the 14th Five-Year Plan," *Chinese Journal of Urban and Environmental Studies* 8, no. 02 (2020): 2050008.

[85] Przemysław CIBOREK, "China's Global Initiatives: Challenges and Prospects," *New Chinese Initiatives for a Changing Global Security*, 2023, 91–110.

in construction, IT, network management, and digital services. Another opportunity is the creation of 5G and the next generation of communication technologies. The 5G technology can facilitate more industrial productivity by automating and using digital monitoring systems to support new digital services such as smart cities, autonomous transportation, and advanced e-commerce. The technologies will enable countries that are members of the DSR to modernize industries and logistics and offer better services to their citizens.

Innovation and technological progress are also encouraged in the Digital Silk Road. Artificial intelligence, cloud computing, big data, and the Internet of Things (IoT) are taking on increasing significance in terms of businesses and governments. These technologies can help countries that participated in the DSR to enhance the decision-making process, manage resources better, and create new products and services. The DSR-supported innovation could result in new industries, increased productivity, and economic competitiveness. The digital ecosystem formed with the help of the initiative is likely to help startups and other technology companies. E-commerce and digital trade will continue to expand in the future. The availability of online markets, digital financial services, and cross-border solutions will enable businesses of different sizes to penetrate and serve the international markets. Development banks, governments, and individual investors should collaborate to achieve sustainable financing. The projects can be stalled or not performed well without a clear agreement and financial planning. Nations should follow sustainable operations, energy-saving technologies, and ethical standards, especially in the case of new technologies, like artificial intelligence and online surveillance. At the same time, this must be well thought out, legal, cooperative, and sustainable to address risks and ensure it makes the best out of it.

9 Conclusion

This chapter has discussed the Digital Silk Road as an extension of the larger Belt and Road Initiative, and this transformation of trade, governance, and social development via the use of digital infrastructure, technology, and connectivity. The goal of the initiative to priorities high-speed internet networks, mobile communication systems, data centers, and cutting-edge technologies, including artificial intelligence, cloud computing, and smart city solutions, has provided countries with more opportunities to engage in the global digital economy. Such advancements have seen businesses have access to international markets, enhanced supply chain efficiency, and also led to innovation in various sectors. The Digital Silk Road has a huge economic effect, especially. Small and medium-sized businesses have been able to break through barriers to trade that existed in old times due to the availability of e-commerce sites, digital payment systems, and online logistics systems to increase their opportunities for venturing and economic diversification.

Chapter 3
Digital Silk Road and Contemporary Theory of Digitalization

Abstract The Digital Silk Road is an important project that is increasing digital connectivity and contributing to economic integration in different regions. The Contemporary Theory of Digitalization (CToD), often known as the theory of digitalization, provides a multidimensional approach that includes technological, institutional, economic, and socio-technical dimensions of the digital transformation. This chapter creates a theoretical connection between DSR and CToD and states that digitalization is not only about the development of the infrastructures, but also about systematic transformation of governance, industrial frameworks, and organizational cultures. It emphasizes that CToD facilitates the transformation of conventional economic systems to digitally integrated systems by harmonizing technological implementation and legal systems, human capital growth, and data management. Special focus is placed on the problems of digital sovereignty, regulatory balance, and technological integration with institutional capacity. The chapter discussed how interoperable standards, digital diplomacy, and cybersecurity collaboration can minimize legal fragmentation and improve coordination across the involved countries. It also takes into account the regulatory voids of new technologies like artificial intelligence, big data, and blockchain, and the need to have certainty in the law to develop digital sustainability.

Keywords Contemporary Theory of Digitalization · Digital Silk Road · Levels of CToD · Socio-technical dimensions · Digitalization

J. Afzal and Y. Chen, *Legal Framework of Digital Economy and Digital Trade Under the Belt and Road Initiative*, https://doi.org/10.1007/978-981-92-4444-7_3

1 Introduction

Although the DSR is expected to close digital divides between different parts of the world, emerging challenges like patchy regulatory environments, overlapping legislations on data sovereignty, and institutional bottlenecks.[1,2] To give a solid outline of the Digital Silk Road, the rational behind the use of the Contemporary Theory of Digitalization (CToD), it is essential to note that the theory does not fit the more traditional, technologically deterministic theories that tend to overlook the localities.[3] Conventional wisdom often presumes that the economic growth effect of digital infrastructure projects will be automatic; CToD acknowledges the developmental effect of technology as conditional, nonlinear, and site-specific. Following this theory, the DSR can be perceived as a scenario-specific process, as the success of digital expansion is closely connected to the quality of existing institutions and the level of social trust. This framework offers a scientifically based foundation of compatibility between digital transformation and social inclusion and governance in such a way that the DSR not only promotes physical connectivity but also long-term, sustainable development.

The CToD offers a rational path to the bends and twists of the global digital development by incorporating different perspectives in a way that the Digital Silk Road is an active ecosystem, which is extremely balanced and resilient.[4] DSR is not simply a system of digital infrastructure initiatives, but a vibrant digital ecosystem that takes into account the communication technologies, monetary arrangements, regulatory customs, and cross-national data transits.[5] The concept of such an ecosystem cannot be properly explained by means of linear or infrastructure-focused models since it presupposes the ongoing process of interaction between technological systems and institutional setups.[6] CToD can particularly be applied in that environment because this method positions digitalization as an evolutionary and co-evolutionary process where technology and governance structures are co-evolutionary rather than evolutionary.[7]

---

[1] Anupam Chander and Haochen Sun, *Data Sovereignty: From the Digital Silk Road to the Return of the State* (Oxford University Press, 2023).

[2] David Gordon and Meia Nouwens, *The Digital Silk Road: China's Technological Rise and the Geopolitics of Cyberspace* (Taylor & Francis, 2022).

[3] Jamil Afzal, "Theory of Digitalization: Contemporary Theory of Digitalization," *International Journal of Discovery in Social Sciences* 2, no. 1 (2026).

[4] Nariman Aliyev, "Artificial Intelligence in Digital Silk Road: Driving Innovation and Economic Transformation," *Euroasia Journal of Social Sciences & Humanities* 12, no. 1 (2025): 95–102.

[5] Andrea Pollio, *Silicon Elsewhere* (University of California Press, 2026).

[6] Abdulaziz I. Almulhim and Tan Yigitcanlar, "Understanding Smart Governance of Sustainable Cities: A Review and Multidimensional Framework," *Smart Cities* 8, no. 4 (2025): 113.

[7] Jamil Afzal, "Nomenclature of the Digital Economy and Contemporary Theory of Digitalization," in *Exploring the New Horizons of International Law Concerning Globalization of Economy* (Springer, 2026).

2 Theoretical Linkage Between DSR and CToD

The applicability of the Contemporary Theory of Digitalization to the DSR could also be elaborated by considering the structural complexity and multi-layered governance environment in which the initiative is implemented. The DSR is not merely a web of digital infrastructure programs; it is an evolving digital ecosystem that combines both communication technologies and financial systems, regulatory practices, and transnational data exchanges.[8] One important factor that contributes to this suitability is that the theory is able to expound regulatory divergence and legal pluralism among the participating countries. The DSR covers both jurisdictions with radically different legal cultures, the ones that are highly regulated digital spaces, and the ones that are loosely regulated or unregulated.[9] This disparity poses a major challenge in regard to coordination, especially in regions like data transfer across borders, taxation requirements through digital means, protection of intellectual property, and cybersecurity needs. CToD provides a methodical way to explore the effects of such regulatory discrepancies in the functioning of digital systems and indicates that technological interoperability must be accompanied by a similar institutional fit. The theory thus makes it possible to further discuss how legal fragmentation can restrain or redefine the course of digital integration under the DSR.

Besides the regulatory aspects, the financial and investment structure of the DSR also shows the applicability of CToD. The digital infrastructure deals are characteristically capital-intensive and have complicated financing structures, such as public–private alliances, state-supported investments, and inter-country financing plans.[10,11] The success of such financial models is strongly connected with transparency in the institutions, risk management systems, and credibility in the governance.[12] CToD represents these interdependences by correlating economic performance with the quality of governance and allows a more detailed evaluation of the impact of financial structures on processes of digital transformation. The issue of power relations and geopolitical factors is another level of complexity that fits the assumptions of CToD. The DSR is not a one-off initiative and is an economic and technological program and strategic instrument that outlines the digital impact and standards in

---

[8] Fakhar Hussain et al., "Infrastructure Development for the Digital Silk Road (DSR) and Its Implications for China under the Belt and Road Initiative," *Asia–Pacific Social Science Review* 23, no. 4 (2023): 7.

[9] David Gordon and Meia Nouwens, *The Digital Silk Road: China's Technological Rise and the Geopolitics of Cyberspace* (Taylor & Francis, 2022).

[10] Ilias Alami, "Foreign Investment Screening Mechanisms and Emergent Geographies of (Post) Globalization," *Dialogues in Human Geography*, 2024, 20438206241278733.

[11] Sarmad Ansari and Muhammad Tayyeb, "Saudi Vision 2030 and Liquidity Constraints: Evaluating Financing Requirements, Aramco Dependency, and Geopolitical Risks to Sustainable GDP Growth," *Social Science Review Archives* 4, no. 1 (2026): 3435–53.

[12] Mohammed Abdullah Ammer and Abdisamat Sattarov, "Enhancing Investors' Decision-Making through Financial Risk Management: Role of Corporate Governance and Financial Communication Transparency," *Decision Making: Applications in Management and Engineering* 8, no. 2 (2025): 376–94.

various areas.[13] The competition of world and regional forces can shape the adoption of technologies, laying down digital standards, and controlling key infrastructure.[14] Such dynamics usually take the shape of technology dependencies, dominance of a platform, and unequal bargaining power between the countries involved.[15] CToD allows studying these dynamics by inserting the digitalization into the broader institutional and political structures and recognizing that technologies are not neutral tools; they are embedded within institutions of power and governance.

The other key aspect is the time dimension of digital transformation, which is directly looked at within the context of CToD. DSR implementation is a process that consists of technological diffusion, institutional adaptation, and long-term changes in society.[16] Connectivity and efficiency in the short run can be temporary unless the institutional and social frameworks are in a position to cope with the technological transformation, which may result in the generation of sustainable development products.[17] Such imprecision of time is capable of generating transition turbulence, such as dislocation of labour, delays of regulations, and social resistance.[18] The immediate impacts of digitalization and the structural changes in the long term associated with the DSR, due to its emphasis on dynamism and evolution, can be analyzed via CToD. Another indication of the need to adopt a multidimensional theoretical approach is the digital platforms that are a part of the DSR.[19] Ecosystems based on platforms, such as e-commerce networks, electronic payment systems, and cloud-based services, exist as a result of complicated user-firm-regulatory body interactions. The platforms create network effects that can hasten economic activity but open the risk of monopoly and data concentration.[20] The regulation of such platforms needs concerted regulatory actions that deal with competition, data protection, and consumer rights.[21] These considerations are also integrated into CToD since technological innovation

[13] Erik Baark, *Powering China's Digital Future: Strategies and Challenges*, 2022.

[14] Anu Bradford, *Digital Empires: The Global Battle to Regulate Technology* (Oxford University Press, 2023).

[15] Donato Cutolo and Martin Kenney, "Platform-Dependent Entrepreneurs: Power Asymmetries, Risks, and Strategies in the Platform Economy," *Academy of Management Perspectives* 35, no. 4 (2021): 584–605.

[16] Vitaly Ambalov and Irina Heim, "Investments in the Digital Silk Road," in *Kazakhstan's Diversification from the Natural Resources Sector: Strategic and Economic Opportunities* (Springer, 2020).

[17] Patrik Söderholm, "The Green Economy Transition: The Challenges of Technological Change for Sustainability," *Sustainable Earth* 3, no. 1 (2020): 6.

[18] Michael Pugh, "Employment, Labour Rights and Social Resistance," in *Whose Peace? Critical Perspectives on the Political Economy of Peacebuilding* (Springer, 2008).

[19] Kevin Hernandez, *Achieving Complex Development Goals along China's Digital Silk Road*, 2019.

[20] Massimiliano Nuccio and Marco Guerzoni, "Big Data: Hell or Heaven? Digital Platforms and Market Power in the Data-Driven Economy," *Competition & Change* 23, no. 3 (2019): 312–28.

[21] Marco Botta and Klaus Wiedemann, "The Interaction of EU Competition, Consumer, and Data Protection Law in the Digital Economy: The Regulatory Dilemma in the Facebook Odyssey," *The Antitrust Bulletin* 64, no. 3 (2019): 428–46.

is associated with the institutional regulation and socio-economic effects, and the opportunities as well as the risks of the system can be considered moderately.

The issues of digital inclusion and inequality, which are directly linked to the socio-technical side of CToD, also have a direct connection to societal implications of the DSR. Digital connectivity may help increase access to information, education, and economic opportunities, but may also support the status quo in the event of unequal access.[22] The barriers to affordability, availability of the infrastructure, and computer literacy may be felt in disadvantaged communities, rural locations, and low-income communities.[23] Such differences may constrain the general performance of DSR initiatives and their contribution towards inclusive development. CToD offers a model to study such inequalities, focusing on the interplay between the use of technology and social structures, and that fair results should be achieved through supportive institutional and policy responses.

3 Layered Approach to Digitalization

3.1 Foundational Digital Order

The first level of CToD consists of 3-Ds; the creation of an orderly regulatory framework is the main goal of Level 1. This foundation layer provides a platform for digital boundaries, creates healthy regulations, and develops effective governance models. This is exactly the level base which would be desirable in the Digital Silk Road paradigm in the development of secure and governable infrastructure in the developing countries. This move will ensure that the states involved do not simply be passive receivers of hardware but are ready to have the sovereign ability to establish and protect their own domesticized digital area by making the design, implementation, and security of the digital standards their ideal. It is not just related to the creation of systems but also the creation of a standard legal environment, which can assist in averting the risks and gaining credibility for organisations.[24] It is also concerned with the urgent need for a coherent set of rules in data localization, policies in cybersecurity, and privacy controls that are yet to be well-developed in the emerging economies.[25] In laying down these principles of governance in the initial stages of the DSR, the framework can help partner countries to avoid the traps of

[22] Tipusultan Alarsaheb Inamdar, "Digital Divide: Analysing the Impact of Unequal Access to Technology on Social Mobility," *Janus* 16, no. 2 (2025).

[23] Omolara Tayo et al., "Impact of the Digital Divide on Computer Use and Internet Access on the Poor in Nigeria.," *Journal of Education and Learning* 5, no. 1 (2016): 1–6.

[24] Phillip H. Kim and Mingxiang Li, "Seeking Assurances When Taking Action: Legal Systems, Social Trust, and Starting Businesses in Emerging Economies," *Organization Studies* 35, no. 3 (2014): 359–91.

[25] Shishir Kumar Shandilya et al., "Navigating the Regulatory Landscape," in *Digital Resilience: Navigating Disruption and Safeguarding Data Privacy* (Springer, 2024).

uncontrolled digital development, which can be systematic vulnerability or ambiguity in the law. This systematic approach to digital maturity has ensured that the infrastructure is not only legally, but also socially responsible to offer a stable platform on which other, more technologically and economically advanced layers will be built in the future.

The practical extension of the operationalization of the 3D aspects of design, deployment, and defense goes beyond the categorization on a theoretical level and is reflected in the practical institutional practices. In the design stage, the policymakers have to take part in regulatory benchmarking, which usually takes references to various models across the world and modify them to suit the local socio-political environment. This involves an exchange of transparency and censorship, particularly about internet regulation, platform regulation, and taxation of the digital space.[26] The administrative complexity involved in the implementation process is that the new regulations to be implemented must be translated into a form of enforceable policies by the regulatory agencies, compliance systems, and digital surveillance mechanisms.[27] This level of establishment is also rooted in the economic consequences. Open and foreseeable digital regulations have direct impacts on the investment flows, especially in such areas as telecommunications, e-commerce, and digital finance.[28] In areas where these factors, such as protection of data, protection of intellectual property, and dispute resolution mechanisms, have been developed appropriately, the investors will have an increased chance of engaging in more activities. On the other hand, regulatory uncertainty will either discourage investment or create predatory deals in which foreign forces take over local digital markets.[29] Level 1 will offer the chance to be equally playing in the digital economy by developing a legal system that will facilitate equal economic participation.

3.2 *Operational Digitalization*

Level 2 operational digitalization (5D Level – 2nd phase of CToD) is the next phase of digital maturity, which is the boundary between the theoretical models and the real involvement of digital projects. This step converts underlying principles into a working reality by emphasizing the implementation of the soft infrastructure, which is an essential element of the long-term plan of the Digital Silk Road. Whereas Level 1 is formed through the establishment of the rules, Level 2 is formed through the

---

[26] Terry Flew et al., "Internet Regulation as Media Policy: Rethinking the Question of Digital Communication Platform Governance," *Journal of Digital Media & Policy* 10, no. 1 (2019): 33–50.

[27] Aadit Sharma et al., "Governance Challenges in Cross-Border Fintech Operations: Policy, Compliance, and Cyber Risk Management in the Digital Age," *IRE Journals* 4, no. 9 (2021): 1–8.

[28] Theo Mbise et al., *Digital Connectivity & E-Commerce: Overview of Financing Flows and Examples of Aid for Trade Support*, 2018.

[29] Anu Bradford, "The False Choice between Digital Regulation and Innovation," *Nw. UL Rev.* 119 (2024): 377.

construction of the functional systems, e-government clouds, advanced digital trade platforms, and regional data centers, which enable the rules to be utilized in real-time. This level is achieved by focusing on the more important components of the 5D, which include more profound interdependence of the data, equipment, and digital processes, to make the physical connectivity offered by the DSR an experience, both to businesses and citizens. This level of operation is important since it is the one that modernizes the day-to-day operations of the state and the market.[30] The introduction of e-government clouds, such as those implemented by partner countries, enables them to digitalize their public services, making them more transparent and less prone to administrative friction.[31] Likewise, the creation of digital trade platforms across borders makes the process of customs and logistics much easier, which directly contributes to the purpose of the DSR, which is to enable the smooth international trade.[32] When countries reach this stage successfully, they have already gone well beyond the stage of mere connectivity, and they can now start to harness the benefits, in a real sense, of an operationalized digital architecture.

Operational Digitalization, or 5D Level, is the stage when the digital governance structures start to become a working system integrated into the state institutions and the economic system. The focus at this level will be on the execution of the system rather than on the regulatory building, and the policies developed during the establishment stage will be converted into operational digital processes. Instead of being bound to legal texts or institutional blueprints, in digitalization, platforms, services, and infrastructures manifest themselves as directly interacting with users, markets, and administrative bodies.[33,34] In the context of the Digital Silk Road, this tier is precisely matched by the creation of the soft infrastructure that supplements the physical infrastructure of connectivity built by means of fiber-optic networks, satellites, and telecom systems. Level 2, as compared to Level 1, involves the data actively used to control and plan economies, as well as optimize services. Using data analytics, governments and organizations can determine trends, anticipate needs, and enhance decision-making.[35] This shift is the start of data-driven governance, in

[30] Stavros Kalogiannidis, "Economic Cooperative Models: Agricultural Cooperatives in Greece and the Need to Modernize Their Operation for the Sustainable Development of Local Societies," *International Journal of Academic Research in Business and Social Sciences* 10, no. 11 (2020): 452–68.

[31] K. Balaji, "E-Government and E-Governance: Driving Digital Transformation in Public Administration," *Public Governance Practices in the Age of AI*, 2025, 23–44.

[32] Yanling Chang et al., "Blockchain in Global Supply Chains and Cross Border Trade: A Critical Synthesis of the State-of-the-Art, Challenges and Opportunities," *International Journal of Production Research* 58, no. 7 (2020): 2082–99.

[33] Julie E. Cohen, "Law for the Platform Economy," *UCdL Rev.* 51 (2017): 133.

[34] Yujia He, "Chinese Digital Platform Companies' Expansion in the Belt and Road Countries," in *China's Digital Expansion in the Global South* (Routledge, 2024).

[35] Rita Uchenna Attah et al., "Leveraging Geographic Information Systems and Data Analytics for Enhanced Public Sector Decision-Making and Urban Planning," *Magna Sci Adv Res Rev* 12, no. 2 (2024): 152–63.

which policies and interventions are more and more informed by real-time data as opposed to fixed reports or past trends.

3.3 Digital Connectivity and Global Interaction

Digital Connectivity and Global Interaction (7D Level – 3rd phase of CToD) makes it possible to make the essential transition to domestic readiness for active cross-border integration. This step can be characterized by the digital growth of functions across national borders to directly support the vision of the Digital Silk Road of fostering deep digital interdependence and regional cooperation. The level allows the countries to align online ecosystems with the global economy by applying the 7D aspects, including global interoperability, cross-border data fluidity, and international collaborative governance. It shifts the emphasis of capacity building in-house towards being part of a shared networked space, in which digital resources and services are distributed across jurisdictions without limitation. The most noticeable real-world impact of this layer can be viewed in terms of the establishment of cross-border e-commerce and the establishment of sophisticated regional digital corridors. In this level, the infrastructure and control that have been offered in the lower levels are utilized in bringing harmony in trade protocols, payment systems, and data-sharing agreements between DSR partners. This form of interaction provides the emerging economies with a chance to leapfrog trade barriers and directly link to global value chains and turn them into local markets into international digital centers.

Actioning in domestic jurisdictions and which enable the infinitely communicating of states, markets, and institutions.[36] This is not a simple change of quantitative nature only (e.g., increased connectivity) but rather a qualitative one, an instance of synchronization of digital infrastructure, policy approaches, and data governance models at a global/regional scale.[37] The layer can be linked within the framework of the Digital Silk Road to the strategic vision of creating a digitally connected world in which the involved countries are no longer separate actors on the digital scene, but the components of a bigger system. It focuses on the empowerment of interoperability of national systems, exchange of data across borders, and the development of common platforms, which could be utilized to supplement economic and administrative programs.[38,39] This phase is enhanced by a touch of controlled digital

[36] Paul Schiff Berman, "The Globalization of Jurisdiction," *U. Pa. L. Rev.* 151 (2002): 311.

[37] Emmanouil Tranos, *The Geography of the Internet: Cities, Regions and Internet Infrastructure in Europe* (Edward Elgar Publishing, 2013).

[38] Susan Ariel Aaronson, "Data Is Different, and That's Why the World Needs a New Approach to Governing Cross-Border Data Flows," *Digital Policy, Regulation and Governance* 21, no. 5 (2019): 441–60.

[39] Joshua Paul Meltzer, "The I Nternet, Cross-Border Data Flows and International Trade," *Asia & the Pacific Policy Studies* 2, no. 1 (2015): 90–102.

interdependence, whereby the functionality of a particular system is more and more interdependent on the functionality of other systems and compatibility between the systems in the network.

4 Legal Theoretical Support for Digital Silk Road

4.1 Foundational Legal Order

4.1.1 Digital Sovereignty & Borders

The CToD enables a rule-based governance model whereby the legal boundaries of the host country are accurately overlaid with the technological assets in a fluid way. This would also ensure that all the levels of the DSR are aligned to the local needs but would also introduce a systematic line towards introduction of Chinese digital standards, to develop a consistent technical environment that would not infringe national sovereignty.[40,41] The profundity of this scheme is in the fact that it can solve the possible conflict between international technical norms and the national legal standards. At this point, the CToD can help partner countries prepare certain definitions of data residency and the local administrative control so that the digital soil on which the infrastructure is placed can be controlled by unambiguous and enforceable regulations.

In the DSR paradigm, the definition of digital sovereignty is a critical legal and strategic issue, especially in a setting where there are asymmetries in the growth of regulatory frameworks.[42] The CToD offers a methodology for the analytical procedures in the explanation of digital territory as not a production of a dreamy and borderless world, but as a territory of jurisdiction, which can be governed by the state. Based on this, it is considered that digital infrastructures (5G networks, cloud ecosystems, and data storage facilities) can be considered a subset of the national regulatory environment, and, thus, can be regulated at the local level with the help of local laws.[43] This re-conceptualization would enable host countries to assume control of the implementation and operation of digital systems within their jurisdiction to ensure that the development of technology goes hand in hand with the national legislation and policy provisions. Simultaneously, it establishes a process by which

[40] Elisa Oreglia and Weidi Zheng, "The Digital Silk Road between National Rhetoric and Provincial Ambitions," *The China Quarterly* 261 (2025): 183–95.

[41] Alex He, *The Digital Silk Road and China's Influence on Standard Setting* (CIGI Papers, 2022).

[42] Mauro Santaniello, "Attributes of Digital Sovereignty: A Conceptual Framework," *Geopolitics* 31, no. 2 (2026): 788–809.

[43] Marja Matinmikko et al., "On Regulations for 5G: Micro Licensing for Locally Operated Networks," *Telecommunications Policy* 42, no. 8 (2018): 622–35.

externally generated standards of technology, in particular with regard to Chinese digital ecosystems, can be integrated into home settings in a highly controlled and systematized fashion. The outcome is not the loss of sovereignty, but the process of integration after a certain degree, through the international technical models being adapted to the local legal framework delimitation.

4.1.2 Digital Regulations

Its implementation of a single system of Digital Regulations, which acts as a regulatory framework of the new digital economies, is one of the major contributions of the CToD to the DSR framework. The conceptual framework provides a methodology for how partner states can evolve domestic laws, data protection, and cybersecurity regulations to be in line with the regulated internet concept.[44] This inclination views legal certainty as a state of secure electronic expansion rather than seeing regulation as an innovation-impediment. By these rules, the DSR can enable host countries to move towards a patchy or nonexistent digital regulation to a general regulatory position that indicates the successful regulatory experience that has been implemented to date in the digital realm of China.[45] The model minimizes the risk of systematic vulnerability and inconsistency of the law by harmonizing the local cybersecurity standards with the technical requirements of DSR infrastructure. The added advantage of such alignment is that it not only makes it easy to implement advanced Chinese technologies but also prepares those countries that participated in it to have a strong, law-based digital society that is in a position to handle the challenges of the advanced information society.

4.2 Operational Regulatory Frameworks

4.2.1 Privacy & Trust

Creating a secure environment within a global collaboration is based on the creation of a digital trust, and the Contemporary Theory of Digitalization enables the formalization of social trust into a legal agreement. This framework would be required in the Digital Silk Road since it would be a systematic framework in the regulation of the cross-border data flows by harmonisation of international privacy standards with

---

[44] Lawal Qudus, "Cybersecurity Governance: Strengthening Policy Frameworks to Address Global Cybercrime and Data Privacy Challenges," *International Journal of Science and Research Archive* 14, no. 1 (2025): 1146–63.

[45] Yizhi Zhang and Muhammad Bilawal Khaskheli, "The Role of Digital Technologies in Advancing Sustainable Economic Development into Intersections of Policy, Law, Environmental Economics, and a Comparative Study of China, the EU, and the USA," *Sustainability* 17, no. 19 (2025): 8666.

robust domestic and international laws, such as the Personal Information Protection Law (PIPL) of China. The theory will be employed to make sure that the security of data mobility is not compromised and that high-level privacy standards are incorporated into the fabric of operation of DSR projects. Rather, it installs an experimental version of a legalized trust in which participants are able to enter into intricate digital relationships with the knowledge that their data are secure within a coordinated and unified regulatory framework. The benefit of such a strategy is that it provides a clear technical-legal guide for making secure data transfers between jurisdictions possible. However, instead of using informal agreements, the CToD promotes the implementation of strict auditing and certification procedures that check adherence to data protection regulations in real-time. This is especially crucial to the Belt and Road areas, where the speed of cloud and fintech solutions implementation presupposes a high level of openness about the manner of personal and sensitive data processing.[46] Through these combined standards, the DSR assists partner countries in developing a robust digital ecosystem in which trust is an inherent structural aspect of the design, to create a more consistent and predictable global digital economy. The creation of trust in digital ecosystems is becoming more reliant on the formalization of privacy safeguards by means of legal and regulatory mechanisms that are enforceable. In this aspect, the CToD is centralized as it changes the abstract concept of trust into a structured and institutionalized aspect of digital government. Such an approach is especially important in the context of the DSR, since it will allow regulating the cross-border flow of data with adequately matched legal norms to offer the safety and responsibility of such data exchange.

4.2.2 Digital Rights & Obligations

A key idea of the Contemporary Theory of Digitalization is the formalization of the relationship between the participants and platform operators, which promotes the idea of the balanced architecture of Digital Rights and Obligations. The Digital Silk Road theoretical design transfers uncertainties in the informal service contracts into the realm of a well-defined legal framework that stipulates the responsibilities of the technology vendors and provides legally binding security to the users.[47] Codification of these roles makes the CToD such that DSR-managed platforms, such as logistics networks, fintech hubs, and so on, are as transparent as possible. Such clarity of structure is needed to minimize the liability risk of the involved businesses since it creates a stable legal space in which compliance is built into the technical and administrative backbone of the platform itself. Another important aspect of this model is that it has moved to a philosophy of governance-by-design, in which the responsibilities of infrastructure providers are not merely reactive but are baked into

[46] Wang Xiaobin et al., "Natural Resources, Trade and Fintech in the Era of Digitalization: A Study of Economies Involved in Belt and Road Initiative," *Resources Policy* 93 (2024): 105082.

[47] David Gordon and Meia Nouwens, *The Digital Silk Road: China's Technological Rise and the Geopolitics of Cyberspace* (Taylor & Francis, 2022).

the operational procedures of the technology. An example is the introduction of a major project of smart cities or clouds in partner countries, in which the CToD offers a model of how to enforce data ethics and service-level guarantees directly into the contract and technical levels. This would ensure the safeguarding of user rights, that is, the digital services are provided in a responsible and rights-respectful way that would be consistent with local requirements and with international best practice.

4.3 Structuring Global Interdependence and Connectivity

4.3.1 Interoperable Standards

To realize both technical and regulatory synergy along the Digital Silk Road, an interoperable standard is required, and the Contemporary Theory of Digitalization suggests this solution to the international legal fragmentation issue. This standard enables the development of standardized standards of different digital products, such that the new technologies developed can communicate easily across sovereign jurisdictions. The development of digital currency systems, e.g., the e-CNY, and the use of smart city standards are one of the key areas of this integration.[48] By balancing these complex systems into a unified technical-legal framework, the CToD makes it possible to have a compatible operational space where cross-border barriers are decreased, and system efficiency is increased. Such standardization has a strategic worth as it will elevate the Chinese digital standards to the international mainstream, which will effectively dictate the international digital standards in the future.[49] Host states that adopt such interoperable models forget lopsided, domesticated systems, which will likely cause technical debt and administrative pain. Rather, they are engaged in the lean network with the rules of the game being universal, clear, and high-performance interaction optimized. This expansion not only enhances the influence of Chinese innovation in the global system of governance but also gives the partner countries a winning model of how they should modernize which they can easily imitate.

Interoperability is also concerned with the problems of national regulation disparities and technological incompatibilities. In the absence of shared standards, digital systems are likely to be created in silos, leading to inefficiencies, increased compliance costs, and barriers to cross-border interaction. CToD is dealing with these problems by promoting the use of standard frameworks that assist in the mutual acceptance of technical standards and regulatory practices. It results in a reduction of legal differences and enables the effortless infiltration of the digital environment into foreign markets. Besides technical alignment, interoperable standards play a critical role in

---

[48] Wenfang Wang et al., "Can E-CNY Pilot Policy Promote Green Innovation? Empirical Analysis Based on Data from Chinese Cities," *Energy & Environment*, 2026, 0958305X261431129.

[49] Stacie Hoffmann et al., "Standardising the Splinternet: How China's Technical Standards Could Fragment the Internet," *Journal of Cyber Policy* 5, no. 2 (2020): 239–64.

institutional alignment between the participating countries. The regulatory agencies, standard-setting agencies, and technology providers need to align their efforts to make sure that common protocols are regularly used and revised.

4.3.2 Digital Diplomacy & Defense

Digital Diplomacy and Defense is part of the Contemporary Theory of Digitalization, and in this instance, the international cooperation in the digital sphere is planned legally, operationally, and strategically. This aspect is put to use in the Digital Silk Road, where digital infrastructure is not only considered an important tool of statecraft, but must be legally protected, institutionally brokered, and coordinated for cybersecurity. One of the largest contributions that CToD has had in the field has been the formalization of mechanisms of cross-border cybersecurity governance. The theory puts cybersecurity in a more expansive frame of diplomatic and legal frameworks that regulate inter-state interactions in the digital realm, instead of regarding it as a one-dimensional technical action. The CToD model can also assist in developing such legal frameworks of digital co-operation in those regions, where the divergent national cybersecurity laws otherwise could lead to gaps in the regulations.

5 Addressing Challenges and Gaps

5.1 Legal Challenges and Gaps

Addressing legal challenges and gaps in the DSR should be done dynamically, where the jurisdiction in which the regulatory mechanisms cannot keep up with the use of technology. The CToD will have a stabilizing effect in most developing countries through a comprehensive approach to the digital economy. This type of conceptual clarity is the foundation for cleaning up legal ambiguity in a legal system and for delivering the requisite legal scaffolding to high-stakes technologies, such as Artificial Intelligence, big data, and blockchain. The CToD will ensure that DSR initiatives are built on a long-term sustainability foundation and are not invented depending on the technical convenience of the moment by closing such regulatory loopholes. Some structural legal problems are discernible in the DSR that is being adopted through various regulatory regimes; notably, in the jurisdictions where digital transformation has been more rapid than the creation of the relevant laws. In this respect, the CToD is an integrative governance model that seeks to address regulatory fragmentation and institutional gaps among the participating developing economies in a systemic fashion. CToD interprets the legal deficiencies not as national issues but as part of a broader imbalance in the system between the accelerator of technology and the modernization of the law that must be dealt with in a concerted and integrated reaction. One of the main contributions of CToD is the ability to create a sense of unity in the fragmented digital governance systems that are fragmented. Most of the partner states of the Belt and Road Initiative have regulatory frameworks of emerging technologies that are either incomplete, inconsistent, or not well-developed.

5.2 *Addressing the Global Digital Divide*

The CToD contributes to the successful transfer of nations that are yet to reach the maturity of the digital transformation process, being able to provide the theoretical legitimation of the intervention of the Digital Silk Road, so that these nations could utilize the highest potential of their more advanced partners (China). This offers an escape route through which new economies will not go through the common bottlenecks of development by adopting ready-made state-of-the-art infrastructure and governance systems. The strength of this strategy is that it has changed to charitable assistance but has taken the approach of symbiotic growth. The CToD offers administrative and legal tools needed to ensure that the technical requirement standards can be aligned across borders so that the integration of hardware will be supported by an effective transfer of knowledge and human capital. The problem of digital divide in the world is an ancient structural complication of the world of the new international digital order, especially after the emergence of technology, which is not uniformly spread over the geographical areas. The Contemporary Theory of Digitalization takes into account such a gap and locates it in the context of controlled digital interdependence, which re-conceptualizes digital inequality as the lack of a deeper systematic imbalance of capabilities, infrastructure, and preparedness to rule. This theoretical inclination provides theoretical legitimacy for the systematic digital cooperation in the Digital Silk Road to decrease asymmetries between the technologically advanced states and the states in the earlier stages of digitalization.

6 Conclusion

Digital Silk Road is an evolutionary extension of the global digital infrastructure and governance, but its deployment is met with complicated technological, legal, and socio-political issues. The findings of this chapter reveal that the Contemporary Theory of Digitalization can offer a multidimensional and holistic approach that can handle these issues in a systematic and sustainable way. CToD redefines digitalization as a systemic change that incorporates governance, human capital, legal frameworks, and economic systems by moving beyond a strictly technological approach. By employing its stratification of digital maturity, CToD fits well within the developmental pathway of the DSR. On the bottom tier, it puts in place definite digital borders and regulatory structures, which are vital to legal certainty and sovereignty. On the operational level, it translates these principles into operational systems that support digital trade, platforms, and digital services. At the connectivity level, it empowers cross-border integration, cross-border interoperability, and digital diplomacy, and digital interdependence of the world. Moreover, CToD is a legal and institutional support that streamlines regulatory principles, improves cybersecurity systems, and builds trust in the digital ecosystems. It is also playing a significant role in closing the digital divide in the world by providing a participatory digital transformation and capacity building to the developing economies. By so doing, the DSR goes beyond infrastructure expansion to the long-term process of socio-economic development.

Chapter 4
Advancing the Digital Economy Under the Digital Silk Road: Legal Perspectives and International Frameworks

Abstract This chapter explores the digital transformation of the economy and society under the BRI, such as a higher level of efficiency in trade relations, the role of medium and small enterprises in cross-border trade, financial inclusion, and the provision of better services to the population. It also highlights the current issues like the digital divide, disparities in technological abilities, and disparities in the digital preparedness of the participating states. The discussion takes into account the engagement of the domestic legal systems and international legal frameworks that affect the digital trade and governance. The chapter also discusses the significance of legal coordination and legal alignment of policies in enabling trust, interoperability, and sustainable development of digital within the BRI framework. The findings of this chapter reveal that consistent implementation of regulations, global collaboration, and the building of capacity are necessary to facilitate safe and inclusive digital economic practices within BRI countries.

Keywords ICT Connectivity · Digital Yuan · Cross-border payment · World Trade Organization

1 Introduction

The advanced ICT infrastructure supports e-commerce across borders, e-finance and smart city building, as well as technology-based innovation centers.[1] With the high digital connectivity, countries are in a better position to enjoy the economic benefits that the digital economy brings, such as boosted trade flows, the sharing of knowledge, and the creation of digital entrepreneurship.[2] On the other hand, poor

[1] Dennis Mwaniki et al., "Towards Smart Economic Development in Nairobi: Evaluating Smart City Economy Impacts and Opportunities and Challenges for Smart Growth," *Smart Economy in Smart Cities: International Collaborative Research: Ottawa, St. Louis, Stuttgart, Bologna, Cape Town, Nairobi, Dakar, Lagos, New Delhi, Varanasi, Vijayawada, Kozhikode, Hong Kong*, 2016, 749–90.

[2] Ikrom Ahmedov, "The Impact of Digital Economy on International Trade," *European Journal of Business and Management Research* 5, no. 4 (2020).

J. Afzal and Y. Chen, *Legal Framework of Digital Economy and Digital Trade Under the Belt and Road Initiative*, https://doi.org/10.1007/978-981-92-4444-7_4

ICT infrastructure may limit the growth of the economy, the digital gap, and the ability of the countries to engage in the full practices of the global digital market.[3] Legal systems are significant during the formation of the digital economy.[4] The level of trust, efficiency, and fairness of digital transactions is determined by issues like data protection, cybersecurity, intellectual property protection, consumer protection, and competition law.

In the BRI, the heterogeneity of the legal system of the participating nations presents both the challenges and opportunities of harmonization, standard-setting, and coordination of policies.[5] There is thus the need to know the legal side of the initiative to realize the optimum potential of ICT-driven economic growth. In addition to the issue of domestic law, there are the international systems and agreements that are on the frontline in facilitating cross-border trade and investment in digital format.[6] The WTO and International Telecommunication Union (ITU) at world trade levels and regional levels of digital trade agreements do offer some guidelines, standards, and best practices that assist countries in navigating the complex digital trade environment.[7] This compatibility of the national laws with these international standards will enable the BRI countries will be able to perform digital trade effectively and address the following problems: the sovereignty of data, privacy, and cybersecurity. Not only do the laws being standardized with the laws across the borders make the ease of transaction easy, but it also creates a feeling of investor confidence and sustainable economic growth. In the chapter, the author refers to the legal and regulatory challenges of developing the digital economy in the framework of the BRI. It explains the association between ICT connectivity and digital trade and the economic integration procedure; evaluates the legal frameworks, both national and international, that govern digital trade and determines the new trends of digital governance.

---

[3] Igor Matyushenko et al., "Assessment of the Digital Gap in Developing Countries," *L. & Innovative Soc'y*, 2024, 130.

[4] Oksana M. Vinnyk et al., "Economic and Legal Policy of the State in the Field of Digital Economy," *International Journal of Criminology and Sociology* 10, no. 1 (2021): 383–92.

[5] Jingxia Shi and Fenghua Li, "Aligning the BRI with Sustainable Development: A Regulatory Framework and Its Implementation," *Journal of World Trade* 57, no. 6 (2023).

[6] Usman Ahmed, "The Importance of Cross-Border Regulatory Cooperation in an Era of Digital Trade," *World Trade Review* 18, no. S1 (2019): S99–120.

[7] Olga Batura, "Liberalisation and Regulation of International Trade in Telecommunications Services Through the WTO," in *Universal Service in WTO and EU Law: Liberalisation and Social Regulation in Telecommunications* (Springer, 2015).

2 The Importance of ICT Connectivity for the Digital Economy

ICT is one of the key drivers of the digital economy that makes it possible to create, transfer, and utilize digital information to facilitate trade, innovation, and economic growth.[8] ICT connectivity facilitates digital trade and e-commerce since any business, be it small or large, can connect to its customers both locally and internationally.[9] Online marketplaces and the digital market allow small and medium-sized enterprises (SMEs) to trade in cross-border trade without the need to be physically present. These operations need to have a good internet connection, a secure payment system, and integrated logistics solutions that can be used to reduce the operation cost and offer transactions to facilitate the operations. ICT enables businesses to enjoy the benefits of delving into foreign markets and consumers and also participate in foreign value-added chains.[10] ICT infrastructure is also applied in digital financial services. Financial resources are available with the use of mobile banking, online payment systems, and digital wallets, which the conventional banking services of the population might not reach.[11] There is a safe and efficient transfer and transfer of finances made possible by ICT, which in turn helps the people to save, transfer, and receive money and enhance entrepreneurship and small businesses. These systems are needed most at locations where physical banking systems are less so as to facilitate better economic inclusion and engagement. The connectivity of ICT is closely related to innovation and the exchange of knowledge.[12] The digital networks allow the cooperation of companies, research organizations, and governments to use each other to exchange information, work on the creation of technologies, and create solutions to cross-border boundaries. Cloud computing, virtual workplace, and the Internet enable communication and research work with no geographical boundaries.[13]

ICT infrastructure is strengthening the delivery of public services and governance. Governments can also make use of ICT to provide these services to the people without the delays that are prevalent in traditional services, which are delivered through

---

[8] Ivana Domazet and Milena Lazić, "Information and Communication Technologies as a Driver of the Digital Economy," *Glasnik Srpskog Geografskog Društva*, 2017, 11–19.

[9] Shouvik Kishore Majumdar et al., "E-Commerce and Digital Connectivity: Unleashing the Potential for Greater India–ASEAN Integration," *Journal of Asian Economic Integration* 2, no. 1 (2020): 62–81.

[10] Guillaume Delautre, "The Distribution of Value Added among Firms and Countries: The Case of the ICT Manufacturing Sector," *ILO Research Department Working Paper* 16 (2017): 18.

[11] Mukul Gupta et al., "Digital Payment Systems and Financial Inclusion: Examine How Digital Payment Systems, Such as Mobile Wallets and Digital Currencies, Can Improve Financial Inclusion by Providing Access to Banking Services for the Unbanked and Underbanked Population," 2023, 725–37.

[12] Lisset Medina et al., "International Connectivity in the Generation of Information and Communication Technology (ICT) in Spain," *Competitiveness Review: An International Business Journal* 30, no. 3 (2020): 355–71.

[13] Sumita Raghuram et al., "Virtual Work: Bridging Research Clusters," *Academy of Management Annals* 13, no. 1 (2019): 308–41.

in-person means.[14] The digital monitoring systems will help in the improvement of urban planning, energy allocation, and transportation, which will maximize the efficiency of the operation of administration and create a more productive environment in which economic activity occurs. Countries are also able to integrate better into the global markets through ICT connectivity. Countries that have developed digital infrastructure will be able to engage in global trade, attract foreign capital, and become members of the global supply chains. The use of ICT in digitalizing the linkage between nations is brought into the limelight by large-scale projects, including the Belt and Road Initiative (BRI), which has facilitated economic, technological, and social integration of various regions.[15] The Internet of Things (IoT), artificial intelligence, blockchain, and big data analytics require connectivity to process data, provide real-time, and automated decision-making. Governments and businesses are opting to invest more in ICT infrastructure to enable them to sustain these services because they offer them economic advantages, accessibility to the necessary resources, and international cooperation. The environment where the digital tools can be effectively used in economic development is formed by policies and investments that make connectivity stronger.

3 Chinese Payment Platforms to Support the Digital Economy Activities

3.1 e-CNY (Digital Yuan)

The multi-layered payment ecosystem is a digital economy that is growing in China.[16] The e-CNY (Digital Yuan) and the Project mBridge are transforming international settlements among themselves on a fundamental level.[17,18] These projects deploy a multi-currency Central Bank Digital Currency (mCBDC) system as an alternative to

[14] Osas-Osayomwanbor Ilawagbon and Adesoye Isiaka Mustapha, "The Role of E-Administration in Enhancing Time Efficiency in Public Service Delivery: A Case Study of the Federal Civil Service of Nigeria Post-COVID-19," *ICONIC Research and Engineering Journals, 7 (12), 445* 457 (2024).

[15] Xin Yue Shen, *Chinese ICT on the Digital Silk Road: A Case Study of Infrastructure Building in Pakistan*, 2020.

[16] Haoli Tan, "Study on Chinese Cross-Border e-Commerce Payments from a" Double Cycle" Standpoint," *Journal of Computing and Electronic Information Management* 16, no. 2 (2025): 46–50.

[17] Xin Chen et al., "Emerging Digital Currency Statecraft with Chinese Characteristics: Chinese Expectations About the Influence of the e-CNY on RMB Internationalization," in *The Geoeconomics of the International Monetary Order: Money and Power in the 21st Century* (Springer, 2025).

[18] Li Zeng and Wee-Yeap Lau, "The Digital Yuan in the Shadow of Dollar Hegemony: Rethinking Asia's Financial Autonomy amid US-China Tensions," *Asia and the Global Economy* 5, no. 2 (2025): 100126.

the SWIFT system that is high-speed and low-cost. This permits direct sovereign-to-sovereign digital dealings in the Digital Silk Road framework.[19] It removes the use of the intermediate corresponding banks that in most cases slow down and add to the expense of transacting money internationally. These fintech projects are financed by institutional players such as the Asian Infrastructure Investment Bank (AIIB) and the BRICS New Development Bank who provide capital and infrastructure to finance the projects.[20,21] The Asia–Pacific and member areas in which the systems operate are financed by them, including the 5G networks, data centers, and digital payment instruments.

3.2 *Cross-Border Payment Systems*

The world of consumers and merchants is subject to the worldwide spread of the super-app and gateways.[22] Alipay+ is a global aggregation that links different regional Asian mobile wallets to one payment gateway with more than 20 currencies.[23] It implies that a businessperson can accept payments in various e- wallets of different countries using a single QR code. WeChat Pay (Weixin Pay) relies on its large social media platform to provide intelligent cross-border trade solutions.[24] It enables small entrepreneurs to access Chinese people with the help of the Mini Programs, which deal with marketing issues and final payment. Huawei Pay is a mobile application that incorporates these digital wallet services into the hardware device to enter emerging markets where Huawei has a huge base of mobile devices.[25] These platforms are becoming compatible with the local systems, including the use of QRIS (Quick Response Code Indonesian Standard). This will help Chinese online tools operate perfectly in local markets and foreign markets without making the merchants purchase costly new technology.[26]

---

[19] Ashley Cordes, *From the Gold Rush to the Cryptocurrency Code Rush? Communication of Currencies in Native American Communities* (University of Oregon, 2019).

[20] Hongying Wang, "The New Development Bank and the Asian Infrastructure Investment Bank: China's Ambiguous Approach to Global Financial Governance," *Development and Change* 50, no. 1 (2019): 221–44.

[21] Ibrar Ahmad et al., "The Geopolitical and Economic Impact of BRICS on the Middle East," *FWU Journal of Social Sciences* 18, no. 4 (2024): 80–95.

[22] D. Kavitha et al., "Super Apps: The Natural Progression in Fin-Tech," *Fintech and Cryptocurrency*, 2023, 383–412.

[23] Yiping Huang and Xun Wang, "Digital Connectivity in China and Asia: The Case of Mobile Payments," *New Dimensions of Connectivity in the Asia–Pacific*, 2021, 203.

[24] Yuwen Zhang, "From Weixin to WeChat: Analysing the Expansion Strategies of a Chinese Social Media Platform," in *Digital Platforms and the Global South* (Routledge, 2023).

[25] Yuanyuan Li, "Research on Huawei Mobile Phone Marketing Strategy Based on Market Segmentation Theory," 2019, 293–300.

[26] Angela Tritto et al., "Governing the Gold Rush into Emerging Markets: A Case Study of Indonesia's Regulatory Responses to the Expansion of Chinese-Backed Online P2P Lending," *Financial Innovation* 6, no. 1 (2020): 51.

3.3 Cambodia-China Tourism Debit Card

The use of sector-specific tools to promote digital adoption, such as the Cambodia-China Tourism Debit Card, can demonstrate the effectiveness of such measures.[27] The particular card simplifies how travelers utilize money in a foreign nation since it eliminates the barrier of exchanging currency and also provides discounts that are localized. These channels do not just affect the transactions; they develop a virtual financial net that decreases friction, stabilizes trade between countries, and solidifies the place of China as a key architect of the digital economy worldwide. Through this digital ecosystem, even the tiniest vendors in the developing countries are able to engage in global e-commerce.[28]

4 Legal Perspectives of ICT Connectivity and the Digital Economy

Digital trade is centered on the role of e-contracts and electronic signatures.[29] The legal systems should accept the validity and enforceability of electronic contracts, signatures, and records.[30] E-contracting legislation minimizes the use of hard copies, simplifies business transactions, and enhances quicker and more productive transactions.[31] The legal status of electronic signatures in the BRI is necessary to facilitate international e-commerce and the provision of digital services.[32,33] Digital economy Regulatory frameworks on emerging technologies are gaining more significance.[34] The concept of artificial intelligence (AI), blockchain, big data analytics, and the Internet of Things (IoT) introduces new legal issues. AI concerns issues of accountability, transparency, and liability of automated decision-making. The use of blockchain necessitates legal enforcement of the smart contracts, ownership of digital

[27] Vannsy Kuon et al., "Cambodia," in *Risk and Tourism Marketing in Asia* (Routledge, 2026).

[28] Nigel Walton, "Digital Platforms as Entrepreneurial Ecosystems and Drivers of Born-Global SMEs in Emerging Economies," in *International Entrepreneurship in Emerging Markets* (Routledge, 2022).

[29] 이지은, *Study on Legal Consideration of E-Contracts in International Digital Trade*, 2023.

[30] Sadam Mohammad Awaisheh, "From Paper to Pixels: The Legal Status and Challenges of Electronic Writing in Administrative Contracts. A Comparative Study of Current Legal Systems," *Electronic Government, an International Journal* 21, no. 2 (2025): 210–26.

[31] Nasir Albalawee, "E-Contracting within Jordan's Legal Framework.," *Pakistan Journal of Criminology* 16, no. 1 (2024).

[32] Christopher Tullis et al., "Electronic Signatures: Enabling Trusted Digital Transformation," *World Bank Digital Transformation White Paper Series*, 2024.

[33] Christopher Tullis, "Public Key Infrastructure: Implementing High-Trust Electronic Signatures," *World Bank Digital Transformation White Paper Series*, 2024.

[34] Marina Larionova and Andrey Shelepov, "Emerging Regulation for the Digital Economy: Challenges and Opportunities for Multilateral Global Governance," *International Organisations Research Journal* 16, no. 1 (2021): 29–63.

assets, and secure ledger systems.[35] The IoT networks generate and process enormous volumes of data, meaning that laws regulating security, privacy, and interoperability are needed. Laws that are developed around the new technology will guarantee that the innovation can continue, and at the same time, keep the ethical values, safety, and trust.[36] One of the key legal issues in digital trade and ICT-based services is cross-border dispute resolution. Some of the areas where disagreements could occur include the terms of the contract, intellectual property, use of data, hacking, or quality of services.

Conflict resolution mechanisms in international arbitration, mediation, and dispute resolution mechanisms that are based on treaties offer predictable mechanisms of resolving disputes.[37] Under the BRI, defining and enforcing the cross-border digital dispute procedures assists in investor confidence and enables long-term engagement in the digital economy.[38] The important legal viewpoints include taxation and the regulation of digital services. Electronic commerce, online services, and digital trade bring a problem to the traditional taxation systems that were based on physical items and localized services. The legal frameworks should be used to deal with taxation of digital transactions, revenue distribution among jurisdictions, and tax evasion. Through introducing clear and equal tax policies on online services, nations will be able to earn income and stabilize the market between companies.[39]

ICT connectivity in the digital economy is formed by the interaction between domestic laws and international agreements. Organizations like the World Trade Organization (WTO), International Telecommunication Union (ITU), and regional agreements have given treaties, conventions, and guidelines that offer the standards in digital trade, data flows, cybersecurity, and electronic commerce. The national regulations will be aligned to international standards; this means that the BRI countries will succeed in entering the international markets, maintaining their sovereignty and the local legal system.[40] Legal convergence helps in interoperability, restricts transaction risks, and enhances best practices.[41] The other legal issue of ICT connectivity is the social and ethical issue. The new issues that should be taken into account and

[35] Jake Goldenfein and Andrea Leiter, "Legal Engineering on the Blockchain: 'Smart Contracts' as Legal Conduct," *Law and Critique* 29, no. 2 (2018): 141–49.

[36] Joost Groot Kormelink, *Responsible Innovation: Ethics, Safety and Technology* (TU Delft OPEN Publishing, 2019).

[37] PK Venkateswaran, "Dispute Resolution Mechanisms in International Trade Law: A Comparative Analysis," *Anusandhanvallari*, 2025, 1255–63.

[38] Engidaw Abriham Ebabu et al., "Opportunities and Challenges in Cross-Border e-Commerce: Strategic Management within the Legal Context of BRI Countries-A Systematic Literature Synthesis and Future Research Directions," *Technology Analysis & Strategic Management*, 2025, 1–20.

[39] Richard M. Bird and Eric M. Zolt, "Tax Policy in Emerging Countries," *Environment and Planning C: Government and Policy* 26, no. 1 (2008): 73–86.

[40] Jingxia Shi and Fenghua Li, "Aligning the BRI with Sustainable Development: A Regulatory Framework and Its Implementation," *Journal of World Trade* 57, no. 6 (2023).

[41] Mohammad Saeed Abdallah ALsheyab, "Legal Analysis of the Merits of Electronic Transferable Records: Toward Cross-Border Trade Digitalization," *International Journal of Law and Management* 67, no. 1 (2025): 145–63.

require legislative attention are privacy, surveillance, the ownership of the data, and the fairness of the algorithms. Ethical law is used to ensure that there is accountable use of technology, the protection of the rights of individuals, and the enhancement of equal treatment of digital services. Such structures facilitate winning the trust of the people in the digital economy and facilitate participation and investment in digital infrastructure.

5 Governing Digital Trade

The e-commerce that includes e-cloud services, e-finance, and sharing of intellectual property, is governed in a complex maze of legal rules across jurisdictions. Such structures establish regulations, norms, and principles to govern the transfers of digital goods, services, and data across borders in order to bring some predictability, equity, and reliability to the global digital economy. Since most countries are relying on digital trade to enable them to grow and be innovative, it is necessary to make sure that policymakers and firms acquire the ins and outs of international agreements, treaties, and regulatory provisions. The BRI, as a project that facilitates regional connectivity and economic integration, indicates the importance of aligning the national regulations with international ones to facilitate digital cross-border trading.[42] The World Trade Organization (WTO) is one of the major international systems that regulates digital trade. The WTO offers a collection of global trade regulations, which are applicable to services, commodities, and, to some extent, to digital products. General Agreement on Trade in Services (GATS) applies to services provided in a digital form, such as telecommunications, finance, and software services, whereas the General Agreement on Tariffs and Trade (GATT) provides the regulation of trading in the cross-border form of goods, which might contain digital elements.[43,44] In recent years, the WTO has embarked on the e-commerce debate through the Joint Initiative on E-commerce that seeks to come up with common principles on the matter related to electronic transactions, consumer protection, data flow across borders, and online privacy. These deliberations present a platform on which nations can devise international regulations that allow them to engage in online commerce and still not violate the issue of sovereignty and safety.

Another important aspect in the regulation of digital trade is regional trade agreements. The agreements include the United States-Mexico-Canada Agreement (USMCA), the Comprehensive and Progressive Agreement for Trans-Pacific Partnership (CPTPP), and the digital financial services, cross-border data transfer, and

[42] Bilal Ahmed, "Cross-Border Connectivity: Strengthening Economic Ties and Regional Integration," *Journal of Regional Connectivity and Development* 3, no. 1 (2024): 70–84.

[43] Ikenga KE Oraegbunam and Chiugo Onwuatuegwu, "Addressing the Challenges in the Contemporary International Trading System: The Limitations of General Agreements on Tariffs Trade (Gatt) and General Agreements on Trade in Services (GATS)," *IJOCLLEP* 5 (2023): 64.

[44] Alla Shlapak et al., "Institutional Provision of Tariff and Non-Tariff Regulation of Cross-Border Trade," *Economics. Ecology. Socium*, no. 7 (2023): 1–23.

e-commerce regulations are defined at the agreement level.[45,46] Such frameworks tend to cover data protection, cybersecurity, intellectual property rights, and dispute resolution mechanisms standards. Regional agreements are supplementary to the multilateral frameworks in that they give more specific provisions that are specific to the economic and technological conditions of the countries involved in the agreements. In the BRI, regional electronic commerce models can be used as examples of harmonization and interaction between involved countries.[47] The regulations of data protection and privacy play a key role in international digital trade. Various nations have different sets of standards regarding the management of data, which may influence a digital cross-border transaction. The General Data Protection Regulation (GDPR) of the European Union is considered to be one of the most powerful legal tools in this field that sets strict regulations concerning the collection, storage, processing, and transfer of personal data.[48]

The other countries, including the BRI members, are either developing or revising data protection systems in order to comply with international standards. International data privacy harmonization also minimizes the obstacles to digital trade, enhances trust between users and businesses, and complies with the legal requirements in various jurisdictions. The other area of digital trade governance is cybersecurity structures. International cooperation in the area of cybersecurity implies the development of norms, principles, and technical standards that prevent cybercrime, protect critical infrastructure, and guarantee the honesty of online operations. Other organizations that establish standards and protocols that determine the national laws and regional cooperation include the International Telecommunication Union (ITU), the International Organization of Standardization (ISO), and the United Nations Office on Drugs and Crime (UNODC).[49,50,51] These structures can make sure that the countries will not be attacked by cyberattacks, that the risks in transactions across borders are minimized, and that people will have more trust in the digital platforms. They are also critical in digital commerce around the world through intellectual property

---

[45] Gary Hufbauer and Steven Globerman, *The United States-Mexico-Canada Agreement: Overview and Outlook* (Fraser Institute Vancouver, 2018).

[46] Terry Wu and Doren Chadee, "Comprehensive and Progressive Agreement for Trans-Pacific Partnership (CPTPP): Implications for the Asia–Pacific Region," in *International Business in the New Asia–Pacific: Strategies, Opportunities and Threats* (Springer, 2022).

[47] Yingying Liang et al., "The Impact of Trade Facilitation on Cross-Border E-Commerce Transactions: Analysis Based on the Marine and Land Cross-Border Logistical Practices between China and Countries along the 'Belt and Road,'" *Water* 13, no. 24 (2021): 3567.

[48] Ziru Li et al., "Impact of the General Data Protection Regulation on the Global Mobile App Market: Digital Trade Implications of Data Protection and Privacy Regulations," *Information Systems Research* 36, no. 2 (2025): 669–89.

[49] Gabriele Balbi and Andreas Fickers, *History of the International Telecommunication Union (ITU): Transnational Techno-Diplomacy from the Telegraph to the Internet*, vol. 1 (Walter de Gruyter GmbH & Co KG, 2020).

[50] Lijuan Yang, "Effects of ISO Technical Standards on China's Digital Exports," *Applied Economics Letters*, 2025, 1–6.

[51] Helen Canton, "United Nations Office on Drugs and Crime—UNODC," in *The Europa Directory of International Organizations 2021* (Routledge, 2021).

(IP).[52] The legal systems must protect online products, software, artistic works, and inventions in technology so that creators and innovative developers can have the right to their work. WTO works with the Agreement on Trade-Related Aspects of Intellectual Property Rights (TRIPS) that provides minimum requirements in the protection of IP.[53]

These include the Commission of International Trade Law (UNCITRAL), which has prepared Model Laws on Electronic Commerce and Electronic Signatures, providing a directive on the national legislation.[54,55] Such systems facilitate businesses and governments to do business contracts, exchange documentation, and authenticate transactions through the electronic system, which helps to build e-commerce and online services in the global arena. Trade facilitation and customs procedures also influence the flow of digital goods and services. The international agreements are concerned with customs duties, electronic documents, and a simpler procedure for electronic transactions.[56] The WTO Trade Facilitation Agreement also provides recommendations to harmonize the customs procedures and trade barriers, including those relating to cross-border digital trade. The capability to easily trade at the digital level implies that the outcome of the digital products, software, and other services can be easily and dependably transported across borders, enhancing competitive advantages and availability in the market. The Digital tax and revenue system is becoming a basic element of the global Digital trade regulatory system.[57] The services provided online are likely to cross national boundaries and, as such, render the traditional taxation systems useless. Multilateral practice, including that held by the Organization for Economic Cooperation and Development (OECD), is aimed at providing policy guidance on the way digital transactions are to be taxed, earnings distributed equally, and a means of avoiding tax evasion.[58,59]

Effective digital taxation frameworks can help governments to collect taxation, as well as allow a level playing field for businesses that undertake international digital

---

[52] J. Suresh Kumar, "E Commerce and Intellectual Property Resolving Disputes in the Digital Marketplace," *Vidyavardhaka First Grade College, Mysuru, Karnataka*, 2023.

[53] Carlos María Correa, *Trade Related Aspects of Intellectual Property Rights: A Commentary on the TRIPS Agreement* (Oxford University Press, 2020).

[54] Kamalesh N., "Analysis of UNCITRAL Model Law Provision on E-Commerce with Respect to Indian Perspective," *Part 1 Indian J. Integrated Rsch. L.* 2 (2022): 1.

[55] Stephen Errol Blythe, *An E-Commerce Law For The World: The Model Electronic Transactions Act: The Model Electronic Transactions Act* (Xlibris Corporation, 2012).

[56] Faye Fangfei Wang, *Law of Electronic Commercial Transactions: Contemporary Issues in the EU, US and China* (Routledge, 2014).

[57] Reuven Avi-Yonah et al., "A New Framework for Digital Taxation," *Harv. Int'l LJ* 63 (2022): 279.

[58] Yrys Abdieva, "Organization for Economic Cooperation and Development (OECD)," in *The Palgrave Encyclopedia of Global Security Studies* (Springer, 2023).

[59] Jeongmeen Suh and Jaeyoun Roh, "The Effects of Digital Trade Policies on Digital Trade," *The World Economy* 46, no. 8 (2023): 2383–407.

trade.[60] The international dispute resolution mechanisms are also necessary to make digital trade enforceable and fair.[61] Controversies can be over the interpretation of the contract, infringement of intellectual property rights, cybercrime, or adherence to regulations. The mechanisms of resolving conflicts are international arbitration, alternative dispute resolution processes that include mediation, and treaty-based dispute resolution processes, which offer efficient and predictable dispute resolution mechanisms. The systems increase trust among trading partners, minimize uncertainties, and promote involvement in cross-border digital markets. The interoperability and technical norms are also covered by international standards. The use of the ISO standards, the ITU recommendations, and other technical frameworks establishes that the digital systems, networks, and software can operate in a global context with minimum interruption. Interoperability facilitates e-commerce across borders, cloud services, and e-communication, and minimizes obstacles in global e-commerce. By harmonizing technical standards, it is easier to invest, transfer technology, and innovate, and businesses and governments achieve this by deploying digital solutions that can align with international systems.

In the BRI, e-commerce and the provision of digital services between countries can only be facilitated through the legalization of electronic signatures across international borders. The legal framework of new technologies is growing more significant in the digital economy. New legal issues include artificial intelligence (AI), blockchain, big data analytics, and the Internet of Things (IoT). AI creates doubts on accountability, transparency, and liability of automated decision-making. Blockchain needs to be recognized by the law in the forms of smart contracts, ownership of digital assets, and safe ledger mechanisms. IoT networks gather and analyze large volumes of information, and the necessary laws are needed to regulate security, privacy, and interoperability. Creation of legal frameworks of the emerging technologies will help ensure that innovation is able to develop and keep ethical standards, safety, and trust. Digital trade and ICT-enabled services are dependent on critical legal issues such as cross-border dispute resolution. The conflict of terms of the contract, intellectual property, the use of data, cybersecurity attacks, or quality of service may be questioned. The mechanisms of international arbitration, mediation, and dispute resolution mechanisms in treaties give certain predictability to the conflict resolution mechanisms. In the BRI, implementing clear and enforceable frameworks of digital cross-border disputes will help investors gain confidence and participate in the digital economy on a long-term basis.

[60] Olubukola Omolara Adebiyi, "Taxation in the Digital Age: An Examination of the Necessity, Feasibility, and Implications of Taxing Virtual Infrastructures," *Asian Journal of Economics, Business and Accounting* 23, no. 23 (2023): 13–35.

[61] Yun Zhao and Hui Chen, "Enhancing Access to Digital Justice: Digital Governance of Dispute Resolution and Dispute Prevention in Online Commercial Activities," *Journal of International Dispute Settlement* 15, no. 2 (2024): 273–304.

6 International Legal Frameworks

6.1 World Trade Organization (WTO) Frameworks

The World Trade Organization (WTO) models play the critical role of developing the digital economy within the Belt and Road Initiative (BRI) through the provision of a uniform system of guidelines in international trade.[62,63] One of the key pillars is the General Agreement on Trade in Services (GATS), as it addresses the "Mode 1" digital delivery.[64] That way, the services such as online banking or distant consultations delivered within the BRI corridors are addressed fairly and transparently. This is augmented by the WTO Work Programme on Electronic Commerce (1998), which keeps the customs duty on electronic transmissions at moratorium. The Digital Silk Road requires this policy as it maintains the cross-border movement of software, data, and digital media as an economical and free flow that is not full of local digital taxes. The physical digital economy is regulated by the Information Technology Agreement (ITA) and the Telecoms reference paper.[65] The ITA also erases tariffs on high-tech devices such as semiconductors, routers, and telecommunication devices, which makes the BRI hard infrastructure more affordable to the third world countries that need to develop partners. Meanwhile, the Telecoms Reference Paper sets out the rules of regulation that avoid examples of network monopoly and provide a smooth connection of various digital systems to one another.[66] These regulations offer the non-formal legal structure that is required to make sure that the fiber optic cables and data centers that are being financed in the BRI are competitive and available to every player in the market.

The Joint Statement Initiative (JSI) on E-commerce (2024) is aimed at modernizing these standards and is in the final phases of its formation having more than 70 members.[67] This plurilateral accord is a significant move in the establishment of global regulations on online signature, consumer protection, and paperless trading. In the case of the BRI, the JSI offers an invaluable connection between the Chinese

62 Zhouying Song et al., "The Trade Network of the Belt and Road Initiative and Its Topological Relationship to the Global Trade Network," *Journal of Geographical Sciences* 28, no. 9 (2018): 1249–62.

63 Carmen Amado Mendes and Xuheng Wang, "The Belt and Road Initiative in Global Governance: Impact on the International World Order," in *The Palgrave Handbook of Globalization with Chinese Characteristics: The Case of the Belt and Road Initiative* (Springer, 2023).

64 Sara Kulsoom and Pritam Banerjee, *Realising The Hong Kong Ministerial Vision: Towards Deeper Mode 1 Liberalisation in Trade in Services*, 2025.

65 KJ Joseph et al., "Information Technology Agreement of WTO: Call for a Revisit," *Centre for WTO Studies Working Paper No* 9 (2013).

66 Jean-Jacques Laffont and Jean Tirole, *Competition in Telecommunications* (MIT press, 2001).

67 Henry S. GAO, *The Joint Statement on E-Commerce: Is This Glass Half Empty or Half Full?* 2024.

digital standards and international ones.[68] Digitalizing the customs documents and identifying electronic authentication; this initiative lowers the administrative strain on small and medium enterprises (SMEs) who are intending to trade across the world. All of these WTO structures offer the legal predictability and international legitimacy needed to transform the Digital Silk Road into an actual, global marketplace that is integrated digitally.

6.2 UNCITRAL Model Laws (Electronic Commerce)

Digital Silk Road uses the necessary legislative templates that are established by the United Nations Commission on International Trade Law (UNCITRAL) to operate in various legal jurisdictions.[69,70] They are not treaties but are gold standard templates which countries can use in their domestic legislation. In the case of the Digital Economy as a part of the Belt and Road Initiative (BRI), these frameworks are the soft infrastructure that allows a signed digital contract to be enforced in other partner countries, such as Kazakhstan or Egypt.[71,72] UNCITRAL is useful in harmonizing different legal systems across the BRI through a common language of law, thereby minimizing the risks and expenses incurred in digital trading across borders.

The Model Law on Electronic Commerce (1996) is the constitution of the whole digital economy.[73] It provided the principle of functional equivalence, which is a revolutionary principle because electronic communications enjoy equal legal protection with paper-based communications. This legislation lays the legal foundation of electronic transactions, specifying regulations for entering into contracts and assigning data messages. Under the BRI framework, this means that e-commerce orders and electronic invoices cannot be ignored, and lack a legal force, just because they are not printed. It enables the huge amount of trade that is transacted online in such websites as Alibaba or JD.com to be legally acknowledged in each and every country that embraces these standards.

---

[68] Daniel Fuchs et al., "China and the Standardization of Digital Technologies–Introduction to the Special Issue," *China Law and Society Review* 10, no. 2 (2025): 75–80.

[69] Maria Gabriela Sarmiento and Katia Fach Gómez, "The United Nations Commission on International Trade Law (UNCITRAL)," *The International Law of Economic Integration, Oxford University Press, DRAFT PRE-PRINT, Forthcoming*, 2023.

[70] Magdalena Łągiewska, "Chinese Approach to Online Dispute Resolution," *Budúcnosť Práva–Právo Budúcnosti II.*, 2022, 47.

[71] Andrew Mazen Dahdal and Adel Abdel Ghafar, "The Digital Silk Road: 'Tech-Diplomacy' as a Paradigm for Understanding Technological Adoption and Emerging Digital Regulations in MENA," *Asian Journal of Law and Society* 12, no. 2 (2025): 163–88.

[72] ЖС Сембаева, "Emerging Green and Digital Sustainable Markets in Central Asia: A Comparative Analysis of Kazakhstan and Uzbekistan within China's BRI framework," *Известия. Серия: Международные Отношения и Регионоведение* 61, no. 3 (2025).

[73] Alan Davidson, *The Law of Electronic Commerce* (Cambridge University Press, 2009).

The Model Law on Electronic Signatures (2001) and the Model Law on the Use and Cross-border Recognition of Identity Management and Trust Services (2022) concern trust and authentication.[74,75] The 2001 legislation allows the legalization of e-signatures by having the requirements of their technical reliability to make them as binding as a signature made with ink. The 2022 model law goes even further by enabling trust in online identity management.[76] This is vital to the digital economy of the BRI since it establishes a system in which the various nations would accept the digital IDs and authentication procedures of each other. This helps to avoid fraud and makes sure that a company or a person involved in a cross-border transaction is who they say they are, which is essential to safe digital payments and government-to-business (G2B) transactions.

The Model Law on Electronic Transferable Records (MLETR) (2017) is one of the most transformative tools of modern global trade.[77] Under this law, one can legally use electronic copies of traditionally paper-intensive documents, including Electronic Bills of Lading (eBLs), promissory notes, and warehouse receipts.[78] The paperless logistics link that the BRI requires is the MLETR. Historically, the transportation of goods along the maritime or overland Silk Road had to be done by physical stacking of the papers between the banks, customs, and ports. Implementing the MLETR, BRI countries will be able to shift to completely digital supply chains, whereby ownership of goods is passed through the use of secure digital tokens or blockchain entries. This has a drastic effect on trade, accelerating it and eliminating the possibility of clerical errors or the loss of physical documents.

6.3 International Standards and Principles

The Digital Silk Road is based on an advanced combination of international standards to compensate for the divergence of national rules.[79] These international principles have the rules of engagement in data privacy, entry of market, and the shift to paperless trade. In the case of the Digital Economy with the BRI, these frameworks will make sure that Chinese-led infrastructure does not obstruct the rest of the world. Adhering to these set standards, BRI associates will be able to create digital solutions that are safe, open, and able to process large volumes of cross-border data flows.

---

[74] Stephen Mason, "Electronic Signatures in Practice," *J. High Tech. L.* 6 (2006): 148.

[75] Ayei Ibor et al., "Considerations for Trustworthy Cross-Border Interoperability of Digital Identity Systems in Developing Countries," *AI & Society* 40, no. 4 (2025): 2729–50.

[76] Thomas J. Smedinghoff, "Is It Legal? Will It Be Trusted? What Are the Rules?–Enabling Electronic Identity Management under the new UNCITRAL Model Law," *Enabling Electronic Identity Management Under the New UNCITRAL Model Law (April 15, 2024)*, 2024.

[77] Henry D. Gabriel, "The UNCITRAL Model Law on Electronic Transferable Records," *Uniform Law Review* 24, no. 2 (2019): 261–80.

[78] Jing Ren, *Stumbling into the Digital Era: How Can Electronic Bills of Lading Achieve Functional and Legal Equivalence to Paper Bills of Lading?* 2023.

[79] Alex He, *The Digital Silk Road and China's Influence on Standard Setting* (CIGI Papers, 2022).

Protection of data is done under the APEC Privacy Framework and OECD Privacy Guidelines.[80,81] APEC structure is an important instrument for the Asia–Pacific, which provides the flexible means of safeguarding personal information and does not hamper the exchange of data across borders. This is necessary for the "super-apps" and e-commerce platforms that run across the BRI, since it will not allow the digital trading to be halted by the inflexible set of laws on data. Meanwhile, the OECD principles establish an international standard on privacy. These combined standards allow BRI nations to build a circle of trust, which ensures that data on users is treated responsibly without restricting businesses in any way.

The G7 Digital Trade Principles govern openness to the market and security in the system.[82] Although these began in G7 countries, they have now become a reference standard of high standard digital commerce worldwide. They stress that the digital markets must remain open, and the systems should not be susceptible to cyber threats. Once BRI projects correspond with these principles, it will be an indication to the international community that the Digital Silk Road is a safe and non-discriminatory place.[83] This has made it very easy to have multinational companies invest in BRI digital projects since they are certain that the regulatory environment adheres to the accepted international best practices. UNCITRAL/WTO Cross-border Paperless Trade Toolkit supports the practical shift towards physical paperwork replacement. This resource is a guidebook in the attempt of governments to modernize their legal systems. It assists countries in embracing the legislation required for digital signatures, digital bills of lading, and automated customs. In the case of a variety of developing nations that make up the BRI, this kit is the key to bypassing the paper-based bureaucracies and going directly to the digital logistics. It offers the technical and legal support to make the vision of the paperless Silk Road a reality.

[80] Graham Greenleaf, "Five Years of the APEC Privacy Framework: Failure or Promise?" *Computer Law & Security Review* 25, no. 1 (2009): 28–43.

[81] Dan Svantesson, "Data Localisation Trends and Challenges: Considerations for the Review of the Privacy Guidelines," *OECD Digital Economy Papers*, no. 301 (2020).

[82] Xuanmei Cheng et al., "Digital Economy, Energy Trade, and the Path to Sustainability: A G7 Perspective," *International Review of Financial Analysis* 109 (2026): 104807.

[83] Heng Wang, "China's Approach to the Belt and Road Initiative: Scope, Character and Sustainability," *Journal of International Economic Law* 22, no. 1 (2019): 29–55.

7 Legal and Regulatory Strategies for Advancing the Digital Economy Under DSR

7.1 Legal Harmonization

The BRI countries have the challenge of balancing a variety of legal systems and promoting innovations, building trust, and creating an environment that supports digital trade and investment.[84] Harmonization of digital trade regulations in BRI countries is one of such strategies. Laws on data privacy, cybersecurity, intellectual property, and e-commerce can cause limitations to cross-border trade in cases of divergence. Legal harmonization refers to national alignment with international policies, the use of similar regulations in electronic transactions, and the coordination of regulations on digital platforms.[85] Coordinated frameworks make it easier to conduct business and invest in a company, increase the compatibility of digital solutions, and enhance cross-border protection of consumers and companies. Harmonization also improves the integration of the region; hence, countries involved in it find it easy to participate in the global digital economy. The data protection and privacy laws are the key to facilitating safe and trustworthy online transactions.

7.2 Robust Data Protection Legislation

Development of effective legal principles of the data collection, storage, processing, and transfer assists in creating trust between the consumers, business and governments.[86] BRI countries can implement policies to ensure the privacy of data, hold accountable the breach of data, and control cross-border data flows. Legal measures can be requirements of consent, localization of data, and violations penalties.[87] With the security of the digital environments, robust data protection legislation will foster the involvement of e-commerce, digital finance, and cloud services. Another important element of digital economy strategies is cybersecurity legislation. Due to the increased ICT networks, there is a high risk of cyberattacks, hacking, and digital fraud as well. Cybersecurity laws nationwide lay out responsibilities and roles of network providers, establish standards for the securing of critical infrastructure, and

---

[84] Jingxia Shi and Fenghua Li, "Aligning the BRI with Sustainable Development: A Regulatory Framework and Its Implementation," *Journal of World Trade* 57, no. 6 (2023).

[85] Irsan Rahman et al., "Harmonization of Digital Laws and Adaptation Strategies in Indonesia Focusing on E-Commerce and Digital Transactions," *Innovative: Journal Of Social Science Research* 4, no. 1 (2024): 4314–27.

[86] Gulbakyt Bolatbekkyzy, "Legal Issues of Cross-Border Data Transfer in the Era of Digital Government," *Journal of Digital Technologies and Law* 2, no. 2 (2024): 286–307.

[87] Bret Cohen et al., "Data Localization Laws and Their Impact on Privacy, Data Security and the Global Economy," *Antitrust* 32 (2017): 107.

offer legal systems to address cybercrime. BRI countries that coordinate cybersecurity matters, including reporting processes of cross-border incidents, sharing knowledge, and collaborative enforcement activities, increase regional resilience. The law approaches can be used to ensure that digital trading is not interrupted, but also that the cybersecurity functions properly to facilitate the healthy functioning of online services. Protection of intellectual property (IP) is a concept that is significant in the enhancement of innovation in the digital economy.[88] The innovations in digital technologies, software, creative materials, and technological and innovative aspects require the laws of protection of rights of creators, fair use, and collaboration. Member states to the BRI can develop policies that bring about the convergence of the IP standards, with the imposition of patents, copyrights, and trademarks, and offer dispute resolution channels to the digital contents and software. Good IP regimes promote research and development, foreign investment, and transfer of technology so that the participating countries can use innovation to develop their economies.

7.3 Competition and Antitrust Regulations

Another part of legal approaches to the development of the digital economy is competition and antitrust regulations. Massive technology firms tend to control the digital markets and establish monopolistic situations. Anti-competitive behavior should be prevented by legal frameworks that encourage open access and fair pricing aspects of the digital ecosystem.[89] Regulations of platform dominance, market concentration, and unfair trade practices can be implemented in BRI countries, and this will create an environment in which new entrants and SMEs can engage and innovate. The issue of competition laws being enforced openly makes markets accessible, efficient, and effective to be able to sustain growth. Electronic trade and e-contract laws are part of the working model of digital trade. Electronic contracts, digital signatures, and electronic records can be recognized legally, and businesses and individuals transact effectively using electronic means as opposed to paper-based transactions. BRI nations can embrace the UNCITRAL model laws and other related frameworks that offer guidelines on how to conduct digital contracting, authentication, and verification. E-contracts have standard rules, which minimize risks on transactions, ease trade across borders and bring some certainty in case of any dispute. The issue of digital taxation and regulatory compliance policies is becoming more significant to countries involved in digital trade. Coordinated electronic tax systems also guarantee fair distribution of revenue and also promote the establishment of a fair business environment among local and foreign firms. New legal approaches to developing technologies, including artificial intelligence (AI), blockchain, and

[88] Muhammed Mahmoud Selwawy Mansy, "The Impact of IPR in Protecting And Enhancing Digital Economy," *Journal of Intellectual Property and Innovation Management* 5, no. 4 (2022): 189–216.

[89] Kseniia Zakharova, "Competitive Strategies in Sustainable Development Ecosystems: Challenges And Opportunities," *Economics, Finance and Management Review*, no. 2 (22) (2025): 16–28.

Internet of Things (IoT), are needed as well. The regulatory systems can establish responsibility in AI-related decision-making, ethical application of algorithms, and liability in automated operations. The blockchain technology demands the establishment of legal regulations for smart contracts, ownership of digital assets, and safe records. The IoT devices produce vast amounts of data, which requires the establishment of regulations on data security, interoperability, and privacy. Establishing a legal clarity of emerging technologies, BRI countries foster their adoption, decrease unpredictability, and promote high-tech investments.

7.4 Cross-Border Dispute Resolution Mechanisms

The digital trade under BRI will be efficiently operating because of the presence of cross-border dispute resolution mechanisms. The e-contract, intellectual property, and cybersecurity-related e-contract and compliance breaches can become disputes.[90] Efficient and predictable results are achieved through legal structures that offer arbitration, mediation, and treaty-related dispute resolutions. It would help in instilling confidence in businesses and investors in the BRI nations because there would be clear rules and enforcement of jurisdiction in the countries, making cross-border digital transactions a good exercise. The elements of legal strategies also include capacity building and institutional development.[91] The effective implementation, monitoring, and enforcement of digital economy regulations requires governments, regulatory agencies, and judicial systems to have training, technical resources, and expertise to be effective. Digital literacy, legal education, and technical skills are programs that help institutions to respond to the changing digital environment.[92] High levels of institutional capacity guarantee that legal frameworks are used in a common way, which assists in adhering to, innovating, and sustainable development.

7.5 Regulatory Strategies for PPP

The public–private partnerships (PPPs) are a significant implementation strategy of the legal and regulatory strategies.[93] The development of effective, flexible,

[90] Andre Wirjo et al., "Assessment of Capacity Building Needs to Support WTO Negotiation on Trade Related Aspects of E-Commerce," in *Assessment of Capacity Building Needs to Support WTO Negotiation on Trade Related Aspects of E-Commerce* (Singapore: Asia–Pacific Economic Cooperation Secretariat, 2020).

[91] LM Hager, "Development Law Capacity Building: Training Legal Professionals for Development," *International Sustainable Development Law-Volume II*, 2010, 258.

[92] Mustafa Kayyali, "Digital Literacy in Higher Education: Preparing Students for the Workforce of the Future," *International Journal of Information Science and Computing* 11, no. 1 (2024): 53–73.

[93] Nutavoot Pongsiri, "Regulation and Public-private Partnerships," *International Journal of Public Sector Management* 15, no. 6 (2002): 487–95.

and business-friendly regulations can be achieved through collaboration among the governments, technology providers, and industry stakeholders. Projects may be assisted by PPPs in infrastructure development, in testing new regulatory models, and also in fostering innovation without violation of legal standards.[94] The effectiveness of the regulations and the facilitation of digital solutions adoption are promoted by legal strategies that promote collaboration between the private and the public spheres.

8 Emerging Legal Trends in the Digital Economy

The high rate of development of digital technologies is still changing the world's economic systems, providing both new opportunities and challenges to various policy makers, regulators, and corporate entities. The new legal tendencies related to this field reveal the necessity to balance economic development, technological progress, customer protection, cybersecurity, and the ethical aspects. The legal frameworks that countries engage in such initiatives as the Belt and Road Initiative (BRI) are increasingly responding to these trends to ensure digital markets do not suffer due to such trends. The growth of data governance structures is one of the major trends. With businesses and governments amassing, processing, and warehousing substantial amounts of data, the laws that govern the privacy of data, the transfer of data, and the localization of data have become increasingly more significant. Nations are heading towards inclusive data protection laws that provide a clear guideline on how personal and business information should be collected, stored, and shared. There is the General Data Protection Regulation (GDPR) of the European Union that has impacted the practices worldwide, as many nations have started to follow similar standards. Newer trends are the stricter cross-border data transfer regulations, the need to express consent, transparency of data usage, and the need to notify data breach. Such rules give companies legal assurance and safeguard consumer rights and any trust in online commerce.

Consumer protection and e-commerce regulation are continuously developing to suit the needs of digital trading across borders. The trends in law are related to transparency, fair competition, dispute resolution, and product liability. The legislation of e-commerce frequently demands clear and transparent information about prices, quality, and delivery conditions, and offers easy channels for complaints and dispute resolution. These innovations improve the level of confidence in online stores and help to promote online trade in BRI nations. Another trend is the regulation of new financial services of a digital nature. Fintech, mobile banking, e-wallets, and cryptocurrencies are changing the way people and businesses receive access to financial resources. Digital economy regulation is gaining more ethical and social concerns.

[94] Dirk Meissner, "Public–Private Partnership Models for Science, Technology, and Innovation Cooperation," *Journal of the Knowledge Economy* 10, no. 4 (2019): 1341–61.

9 Conclusion

In this chapter, the building of the digital economy within the Belt and Road Initiative (BRI) has been discussed in a variety of aspects, such as ICT connectivity, legislative practices, and new trends. Facilitating cross-border trade, financial services, e-commerce, and innovation development is based on the integration of high-level digital infrastructure in the involved countries. Under the knowledge exchange, smart services, and regional economic integration, ICT connectivity ensures technical support of digital markets. Quality networks, high-speed internet, and new technologies, including cloud computing, artificial intelligence, and blockchain, allow businesses and governments to efficiently operate and provide an opportunity to trade with others around the globe digitally. Legal and regulatory frameworks are very important factors in the digital economy. Encrypted data, online security, copyright, competition, consumer, and taxation are all critical elements of a healthy digital ecosystem. The alignment of laws in BRI countries will help to increase the level of interoperability, build trust, and eliminate obstacles to cross-border digital transactions. The alignment of the regulatory frameworks, capacity building, and the government-private sector collaboration may be considered the strategies that will ensure that the legal frameworks can also keep pace with the emerging technologies.

Chapter 5
Scrutiny of Challenges Regarding the Digital Economy Within the Digital Silk Road

Abstract This chapter investigates technological and infrastructural constraints, such as the lack of digital connection, cybersecurity threats, and disparities in access to high-tech technologies. The chapter also discusses legal and regulatory issues, especially fragmented regulatory frameworks, issues on data protection, and jurisdictional issues in digital cross-border operations. Besides, geopolitical and diplomatic issues, including digital sovereignty, strategic competition, and regulatory divergence, are addressed, as well as financial and investment barriers to building digital infrastructure. This chapter suggests possible solutions and policy proposals that revolve around harmonization of regulation, capacity development, multilateral co-operations, and sustainable investment strategies.

Keywords Cybersecurity and E-Commerce · Intellectual Property Rights · Diverse legal environments · Dispute resolution challenges

1 Introduction

The lack of technological and infrastructural barriers, including a lack of broadband connectivity and unequal access to sophisticated digital resources, is an obstacle to the seamless integration of digital services.[1] Interpretation of laws and regulatory issues, as well as discrepancies in data protection regulations and uncoordinated jurisdictional boundaries, make cross-border digital business complicated.[2] The digital literacy and workforce skills divide prevents the complete access and use of digital efforts by the local communities.[3] These problems are also compounded

[1] IAP Nirmani, "Barriers to Digital Participation in Developing Countries: Identifying Technological, Social, and Cultural Obstacles to Community Involvement," *GSC Advanced Research and Reviews* 23, no. 2 (2025): 061–071.

[2] Bryan Mercurio and Ronald Yu, *Regulating Cross-Border Data Flows: Issues, Challenges and Impact* (Anthem Press, 2022).

[3] Andrew Enaifoghe, "Bridging the Digital Divide in the South African Public Sector: Assessing Digital Literacy Gaps and Capacity-Building Strategies," in *Digital Equity and Literacy* (IntechOpen, 2025).

J. Afzal and Y. Chen, *Legal Framework of Digital Economy and Digital Trade Under the Belt and Road Initiative*, https://doi.org/10.1007/978-981-92-4444-7_5

by the geopolitical tensions, the complexities of the diplomatic relationships, and the national priorities of the countries, and the financial and investment barriers become the major barriers on the way to the implementation of the sustainable projects.

Social and environmental sustainability is a key problem that contributes to the ultimate success of digital BRI projects.[4] Under the BRI, the digital economy, which is commonly termed the Digital Silk Road, is meant to improve connectivity beyond physical infrastructure through faster exchange of information, making cross-border trade more efficient as well as innovation-driven expansion. In the case of many developing and emerging economies that are members of the BRI, digital transformation is a chance to address the traditional barriers of development and take a more active part in the global economy.[5] One of the continuous challenges has been to ensure that the digital growth is in line with other economic, social, and environmental objectives. Balanced governance, mutual trust, inclusive growth, innovation, cooperation, transparency, stability, and prosperity are some of the areas of focus of this perspective.

2 Technological and Infrastructure Challenges

Availability and quality of technological and digital infrastructure are closely associated with the growth of the digital economy as a part of the Belt and Road Initiative.[6] Digital infrastructure forms the backbone of modern economic activities, facilitating communication, the exchange of data, online services, and digital trade across borders.[7] Nevertheless, the issue of the unequal degree of technological and infrastructural advancement between countries participating in the digital aspect of the BRI is one of the most urgent problems of the digital dimension. Further trends are the implementation of new and superior communication technologies, namely, the fifth generation (5G) networks.

The other essential element in the digital economy is data infrastructure, such as data centers and cloud computing infrastructure.[8] The use of digital channels, artificial intelligence, and online services is based on the processing and storage of

---

[4] Shuhong Peng et al., "Technological Cooperation for Sustainable Development under the Belt and Road Initiative and the Sustainable Development Goals: Opportunities and Challenges," *Sustainability* 17, no. 2 (2025): 657.

[5] Sainan Zhao et al., "Dynamic Influence of Digital and Technological Advancement on Sustainable Economic Growth in Belt and Road Initiative (BRI) Countries," *Sustainability* 14, no. 23 (2022): 15782.

[6] Jinzhu Zhang et al., "The Impact of Digital Economy on the Economic Growth and the Development Strategies in the Post-COVID-19 Era: Evidence from Countries along the 'Belt and Road,'" *Frontiers in Public Health* 10 (2022): 856142.

[7] Odilile Ayodele, "Digital Infrastructure: Creating the Backbone for Development," in *The Quest for Unity* (Routledge, 2024).

[8] Kehinde Abiodun, "Digital Infrastructure & Sustainable Data Centers Investment in Africa: Role of Tier III & Tier IV," *Int. J. Multidiscip. Res. Growth Eval* 6 (2025): 1878–88.

large amounts of data. Most BRI countries, however, lack the capacity to store their data in domestic data centers and rely on the facilities in other countries. Poor cybersecurity systems augment the chances of information intrusions, economic fraud, and system failures.[9] These weaknesses make digital systems less trusted and digital infrastructure less likely to be invested in. The presence of cyber risks is especially troubling when the digital systems are connected to such critical areas as energy, transportation, and finance. The maintenance and upgrading of digital infrastructure in the long term is also quite challenging.[10] The infrastructure construction is just a starting point since maintenance of networks, modernization of old technologies, and reliability of systems will require constant investment and experienced individuals. The institutional capability to manage infrastructure in most of the BRI countries is quite poor, and infrastructure is underfunded in terms of maintenance.[11]

Consequently, online systems can be damaged within a short period, creating service interruptions and higher expenses in the long term. The speed of technological development also exacerbates the maintenance work since infrastructure may become outdated in the near future.[12] The geographical and environmental influences also have an impact on the formation of the digital infrastructure. Mountains, deserts, islands, and areas with few people make it harder and more expensive to roll out digital networks technically. In these regions, the private sector investments might be minimal since the commercial returns are very low, and the community will be left behind. Besides this, digital infrastructure can be harmed by climate-related risks like floods, extreme heat, and storms, as well as disrupted service.[13] These environmental issues demonstrate that a vibrant and flexible infrastructure planning is necessary. The dependence on outsourcing infrastructure development to external providers of technology is also another major concern. Most BRI nations rely on foreign firms in terms of equipment, software, and technical skills.[14] Although international collaboration could hasten the implementation of infrastructure, overreliance on this could restrain the growth of local technologies.[15] It is also capable of generating vulnerabilities in terms of supply chains, maintenance of the systems, and geopolitical

---

[9] A. Shaji George et al., "Cyber Threats to Critical Infrastructure: Assessing Vulnerabilities across Key Sectors," *Partners Universal International Innovation Journal* 2, no. 1 (2024): 51–75.

[10] Xiaolong Li et al., "Digital Infrastructure," in *Development Practice of Digital Business Environment in China* (Springer, 2022).

[11] Junaid Ashraf et al., "Do BRI Policy and Institutional Quality Influence Economic Growth and Environmental Quality? An Empirical Analysis from South Asian Countries Affiliated with the Belt and Road Initiative," *Environmental Science and Pollution Research* 29, no. 6 (2022): 8438–51.

[12] Steven J. Jackson, "Speed, Time, Infrastructure," *The Sociology of Speed: Digital, Organizational, and Social Temporalities* 169 (2017).

[13] Giovanni Bettini et al., "Clouded Skies: How Digital Technologies Could Reshape 'Loss and Damage' from Climate Change," *Wiley Interdisciplinary Reviews: Climate Change* 11, no. 4 (2020): e650.

[14] Yujia He, "Chinese Digital Platform Companies' Expansion in the Belt and Road Countries," in *China's Digital Expansion in the Global South* (Routledge, 2024).

[15] Rajneesh Narula, *Globalization and Technology: Interdependence, Innovation Systems and Industrial Policy* (John Wiley & Sons, 2014).

tensions. The development of domestic capabilities in digital technologies is a long-term challenge for many countries engaged. Another complexity in the development of digital infrastructure is coordination among the stakeholders. Digital projects typically have various stakeholders, such as governments, commercial entities, financial as well as international collaborators.[16] Regulatory systems, institutional interests, and governing systems differ, which can slow down project implementation and efficiency.[17] Poor coordination can lead to fragmented systems, overlapping investments, or inconsistency of goals and, as such, diminishes the overall effectiveness of digital infrastructure programs. The institutional and policy capacity is also very critical in influencing the outcome of technology.[18] There is an inadequate notion of implementation, performance standards, and most importantly, monitoring mechanisms in digital strategies in certain BRI countries. Inadequate technical knowledge in the institutions of the government may be a barrier to the proper planning and management of digital infrastructure projects. Investments in technology cannot bring desired economic and social returns without sound institutional structures.

3 Legal and Regulatory Challenges

3.1 Regulatory Environments Differences

Legal and regulatory environments of the countries where the Belt and Road Initiative exist has a strong impact on the expansion of the digital economy.[19,20] E-commerce, e-finance, and data exchange, as well as online services, are digital activities that take place across national borders, but the legal frameworks that regulate such activities are mostly still national and very diverse. This regulatory divergence poses serious problems to the digital cooperation within the BRI and influences the trust of the governments, companies, and investors in digital projects. Among the most eminent legal issues is regulatory fragmentation between BRI countries.[21] The laws of each

[16] Federico Brunetti et al., "Digital Transformation Challenges: Strategies Emerging from a Multi-Stakeholder Approach," *The TQM Journal* 32, no. 4 (2020): 697–724.

[17] Yumin Qiu et al., "Governance of Institutional Complexity in Megaproject Organizations," *International Journal of Project Management* 37, no. 3 (2019): 425–43.

[18] Ekaterina Domorenok et al., "Introduction: Policy Integration and Institutional Capacity: Theoretical, Conceptual and Empirical Challenges," *Policy and Society* 40, no. 1 (2021): 1–18.

[19] Rong Zhixie et al., "Impact of the Digital Economy on Technical Regulations and Standardization in the Context of the Belt and Road Initiative," *Роль Технического Регулирования и Стандартизации в Эпоху Цифровой Экономики.—Екатеринбург, 2023*, 2023, 444–52.

[20] Jinzhu Zhang et al., "The Impact of Digital Economy on the Economic Growth and the Development Strategies in the Post-COVID-19 Era: Evidence from Countries along the 'Belt and Road,'" *Frontiers in Public Health* 10 (2022): 856142.

[21] Haisheng Hu and Jernej Pikalo, "Fragmented Governance in the Belt and Road Initiative: Aligning Policy with SDGs 8 and 9," *Global Policy* 16, no. 5 (2025): 1004–20.

country in which this is conducted will regulate digital trade, data protection, cybersecurity, consumer rights, and intellectual property. Prices of compliance are high, especially for small and medium-sized businesses that might not have the means of operating within two or more regulatory systems.

3.2 *Cybersecurity and E-Commerce Regulation*

Despite the consensus that cybersecurity is an important issue for the safety of the digital infrastructure and the data of people, the legal frameworks of the BRI countries vary widely.[22] In certain countries, the cybersecurity regulations and enforcement systems have been well established, and in others are basing their efforts on piecemeal or even outdated regulations. Laws with weak cybersecurity make the systems susceptible to cyberattacks, data breaches, and system failures.[23] Meanwhile, too strict cybersecurity policies may restrict creativity and deter foreign direct investment in case the compliance conditions are ambiguous or overwhelming. The problem of the regulation of e-commerce is even more legal. Differences that affect the international online trade include consumer protection, taxation policies, regulation of digital payment, and product liability.[24] This unfair treatment can disorient the customers as well as the companies and make the digital markets less credible. Using the case in point, one might not be able to offer equal competition and trust to the consumer in different countries because of the differences in the refund policy, dispute resolution systems, or online advertising standards. Such problems are especially problematic to emergent digital markets whose regulatory frameworks are in the process of development.

3.3 *Intellectual Property Rights*

Another legal concern that is essential to the digital economy is the protection of Intellectual Property Rights (IPR).[25] Using digital technologies, it is possible to quickly duplicate and disseminate content, software, and innovations, and enhance the threat of intellectual property violation. The enforcement capacity of many BRI countries is limited, or their IPR laws are obsolete, failing to keep pace with the

[22] Hairong Tang, "Research on Investment Protection Mechanisms within the International Legal Framework of the Belt and Road Initiative," *Science of Law Journal* 3 (2024): 147–51.

[23] Ömer Aslan et al., "A Comprehensive Review of Cyber Security Vulnerabilities, Threats, Attacks, and Solutions," *Electronics* 12, no. 6 (2023): 1333.

[24] Fajar Sugianto et al., "Comparison of Legal Consumer Protection Systems in E-Commerce Transactions To Support Digital Economic Growth in Indonesia," *Dalat University Journal of Science*, 2022, 39–51.

[25] Asif Kahn and Ximei Wu, "Impact of Digital Economy on Intellectual Property Law," *J. Pol. & L.* 13 (2020): 117.

digital reality.[26] Lack of strong intellectual property will deter innovation, hinder foreign investment, and block the sharing of knowledge.[27] Such an unequal regulatory approach erodes confidence in the digital markets as well as diminishes the efficiency of legal frameworks that exist to promote the digital economy.

3.4 Value-Added Tax Regulations

Digital services are frequently inconvenient to fit within a conventional taxation framework used to collect taxes on tangible commodities and services. The cross-border digital transactions may face obstacles due to the differences in digital taxation policies and the value-added tax regulations, as well as the customs regulations.[28] Poor or ambiguous taxation laws can result in either double taxation or tax evasion, thus impacting the government revenue and the business.[29] Law transparency and predictability are necessary to create confidence in digital cooperation.

4 Jurisdictional and Regulatory Jurisdiction Issues

4.1 Diverse Legal Environments

The Belt and Road Initiative is a complicated patchwork of countries in the expansion of the digital economy.[30] These countries embody a large range of economic progress, with the highest-income digital centers on one end and the developing economies with the emergent technological markets on the other end. Therefore, these environments are not equally mature in terms of the law. This often presents new regulatory frameworks that are not provided by international norms to investors and digital service providers. In most jurisdictions, there are no specialized digital courts or tech-law experienced practitioners, which can make a difference in terms of the enforcement of a contract. This doubt is normally escalated by the level of

---

26 Andrew Mazen Dahdal and Adel Abdel Ghafar, "The Digital Silk Road:'Tech-Diplomacy' as a Paradigm for Understanding Technological Adoption and Emerging Digital Regulations in MENA," *Asian Journal of Law and Society* 12, no. 2 (2025): 163–88.

27 J. Afzal et al., *Statistical Analysis of Foreign Investment Using Neutrosophic Interval Based Approach. Neutrosophic Sets and Systems, 79 (1), 14*, 2025.

28 Momchil Antov, "Challenges to Customs Imposed by the New European Union Value-Added Tax Rules on Cross-Border E-Commerce–the Case of Bulgaria," *World Customs Journal* 17, no. 1 (2023): 33–53.

29 Md Harun Ur Rashid et al., "Doing Business and Tax Evasion: Evidence from Asian Countries," *Sage Open* 12, no. 4 (2022): 21582440221131280.

30 Wei Ma et al., "Inhibit or Promote: Assessing the Impact of Digital Economy on Poverty Reduction in the Belt and Road Initiative Countries," *Applied Spatial Analysis and Policy* 18, no. 4 (2025): 132.

bureaucratic corruption that ranks high and tends to create obstacles in authorizing projects and playing unequal fields to foreign firms. The primary problem the Digital Silk Road has is that no international multilateral treaty or other hard law instrument that governs the rights to digital investment exists.[31] This program has become highly reliant on non-binding Memorandums of Understanding (MoUs) and elevated political elucidations.[32] These papers are suggestive, not granting the lawful protection that is available in the conventional trade blocs. On the issue of resolving the dispute, one tends to resort to a comprehensive network of bilateral investment treaties (BITs), the vast majority of which were developed decades ago. The treaties discussed will often be outdated and fail to address a brand-new digital issue, such as the portability of information, the liability of cloud storage, or the transparency of algorithms, which have resulted in a major legal gap in the high-tech industry.

Infrastructure, including 5G base stations or regional data centers, is very sensitive to changes in politics because these investments are very large and long-term. In most BRI zones, the feasibility of a project can not only change at short notice due to the amendment of local laws.[33] The threat to the physical assets and the survival of digital services is caused by political instability and high-risk domestic environments. Governments can suddenly alter data localization policies or country security measures and leave investors with a decision between expensive technical upgrades or just leaving the market. These threats generate a lack of trust that will be a disincentive to the private capital that will sustain digital development. Weak courts tend to limit the imposition of legal rights in online trade across borders. Although international arbitration is a typical aspect of the BRI contracts, the issue of the enforcement of arbitral awards in the host countries is a problem. Litigation often occurs in parallel due to the border lessness of the digital economy.[34] Several countries can take jurisdiction over the same data breach or contractual dispute, leading to conflicting court orders, higher expenses in legal proceedings, and continued uncertainty for all parties.

There are usually disputes over the law to use in BRI digital contracts.[35] Such agreements are commonly signed between the Chinese State-Owned Enterprises (SOEs) and local government bodies or privately-owned firms of the host country.[36] There are also frequent eruptions of controversial issues on whether the contract

---

[31] Magdalena Łągiewska, "Legal Aspects of the Digital Silk Road: Trends and Challenges," *Routledge Handbook of Chinese and Eurasian International Relations*, 2024, 405–16.

[32] Marina Kolb, "The Memorandum of Understanding," in *The European Union and the Council of Europe* (Springer, 2013).

[33] Nguyen Thi Lan Anh and Mai Ngan Ha, "Legal Challenges to the Belt and Road Initiative," in *Critical Reflections on China's Belt & Road Initiative* (Springer, 2020).

[34] Naeem AllahRakha, "Rethinking Digital Borders to Address Jurisdiction and Governance in the Global Digital Economy," *Int. J. Law Policy* 2, no. 1 (2024).

[35] Julien Chaisse and Jamieson Kirkwood, "Smart Courts, Smart Contracts, and the Future of Online Dispute Resolution," *Stan. J. Blockchain L. & Pol'y* 5 (2022): 62.

[36] Edmund Terence Gomez, "State-Business Relations and Public-Public Partnerships: China's State-Owned Enterprises in Southeast Asia," *Malaysian Journal of Economic Studies* 61, no. 1 (2024): 141–57.

should be regulated by Chinese law or by the law of the host country. These uncertainties also get to the matter of the selection of the forum; parties may not agree on whether cases ought to be heard by Chinese courts or local host courts, or the third-party hubs such as Singapore or Hong Kong. These jurisdictional battles may paralyze a project implementation for years without any express conditions. The larger the digital projects, the greater the financial commitments. Where debt sustainability is an issue, the issues of sovereign immunity are frequently brought up in cases of debt repayment. State-owned organizations in BRI nations can claim that they are not subject to foreign court jurisdiction, and it is exceedingly hard to get lenders/partners to take legal action.[37] This complexity is more specifically seen in the high-value construction and technology transfers, as the borderline between a commercial organization and a governmental one is indistinct. The BRI often has the use of independent guarantees to provide performance on high-value digital and physical construction projects. Legal problems become major when it involves fraud claims. Various jurisdictions define what amounts to fraud that is enough to terminate a payment by a bank differently. The result of this is jurisdictional forum shopping, where parties apply to have an injunction granted in a court where the standards are laxer or the power to freeze payment is otherwise broader. Failure to harmonize the independent guaranteed system poses a financial threat to the contractors and banks funding Digital Silk Road projects.[38]

4.2 *Absence of Comprehensive Legal Framework*

The main obstacle of the Digital Silk Road is that there is no single, comprehensive multilateral treaty or hard law tool to coordinate the rights of investment in the digital sphere on the whole network. The Belt and Road Initiative is presently based on non-binding Memorandums of Understanding (MoUs), unlike the European Union, which has a centralized legal framework, or the USMCA. Although such documents are an indication of political intent and cooperation at a high level, they lack the binding legal protection and uniformity of procedures that are present in conventional trade blocs. This lack of a codified legal framework implies that there exists no single standardised framework of dealing with digital property, intellectual property, and investor-state relations in respect of the unique challenges of the present-day digital economy.[39]

Due to such a deficiency of a dedicated BRI-wide legal framework, dispute resolution usually reverts to a patchwork quilt of the available Bilateral Investment Treaties

[37] Wenjuan Nie, "China's State-Owned Enterprises: Instruments of Its Foreign Strategy?" *Journal of Contemporary China* 31, no. 135 (2022): 383–97.

[38] Kevin Hernandez, *Achieving Complex Development Goals along China's Digital Silk Road*, 2019.

[39] Asif Khan, "Rules on Digital Trade in the Light of WTO Agreements," *PhD Law Dissertation, School of Law, Zhengzhou University China*, 2023.

(BITs). Numerous these treaties were written many decades ago, when the emergence of cloud computing, artificial intelligence, or transnational e-commerce was unheard of. All these archaic legal instruments are not always applicable to new digital problems, such as the portability of data, the liability of automated services, or the legality of digital tokens. Therefore, in case of a dispute concerning a high-tech project, investors and host nations are normally obliged to make do with legal terminology that lacks the technical proficiency of the twenty-first century.

This reliance on an informal system of ancient agreements provides the high-tech businesses with loopholes.[40] In the absence of a well-designed and updated framework, the digital service providers do not have a lack of functional equivalence in legal protections across various borders. As an example, a contract that is valid under one BRI jurisdiction and invalid under another due to the varying meaning of a treaty. Such discontinuity of the law renders it costly to conduct business in that firms must carry out a due diligence exercise as daunting as it can be because of every and every nation rather than operating under a set of rules that can be predicted. This is a big challenge to scaffolding the Digital Silk Road to an operational international market.

4.3 Regulatory & Political Risk

The Digital Silk Road risks experienced in the category of Regulatory and Political Risks have been taking on a multi-dimensional issue as the project expands.[41] These dangers are no longer merely about the unexpected turn of the policy; they are being closely correlated with the changing strategic interests of the giant world forces and the business needs of the technology giants. This gives a platform whereby the rules of engagement are subject to continuous change to investors and partner countries. Such massive infrastructure as subsea cables, 5G networks, and data centers are of particular interest since they have become the center of an acute competition in the global technology arena.

The threat of debt distress creates a problem with diplomatic and regulatory relations.[42] Other parts were much involved, but there exist acute declines in other parts because of economic exposure and instability in the areas. Technological projects are important to growth, but are very expensive in cost, which could be unbearable to the budget of developing countries. The problems of diplomatic controversy in case

[40] Gillian K. Hadfield and Iva Bozovic, "Scaffolding: Using Formal Contracts to Support Informal Relations in Support of Innovation," *Wis. L. Rev.*, 2016, 981.

[41] Jani Grey Kasunda, "The Digital Silk Road in a Cash-Limited Society: A Critical Analysis of Chinese Fintech Expansion and Its Impact on Financial Sovereignty in Malawi," *Journal of Economic Development, Innovation and Policy* 2, no. 1 (2026): 34–52.

[42] Mansoor Dailami and Mansoor Dailami, *Sovereign Debt Distress and Corporate Spillover Impacts* (World Bank, 2010).

of a debt crisis in a country are the digital assets, such as data centers or telecommunication networks. This leads to a lack of trust that paralyzes innovation, and future investments become extremely difficult to raise.

4.4 Dispute Resolution Challenges

The Digital trade has been a significant bottleneck to the Digital Silk Road, primarily due to the vast difference in the manner in which the courts conduct their operations across the initiative as a result of applying legal rights to the Digital trade across borders. Even though in practically all the digital contracts with a high value, the clause of international arbitration is not less than a standard clause to be included in the contract, the feasibility of the enforcement of such arbitral awards in the host countries is also a significant issue. The courts of most of the countries involved are either weak or underdeveloped to have the technical expertise to solve complex online cases. This knowledge gap can create a lot of delays, since local judges can have difficulties reading between the lines of software licensing, data ownership, or algorithmic liability. The success of arbitration is greatly concerned with the compliance of a country with the international frameworks, such as the New York Convention on the Recognition and Enforcement of Foreign Arbitral Awards. Although there are numerous partners in the Belt and Road Initiative (BRI) who are signatories, they tend to be inconsistent in implementing the convention practically. Other jurisdictions permit local courts to decline to enforce a foreign award because the award violates vague and amorphous exceptions of an undefined "public policy". This presents a situation, whereby a technology provider may prevail in an arbitration court in a neutral centre such as Singapore or Hong Kong, but will not be in a position to enforce that against the assets or damages in the host country where the digital infrastructure is really based.

The situation is further complicated by the fact that international lawyers do not have the same understanding of the international legal conventions, making it a difficult place to be a digital investor. In most of the emerging markets, the legal culture is local and incomprehensible to outside judicial authority. This may result in judicial protectionism in which local courts will prefer local things or state-owned enterprise to foreign technology companies. Political stakes are stakes where the struggle is about a significant element of digital infrastructure, such as a national 5G backbone or a centralized data centre.[43] The local courts may be under extreme pressure to ignore the international decision-making through the arbitral system in favour of the national interests that render the protection of the original agreement useless in practice.[44]

---

[43] Robin Mansell and Jean-Christophe Plantin, "Imagining 5G Networks: Infrastructure and Public Accountability," *International Journal of Communication* 16 (2022): 19–19.

[44] Jeffrey Waincymer, *Procedure and Evidence in International Arbitration*, 2012.

The digital economy is an intangible and borderless industry that only adds to these enforcement challenges. A physical bridge or a railway can be moved or covered with trouble, but a relocation or covering of digital items like data, code, and cloud-based services can be duplicated with ease. When the judicial system in a host nation is slow to act or fails to establish some form of interim relief like an injunction, then the digital property in the midst of the dispute may be lost or otherwise utilized until a judgment is made. Such an inability of weak judiciaries to use their legal agility leaves it nearly impossible to recover financial losses or defend the intellectual property of a company.

4.5 *Parallel Litigation*

The borderless nature is frequently described as a feature of the digital economy, and the parallel litigation: the same case is taken to court in a number of other countries simultaneously. Because digital services, data storage, and interactions between a user may be performed in two or more territories at the same time, the courts of various countries can assert the right to hear a case.[45] To a firm that is on the Digital Silk Road, one instance of a breach of data or a dispute of the contract may result in legal suits in the country in which the servers are situated, in the country in which the firm is located, and in the country in which the end-users are situated. This interference leads to a disordered legal practice where a company may have to defend its case in more than one language, in other legal systems, and in front of more than one judge concurrently. The consequence of parallel proceedings is that there is an enormous legal uncertainty for all parties concerned.[46] When cases are handled by two courts of different countries over the same case, the chances of getting contradicting decisions are very high. To illustrate, the judgment in a case in one of BRI partner countries may be to the effect that a digital contract was valid, whereas a similar contract in another country may be to the effect that the contract was void. These inconsistent results ensure that the businesses do not know what rules to adhere to and, in fact, paralyze their activity, being unable to plan it in the long-term perspective. Such a jurisdiction war on the stability of the digital economy, as the absence of a definite, final decision will not encourage further investment to be made in cross-border infrastructure.

The economic costs of the defense of parallel litigation are high, resulting in higher costs that may cause the collapse of smaller technology companies.[47] A large number of lawsuits in different jurisdictions has necessitated the employment of

[45] Jane Donoghue, "The Rise of Digital Justice: Courtroom Technology, Public Participation and Access to Justice," *The Modern Law Review* 80, no. 6 (2017): 995–1025.

[46] Bernardo M. Cremades and Ignacio Madalena, "Parallel Proceedings in International Arbitration," *Arbitration International* 24, no. 4 (2008): 507–40.

[47] Bernard A. Burk and David McGowan, "Big but Brittle: Economic Perspectives on the Future of the Law Firm in the New Economy," *Colum. Bus. L. Rev.*, 2011, 1.

different legal teams, the costly long-time translation of documents, and the expensive costs of administrative fees of different court systems. These costs can be very high compared to the cost of the project itself. Moreover, the resources spent on handling these conflicting cases do not allow the corporate leadership to concentrate on innovation and expansion and transform a technological venture into a long-lasting court battle. To most small and medium-sized firms (SMEs) in the BRI region, the threat of such huge legal expenses is a significant deterrent to their venture into foreign markets.[48] The problem of parallel litigation is regularly driven by strategic forum shopping. With a conflict over digital property or intellectual property, one side might be in a hurry to initiate a lawsuit in a nation that has more favorable laws regarding the particular stance. This compels the other party to bring a counter-suit in another jurisdiction in an attempt to safeguard themselves. This court rush has led to a piecemeal court system where the decision of a case is made more about its place of hearing than about the facts involved in the case. The Digital Silk Road is a high-risk environment where the complexity of law can easily surpass technological advantage without a harmonized international accord to govern these jurisdictional overlaps.[49] To address these risks, the digital contracts today often contain such clauses as exclusivity or anti-suit injunction. They are created to compel any disagreements to one already agreed court or arbitration facility. But these clauses cannot be fully enforced when one of the concerned countries does not acknowledge the authority of another one.

4.6 In-Depth Due Diligence

The growth of online projects within the Belt and Road Initiative requires a certain degree of due diligence that extends beyond the financial audit.[50] Since digital infrastructure is closely connected with national security, data privacy, and long-term state contracts, the risks of inappropriate vetting are increased. The initial line of operation in the prevention of operational failure is proper investigation of local partners. Most of the BRI projects consist of collaborating with local companies that might have shady ownership or unreported relationships with political leaders.[51] Devoid of a strict deep-delve into the ultimate beneficial owners of such companion firms.

---

[48] Samuel Gyamerah et al., "The Belt and Road Initiative and East African Small and Medium-Sized Enterprises: Benefits, Drivers and Particular Sectors," *International Journal of Emerging Markets* 18, no. 2 (2023): 463–82.

[49] David Gordon and Meia Nouwens, *The Digital Silk Road: China's Technological Rise and the Geopolitics of Cyberspace* (Taylor & Francis, 2022).

[50] Mohamad Zreik, "The Belt and Road Initiative: Vision, Objectives, and Complexities," in *Qatar's Role in China's Belt and Road Initiative: Bridging Two Economic Titans* (Springer, 2025).

[51] Jiatao Li et al., "Foreign Direct Investment along the Belt and Road: A Political Economy Perspective," *Journal of International Business Studies* 53, no. 5 (2022): 902–19.

Foreign investors stand a risk of being entangled in politically prone disputes that may result in changes or the sanctioning of licenses when the political weather changes locally. Research on the regulatory environment of a host country is also important in ensuring compliance in the long run. The online environment is notoriously unstable, and the legislation that regulates the cybersecurity measures, the localization of the data, and encryption evolves quickly. Due diligence demands a prospective approach to the analysis of the legislative path of a country, rather than the existing legislation.[52] This is the evaluation of the autonomy of local regulatory bodies and the openness of the decision-making process. In case one of the host countries has a record of enacting emergency decrees that ignore the usual procedure of lawmaking, a digital project can end up out of compliance overnight. The investors also need to assess the local legal framework on whether it offers enough protection of intellectual property, as well as whether the government has clear procedures for data requests.

The reduction of corruption risks is, perhaps, the most difficult part of due diligence in the BRI context. The border between legal government facilitation and illegal bribery may also be unclear in most of the emerging markets.[53] Digital contracts with high value, like those of national 5G rollouts or systems to monitor Smart Cities, frequently have enormous procurement budgets, which are prone to rent-seeking behaviour.[54] The due diligence should be comprehensive, with on-the-ground intelligence to check the compliance of local partners with the international anti-corruption norms, including the UN Convention on Anti-Corruption. This also involves auditing the internal compliance programs and history of interaction of the partner with state officials to make sure that the project is constructed on the principle of integrity and not backroom deals. The threat of non-conformance goes to international standards and technical certification. To achieve success in a Digital Silk Road project, it has to interface with the global networks frequently. The due diligence should ensure that local partners are able to match the high standards of technical and security needed to achieve international interoperability. This involves ensuring that their cybersecurity measures, data management credentials, and their capacity to maintain the life of the software and the security patches are in place. An absence of such technical due diligence detail might result in a digital silo where the local back end fails to be linked to the global one, and the investment is old-fashioned.

---

[52] Vincent Dupont et al., "A Step in the Right Direction, or More of the Same? A Systematic Review of the Impact of Human Rights Due Diligence Legislation," *Human Rights Review* 25, no. 2 (2024): 131–54.

[53] Kimberly Kay Hoang, "Risky Investments: How Local and Foreign Investors Finesse Corruption-Rife Emerging Markets," *American Sociological Review* 83, no. 4 (2018): 657–85.

[54] Peter F. Cowhey and Jonathan D. Aronson, *Digital DNA: Disruption and the Challenges for Global Governance* (Oxford University Press, 2017).

4.7 Choice of Governing Law and Jurisdiction

One of the most controversial legal obstacles in the Digital Silk Road is the decision of Choice of Governing Law and Jurisdiction, in part due to the fact that it determines the law of one country or another to be used when a high-stakes digital project goes haywire.[55] In most of the Belt and Road Initiative (BRI) deals, agreements are made between the large Chinese State-Owned Enterprises (SOEs) and the local governments or businesses in the host country. Such deals tend to emphasize technical requirements and monetary payments without paying much attention to the small print of lawsuits. Failure by a contract to expressly provide the laws of a given country that the contract will be governed by will leave a huge vacuum in the law. This ambiguity causes delay of debates as to whether the native law to use is Chinese law, the local law of the host country, or the laws of a neutral third-country jurisdiction. The conflict is usually caused by the conflict between the basic legal cultures and national interests. Chinese SOEs usually adhere to Chinese laws due to their familiarity with Chinese laws and because the Chinese judicial system is viewed as stable. On the other hand, the entities in the host countries tend to demand their own local laws in order to safeguard their national sovereignty and make sure that the project meets the local labor regulations, environmental laws, and data privacy regulations. This is especially delicate in the digital realm; in the case of a dispute over the ownership of the data in a Smart City project, the legal result might be completely different should it be considered under the Data Security Law of China or under new privacy regulations of a host country. In the absence of a predetermined selection of law, the parties waste more time arguing over the rules of the game as compared to the facts of the dispute.

The absence of clear legal requirements poses a serious issue in transparency and risk evaluation of international investors and insurers. In case the ruling law is vague, it becomes almost impossible to estimate the legal risks of a project correctly. Such uncertainty increases the price of financing and insurance premiums since the lenders are forced to make their worst-case scenario the complete breakdown of the law. To develop the Digital Silk Road into a mature and fully global, trustworthy ecosystem, the stakeholders need to consider standardized, so-called bulletproof contractual clauses that properly stipulate the governing law, as well as the jurisdiction-specific courts or arbitration centers. The only means by which such a technological alliance can be avoided is by creating this legal transparency in the first place before the technology partnership becomes a diplomatic and legal scandal.

---

[55] Xin wei Chen, "The Legal Protection of" Silk Road E-Commerce": Challenges, Approaches, and Solutions," *International Journal of Law and Politics Studies* 7, no. 3 (2025): 01–14.

4.8 Sovereign Immunity and Debt Disputes

The meeting of the sovereign immunity and debt issues is a legal gray zone to the Digital Silk Road that places a critical bottleneck when the capital needs of 5G and data center initiatives impose an enormous financial strain on the national financial systems.[56] When a recipient state is unable to service its loans to digital infrastructure, the resulting litigation is likely to result in what is known as a jurisdictional stalemate relying on the doctrine of sovereign immunity.[57] This is a rule of international law that usually shields a state against lawsuits in the courts of a different nation without its express permission, and such is the heinousness of it that lenders can be Chinese policy banks or foreign investors, failing to find easy service recouping their debts or growing their estates using the more conventional foreign judicial methods. The fact that in the case of the Silk Road, the line between commercial and sovereign activity of state-owned corporations is indistinct also makes these conflicts even tougher.[58] Using the restrictive theory of immunity, a state is usually only safeguarded over its official activities; nonetheless, due to the Digital infrastructure often being classified as a national security concern or essential to the populace, debtor countries can have the argument that the loans behind it are sovereign in nature. This will help them to invoke immunity to avoid foreclosure of strategic assets like satellite ground stations or telecommunications hubs. This legal loophole creates an ongoing imposed lacuna in implementation, where the actual on-the-ground infrastructure remains intact, but the legal frameworks to actualize the financial value of the infrastructure cannot be acted upon because of the complexities of international law.

These strains have been enhanced by the lack of uniform conditions regarding waiver of immunity in the majority of the original Digital Silk Road memoranda of understanding. Without any written and explicit waiver, the foreign courts are unlikely to agree to a suit against a sovereign state on the basis that diplomatic goodwill and traditional etiquette are not violated. This usually forces the dispute into international arbitration, which, although more objective, is usually long and costly to maintain, postponing the settlement of the case by years. In the case of the host country, the imminent risk of an unresolved litigation may result in a credit freeze, with international markets reluctant to extend further investment until the immunity claims are resolved to put a hold on the digital modernization of the country.

---

[56] David Gordon and Meia Nouwens, *The Digital Silk Road: China's Technological Rise and the Geopolitics of Cyberspace* (Taylor & Francis, 2022).

[57] W. Mark C. Weidemaier, "Sovereign Immunity and Sovereign Debt," *U. Ill. L. Rev.*, 2014, 67.

[58] Ping Xiong and Roman Tomasic, "Soft Law, State-Owned Enterprises and Dispute Resolution on PRC's Belt and Road-towards an Emerging Legal Order," *Hong Kong LJ* 49 (2019): 1025.

4.9 Independent Guarantee Fraud Disputes

Digital and physical infrastructure projects of high value under the Belt and Road Initiative are often based on independent guarantees (such as performance bonds or standby letters of credit), as a way of addressing financial risk. They are all intended to work independently of the construction contract underlying them, i.e., the bank has to pay to the beneficiary on demand without inquiring whether a breach of contract actually took place. Nevertheless, the main legal tool that is applied to prevent such payments is the fraud exception.[59] When a party makes a claim that a payment demand is fraudulent, e.g., when a contractor asserts the work is done, but the employer enforces a guarantee despite the latter, the issue that the court system of either country has the jurisdiction to grant an injunction to freeze the funds is frequently the focus of a legal contest. Since BRI projects are the ones in which different legal systems are involved, no agreement is usually reached on which court has the authority to halt a payment.[60] A Chinese contractor may want a court in Beijing to issue an injunction against a Chinese bank to pay out, whereas the local project employer in a country such as Indonesia or Kenya may claim that only their local court may impose jurisdiction over the issue. This results in contradictory legal directions, with one court ordering a bank to make a payment and another court prohibiting it, which places the financial institution in an impossible legal situation and jeopardizes the funding of the project.

The use of the standard of proof of fraud differs dramatically among the jurisdictions of the BRI, which leads to the possibility of forum shopping.[61,62] The fraud must only be evident, and in certain legal systems, an injunction can be won and millions of dollars frozen on an arguable case only. In others, the level is far greater, and there has to be clear evidence of deliberate deception. The absence of a standardized standard implies that a party that perceives an issue at hand will seek to have an injunction in a jurisdiction that has the most lenient rule. In the Digital Silk Road, where projects are quick and cash flow is paramount, these stop-payment orders can bring business to a standstill and cause delays, and the technological equipment is becoming obsolete before it is even attached. More so, these fraud accusations are further complicated by the role of State-Owned Enterprises (SOEs). Where an independent guarantee is referred to a government-related organization, an injunction application is sought to restrain payment, and it may be viewed as a political and not a commercial action. This may invite judicial interference, in which local courts

---

59 Zaid Aladwan, "The Implementation of the Fraud Exception Rule: A Comparative Study," *Journal of Financial Crime* 27, no. 3 (2020): 977–93.

60 Veltrice Tan, "Belt and Road Initiative: The Interplay between Corruption, Plea-Bargaining and Civil Alternative Dispute Resolution," *Journal of Financial Crime* 30, no. 3 (2023): 603–17.

61 Chen Siqi et al., "Application of Blockchain Technology in Cross-Border Telecommunications Network Fraud to Ensure China's Judicial Justice," *Jurnal IUS Kajian Hukum Dan Keadilan* 12, no. 3 (2024): 472–86.

62 Yaolin Zhang, "Developing Cross-Border Blockchain Financial Transactions under the Belt and Road Initiative," *The Chinese Journal of Comparative Law* 8, no. 1 (2020): 143–76.

might be reluctant to issue an injunction to obstruct a strong beneficiary of the state, or vice versa, might be so quick to create an injunction to shield a local company against a foreign competitor. The fact that there is no neutral, internationalized standard of dealing with the issue of independent guarantee fraud in the BRI context compromises the autonomy of said financial instruments, as it is not as effective a means of conducting international trade.

5 Digital Literacy and Skills Gap

Availability of skilled human resources is a major factor in the expansion of the digital economy in the BRI.[63] The digital literacy and technical skills are prerequisites to engagement on online platforms, administration of digital systems, and manipulation of modern technologies, including cloud computing, artificial intelligence, and big data analytics. Nevertheless, the fact that many countries in the BRI have a wide digital skills and literacy gap is also one of the most serious problems, as it restricts the participation of these countries in the digital economy and the cross-border digital initiatives. Digital literacy is the skill of people to learn, shift, and make use of digital technologies.[64] It encompasses not only the basics, including the use of computers, smartphones, and the internet, but also more advanced skills, including knowledge of cybersecurity, handling digital materials, and software apps. A substantial number of the population in most of the BRI countries, especially the less developed and developing countries, are not endowed with such skills. Poor digital literacy will limit access to e-commerce, digital finance, online learning, and telemedicine, and place a significant number of individuals on the sidelines of the contemporary economy and social life. The skills gap is not limited to the essential aspect of digital literacy. High-tech digital skills, including programming, data analysis, network management, and cybersecurity skills, are important in the development and maintenance of digital infrastructure by businesses and governments. There is a lack of professionals with such competencies in many BRI countries.

Both the public and the private sectors place the governments in the position of incapacity to effectively carry out digital policies, as well as the businesses that are not able to develop innovative products or services. There will be no digital economy's full potential without a skilled workforce, and the risk of losing global competitiveness in the digital world is incumbent upon the countries. Many BRI countries have education and training systems that are usually not able to keep up with

---

[63] Aamir Shahzad et al., "The Belt and Road Initiative: Catalyzing Human Capital Development and Technological Innovation for Sustainable Growth," *China Quarterly of International Strategic Studies* 9, nos. 01–04 (2023): 361–80.

[64] Hasan Tinmaz et al., "A Snapshot of Digital Literacy," *Library Hi Tech News* 40, no. 1 (2023): 20–23.

technological advancements.[65] Schools and universities might not focus on digital skills and practical training of the new technologies in their traditional curriculum. It is necessary to bridge these gaps to make sure that every part of the population is able to engage in the digital economy and enhance social and economic inclusion. The digital literacy and skill growth are also impacted by infrastructure and access. People will have no opportunity to practice or learn digital skills without proper internet, computers, or mobile devices. The rural and remote regions are usually poorly connected, and it is hard to get students, employees, and small businesses to experience using digital technologies. To develop a universal digital literacy, there is a need to expand digital infrastructure and make the devices accessible to everyone at a low cost. Another factor related to the digital skill development is language and content barriers. A large number of digital training, software, and online resources are distributed in a small number of languages. The availability of resources to citizens in BRI countries may differ among countries that have diverse languages.

6 Geopolitical and Diplomatic Challenges

6.1 Technological Cold War

A major geopolitical irritant of the Digital Silk Road (DSR) is the Technological Cold War, which, instead of a globalized technology marketplace, has turned into a highly polarized one.[66] This is a battle based on the understanding that the United States and its allies feel that the DSR is not a business undertaking but a strategic Trojan horse.[67] China is seen as installing its own technical standards and surveillance capacities in the sovereign networks of Silk Road partner countries by exporting low-cost, high-efficiency, and digital infrastructure, whether 5G equipment provided by Huawei and ZTE or undersea cables offered by HMN Tech. It has resulted in the formation of a bipolar world digital order where states are more and more coerced into picking either a Western-led Clean Network or a Chinese-led digital ecosystem. The technological disparity can be seen within the limits of the Silk Road worlds in the digital supremacy and global standardization setting battle.[68] The integrators of the Western policies claim that the integration of Chinese hardware into what they refer to as the hard infrastructure of the Silk Road would provide Beijing with the opportunity to gain backdoor access to sensitive information that would threaten the

[65] Ruirui Wang et al., "Unveiling the Power of Education, Political Stability and ICT in Shaping Technological Innovation in BRI Nations," *Heliyon* 10, no. 9 (2024).

[66] David Gordon and Meia Nouwens, *The Digital Silk Road: China's Technological Rise and the Geopolitics of Cyberspace* (Taylor & Francis, 2022).

[67] Jonathan E. Hillman, *The Digital Silk Road: China's Quest to Wire the World and Win the Future* (Profile Books, 2021).

[68] Kevin Hernandez, *Achieving Complex Development Goals along China's Digital Silk Road*, 2019.

intelligence-sharing patterns of the West. The U.S. has responded by intensifying diplomatic efforts to assist in recruiting the members of BRI in Europe, Southeast Asia, and the Middle East to de-Chinese their key networks.[69] This enemy-us-villain environment has literally separated the Silk Road into two contrasting technology spheres, whereby interoperability is sacrificed on the altar of national security as perceived.

This strategic rivalry has at last been able to question the situation of the Silk Road as a trade bridge. In some places, such as Central Asia or Africa, where DSR is the only cheap route to high-speed connectivity, the Technological Cold War will form a digital dilemma. These nations will find themselves ostracized by the Western high-tech supply chains and financial markets when such countries implement Chinese 5G or AI-based solutions of the Smart City. On the other hand, their domestic digital transformation can be paralyzed by denying the DSR investment. This pressure has turned the Silk Road into a cyber sovereignty trial as China develops an image of a state-managed internet that is so diametrically opposite to the vision of the West of an open and decentralized internet. The growth of the DSR also promotes regulatory dispersion along the Silk Road. By using its multilateral platforms to establish new norms in 6G, in satellite navigation (BeiDou), and governance of AI, China is establishing a de facto standard to the global south that does not rely on the Western-led institutions such as the IEEE or the ITU. This division is causing a divided digital reality in which the software, data protocols, and security certifications applied in a DSR-aligned nation may not be compatible with those applied in the West. Such a digital language disunity poses a danger of reversing the connectivity that the original Belt and Road Initiative was supposed to bring.

6.2 Regional Instability

The growth of the Digital Silk Road (DSR) is often hindered by the unstable political environment of the countries involved, in which the issues of regional instability can radically change the aim of imported technology.[70] In most Belt and Road Initiative (BRI) jurisdictions, the implementation of a modernized digital infrastructure, including Smart City platforms, facial recognition technology, and high-speed telecommunications, is first introduced as an urban management and traffic control tool, and even as a safety aid to the population. But when there is some political crisis in a host country- a coup or a mass demonstration, or ethnic unrest, the high-tech systems are commonly used to suppress the local population. It is a paradigm shift between the civic utility and the state control that has brought a fundamental political dilemma to the receiver and the provider nation. Another notable case of this dynamic

---

69 Lars Erslev Andersen, *One Belt One Road'and China's Westward Pivot: Past, Present and Future*, 2017.

70 Bora Ly, "Challenge and Perspective for Digital Silk Road," *Cogent Business & Management* 7, no. 1 (2020): 1804180.

was the political turmoil that occurred in Kazakhstan at the beginning of 2022.[71] When the government was experiencing mass protests, the digital instruments that were once installed in the name of modernizing the Silk Road were reportedly used to spy on dissidents, trace individual movement, and impose digital blackouts. This change brings a significant threat to the DSR: the technology designed to promote economic connectivity can be transformed into an authoritarian resilience tool. To the citizens of these countries, the digital layer of the Silk Road is not connected with prosperity, but the increase of state surveillance, which results in a lack of trust that may then turn to an anti-government attitude over the long-term, as well as making the establishment of international collaboration more difficult.

Such reuse of technology puts Chinese technological giants and the Silk Road project in an awkward diplomatic and ethical situation. Although China has a policy of non-intervention in the internal affairs of other countries, the crackdowns through its technology in cases of instability in the region attract international reproach. These are used by Western critics as an indication that the DSR imposes a model of digital authoritarianism on its trade routes. To the host government, the dilemma is no less acute: although the technology offers the government a short-term tool to preserve order, its application against the citizens may lead to the legitimization of the government and international sanctions, which may further isolate the country from the world markets and increase its reliance on one technological supplier.

Moreover, the physical and electronic security of Silk Road assets is usually at risk due to instability in the region. In times of unrest, sabotage or even a cyberattack on data centers and fiber-optic cables by opposition groups that consider the infrastructure as an instrument of the ruling elites may occur. Such instability presents an extremely volatile situation to investors who need to consider the fact that their multi-billion-dollar digital projects may be appropriated, shut down, or destroyed in a localized conflict. The absence of a predictable political situation also renders it almost unfeasible to perform the correct long-term risk evaluations, which increases the cost of insurance and discourages the involvement of the private sector needed to make the DSR sustainable.

6.3 AI Governance Conflict

The AI Governance Conflict is a basic battle concerning the ethical and legal principles of the future global economy, in this case, concerning the DSR.[72] With the advent of Artificial Intelligence (AI) as the operating system of the modern infrastructure, which not only includes the Smart Ports in Piraeus but also automated logistics hubs

[71] Diana T. Kudaibergenova and Marlene Laruelle, "Making Sense of the January 2022 Protests in Kazakhstan: Failing Legitimacy, Culture of Protests, and Elite Readjustments," *Post-Soviet Affairs* 38, no. 6 (2022): 441–59.

[72] Nariman Aliyev, "Artificial Intelligence in Digital Silk Road: Driving Innovation and Economic Transformation," *Euroasia Journal of Social Sciences & Humanities* 12, no. 1 (2025): 95–102.

in Southeast Asia, the world is seeing a collision between two mutually irreconcilable conceptions of how it should be regulated. China has become an advocate of an "inclusive" model of AI governance, which highlights the sovereignty of the state and the entitlement of developing countries to use AI to stabilize the economy and ensure social security. Contrary to that, the United States and its allies advocate a "human-centric" model based on liberal democratic principles, establishing a fresh "AI divide" that will bifurcate the Silk Road into incompatible technology rings.

In the context of the Silk Road, China uses its multilateral technologies, including the Global AI Governance Initiative, to establish an alliance of rule-makers among the emerging economies.[73] By being able to provide BRI partners with AI-backed surveillance, facial recognition, and predictive policing services, Beijing sets a de facto precedent of how AI ought to interface with society. The inclusive approach of this model is appealing to most countries in the Silk Road since they are interested in getting developed quickly and maintaining internal peace without the strict human rights or transparency conditions that come with Western technology transfers. Nevertheless, it poses a serious legal and moral dilemma, with AI providers being trained and governed in accordance with Chinese norms, and not necessarily being up to the safety or privacy standards needed to enter the markets of the West.

It is not just a technical dispute between the U.S. and these standards, but a strategic protection of online leadership. The U.S. claims that the inclusive standards that have been promoted throughout the Silk Road put more emphasis on state regulation than individual freedom, which could introduce some algorithmic bias or encourage mass surveillance. This opposition is reflected through the formation of closed AI networks, e.g., the Hiroshima AI Process by the G7 or the OECD AI Principles, which focus on the establishment of high-safety standards that tend to marginalize technologies that are aligned with DSR. In the case of a country located on the Silk Road, such a conflict will form a bipolar regulatory landscape: by following Chinese AI standards, trade with Beijing may be simplified, but may provoke a series of tech sanctions or isolation in Western AI research and development circles.

This governance war speeds up a new digital divide with the focus on AI Readiness. The development of high-end AI needs a huge amount of computing power and specialized semiconductors, which are the center of export controls and trade wars today. With the U. S. limiting the export of high-performance AI chips to China and its allies, the Digital Silk Road may be divided into an AI-rich and AI-constrained group with access to Western hardware and Chinese-based hardware, respectively. This gap is certain to make the very idea of connectivity, which the original Silk Road boasts of, be compromised by a lack of algorithmic interoperability, where an artificial intelligence-based logistics system in one nation cannot interact with the security measures of another.

[73] Gyan Prakash Tripathi, *Geopolitics of AI Standardisation and Its Impact on Fundamental Rights*, 2025.

6.4 Espionage Fears

The Digital Silk Road is regularly stalled by a basic failure to understand the local situation by the Chinese technology vendors.[74] Although these companies are international leaders in the use of fast infrastructure implementation, they often lack cultural and administrative flexibility to traverse local labor legislation and social demands of various BRI countries. This information disconnect creates a deficit of trust, resulting in a situation where local communities and political authorities can perceive high-technical installations as alien and forced products, instead of a concerted effort. The failure of the management styles or data-handling practices to match the local norms will result in a local pushback that will not only make the diplomatic relations complicated but will also stall the incorporation of digital services into the local economy. Sustainability of debt is also an issue of concern when it comes to the long-term success of the Digital Silk Road because the price of 5G networks and data centres is very high and may burst the budget of developing countries. Digital assets, unlike the conventional physical infrastructure, are expensive to maintain and continually updated with technical measures, which are ongoing and costly, forming a never-ending financial liability. The high dependence on the Chinese policy banks' loans in most cases has contributed substantially to the debt-to-GDP ratios of the partner countries, leading them to the brink of debt distress. This economic burden can cause tensions in diplomacy because the countries hosting them are torn between the necessity to develop modern connectivity and the fact that they cannot afford to unemployed debt payment timelines.

These projects have macroeconomic risks that are even aggravated by the Iron Triangle of non-transparent financing systems. Since a large number of DSR projects are a combination of Chinese equipment, labor, and tied loans, it is easy to conceal the real long-term costs and risks of investment under local scrutiny. This is not very transparent and may result in poorer-than-expected economic payoffs in those areas where the power grid or consumer demand is not adequate to serve high-end digital services. Also, there is extreme currency volatility in emerging markets, which would result in the real value of such debts skyrocketing, and the financial recovery of digital investments would be more vulnerable to both the lender and the borrower. There are also operational challenges due to the challenges of asset monetization in the various markets of the Silk Road. Although Smart City and 5G projects introduce massive data, it is often hard to transform the data into a lucrative business model due to local regulatory constraints or societal disapproval of surveillance-based services. In the absence of a clear road to profitability, most high-tech projects are likely to become white elephants, glamorous technological developments that cannot be translated into the type of commercial value that can overall justify their original expense. To be sustainable, the DSR should not be focused on hardware laying but towards a model that guarantees financial transparency and produces real economic growth for all the stakeholders involved.

---

[74] Hong Shen, "Building a Digital Silk Road? Situating the Internet in China's Belt and Road Initiative," *International Journal of Communication* 12 (2018): 19–19.

7 Financial and Investment Challenges

7.1 Macroeconomic and Debt Sustainability Risks

Another trend is taking shape in the financial structure of the Digital Silk Road, that there exists a high degree of systematic credit risk, which is largely owed to the fact that the projects are being financed through non-concessional lending by the Chinese policy banks. It is a capital-intensive model, which has created an acute rise in the debt-to-GDP ratio of various host countries, which is more likely to put emerging economies on the brink of severe debt distress. A digital infrastructure cannot be merely any physical infrastructure like a road, but the process of cyclic replacement of expensive technology and specific support, it creates a constant liability on the national budget of a host country. This financial strain becomes a thorn in the flesh of diplomacy when the default of debt-service is taken in the context of the potential loss of sovereignty, due to which urgent attention is paid to the regulatory terms that support loans is paid in the international arena.

The Debt-Trap Diplomacy story has become a central topic of criticism of critics of the Digital Silk Road, who think that the program is effective in allowing Beijing to have strategic benefits over partner countries.[75,76] The worry is that when one country is unable to cover its repayment terms, it may be forced to give up the control of important digital property, such as the national data centres, land stations of the ground locations of the satellites, or landing points of undersea cables. This loss of potentially valuable infrastructure poses a substantial risk premium to host governments, since the loss of digital resources can undermine national security and future economic independence. On the one hand, supporters of the DSR note that it can be used to address the global digital divide, but on the other hand, the risk of seizing the assets is one of the significant obstacles to developing deep and long-term confidence between investors and recipient states.

A high level of extreme currency and exchange rate volatility in the emerging markets is an additional risk to the long-term stability of digital investments along the Silk Road. Because such infrastructure loans are often issued in foreign currency, such as the U.S. dollar or Chinese yuan, any major depreciation of the domestic currency of a host nation can exponentially lead to a rise in the actual cost of servicing the debt. To technology providers and financiers, such volatility can turn a seemingly profitable project into a net loss during a single fiscal quarter, where the revenue collected in the local currency will not be sufficient to cover the expenses of the foreign-denominated debt anymore. This financial turbulence requires the adoption of multi-faceted and costly hedging measures, which in turn escalate the overall cost

[75] Michal Himmer and Zdeněk Rod, "Chinese Debt Trap Diplomacy: Reality or Myth?" *Journal of the Indian Ocean Region* 18, no. 3 (2022): 250–72.

[76] Lee Jones and Shahar Hameiri, "Debunking the Myth of 'Debt-Trap Diplomacy,'" *Chatham House* 19, no. 2020 (2020): 657–71.

of digital access and could discourage the mass participation of the private sector needed to make the initiative mature.

These macroeconomic pressures at the operational level are compounded by the existence of opaque financing mechanisms and bundled procurement contracts. The absence of clear, competitive bidding systems tends to obscure the real long-term costs of the 5G rollouts and the operation of a data center, leading to an inefficiency premium that may nullify the initial investment by the host country. Moreover, the economic feasibility of these high-technology projects is often compromised by the lack of fit between the high-tech abilities of the technology and the current softer infrastructure available in the host nation, in terms of poor power grids or low digital literacy levels. It is this imbalance that frequently results in the establishment of technological enclaves that cannot provide the localized economic returns to cover the enormous capital cost and leaves the host country with a highly advanced resource but no means of covering the cost.

7.2 *Operational and Investment Risks*

The Digital Silk Road and its operational environment are becoming more conceptualized by the existence of opaque financing systems, commonly known by pundits as the Iron Triangle.[77] This arrangement often entails a strongly packaged deal of Chinese state-supported loans, Chinese technology suppliers, and Chinese manpower, which in effect constrains the competition bidding and the local control. To international investors and partner countries, such non-transparency is a way of hiding major fiscal risks over the long run, as the actual cost of infrastructure maintenance and payment of debts is often hidden by the ease of the turnkey solution in the first place. These projects may turn into financial black boxes without open and standardized accounting, and it is almost impossible to perform accurate risk assessment or to convince that the digital assets are actually delivering value to the capital invested.

Moreover, numerous DSR projects are at constant risk of reduced economic returns and construction delays, especially where they are implemented in the underdeveloped areas where the supporting infrastructure is lacking. The viability of high-tech infrastructure (such as 5G base stations or regional data centers) solely relies on a stable power infrastructure and high rates of local digital literacy, neither of which is likely to be present in the frontier markets. These logistical challenges raise the cost of construction and the time to finish the project, this is as the real-business need of the high-quality digital services is often not as attractive as it was originally estimated. This discrepancy between the sophisticated functions of the technology

[77] Richard Ghiasy and Rajeshwari Krishnamurthy, "China's Digital Silk Road," *Institute of Peach and Conflict Studies, Leiden Asia Center* 26 (2020).

and the real economic demands of the locals frequently leads to the creation of the so-called technological enclave that has little trouble being profitable to support its own operations.

8 Multilateral Determination

China has put in place more than 20 multilateral platforms to promote the implementation of the New Infrastructure. These sites are the nerve centers in which 5G networks, hyperscale data centers, and the Peace Cable network connecting Asia and Africa, as well as Europe, are built. Such forums will enable the standardization of the implementation of "Smart City" and AI solutions, whereby involved countries can discuss the best practices and technical blueprints. The horizontalization of these projects across several countries at a time brings about economies of scale that allow the highly advanced surveillance and city management tools to be made available to developing economies that had, in the past, been prohibitively expensive to access the Western technological market.

The key aim of this multilateral push is the strategic shift of China towards being a rule-taker to rule makers in the global technology environment. The Western companies established the standard protocols of the internet over the decades, but with the DSR, China is capitalizing on its extensive deployment base to establish the next-generation technologies. Through multilateral platforms to create consensus amongst the countries of the "Global South", Beijing is effectively selling its own technical specifications on anything but the facial recognition algorithms, but on Internet of Things (IoT) protocols. It is a norm-setting authority that will see to it that the future of global connectivity will be anchored on Chinese architectural principles that will produce a long-term lock-in effect on any country that will have become part of the digital landscape of the Silk Road.

This trend presents a unique alternative form of governance to the Western paradigm of the Open Internet, which focuses on such notions as cyber sovereignty and data localization. The model targets the African, Southeast Asian, and Middle Eastern leadership, in particular, because it puts the right of the state to regulate the digital borders and the control of internal data without the external intervention of tech giants or international non-governmental organizations first. The DSR supplies the physical hardware and the legal basis for a state-led digital management and therefore provides a turnkey means of digital modernization that does not threaten the political status quo of recipient countries.

9 Potential Solutions and Recommendations

To tackle the challenges of the digital economy in the framework of the Belt and Road Initiative (BRI), it is necessary to find effective ways of solving problems and develop specific solutions. The problems are technological, legal, financial, skills, sustainability, and diplomatic, and therefore the solutions need to be integrated, global, and flexible. Powerful strategies can enhance digital infrastructure, participation, minimize risks, and grow in the long run in the BRI region. Improving digital infrastructure is one of the most significant solutions. The development of high-speed internet infrastructure, the creation of stable data centers, and the implementation of contemporary systems of communication, including 5G, may provide new opportunities in terms of connectivity and facilitating the growth of digitalization. Nations can emphasise on the partnerships between the state and the companies to share the expenses and knowledge. The infrastructure planning across BRI countries is coordinated so that the networks are compatible, secure, and able to meet the technological requirements in the future. Green technologies and energy-efficient infrastructure that are also invested in are part of sustainability.

The other recommendation is to improve the regulatory and legal structure. Unambiguous and regular data protection, cybersecurity, e-commerce, and cross-border digital trade regulations and policies diminish the uncertainty among businesses and governments. The coordination of regulations in the BRI countries would make it easier to comply and facilitate digital transactions. The creation of cross-border dispute settlement systems, intellectual protection, and standards recognition can enhance confidence in digital cooperation. Governments may establish dedicated regulatory authorities to monitor the operations of the digital economy and liaise with other agencies to ensure that there are no overlaps. Enhancing digital literacy and technical skills is very important in the survival of the digital economy. Digital skills ought to be imparted into the curriculum across the board, either at schools, vocational training centers, or universities. Online learning platforms, hands-on workshops, and professional development programs may be made available to people and employees to acquire skills in coding, data analysis, cybersecurity, and digital business operations. The systems set to monitor progress, measure effectiveness, and identify challenges enable policymakers and other stakeholders to make amendments where necessary.

The exchange of lessons learned and best practices between the BRI countries encourages learning and avoids recurring errors, as well as boosts the process of digital development. Regional cooperation may be enhanced through collaborative platforms, conferences, and the sharing of knowledge, and make sure that practical experience informs solutions. Promoting the interests of the private sector is also a good suggestion. Companies are very instrumental in offering technology, investment, and innovation. The establishment of easy-to-understand policies, incentives, and public–private collaborative structures will make businesses engage in digital projects. Further competition, better service quality, and entrepreneurship in the BRI region are all already supported by the establishment of small and medium-sized enterprises, startups, and local innovators.

10 Conclusion

The Belt and Road Initiative (BRI) has a digital economy that presents immense economic development, technological transformation, and cooperation in the region. Meanwhile, it has many obstacles that should be considered. These issues are technological infrastructure, legal and regulatory framework, financial constraints, digital literacy, geopolitical tensions, and sustainability issues. This knowledge of these issues is critical in helping governments, businesses, and other parties to make sound decisions and actively engage in the digital initiatives carried out by the BRI. The digital economy needs a secure technological platform. Regulatory and legal frameworks have an impact on the involvement of countries in the digital economy. The skilled workforce enhances productivity and growth of the business, and it also motivates more individuals to participate in the digital economy. The issues that are involved demand planning, investment, and collaboration to arrive at the success of the BRI digital economy.

Chapter 6
Digital Operations Legal Issues and Digital Dispute Resolution Mechanism

Abstract An increase in digital operations in the BRI countries poses a few complex legal, regulatory, and operational challenges. The difference in data protection laws, such as the EU GDPR and the Chinese PIPL, is a challenge to multinational companies and offers more grounds for conflict. The legal issues surrounding the use of digital operations are typified by technical sophistication, transnational forces, and electronic data, proving the limitations of the traditional dispute resolution process. The findings of this chapter reveal that new technologies, such as Online Dispute Resolution (ODR) platforms, blockchain, and smart contracts, can be used to propose new ways to effectively, transparently, and safely resolve digital disputes. They can be scaled and made available through the combination of technology automation and legal control, which is one of the ways through which conflicts can be resolved, particularly when cross-border cases are involved.

Keywords Dispute resolution mechanism · Online Dispute Resolution · GDPR versus PIPL · Cybersecurity Law · Data Security Law

1 Introduction

The development of the digital economy raises a complex set of legal, regulatory, and operational concerns.[1] Digital technologies are not geographically bound, unlike physical infrastructure; thus, national laws can conflict with one another.[2] The ambiguity may be found in data management, data privacy, intellectual property, cybersecurity, and cross-border compliance in companies that exist in different jurisdictions.[3] As an illustration, a digital transaction between one party in China, Pakistan, and

[1] Guillaume Beaumier et al., "Global Regulations for a Digital Economy: Between New and Old Challenges," *Global Policy* 11, no. 4 (2020): 515–22.

[2] Naeem AllahRakha, "Rethinking Digital Borders to Address Jurisdiction and Governance in the Global Digital Economy," *Int. J. Law Policy* 2, no. 1 (2024).

[3] Jatish Gulia, "Cross-Border Data Transfers: International Cooperation and Conflicts," *Legal Lock J.* 4 (2024): 263.

J. Afzal and Y. Chen, *Legal Framework of Digital Economy and Digital Trade Under the Belt and Road Initiative*, https://doi.org/10.1007/978-981-92-4444-7_6

Malaysia could harbor data that is stored in different countries and thus have different legal provisions to maintain, store, and transfer the data. These disparities present ambiguity to the multinational operations and may lead to the possibility of conflict.

Data has now also become a controversial political and legal matter in addition to its economic worth.[4] The governments are increasingly appreciating the fact that the information that is produced within the territories is highly informative about the citizens, the institutions, and the activities in which the economy is involved. This acknowledgment has led to the emergence of data sovereignty. The concept of data sovereignty represents the notion that states must retain the right to control how data is gathered, stored, processed, and transferred, despite the fact that digital operations may cross-border boundaries.[5] The correlation between the data flows across the border and the data sovereignty is described by a dilemma of transparency and regulation.[6] On the one hand, free data flows may put states at economic, political, and security risks. Governments worry about foreign spy desires, cyber espionage, unauthorized access to sensitive information, and the rise of multinational technology companies. There is also the fear that the domestic data will probably be commercially exploited in other nations.[7] Such concerns have induced many states to adopt regulatory policies, which will boost national control over data. Data localization is another regulation model that is commonly embraced and demands that some groups of data be stored or processed in a country. The reasons of national security, protection of privacy, regulatory control, and capabilities of law enforcement usually support the localization of the data.

Jurisdictional control of data is another major challenge. In the case of information stored in foreign servers or information being processed by Multinational Corporations (MNCs), there is no understanding of the jurisdiction of the law of any particular country, and the legal access to the information. This may be complicated by the fact that there may be conflicts between the jurisdictions on the same information between two or more states, especially in regard to a criminal investigation, taxation or even enforcement of regulations.

In the global economic outlook, limitations on the cross-border movement of data can also be an issue of concern regarding trade and investment. The digital trade is heavily relying on the free movement of data, and the barriers to trade in services

[4] Michael Wojatzki et al., "Quantifying Qualitative Data for Understanding Controversial Issues," paper presented at Proceedings of the Eleventh International Conference on Language Resources and Evaluation (LREC 2018), 2018.

[5] Luca Belli et al., "Data Sovereignty and Data Transfers as Fundamental Elements of Digital Transformation: Lessons from the BRICS Countries," *Computer Law & Security Review* 54 (2024): 106017.

[6] W. Gregory Voss, "Cross-Border Data Flows, the GDPR, and Data Governance," *Wash. Int'l LJ* 29 (2019): 485.

[7] John Selby, "Data Localization Laws: Trade Barriers or Legitimate Responses to Cybersecurity Risks, or Both?," *International Journal of Law and Information Technology* 25, no. 3 (2017): 213–32.

may be operated by the restrictions on data.[8] This has occasioned increasing arguments regarding the way of balancing data sovereignty with international economic obligations, especially in the circumstances of the digitalized trade rules and cross-border services. Regulatory methods that concern regulated or trusted data flows have become more popular in response to these issues. These methods aim to permit cross-border data transfers whilst ensuring that they are conducted within legal and technical limitations rather than encouraging complete openness or severe localization.

2 Data Flow and Data Sovereignty: GDPR Versus PIPL

2.1 Overview of General Data Protection Regulation

The European Union established the General Data Protection Regulation (GDPR) in 2018, which establishes a complete framework of regulations regarding how to gather, process, and transfer personal data in a digital environment that is increasingly becomes interconnected.[9] Among the most significant aspects of GDPR, the fact that the regulation is applicable to non-EU organisations that process the personal data of EU citizens must be mentioned. This is particularly relevant to the Digital Silk Road activities, where European consumers tend to consume cross-border digital services such as e-commerce, cloud, and smart-city systems.[10,11] Companies that work in these networks must make sure that their data governance structures follow GDPR rules. This implies that their technology should be in line with their daily activities. The regulation is based on a few main ideas, such as being open, limiting the purpose of the data, keeping it to a minimum, being accurate, and protecting the integrity and privacy of the data. These principles establish rules regarding the scope, purpose, and extent of data processing, which assist big digital infrastructures in handling their data in a more structured manner. The rights of individuals are also enhanced by GDPR because users have the right to access, rectify, erase, and transfer their own information.[12] This contributes to data-driven systems being more responsible.

---

[8] Nikita Melashchenko, *Data Barriers to International Trade*, 2022.

[9] Jamil Afzal, "Legal Challenges Regarding Digital Operations," in *Implementation of Digital Law as a Legal Tool in the Current Digital Era* (Springer, 2024).

[10] Matthew S. Erie and Thomas Streinz, "The Beijing Effect: China's Digital Silk Road as Transnational Data Governance," *NYUJ Int'l L. & Pol.* 54 (2021): 1.

[11] Andrew Mazen Dahdal and Adel Abdel Ghafar, "The Digital Silk Road: 'Tech-Diplomacy' as a Paradigm for Understanding Technological Adoption and Emerging Digital Regulations in MENA," *Asian Journal of Law and Society* 12, no. 2 (2025): 163–88.

[12] Maria Bottis et al., "The Right to Access Information under the GDPR," *International Journal of Technology Policy and Law* 3, no. 2 (2019): 131–42.

The transfer of data across borders is regulated by GDPR.[13] As an example, personal data may only be transferred outside the EU with the proper protection or the right measures. This imposes regulatory consequences on Digital Silk Road projects that operate across a country or countries, particularly those in countries that are not adequately regulated by the EU. One of the compliance requirements is the internal governance, risk assessment, and enforcement mechanisms, which are supported by severe penalties in case of violation of the rules. This framework renders the GDPR a major regulatory force in the Digital Silk Road. It influences the way digital infrastructure is operated, the organization of data flows, and the realization of international norms of privacy and security in digital cross-border systems.

2.2 Overview of Chinese Personal Information Protection Law

In the year 2021, China enacted the Personal Information Protection Law (PIPL).[14] This legislation establishes the guidelines on how to manage individual information within the fast-evolving Chinese digital economy. It is not just vital to domestic regulation, but also directly assists China in its digital development plan with the Digital Silk Road, which is a major component of the Belt and Road Initiative.[15] The Digital Silk Road initiatives are developing transnational digital infrastructure such as 5G networks, smart cities, cloud services, and e-commerce. The PIPL law governs and manipulates data that is input by these systems. Another aspect that makes PIPL prominent is its emphasis on data sovereignty that resembles the strategic objectives of the Digital Silk Road greatly.[16] The law is applicable to the data processing operations in China as well as to the businesses outside China that process the personal data of Chinese citizens.[17] The foreign companies and host countries, in collaboration with the Chinese digital platforms or infrastructure, are to adhere to the Chinese

---

[13] Clare Sullivan, "EU GDPR or APEC CBPR? A Comparative Analysis of the Approach of the EU and APEC to Cross Border Data Transfers and Protection of Personal Data in the IoT Era," *Computer Law & Security Review* 35, no. 4 (2019): 380–97.

[14] Barbara Verri, "The Chinese Frontiers of Data Protection: The Personal Information Protection Law (PIPL)," in *Quo Vadis, Sovereignty? New Conceptual and Regulatory Boundaries in the Age of Digital China* (Springer, 2023).

[15] Magdalena Łągiewska, "Legal Aspects of the Digital Silk Road: Trends and Challenges," *Routledge Handbook of Chinese and Eurasian International Relations*, 2024, 405–16.

[16] Anupam Chander and Haochen Sun, *Data Sovereignty: From the Digital Silk Road to the Return of the State* (Oxford University Press, 2023).

[17] Igor Calzada, "Citizens' Data Privacy in China: The State of the Art of the Personal Information Protection Law (PIPL)," *Smart Cities* 5, no. 3 (2022): 1129–50.

data governance standards. This is because the Digital Silk Road has an extraterritorial scope. PIPL gives China an extension of its regulatory jurisdiction over BRI digital networks, thereby enhancing its dominance over data movement over these systems.[18]

PIPL relies on such principles as legality, necessity, and specification of purpose.[19,20] This implies that personal information should be obtained with clear and direct purposes. Surveillance systems, logistics platforms, and digital services have the capacity to create a significant amount of data on a daily basis, which is generated by Digital Silk Road projects. These values will regulate the use of such data and remain in accordance with the priorities of the state. User consent is needed to collect data, particularly sensitive data, but the overall governance framework is closely associated with regulatory control and national policy objectives. This legislation gives people the right to access, correct, and remove their personal data, which is an evolving data protection system in China. Nevertheless, in the Digital Silk Road, these rights are practiced in unity with the interests of the state overall, especially in the infrastructural works, where they are combined with the public security systems, urban management technologies, and data platforms.[21] This sets a trend of government where personal data protection is provided, but at the expense of centralization.

The export of data outside China is very restricted as far as regulatory approvals, like security checks and compliance certificates, are concerned.[22] The localization needs of the data in the majority of cases are as follows: crucial data will be stored in China. Such limits affect the architecture of Digital Silk Road networks, usually promoting the creation of locally managed data systems in place of complete global flows. This implies that the information produced under the BRI digital infrastructure will be more likely to remain within the controlled jurisdiction, which underpins the strength of digital connectivity. PIPL also has compliance requirements, including data management systems, security, and regulatory reporting internally. In the scenario of companies that took part in the Digital Silk Road programs, the key to remaining in operation on the Chinese technologies and markets is adherence to these requirements. Enforcement mechanisms also strengthen regulatory authority through the imposition of fines and limitations on operations. PIPL is an essential pillar of the Digital Silk Road regulation, and it brings data sovereignty, controlled data flows, and state-based regulation to the cross-border digital infrastructure, which is developed within the framework of the Belt and Road Initiative with these provisions.

---

[18] Ziwen Tan and Channing Zhang, "China's PIPL and DSL: Is China Following the EU's Approach to Data Protection?," *Journal of Data Protection & Privacy* 5, no. 1 (2021): 7–25.

[19] Zhang Yi-Chen, "China's Personal Information Protection Law (PIPL) 2021: An Analysis," *Modern Jurisprudence* 3, no. 3 (2025).

[20] Rachele Torrisi, *China's New Personal Information Protection Law (PIPL): Implications for Companies and Human Resources Management*, 2023.

[21] Adrian Shahbaz, "The Digital Silk Road and Normative Values," *Adelphi Series* 60, nos. 487–489 (2020): 107–30.

[22] Giulia Bonardi, *Outbound Data Transfer from China: Implications for National Security and Foreign Businesses*, 2023.

2.3 Similarities Between GDPR and PIPL

Despite the fact that they belong to different political and regulatory frameworks, both the General Data Protection Regulation (GDPR) and the Personal Information Protection Law (PIPL) have a number of structural and functional similarities, particularly in their regulation of personal data in the framework of more and more globalized digital networks.[23,24] These similarities play a critical role in the context of the Digital Silk Road in terms of interoperability of data governance practices between the regions that are interlinked with the European and Chinese digital spaces. The scope of the law is not limited because both GDPR and PIPL have an observable extraterritorial scope.[25] The laws apply to all organizations outside their jurisdiction as they handle personal data about people in their jurisdictions, especially when they are offering goods and services or monitoring user activities. This similarity is particularly relevant in the context of the activities of the Digital Silk Road, in which companies tend to operate in many different jurisdictions. Firms that get involved in cross-border e-commerce, digital platforms, and smart infrastructural projects must consider that they have to comply with both regulatory frameworks when working with the European and Chinese data environments.

There are also similar underlying principles in both regulations that lead to data processing processes. The lawfulness, fairness, transparency, purpose limitation, and data minimization are the main concepts of the two frameworks that create a structured framework on how personal data is gathered and utilized. All these principles allow some kind of regulatory convergence of Digital Silk Road projects, where the telecommunications networks, logistics networks, and urban technologies are used to produce the huge volumes of data, although their use may be different. GDPR as well as PIPL define what constitutes personal information using broad terminology, such as any data that can identify the person, either directly or indirectly.[26] This includes names, identification numbers, localization data, online identifiers, and other online indications. Such a broad definition is particularly essential within the framework of the Digital Silk Road, where emerging technologies such as artificial intelligence, Internet of Things (IoT), and big data analytics are regularly generating various forms of identifiable information. One of the greatest similarities between both laws is the right to protect individual rights. Both models also provide individuals with the right to their data, request corrections, copies, deletion, and limit specific processing, as well as withdraw their consent. These rights impose some sense of responsibility

---

[23] Wenlong Li and Jiahong Chen, "From Brussels Effect to Gravity Assists: Understanding the Evolution of the GDPR-Inspired Personal Information Protection Law in China," *Computer Law & Security Review* 54 (2024): 105994.

[24] Igor Calzada, "Citizens' Data Privacy in China: The State of the Art of the Personal Information Protection Law (PIPL)," *Smart Cities* 5, no. 3 (2022): 1129–50.

[25] Christopher Kuner, "Data and Extraterritoriality," in *Research Handbook on Extraterritoriality in International Law* (Edward Elgar Publishing, 2023).

[26] Jun Yang, "An Overview of the Chinese 'Personal Information Protection Law,'" *Pin Code* 10, no. 1 (2022): 8–13.

on the organizations involved in the Digital Silk Road systems and require them to have user-centric processes of data management in platforms that are likely to be large-scale and of a cross-border nature.

An institutional responsibility is also backed by the necessity to assign responsible persons to address data protection. The GDPR mandates the appointment of a Data Protection Officer (DPO) in specific cases, as compared to PIPL, which does the same for organizations handling large volumes of data. This will allow organizations that are part of the Digital Silk Road activities to possess internal governance systems that will be capable of tracking compliance with the demands of data protection. The requirements for notification about data breaches also exist in the two regulations. Companies are required to report the instances of unauthorized access, loss, or leak of personal information to the government and, in other cases, to the individuals who were affected.[27] This is especially essential in Digital Silk Road infrastructures, where interrelated systems expand the magnitude and possibilities of the effects of data breaches across a variety of nations. Another area of coordination is risk management since both GDPR and PIPL obligate organizations to perform impact assessments prior to the involvement in high-risk data processing operations or transferring data to foreign countries. These tests determine possible threats to personal privacy and information security and make sure that the necessary precaution is taken. These requirements are reflected in the design and deployment of technologies in Digital Silk Road projects, namcly, in the areas of surveillance systems, smart governance platforms, and cross-border digital services.

The other similarity between the two frameworks is that sensitive data ought to be more secure. GDPR is aware of special categories of personal data, whereas PIPL is aware of sensitive personal information, including health-related, biometric, and financial status information, and location-related data. Stricter terms are also provided in the processing of such data, and it is a sign of higher risks of abuse. These safeguards are necessary in the establishment of responsible data practices of Digital Silk Road applications, where sensitive information is often integrated into massive digital platforms. These common characteristics show that even though there are some variations in the philosophy of governance, GDPR and PIPL overlap in some fundamental areas of data protection. This intersection is part of a partial regulatory compatibility in the Digital Silk Road and influences how cross-border businesses organize their compliance strategies, as well as the evolution of cross-border digital ecosystems in the broader context of the Belt and Road Initiative.

[27] Vera Zinovieva et al., "Legal Issues of Protection of Personal Data: Cases of Transport Data Leaks," *Transportation Research Procedia* 68 (2023): 461–67.

2.4 Distinction of PIPL

2.4.1 Strict Data Localization

The Personal Information Protection Law (PIPL) is the cornerstone of Chinese digital governance, and it has provided a regulatory framework that is vastly different from the European General Data Protection Regulation (GDPR). Although both laws have the same goal of safeguarding the privacy of individuals, the PIPL also includes an obligation of high-grade data localization, which obliges organizations that process large amounts of personal data to store the latter physically within Chinese territory.[28] In contrast to the GDPR system of the so-called adequacy decisions, which enables relatively fluid data transfers between trusted jurisdictions, the PIPL regards the export of personal information as a high-level matter. Any data transfer across borders requires a formal security evaluation by the Cyberspace Administration of China (CAC), which essentially forms an online border that replicates the physical sovereignty that is the main theme of the historical and contemporary Silk Road trading routes.

2.4.2 Consent-Focused

The PIPL is much more consent-minded and restrictive in its position compared to the European one. Although the GDPR permits data processing based on a loose legal justification, legitimate interest, the GDPR permits businesses to operate without express permission in some low-risk situations, the PIPL does not permit this loophole.[29] This establishes a high-quality compliance environment in which platforms have to obtain individual approval of specific, high-stakes actions, like processing sensitive data, information sharing with third parties, or international transfers. For countries and companies becoming part of the Digital Silk Road, which provides a fine-grained measure of control, it requires a strict compliance architecture centered around state-vetted protocols instead of the Western approach of open-data. The definition of sensitive data of the PIPL is significantly broader than that of international standards and includes not only the personal information of all minors, but also those who are less than 14 years old, and extremely narrow data of the location of an individual, including his or her exact location. This broadened coverage shows the state-centric nature of the law, where individual rights are weighed against and are often weighed by national security and the common good. This model is quite appealing to most of the Silk Road partner states, who embrace the concept of cyber sovereignty, as it gives them a roadmap to a digital economy in which the state is the ultimate information adjudicator.

---

[28] Ziwen Tan and Channing Zhang, "China's PIPL and DSL: Is China Following the EU's Approach to Data Protection?," *Journal of Data Protection & Privacy* 5, no. 1 (2021): 7–25.

[29] Monique Taylor, "The Party-Led Internet Economy," in *China's Digital Authoritarianism: A Governance Perspective* (Springer, 2022).

2.4.3 Higher Penalties and State-Centric Approach

The PIPL has more of the highest penalties and stricter deterring measures than practically any other privacy law around the world in order to make sure that there is overall compliance. Penalties in case of non-compliance may go as high as 5 percent of the annual earnings of a company, which is higher than the 4 percent limit in the GDPR.[30,31] More importantly, the PIPL might present employees with personal liability, i.e., individual managers could be legally and financially liable when a company fails in its data. This forms a strong motivation for the firms working in the Silk Road ecosystem to comply with CAC principles strictly. With these standards in place, China is no longer a rule-taker when it comes to international privacy, but a rule-maker, with an alternative legal architecture that alters the ways information is secured and enforced throughout the modern Silk Road.

3 Legal Support for Digital Operations by China

3.1 Core Legal Pillars of DSR Data Protection

Having become one of the pillars of digital governance in China, the Personal Information Protection Law (PIPL) establishes a regulatory framework.[32] In contrast to the GDPR system of adequacy decision, where the relatively free flow of data may be permitted between jurisdictions that are approved, the PIPL categorizes the export of personal information as a state concern. Any data flow across borders must be formally evaluated by the Cyberspace Administration of China (CAC), which has the effect of organizing a digital border that resembles the physical sovereignty at the heart of the historical and contemporary trade routes of the Silk Road.[33]

The PIPL does not provide an alternative to explicit permission by taking a much more consent-based and restrictive pose than its European counterpart. Where the GDPR permits data processing under the banner of the legitimate interest, a broad legal provision, which permits businesses to conduct business in some low-risk situations, the PIPL mandates a high-compliance standard where platforms make specific, high-stakes decisions, they must obtain separate consent. Such actions are processing

---

[30] Josephine Wolff and Nicole Atallah, "Early GDPR Penalties: Analysis of Implementation and Fines through May 2020," *Journal of Information Policy* 11 (2021): 63–103.

[31] Morgana Mo Zhou et al., "Understanding Chinese Internet Users' Perceptions of, and Online Platforms' Compliance with, the Personal Information Protection Law (PIPL)," *Proceedings of the ACM on Human–Computer Interaction* 8, no. CSCW1 (2024): 1–26.

[32] Ming-Ting Oceanus Kam, "A Comparative Analysis of Customer Data Privacy Protection under the European Union's General Data Protection Regulation and the People's Republic of China's Personal Information Protection Law," *Beijing L. Rev.* 16 (2025): 1721.

[33] A. Portrait, "The Cyberspace Administration of China," *The Emergence of China's Smart State*, 2023, 9.

sensitive data, the transfer of information to third parties, and international transfers. To countries and businesses that join the Digital Silk Road, this is both a more detailed level of control and a compliance structure that requires strict adherence to protocols vetted by the state, and not the Western open-data approach to computing.

3.2 Cybersecurity Law (CSL – 2017)

The Cybersecurity Law (CSL – 2017) is the main legal tool to regulate the domestic and international scope of the Chinese internet infrastructure, as it implements a background of digital monitoring.[34] The law has put in place strict security standards on sectors that are perceived as of critical national security, including telecommunication, energy, and finance. One of the central elements of this legislation is real-name registration, where users are required to present government-issued identification to use the online services. The policy is an effective way to restrict online anonymity and trace digital activities, which makes the environment highly controlled and focuses more on the security of the state rather than on the privacy of the individual.

The Digital Silk Road (DSR) incorporates the CSL into its standards of domestic security brings these standards to the international projects and influencing the way the partner countries will operate their networks. Since Chinese companies are exporting 5G technology, data centers, and so-called Smart City platforms, the architectural specifications tend to resemble the same security-first principles that were included in the 2017 law. In the case of countries located on the Silk Road, the need to implement this infrastructure will often require the implementation of related real-name schemes and infrastructure safeguards, making it easier to have a common approach to cyber sovereignty. This correspondence makes it easier to technologically integrate the DSR more smoothly and can set a unified base for how the state authorities can track and secure the digital corridors of the contemporary Silk Road.

By exporting these legal and technical standards, China is gradually transforming from a rule-taker in the global cybersecurity to a rule-maker in the developing world. The CSL is a turnkey approach to countries that want to bring their digital economies up to date without having to embrace the Open Internet philosophy that is heavily dominated by the West. The law provides an exciting alternative to governments in Southeast Asia, Africa, and the Middle East that are more interested in state control of information and internal stability and national security.

[34] Rogier Creemers, "Cybersecurity Law and Regulation in China: Securing the Smart State," *China Law and Society Review* 6, no. 2 (2023): 111–45.

3.3 *Data Security Law (DSL – 2021)*

The Data Security Law (DSL – 2021) was established to enhance the legal framework of the digital economy of the country by acting as a complex set of rules that govern the process of data management throughout the entire life cycle.[35,36] This bill creates a special group referred to as important data, which includes any information that may affect national security, economic stability, or the interest of the people in case it is leaked. The DSL will make sure that strategic information is not left outside state control by making the transfer of such data subject to strict security evaluations. Moreover, the legislation introduces tight restrictions concerning the delivery of data to foreign courts or law enforcement bodies, effectively not allowing domestic organizations to respond to foreign legal requests in advance without the confirmation of the Chinese government.

The DSL is part of the overall picture of the Digital Silk Road (DSR), and it is a standardized legal framework to operate the enormous data flows produced by the infrastructure across boundaries. As Chinese corporations launch subsea cabling, satellite networks, and regional data centers, the idea of the 2021 law that gives more emphasis to security is exported as a piece of the technological bundle. This model offers a blueprint for data sovereignty to the partner countries along the Silk Road, where governments exert a high degree of control over the digital assets operating within their borders. It is easier to have a single set of data corridors that is being managed as a piece of national significance than as a commodity that is being freely traded using this synergy.

4 Mechanisms for Data Protection and Privacy

4.1 *Data Localization*

One of the pillars of the greater cybersovereignty approach of China is the data localization principle, according to which the physical location of data generated on the territory of a country should be stored in local servers.[37] This is a legal criterion that is included in major legislations like the Cybersecurity Law and the PIPL, which ensure that sensitive information, either financial information or personal identifiers, does not end up in the possession of foreign intelligence or other technology giants.

---

[35] Jihong Chen and Jiabin Sun, "Understanding the Chinese Data Security Law," *International Cybersecurity Law Review* 2, no. 2 (2021): 209–21.

[36] Ziwen Tan and Channing Zhang, "China's PIPL and DSL: Is China Following the EU's Approach to Data Protection?," *Journal of Data Protection & Privacy* 5, no. 1 (2021): 7–25.

[37] Heylyung Yun, "China's Data Sovereignty and Security: Implications for Global Digital Borders and Governance," *Chinese Political Science Review* 10, no. 2 (2025): 178–203.

These geographic boundaries of digital information will enable the state to conduct security audits more effectively, introduce local privacy standards, and ensure that the new oil of the digital economy is utilized to serve the development of local areas, and not lose it to foreign clouds. Relating this localized model to the Digital Silk Road (DSR), China also actively enforces the same policies on other countries as a way of securing national dominance over their online destinies. In the process of constructing the physical infrastructure of the Silk Road, including the "Peace Cable" or regional data centers in Southeast Asia and Africa, Chinese firms tend to export with them the legal philosophy that data is a sovereign resource. To most developing economies, this is a potent substitute to the Western system, where data is usually stored in remote Silicon Valley-controlled servers. Through localization, the partners of the Silk Road have the technical and legal ability to establish a fencing in of their national data so that their digital trade across borders does not escape their direct jurisdiction.

4.2 Standardized Cross-Border Transfers

The Cyberspace Administration of China (CAC) has a stringent control mechanism on all the outbound data flows, in order to regulate the flow of digital assets within its borders. Such a system is established based on compulsory security evaluation, as well as the establishment of so-called Standard Contracts on cross-border data exchange, which serve as legally binding instruments between home exporters and abroad. Such contracts are particularly formulated in such a manner that any foreign party accessing Chinese data offers a data protection level that is at least equivalent to that of the protections provided by the PIPL. Through these requirements, the state will ensure that its privacy and security standards do not become diluted as its information goes beyond its physical bounds and therefore its domestic law jurisdiction is projected into the international marketplace of the digital world. Relating this standard of practice to the Digital Silk Road (DSR), China leverages such regulatory instruments to synchronize the information movement throughout its vast system of partner countries. These legal provisions make sure that data traveling in and out of the Chinese firms remains in a "trusted zone of compliance" as Chinese firms implement e-commerce systems and cloud services in Southeast Asia, Africa, and the Middle East. Such alignment ensures that the participating states can be incorporated into a high-tech trade route without violating their national security and the privacy of their citizens.

4.3 Regulatory Exportation

Marketing its Internet+, Artificial Intelligence, and Big Data protocols, China actively exports regulations that alter the digital terrain of its partner countries.[38] It is often called the Beijing Effect, where recipient countries adhere to the legal and technical systems that mimic those that exist internally in China in order to ensure an easy integration with the Chinese technology.[39] China offers the physical infrastructure of 5G networks and cloud computing, and thus, at the same time, offers the software of governance, the regulation, moral code, and security standards according to which these technologies are to be administered and enforced. Relating this regulatory change to the Digital Silk Road (DSR), the exportation of such standards is a contemporary version of the harmonization of trade in the ancient Silk Road. The need to switch to these turnkey Chinese standards is a practical decision by many developing countries of Southeast Asia, Africa, and the Middle East, as it would make their systems fully compatible with the globally leading provider of low-cost infrastructure.

4.4 Data Classification and Grading

The Data Classification and Grading system is a complex system of implementing granular security measures throughout the digital economy by establishing a systematic approach to information management.[40] In this model, data is classified into hierarchical groups, namely, general, important, and core data, according to how it affects national security and people's interests. Although the general data are covered by regular protection, there are strict security measures that include the core and important data, which are closely monitored by the state. This level of organization enables the specialized treatment of high-stakes data, including biometrics, health records, and financial data, where the most sensitive assets are enclosed in the most formidable legal and technical protection. Incorporating this systematic solution in the Digital Silk Road (DSR), China advocates this classification framework to its partner countries as an example of contemporary data sovereignty. With Chinese companies implementing the technologies and digital healthcare solutions of the Smart Cities in Southeast Asia, Africa, and the Middle East, the possibility to classify data becomes crucial to the stability within the company. To these nations, a tiered grading scheme is a clear guide on how to safeguard their most important national assets without

[38] Chunqiang Tang and Rozaini Rosli, "Internet Technology in Legal Economics and Policy: Strategic Enterprise Innovations in the US-China Trade Relationship," *China and WTO Review* 10, no. 1 (2024): 28–45.

[39] Robert D. Williams, *International Law with Chinese Characteristics: Beijing and the "Rules-Based" Global Order* (Brookings Institution, 2020).

[40] Sheela Kakanur Shivayogi, "Data Classification Methodologies and Implementation," *Journal of Computer Science and Technology Studies* 7, no. 5 (2025): 202–10.

suffocating the development of the greater digital economy. This alignment will result in a common language of security along the Silk Road, where states involved in it can coordinate the level of protection of sensitive information between borders.

5 Digital Trade Agreements and Compliance for Digital Operations

Digital trade agreements are a significant tool that can help to regulate economic operations within the digital economy.[41,42] Digital trade agreements provide certainty to the law by making identical rules regarding cross-border digital transactions, electronic commerce, electronic flow of data, and electronic services. Cross-border digital trade and the minimization of regulatory barriers are some of the main aims of digital trade agreements. Some of the issues that may be covered in these agreements would include electronic contracts, electronic signatures, consumer protection, and online payments. They encourage the expansion of cross-border e-commerce and digital services since they acknowledge the legalism of digital transactions. This is especially so with small and medium-sized enterprises, which depend on digital platforms to reach global markets. One of the key elements of digital trade agreements is the provision of data. A number of accords are encouraging free spatial movement of information across borders to facilitate digital commerce and inventiveness. Meanwhile, they tend to acknowledge the right of states to restrict data to justifiable purposes of the state, like privacy and national security. In the case of developing economies, there may be restricted technical competence and regulatory ability that may make it especially hard to comply.

The other important compliance concern is institutional coordination. Different government bodies usually deal with digital trade requirements that cut across several policy fields. They can result in inconsistency and loopholes in regulations when there is poor coordination. Good compliance, therefore, entails good division of roles, inter-agency consideration, and always observing the trend of regulations. In the business case, the digital trade agreements can facilitate business activities across borders because they provide legal predictability. Nevertheless, the compliance may remain complicated even in those cases when business organizations are situated in several jurisdictions and have trade obligations that overlap or diverge. Existing variations in definition, standards, and enforcement mechanisms may lead to a cost of compliance and jurisprudent ambiguity. Small businesses might have certain challenges that are caused by low resources. The mechanisms of enforcement are important to the compliance with digital trade agreements. Dispute settlement procedures give

---

[41] Michael A. Peters, "Digital Trade, Digital Economy and the Digital Economy Partnership Agreement (DEPA)," *Educational Philosophy and Theory* 55, no. 7 (2023): 747–55.

[42] Li Sheng, "The World Trade Organization and the Digital Economy Partnership Agreement: Analog Trade Rules in a Digital Era," in *Big Tech Firms and International Relations: The Role of the Nation-State in New Forms of Power* (Springer, 2022).

states a chance to solve the alleged violations and clear up the rules of digital trading interpretation. The success of these mechanisms is, however, dependent on political goodwill, institutional capabilities, and technical skills of the dispute resolution institutions. In other instances, there is poor enforcement of rules, which limits the practical consequences of agreed-upon rules. This kind of support is especially relevant to the countries that want to become a part of the digital economy of the world but preserve their domestic governance. Compliance is also enhanced by transparency and involvement of the stakeholders. Digital trade can be enhanced by clarity in communicating the digital trade rules, consultation with businesses, civil society, and technical experts to understand how to implement these rules. As digital trade is still developing, the agreements and compliance systems need to be adaptable and adapt to the technological and economic changes.

6 The Need for a Digital Dispute Resolution Mechanism

With the growing use of digital technologies to transform business and other interactions between people, there has been a growing number of disputes that occur in the context of digital activity, and the complexity of such disputes.[43] Conventional dispute resolution procedures, including a court or a conventional arbitration, are in most cases not able to manage the peculiarities of a digital dispute.[44] Digital services and platforms can be long-distance having the parties located in different jurisdictions. This poses complicated legal issues on the law to apply, jurisdiction, and implementation of rulings. The conventional dispute resolution systems tend to be territorial in nature, and they might not effectively solve multi-national disputes. Disruptions in jurisdictional decisions and implementation would decrease the efficiency of the legal solutions and raise expenses for all stakeholders. The digital economy in particular places great value on speed and efficiency since it is the difference between a loss of considerable amounts of money and time.[45] As an example, a malfunction of an online platform or the cloud service may interfere with business and affect thousands of users. These losses may be added to by delays in settling disputes by the traditional courts. A specialized digital dispute resolution mechanism may offer quicker, more adaptable processes that satisfy the immediacy of digital disputes without any prejudice or responsibility. Another reason that has prompted the need for digital dispute resolution mechanisms is cost. Small and medium-sized businesses

[43] Bhupinder Singh, "Unleashing Alternative Dispute Resolution (ADR) in Resolving Complex Legal-Technical Issues Arising in Cyberspace Lensing e-Commerce and Intellectual Property: Proliferation of e-Commerce Digital Economy," *Revista Brasileira de Alternative Dispute Resolution-Brazilian Journal of Alternative Dispute Resolution-RBADR* 5, no. 10 (2023): 81–105.

[44] Ekaterina P. Rusakova and Evgenia E. Frolova, "Digital Disputes in the New Legal Reality," *RUDN Journal of Law* 26, no. 3 (2022): 695–704.

[45] Erik Brynjolfsson and Avinash Collis, "How Should We Measure the Digital Economy," *Harvard Business Review* 97, no. 6 (2019): 140–48.

or individuals who use it cannot afford conventional litigation or international arbitration, as it is likely to be very expensive. Online interactions may be characterised by comparatively minor financial weight, and big volumes of respondents.

Digital mechanisms would be able to utilize technology to simplify processes, lower administrative expenses, and make justice more approachable to everyone. Users and businesses will tend to undertake digital commerce when they have the impression that conflict is easy to solve amicably and effectively. Lack of efficient resolution mechanisms may make the participants reluctant to use the digital services or may not engage in cross-border transactions at all. A digital dispute resolution system inspires confidence in digital markets by offering predictable and transparent solutions.

7 Online Dispute Resolution (ODR) Systems

Online Dispute Resolution (ODR) systems have become a successful technique of dealing with disputes in the online space.[46] ODR means this online utilization of digital platforms, tools, and processes to deal with conflicts, usually without the need to be physically present in a courtroom or other traditional arbitration space.[47] These systems integrate technology, legal and procedural frameworks, and solve conflict issues in an efficient, transparent, and fair manner. ODR systems are also specifically applicable in conflicts that are the result of e-commerce, online contracts, and online services. With the growth of online transactions, parties tend to disagree with each other over payment, quality of products, and problems of delivery or performance of services. Conventional dispute resolution techniques are most likely to be inefficient, slow, and inaccessible to users working in other countries. ODR is a viable alternative as it is a quicker and more convenient method of dispute resolution. Automation and integration of technology are major characteristics of ODR. Artificial intelligence, automated negotiation algorithms, and decision-support systems are some of the tools that are applied in many ODR platforms to resolve disputes. These tools may assist in finding areas of congruency, offer solutions, and facilitate communication between parties. Technology does not eliminate the need to have human judgment, but it can save on time and money, and resolve the dispute becomes easier and more affordable, particularly in cases of low-value disputes.

ODR systems are as well meant to deal with cross-border disputes. Online transactions tend to connect two or more parties in various nations, which leads to jurisdictional and legal issues. ODR platforms may offer a neutral ground to settle such conflicts and sets of standard procedures and rules to which both sides to the conflict would adhere. ODR streamlines cross-border enforcement, therefore, increasing the

---

[46] Karolina Mania, "Online Dispute Resolution: The Future of Justice," *International Comparative Jurisprudence* 1, no. 1 (2015): 76–86.

[47] Daniel Rainey et al., *Online Dispute Resolution-Theory and Practice: A Treatise on Technology and Dispute Resolution*, 2021.

predictability and reliability of international digital commerce. ODR systems often include negotiation, mediation, and arbitration. The instruments of negotiating enable the parties to communicate directly via the online platform, to propose, and to talk to each other safely. In mediation, there is a third party that is neutral and assists in the dialogue to allow the parties to come up with a voluntary agreement. In an online arbitration, there is a more formal approach in which evidence is examined by an arbitrator and a decision is made that is binding. All these processes may be modified to the digital setting, utilizing online communication, digital exchange of documents, and safe evidence management.

8 International ODR Systems

8.1 UNCITRAL

As a global rule-maker, China has become more and more involved in incorporating its national Online Dispute Resolution (ODR) capacities into the Digital Silk Road (DSR) framework.[48] The Chinese courts have produced a blueprint for technology in solving e-commerce and data disputes by establishing specialized "Internet Courts" in cities such as Hangzhou, Beijing, and Guangzhou to deal with all such cases using all digital platforms.[49] These courts are powered by AI-mediation and blockchain-based evidence retention, which provides a degree of technical complexity that is currently being imitated and exported to partner countries across the Silk Road. These ODR systems, placed at the center of the Silk Road Legal Infrastructure, are intended to accommodate the friction of giant transnational trade without the stalling of the conventional physical courts. To the countries in Southeast Asia, Africa, and Central Asia that are becoming part of the digital ecosystem of China, the use of similar standards of ODR would guarantee that their local businesses can easily resolve disputes with Chinese suppliers. This correlation minimizes the legal distance between the disparate markets, just as the ancient Silk Road applied to the use of standardized caravanserais to offer safe havens and predictable regulations to merchants as they travelled thousands of miles.

As another sign of strategic change towards Cyber Sovereignty, the promotion of ODR in China is also focused on the state administration of digital justice. Whereas in the West, the system is mostly based on the idea of private arbitration, the DSR model is often focused on the court-affiliated mediation that is still regulated by the national authorities. This is a strategy that Silk Road partners like internal stability and desire to have their digital trade routes under transparent and efficient yet state-vetted systems.

[48] Magdalena Łągiewska, "Chinese Approach to Online Dispute Resolution," *Budúcnosť Práva–Právo Budúcnosti II.*, 2022, 47.

[49] Meirong Guo, "Internet Court's Challenges and Future in China," *Computer Law & Security Review* 40 (2021): 105522.

8.2 APEC ODR Framework

As a coordination system of the contemporary digital economy, the APEC Collaborative Framework of Online Dispute Resolution (ODR) of Cross-Border B2B Disputes provides a simplified route through which companies resolve legal disputes.[50,51] The framework particularly focuses on the Micro, Small, and Medium-sized Enterprises (MSMEs), which may not have the financial means to overcome the prohibitive nature of international litigation. The APEC model substitutes national laws that are often fragmented with a single, three-step process: negotiation, then mediation, and finally binding arbitration by applying a common set of Procedural Rules. This digital-first strategy makes sure that the commercial friction does not suffocate the development of small businesses working in the globalized market.

By introducing this model of collaboration into the Digital Silk Road (DSR), China and its APEC partners have developed a safety net of digital dimensions regarding the huge amount of trade passing through the Asia–Pacific axis.[52] Through the encouragement of such mutual procedural rules, the DSR helps to create a so-called trusted trade zone in which MSMEs in Southeast Asia and elsewhere may interact with Chinese suppliers within a legal umbrella that is predictable. This coordination decreases the legal distance between incomparable markets and reflects how the ancient Silk Road depended upon standardized caravanserais to offer secure shelters and predictable regulations to merchants making a thousand-mile journey.

8.3 EU ODR Platform

The EU ODR Platform is a centralized multilingual portal, created by Regulation (EU) No. 524/2013, to facilitate the settlement of consumer-trader disputes.[53] This online gateway operated by connecting parties to a range of Alternative Dispute Resolution (ADR) entities, enabling them to have a streamlined out-of-court settlement procedure on a cross-border basis in Europe.[54] The portal would also help in

[50] Wenny Huang and Yoshihisa Hayakawa, "The APEC Collaborative Framework for Online Dispute Resolution (ODR) of Cross-Border B2B Disputes: An Overview and Analysis (Part 1)," *Dispute Resolution International*, no. 100 (2025).

[51] Nadja Alexander and Alvin Leu Jun Kang, "Das Neue ODR-Rahmenwerk Der APEC Als Wegbereiter Für Internationale Online-Streitbeilegung," *Zeitschrift Für Konfliktmanagement* 25, no. 6 (2022).

[52] Pramila Paudel, "Connecting Asia: The Rise of China's Digital Silk Road in ASEAN Countries," *Realism: Law Review* 3, no. 2 (2025): 70–94.

[53] Aiymgul Kachyke, *The Use of Information Technologies in the European Union's Special Regulations on Cross-Border Civil Procedure: Regulations on the Order for Payment, Small Claims, Service of Documents and Taking of Evidence*, 2026.

[54] Pablo Cortés, "Embedding Alternative Dispute Resolution in the Civil Justice System: A Taxonomy for ADR Referrals and a Digital Pathway to Increase the Uptake of ADR," *Legal Studies* 43, no. 2 (2023): 312–30.

improving consumer confidence in the online single market by offering one location for lodging complaints. Nonetheless, in keeping with the move towards more specialized and agile instruments, the EU ODR platform was formally dissolved on 20 July 2025, as the European Union started to move towards more modern, decentralized digital solutions to consumer protection.

Incorporating this European experience into the transformation of the Digital Silk Road (DSR), the emergence and following disintegration of the EU platform presents a crucial case study to the countries of the Silk Road partners. By developing their own digital bridges, as China and its DSR partners in Southeast Asia, Africa, and the Middle East are doing, they can see how justice systems are being transformed to feature more centralized points of contact to be more integrated and driven by AI. The dispute resolution method of the DSR is frequently reflective of the initial objectives of the EU to achieve harmony across borders without the drawbacks of a single platform but includes the incorporation of Smart Courts and blockchain-based arbitration directly into the e-commerce framework. This coherence will make sure that the digital trade routes of the contemporary Silk Roads are steady and flexible to the speed at which technology is evolving.

8.4 *India's ODR Landscape*

Being placed as a world leader in the digital justice arena, the ODR landscape in India is one of the few places with a strong Digital Public Infrastructure (DPI) integration.[55] India has developed a frictionless dispute resolution environment by using its foundation tools, such as Aadhaar to secure identity authentication and Unified Payments Interface (UPI) to make financial settlements. The leaders of the private innovation are the private platforms like Sama and Presolv360, whereas the public sector has offered specific portals, such as the SMART ODR portal offered by SEBI, to allow investors to file grievances and MSME SAMADHAAN to settle delayed payments to small businesses. The outcome of this combination of state-provided infrastructure and the dynamism of the private sector is that legal recourse can easily be provided and can be scaled in a rapidly digitalizing economy.

Even though the DSR is inclined to a top-down, state-centric regulatory export, the model of India demonstrates how open-source, interoperable, public goods can help to create a decentralized network of dispute resolution providers. As digital trade corridors are propagating across South Asia, Southeast Asia, and the Middle East, the philosophy of the India Stack provides a technical language through which cross-border e-commerce may be controlled without requiring the utilization of an exclusive proprietary platform.

[55] Desh Gaurav Sekhri and NITI OSD, "Designing the Future of Dispute Resolution: The ODR Policy Plan for India," *Message Posted To*, 2020.

8.5 *International Centre for Appropriate Dispute Resolution and Prevention (ICADRP)*

The International Centre of Appropriate Dispute Resolution and Prevention (ICADRP) has introduced the first specific Online Dispute Resolution (ODR) platform in Pakistan.[56,57] This is a fully online system built upon a strategic collaborative approach with the Pakistan-U.S. Alumni Network (PUAN), which is a stable, web-based platform that aims at settling commercial and civil conflicts at a distance. Through mediation and arbitration automation, the platform will aim at saving the long backlog that has always existed in the conventional courts, providing an alternative that is more streamlined and is both affordable and accessible to the general population and the business community in general. As part of the growing network of the Digital Silk Road (DSR), the ODR initiative in Pakistan can play a key role in cross-border stability by integrating this digital infrastructure into the network. As the China-Pakistan Economic Corridor (CPEC) is relatively young, the volume of digital trading and investment requires a legal safe valve functioning as swiftly as the existing business.[58] The ICADRP platform ensures that the "digital bridges" between Pakistan and the other Silk Road members are reinforced through the provision of a sound conflict management mechanism, by providing a secure digital space where the disputes can be solved. This uniformity allows the international investors as well as the local entrepreneurs to conduct trade without fear that their trade interests can be compromised by an inefficient, opaque, and state-of-the-art system of law.

9 Digital Silk Road ODR Systems

The conventional litigation in various jurisdictions tends to be lengthy, costly, and complex because of the disparities in legal, language, and regulatory standards. As a way of handling such challenges, China has established Online Dispute Resolution (ODR) systems through which digital technologies are used to deliver quick, transparent, and enforceable resolution to cross-border commercial transactions.

---

[56] Serkan Kaya and Muhammad Danyal Khan, "Online Dispute Resolution in Pakistan: Challenges and Opportunities," *Journal of Nusantara Studies (JONUS)* 7, no. 2 (2022): 103–19.

[57] Daniyal Shoukat, "Resolving Civil-Commercial Disputes through Mediation in Pakistan: Legal Framework, Sector-Specific Application, and Digital Trends," *Journal for Social Science Archives* 3, no. 2 (2025): 10–59075.

[58] Ma Zhong et al., "China Pakistan Economic Corridor Digital Transformation," *Frontiers in Psychology* 13 (2022): 887848.

9.1 *eBRAM International Online Dispute Resolution Centre*

The rapid expansion of cross-border trade along the Digital Silk Road, which is one of the primary elements of the Belt and Road Initiative, has generated a strong need for effective and efficient ways of settling commercial disputes. In response to this requirement, the International Online Dispute Resolution Centre (eBRAM) was created in Hong Kong to offer a digital mediation and arbitration resolution.[59] Developed to support both businesses that have been involved in Belt and Road projects and those involved in the Greater Bay Area (GBA) development strategy, eBRAM is a combination of innovative technology and legal expertise to simplify the process of dispute resolution, and this saves time and money that would have been involved in conventional litigation. The use of blockchain technology is one of the most innovative features of the platform. eBRAM makes all transactions transparent, tamper-proof, and verifiable by storing contracts, arbitration agreements, and mediation results on an immutable and secure ledger. The Digital Silk Road is one area where this technology is of great importance since transactions may involve more than one jurisdiction with different legal systems. Blockchain not only increases the trust between parties across countries, but it also reduces the risks of fraud or contractual issues in high-value cross-border projects, such as infrastructural, logistical, and digital commerce projects. In addition to dispute resolution, eBRAM is a full-fledged Deal Making platform, which allows businesses to handle the agreements, track the contractual commitments, and even negotiate online. This feature promotes the overall objectives of the Digital Silk Road because it will enable the smooth flow of commercial activities amongst BRI nations. E-commerce companies, smart city initiatives, or foreign investment may use eBRAM to achieve legal transparency, operational ambiguity, and regulatory adherence as they engage in the multifaceted cross-border trade network enabled by the Chinese digital economy.

9.2 *APEC ODR Procedural Rules Platform (B.Ming Casettle)*

The proliferation of micro, small, and medium enterprises (MSMEs) along the Digital Silk Road has placed an urgent demand for affordable and available dispute resolution systems. Numerous MSMEs encounter special obstacles to cross-border trade, such as a lack of legal resources, language barriers, and difficulties with the functioning of a complicated regulatory environment in various jurisdictions. To solve these problems, the Ministry of Justice of China, together with Beiming Software, designed the APEC Online Dispute Resolution (ODR) Procedural Rules Platform, called B.Ming

[59] Yang Lin, "E-Commerce and Online Dispute Resolution in Hong Kong: The Case of eBRAM," *Amicus Curiae* 4 (2022): 542.

Casettle.[60,61] The site is specifically established to support MSMEs that carry out cross-border transactions to facilitate hassle-free processes of mediation, arbitration, and settlement of business disputes on an online platform. B.Ming Casettle is adapted to the operational realities of the Digital Silk Road, where MSMEs are increasingly engaged in e-commerce, logistics, and supply chain networks that span across Asia, Europe, and other areas linked by the Belt and Road Initiative. The site enables companies to start, administer, and settle a dispute all online, keeping business time, cost, and red tape to a minimum, traditionally associated with legal disputes. This feature is especially significant to MSMEs, which frequently do not have sufficient financial and human resources to undertake protracted litigation across borders. The design of the platform is made to be user-friendly, efficient, and transparent, so that more small businesses will be able to engage in global business and reduce the risks of legal complications.

9.3 China International Commercial Courts (CICC) ODR Integration

As a high-tech court of the contemporary era, the China International Commercial Courts (CICC) offers a simple, one-stop dispute resolution system, which is directly designed to support international trade.[62,63,64] The CICC was established by the Supreme People Court, and it combines negotiation, mediation, and arbitration into one digital platform, which practically avoids the divisive aspect of traditional litigation. It is a professional system, which is supposed to handle high-stakes business conflicts in an efficiency-based way, with the use of a pool of international experts, to ensure that verdicts are technically reliable as well as internationally esteemed. The CICC is an important legal clearinghouse for the complex infrastructure and investment undertakings that define the Belt and Road Initiative (BRI) as a component of the Digital Silk Road (DSR). As there is increased growth of digital trade corridors in Southeast Asia, Africa, and Central Asia, CICC has provided the legal

---

[60] Cao Yanyan and Nabeel Mahdi Althabhawi, "China's Online Dispute Resolution Mechanism for Cross-Border E-Commerce: Challenges and Solutions," *Pakistan Journal of Life & Social Sciences* 22, no. 2 (2024).

[61] Cao Yanyan and Nabeel Mahdi Althabhawi, "China's Online Dispute Resolution Mechanism for Cross-Border E-Commerce: Challenges and Solutions," *Pakistan Journal of Life & Social Sciences* 22, no. 2 (2024).

[62] Wenhua Shan and Yunya Feng, "The China International Commercial Court: Towards an Integrated Dispute Resolution System," *Asia Pacific Law Review* 29, no. 1 (2021): 107–28.

[63] Xiangzhuang Sun, "A Chinese Approach to International Commercial Dispute Resolution: The China International Commercial Court," *The Chinese Journal of Comparative Law* 8, no. 1 (2020): 45–54.

[64] Kashif Imran Zadi et al., "China International Commercial Court (CICC) in the Context of Commercial Disputes under Belt and Road Initiative: Organizational Structure, Rules and Jurisdiction," *Pakistan Languages and Humanities Review* 5, no. 2 (2021): 601–12.

certainty that is so desired by state-owned enterprises and individual investors. The court removes the geographic stranglehold that had stalled transcontinental trade by availing a digital-first environment, where evidence can be uploaded, or proceedings can be conducted remotely. This coordination will ensure that the digital bridges of the Silk Road are not only the tool of circulating capital, but also that a sound and stable system of the judicial architecture controls it.

9.4 *Digital Online Dispute Resolution (DODR) Project*

The emergence of the digital trade wave along the Digital Silk Road has further highlighted the necessity of instating responsive and technology-driven processes to resolve transnational business disputes.[65] To address these issues, a joint venture between UNCTAD and China Silk Road Group Limited led to the establishment of the Digital Online Dispute Resolution (DODR) Project.[66] The project will enhance international trade and e-commerce through the integration of digital trading infrastructure and online dispute resolution systems to offer a systematic and dependable framework through which businesses involved in Belt and Road activities will operate. The platform will serve the needs of the Digital Silk Roads trade, where transactions are often multi-jurisdictional, multi-regulatory, and multi-currency. DODR enables parties to have disputes resolved effectively by combining online mediation, arbitration, and automated procedural advice, eliminating time wastage that comes with traditional litigation. This method is especially useful with enterprises of any size, such as SMEs that can hardly afford high legal rates and do not have sufficient access to international arbitration funds. Through this, DODR will ease barriers to smaller players in the Digital Silk Road trade to be able to participate with confidence in cross-border trade.

9.5 *Hangzhou Internet Court System*

One example of the change in the judicial system in China so that it can be compliant with the requirements of the digital economy is the creation of the Hangzhou Internet Court, one of the first smart courts in the country.[67,68] Having been created to address the conflicts that occur due to e-commerce, intellectual property, and other online

[65] Zeng Wei, "China's Innovative Dispute Resolution under the "Belt and Road" Initiative," *Public Health Policy and Laws Journal* 10, no. 1 (2024): 153–68.

[66] Jiaqi Song, *Reforming Mechanisms for Investment Dispute Settlement under the 21st Century Maritime Silk Road Initiative: With Special Reference to Disputed Maritime Areas*, 2025.

[67] Changqing Shi et al., "The Smart Court—A New Pathway to Justice in China?," 12 (2021): 1.

[68] Alex Chung and Ying Yu, "Delivering Justice in the Digital Economy," *Digitalization and Artificial Intelligence in Courts: Opportunities and Challenges*, 2025, 157.

dealings, the court uses innovative technologies like artificial intelligence, big data analytics, and digital evidence systems to deliver fast, precise, and transparent judgments. Its operational model has been broadly viewed as a model of what has been termed as ODR + solutions, a combination of traditional legal procedures with digital platforms to form a hybrid model to fit the new digital economy. Hangzhou Internet Court is directly related to the Digital Silk Road within the Belt and Road Initiative. Due to the growth of the digital trade, e-commerce, and online trans-border services offered by BRI countries, intellectual property, digital contracts, and online dispute issues are becoming increasingly frequent. The court shows how a technologically advanced legal system can effectively regulate these disputes, providing lessons and examples that Digital Silk Road partners interested in creating such systems should follow. The processing of cases digitally reduces the amount of time that is wasted and facilitates access to justice, particularly to those businesses that are engaged in digital trade (both cross-border and within a single country), such as SMEs, which would otherwise face limitations in legal resources.

9.6 *Smart Settle*

With the increasing cross-border digital trade along the Digital Silk Road, businesses are encountering more and more complex disputes that demand flexible and multi-layered systems for resolving them. To overcome these difficulties, a computer-assisted negotiation system has been created that offers a framework for a structured and adaptable way of conflict resolution. This system is an alternative to the conventional dispute resolution procedures, and as such, it uses computational algorithms and decision support systems to take the parties through a series of negotiation steps, providing mediation, conciliation, and arbitration services on a digital platform. This multi-level strategy will provide the guarantee that the conflicts may be solved effectively at the earliest stage, by which the probability of their further development into expensive or time-consuming legal actions can be minimized. The system is especially applicable to the Belt and Road Initiative, where businesses working along Digital Silk Roads usually have to address several stakeholders in various nations, regulatory frameworks, and business customs. The platform helps businesses to find the best solutions, discuss the options of compromise, and transparently see the negotiation process by automating procedural guidance and providing decision-support analytics.

10 Blockchain and Smart Contracts in Dispute Resolution

The digital economy is increasingly defining dispute resolution in blockchain technology and smart contracts.[69] Blockchain is a decentralized digital register that keeps records of transactions in many computers, such that records are secure, transparent, and unchangeable.[70] Smart contracts are programs that are automatically executed and kept on the blockchain and enforce the terms of an agreement once predetermined conditions are satisfied. An aggregate of these technologies opens new avenues of preventing and solving conflicts, especially in online and inter-country dealings. The improved transparency and security that come with the use of blockchain are one of the major benefits of blockchain as a dispute resolution method. All the operations made on a blockchain are irreversible, time-stamped, and publicly verifiable. This leaves a clear and trustworthy record of what has been done, and it is simpler to find out violations of a contract, an unauthorized action, or even a misdemeanor in transactions. Blockchain provides a reliable and immutable solution in cases where evidence integrity is required. Smart contracts minimize the chances of controversies by automating the performance requirements. Conventional agreements may have to be enforced manually and hence may incur delays, misinterpretations, or a lack of adherence.

Smart contracts are automatically executed once the terms are fulfilled, and thus the payments, transfers, or any other activities take place as the two parties agreed.[71] As an illustration, in supply chain management, a smart contract may automatically send money after a delivery confirmation is registered on the blockchain, decreasing the possibility of non-payment or non-performance. Blockchain-based dispute resolution boasts of cross-border transactions. The digital trade may also include parties in various jurisdictions, posing a challenge to the laws and enforcement issues, and jurisdiction. Smart contracts and blockchain records are not limited by national borders, which offers a neutral and universal system of implementing transactions and collecting evidence. This makes it less complex and expensive to settle international disputes. The blockchain technology has integrated dispute resolution mechanisms as well. Some platforms integrate built-in conflict resolutions in blockchain. As an example, smart contracts may also contain provisions that initiate arbitration or mediation in case of a dispute over certain conditions. This may then be a dispute resolution that is carried out online, and results are documented on the blockchain to be transparent and enforceable. Such integration enables the cases to be solved faster and with less resort to the conventional courts. Enforcement challenges are another issue that is important. After a smart contract is executed, the

[69] Sergei A. Sinitsyn et al., "Smart Contracts in the Digital Economy: Contractual Regulation and Dispute Resolution," in *Smart Technologies for the Digitisation of Industry: Entrepreneurial Environment* (Springer, 2021).

[70] Shi Dong et al., "Blockchain Technology and Application: An Overview," *PeerJ Computer Science* 9 (2023): e1705.

[71] Silas Mutie Nzuva, "Smart Contracts Implementation, Applications, Benefits, and Limitations," *Journal of Information Engineering and Applications*, 2019.

outcomes are automatically imposed without outside influences. This will reduce the chances of non-compliance and lower the pressure on the legal system. In situations where human control is mandatory, blockchain will ensure that all data is precise and accessible to everyone, and its enforcement is easier and more trustworthy.

11 Conclusion

The high pace of the digital economy has transformed the interaction of governments, businesses, and individuals in terms of unprecedented opportunities and challenging issues. It has become apparent in this chapter that legal, regulatory, and technological frameworks that regulate digital operations need to be altered to reflect issues of cross-border data flows, data sovereignty, data security, intellectual property, and compliance with digital trade. These spheres are intertwined to prove that the holistic approach to the management of the risks and the maximization of the benefits of digitalization is necessary. The outflows of data across the borders represent the contradiction between the encouragement of innovation and protection of national interests. The development of plausible structures and facilitating global collaboration are not the only steps towards the path of balancing openness and regulation. The international agreements must be adhered to help in cross international transactions and also to provide a predictable business environment and consumer environment. The increasing cases of digital conflicts underscore the importance of special resolution plans. Online Dispute Resolution systems, blockchain and smart contracts provide the tools of efficient, secure and transparent conflict resolution, particularly in the case of cross-border or technical disputes.

Chapter 7
Digital Financial Inclusion and Fintech Innovations in DSR and Regulatory Issues

Abstract Online monetary access and fintech innovations have become the center of focus in terms of economic growth in Belt and Road Initiative economies. Digital financial inclusion is the delivery of affordable, convenient, and safe financial services via digital technologies to less privileged individuals and companies that are excluded by the formal financial system. Digital financial inclusion enhances economic inclusion by improving access to finance, facilitating the operation of small businesses, empowering marginalized populations, and minimizing poverty. The relevance of Fintech innovations in facilitating digital financial inclusion is vital. Mobile money, digital payment systems, online lending, peer-to-peer lending, blockchain-based systems, and artificial intelligence applications have changed the nature of the delivery of financial services. This chapter emphasizes that digital financial inclusion through fintech solutions and effective regulatory frameworks can lead to inclusive economic growth, enhance financial accessibility, and social and economic resilience in economic activities in BRI economies.

Keywords Digital financial inclusion · Fintech innovations · Digital transactional platforms · Digital literacy and capability

1 Introduction

Digital financial inclusion has gained significance in the current world economy.[1] Digital financial inclusion aims to achieve affordability, access, and safety of financial services for all, including the low-income groups and small businesses.[2] In most of the developing and emerging economies, many individuals remain unincorporated into the formal financial system. They lack bank accounts, credit facilities, and secure

[1] Arnesh Telukdarie and Aviksha Mungar, "The Impact of Digital Financial Technology on Accelerating Financial Inclusion in Developing Economies," *Procedia Computer Science* 217 (2023): 670–78.

[2] Lee-Ying Tay et al., "Digital Financial Inclusion: A Gateway to Sustainable Development," *Heliyon* 8, no. 6 (2022).

J. Afzal and Y. Chen, *Legal Framework of Digital Economy and Digital Trade Under the Belt and Road Initiative*, https://doi.org/10.1007/978-981-92-4444-7_7

payment systems. Such a case is typical of certain Belt and Road Initiative economies, in which financial infrastructure is usually scarce and not spread evenly. Some of the most impacted populations are rural populations, women, informal workers, and small and medium-sized enterprises (SMEs).[3] Consequently, cash-based transactions and informal financial operations become the main source of financial risks and restrict economic development for many. The Belt and Road Initiative has countries in Asia, Africa, Europe, and the Middle East. These nations vary with regard to economic development, institutional capacity, and technology preparedness.

Nevertheless, the most common problems regarding financial inclusion in many BRI economies are poverty, income inequality, insufficient bank reach, and poor financial literacy.[4] Meanwhile, these nations are seeing a fast increase in online connectivity. The rising use of mobile phones and internet services has offered new avenues to provide financial services in a digital form, even in new locations where banking services are not available.[5] Conventional banking services have not been in a position to meet the requirements of the underserved groups in BRI economies.[6] The physical bank branches tend to be concentrated in urban localities, which are not easy to access for those who are in remote areas.[7] The costs of transacting are high, documentation needs are strict, and people do not trust financial institutions, which further demoralizes people to use formal banking services. In the case of small businesses, access to credit is a significant impediment to growth and innovation. These shortcomings have made it necessary to seek alternative financial solutions that are more accommodating and flexible. Fintech innovations have been developed as a potential way out of these problems. Fintech is the application of digital technologies to enhance and automate financial services.[8,9] The examples are mobile money platforms, digital wallets, online lending platforms, blockchain-based transactions, and artificial intelligence-powered financial tools.

---

[3] Zhao Xu et al., "Availability and Access to Livelihood Capital Assets for Development of Sustainable Livelihood Strategies of Fishermen: A Case Study of Manchar Lake Pakistan," *Heliyon* 9, no. 12 (2023).

[4] Xiaoling Song et al., "Creating Financial Inclusion in 'Belt and Road' Countries in Europe, Asia and Africa: Regulation, Technology and Financial Literacy," *Journal of Financial Regulation and Compliance* 32, no. 4 (2024): 445–61.

[5] Faisal Akbar et al., "The Impact of Financial Scams on Consumer Trust in the Banking Sector: A Qualitative Analysis," *International Journal of Discovery in Social Sciences* 1, no. 1 (2025).

[6] Wasi Ul Hassan Shah et al., "Evaluating the Role of Banking Efficiency, Institutions and Financial Development for Sustainable Development: Implications for Belt and Road Initiative (BRI)," *Plos One* 18, no. 10 (2023): e0290780.

[7] Rini Rachmawati et al., "The Advantages and Analysis of the Location of Branchless Banking in Urban and Rural Areas in Yogyakarta Special Region, Indonesia," *Journal of Urban and Regional Analysis* 11, no. 1 (2019): 53–68.

[8] Joseph Bamidele Awotunde et al., "Application of Big Data with Fintech in Financial Services," in *Fintech with Artificial Intelligence, Big Data, and Blockchain* (Springer, 2021).

[9] Kelvin Leong and Anna Sung, "FinTech (Financial Technology): What Is It and How to Use Technologies to Create Business Value in Fintech Way?," *International Journal of Innovation, Management and Technology* 9, no. 2 (2018): 74–78.

The innovations enable quicker, more efficient, and cheaper delivery of financial services. Fintech has been important in increasing the financial access of people who were not formally part of the financial system in many BRI countries.[10] There are various advantages of digital financial inclusion on an individual level, a business level, and a national level. To the individuals, it offers a secure method of saving money, paying money, and credit access. The digital financial services also minimize the risks of carrying cash and enhance financial security. In the case of SMEs, digital finance enhances the availability of working capital, facilitates online operations, and promotes efficiency in operations.[11] Digital financial inclusion, on a national level, facilitates economic inclusion, aids in formalizing an economy, and leads to sustainable development.[12]

This chapter explores that digital financial inclusion can be a strong instrument of inclusive growth in BRI economies. Digital finance has the potential to decrease inequality, enhance economic engagement, and change the lives of millions of individuals when properly supported by efficient fintech solutions and regulatory frameworks. Digital financial inclusion allows BRI countries to adopt long-term and sustainable development by targeting easy access, trust, and innovation.

2 Understanding Digital Financial Inclusion

2.1 Digital Transactional Platforms

Digital financial inclusion relies on the operational support of digital transactional platforms that facilitate individuals and companies to conduct financial transactions via mobile wallets, digital payment applications, and online banking platforms.[13] These platforms, in BRI, serve as a direct point of access to formal financial services, especially in places where traditional banking infrastructure is restricted or unavailable. Most Belt and Road Initiative (BRI) economies rely heavily on cash-based and informal financial systems because of structural gaps in access to banking. Digital transactional solutions mitigate this constraint by providing affordable and readily available financial services using mobile phones and the internet. They can enable a wide variety of transactions, such as peer-to-peer transfers, merchant payments, settling utility bills, and government-to-person disbursements, enabling users to

---

[10] Wang Xiaobin et al., "Natural Resources, Trade and Fintech in the Era of Digitalization: A Study of Economies Involved in Belt and Road Initiative," *Resources Policy* 93 (2024): 105082.

[11] Vivian Chilee Osuji et al., "Seamless Integration of Digital Supply-Chain Platforms with Commercial Banking to Enhance Working Capital Efficiency for SMEs," *Journal Not Specified*, 2023.

[12] Lee-Ying Tay et al., "Digital Financial Inclusion: A Gateway to Sustainable Development," *Heliyon* 8, no. 6 (2022).

[13] Douglas W. Arner et al., "Fintech for Financial Inclusion: A Framework for Digital Financial Transformation," *UNSW Law Research Paper*, nos. 18–87 (2018).

transact in formal financial systems without necessarily having a physical interaction with their banks. Other digital ecosystems that can be incorporated with financial services through digital transactional platforms are e-commerce and online lending systems.[14] Such integration enhances the efficiency in transactions, lessening the barriers to operations, and facilitates financial connectivity in various regions within the BRI framework, such as inter-border financial interactions, which are vital in trade and economic collaboration.

2.2 Retail Agents

The retail agents are key players in promoting digital financial inclusion because they bridge the digital financial system and cash-based economies.[15] These agents are the physical points of access through which users can exchange cash into digital value (cash-in) and digital funds into cash (cash-out), especially where formal banking infrastructure is either unavailable or scarce.[16] The percentage of cash transactions among the population remains considerably high in most BRI economies because most people lack confidence in digital platforms and access to banking facilities. Through local shops, retail agents operate through a kiosk or small business and increase the coverage of financial services to the rural and underserved regions by providing face-to-face interaction and coverage. Retail agents offer a host of services other than the basic cash-in and cash-out services, including opening an account, paying bills, refilling a mobile phone, and even microfinance services. This model can guarantee continuity in the delivery of financial services in BRI economies, which might not have sufficiently advanced digital infrastructure, and it is conducive to the shift to completely digital systems.

2.3 Mobile Technology and Digital Infrastructure

Mobile technology and digital infrastructure are some of the basic enablers of digital financial inclusion, as they offer the technological platform upon which financial services are accessed and delivered.[17] With Digital Financial Inclusion and Fintech

---

[14] Daniel Fasnacht, "Banking 4.0: Digital Ecosystems and Super-Apps," in *Theories of Change: Change Leadership Tools, Models and Applications for Investing in Sustainable Development* (Springer, 2021).

[15] Eni Minarni, "Impact of Digital Payment Systems on Financial Inclusion and Small Business Growth in Developing Economies," *International Journal of Innovation and Thinking* 2, no. 1 (2025): 1–12.

[16] Ceyla Pazarbasioglu et al., "Digital Financial Services," *World Bank* 54, no. 1 (2020): 1–54.

[17] Vrajlal Sapovadia, "Financial Inclusion, Digital Currency, and Mobile Technology," in *Handbook of Blockchain, Digital Finance, and Inclusion, Volume 2* (Elsevier, 2018).

Innovations in BRI Economies, the ubiquity of mobile phones, especially smartphones, has changed how financial services can be accessed by underserved populations, lessening the reliance on physical banking systems.[18] The development of mobile networks and internet accessibility in most BRI economies has opened new possibilities to provide financial services in remote and unreachable areas. The mobile money services enable users to carry out transactions, including payments, transfers, savings, and even borrowing, using their mobile phones. This distance access removes geographical limits and greatly reduces the cost and time of conventional banking services. Another transformative role of mobile technology is women's financial inclusion in BRI economies. Women are usually restricted in accessing traditional financial institutions due to social, cultural, and mobility limits.[19] Mobile financial services offer a personal and autonomous way of dealing with money, which enables women to save, remit money, and participate in business.[20] Such access promotes financial independence and leads to even greater socio-economic empowerment.[21]

2.4 Digital Literacy and Capability

As the cornerstone to sustainable economic development, digital literacy and capability are the key factor to the difference between merely possessing financial means and actually using them to enhance livelihoods.[22] The digital literacy promotion, which is a mechanical prerequisite to the success of the Digital Silk Road (DSR), is strategically placed within the framework of the Digital Financial Inclusion and Fintech Innovations in BRI Economies.[23] In the BRI economies and especially in emerging markets in Central Asia and Africa, digital literacy programs are being made available so that the shift of a cash-based society to a digital-first ecosystem does not leave vulnerable populations behind. With a stable and informed user base, such alignment makes a reliable digital corridor possible when the pace of Fintech

[18] Olumide Olumayowa Fowowe et al., *The Role of FinTech in Expanding Access to Finance for Underserved Communities: A Policy-Focused Study Linking Digital Financial Services to Economic Inclusion*, 2025.

[19] Jamil Afzal and Muhammad Adeel Afzal, "Leveraging ICT for Social Sustainability in Pakistan through the Mediating Role of Gender Empowerment and Institutional Support," *Quality & Quantity*, 2026, 1–25.

[20] Kyungha Kim, "Assessing the Impact of Mobile Money on Improving the Financial Inclusion of Nairobi Women," *Journal of Gender Studies* 31, no. 3 (2022): 306–22.

[21] Id Bouhou Mohamed and Ikram Ben Ali Kaddour, "Protection for Working Women: Comparative Study of Moroccan and Chinese Regulations," *International Journal of Discovery in Social Sciences* 2, no. 1 (2026).

[22] Gorrettie Nakyeyune Kyeyune and Joseph Mpeera Ntayi, "Empowering Rural Communities: The Role of Financial Literacy and Management in Sustainable Development," *Frontiers in Human Dynamics* 6 (2025): 1424126.

[23] Huma Iftikhar et al., "A Multi-Dimensional FinTech Composite Integrating Infrastructure, Access, Usage, Knowledge Transfer, and Governance-by-Technology: The Role of Digital Silk Road Policy in BRI Economies," *Technology in Society*, 2025, 103162.

innovation is aligned.[24] Just as the ancient merchants should have had an extensive knowledge of the regulations of the road to avoid the carnivorous pitfalls of the desert, the literacy of the members of the present-day DSR is the source of its stability. Introduction of these educational programs and high-speed fiber-optic cables will also ensure that the digital bridges of the new Silk Road are not only a data highway but also have an integrated and smart economic structure. This commitment of the government towards capacity building makes the Silk Road a formidable ecosystem wherein connectivity is predetermined by a lexicon of security, effectiveness, and established trust.

2.5 Customer-Centric Products

Digital financial inclusion involves customer-centric products and aims at designing and providing financial services that consider the needs, preferences, and abilities of the users.[25] This strategy is critical in making sure that the digital financial services are not merely accessible but also viable, applicable, and feasible to various populations, especially those who are just getting into the formal financial sector. The difference between the various user categories in most BRI economies is vast in terms of income level, literacy, digital skills, and availability of technology. The standardized financial products can hardly accommodate these differences, which results in low adoption and low usage.[26] The solution to this gap is customer-centric design, which creates simplified interfaces, local language accessibility, minimal transaction requirements, and customized financial products like micro-savings, small-scale credit, and customized insurance products. These characteristics increase the accessibility of digital financial services by low-income users, rural populations, and first-time adopters, as well as simplify their use.

2.6 Regulatory Frameworks and Risk Management

Regulatory frameworks and risk management systems play a vital role in making sure that the digital financial inclusion process is safe and sustainable, especially in the framework of Digital Financial Inclusion and Fintech Innovations in BRI

---

[24] Nalabothu Raviteja, "Financial Technology (Fintech) and Banking Industry Transformation: A Symbiotic Evolution into the Digital Era," *Transactions* 1, no. 2 (2024): 23–29.

[25] Priscilla Samuel Nwachukwu et al., *Marketing Financial Products in Emerging Economies: Global Strategies, Effectiveness, and a Conceptual Customer-Centric Banking Model*, 2023.

[26] Stefan Koch and Duygu Inanc, "Mass Customization for Financial Services: An Empirical Study of Adoption and Usage Behavior," *Journal of Services Marketing* 29, no. 3 (2015): 235–43.

Economies.[27,28] These frames establish a rigid system of rules regarding the financial service providers and fintech firms that balances the need to be innovative with the security of users, financial system stability, and removal of operational risk. The adoption of digital financial services in economies in the BRI has been high, and this poses potential vulnerability to fraud, cyberattacks, money laundering, and operational failure. The regulatory systems define the licensing terms and conditions, capital adequacy, and reporting requirements in such a way that the service providers are responsible and transparent in nature. They also possess the tools for tracking the digital payment systems, safeguarding customer data, and establishing the dispute resolution process. An addition to regulation is risk management policies since they assist in identifying, monitoring, and mitigating the potential risks in operations and financial. This involves the implementation of cybersecurity regulations, fraud detection machinery, and real-time monitoring of transactions. Disciplined risk management makes the users of the digital platforms more confident, which is crucial to be embraced by the populations that are traditionally out of the informal financial services.

2.7 *Interoperability*

An important feature of digital financial inclusion is interoperability, enabling various digital platforms, payment systems, and financial service providers to interoperate with each other.[29] In the Digital Financial Inclusion and Fintech Innovations in BRI Economies context, interoperability can permit users to transact between many networks, devices, and institutions without limits and make up a cohesive and effective digital financial universe. Mobile money operators, fintech startups, and payment platforms join banks to provide financial services in most BRI economies.[30] In the absence of interoperability, users experience a challenge of transfer of funds across systems, restricted access to services, and increased transaction costs. Interoperable platforms allow customers to transfer money between networks or receive money between networks, make payments to merchants regardless of the service provider, and receive banking services in many ways, making it more convenient and expanding financial inclusion. The efficiency and scalability of fintech ecosystems are also promoted through interoperability. It enables the real-time settlement of transactions,

---

[27] Ross P. Buckley et al., "Sustainability, FinTech and Financial Inclusion," *A Research Agenda for Financial Inclusion and Microfinance*, 2019.

[28] Huma Iftikhar et al., "A Multi-Dimensional FinTech Composite Integrating Infrastructure, Access, Usage, Knowledge Transfer, and Governance-by-Technology: The Role of Digital Silk Road Policy in BRI Economies," *Technology in Society*, 2025, 103162.

[29] Marc Bourreau and Tommaso Valletti, "Enabling Digital Financial Inclusion through Improvements in Competition and Interoperability: What Works and What Doesn't," *CGD Policy Paper* 65 (2015): 1–30.

[30] Yuan Zhu, *Bridging the Gap: Strategies and Roles of Chinese Fintech Entrepreneurs and Startups in Sub-Sahara African Markets*, 2025.

eliminates duplication of infrastructures, and decreases provider operational costs. To achieve regional economic integration, interoperable systems are used to support faster, secure, and cost-effective remittances and trade transactions to cross-border payments in BRI economies.

3 Importance of Digital Financial Inclusion

The concept of digital financial inclusion the utmost importance to the economies of the BRI since most of these nations struggle with severe financial and economic hardships. Big segments of the people in BRI economies are not within the formal matter of the money system because of poverty, geographic alienation, and poor financial infrastructures. Digital financial inclusion presents an effective solution to reaching out to these groups with the necessary financial services and promoting inclusive economic growth. Reduction of poverty through digital financial inclusion is one of the reasons why it is important in BRI economies. Once individuals are able to access digital financial services, they are able to save their money in a safe manner, make and get payments in an effective manner, and even take small loans when there is an emergency. Through the digital platforms, governments and development agencies are finding it easy to transfer social welfare payments to individuals by direct means, thus reducing leakage and delays. It is the direct entry to the financial services that allows the low-income households to manage the financial risks, along with the ability to improve their living conditions. Another major beneficiary of digital financial inclusion is the small and medium-sized enterprises (SMEs), which also form a great share of the number of jobs in the BRI economies.[31]

In BRI economies, much economic action is performed in the informal sector. The informal workers are used to cash transactions and have no access to formal financial security. Digital financial inclusion assists in drawing informal economic practices into the formal system by promoting digital payments and record-keeping. This formalization enhances transparency and enables the workers to access financial services, including insurance services and pension services, which increases economic security. Another notable area of BRI economies is women's financial inclusion. Women in most of the countries encounter cultural, legal, and social challenges that tend to restrict their access to financial services. Online financial services also minimize these obstacles by ensuring women can access financial services using mobile phones on their own. It gives women more power to manage their finances, encourages entrepreneurship, and promotes gender equality.[32] Digital financial inclusion is also required in rural development in BRI economies. Due to high operation costs and population density, the physical access to bank branches in rural settings

---

[31] Xiaoyan Zhang et al., "Digitalization, Financial Inclusion, and Small and Medium-Sized Enterprise Financing: Evidence from China," *Economic Modelling* 126 (2023): 106410.

[32] Jamil Afzal et al., "Analyzing the Role of Foreign Direct Investment, Human Welfare, and Gender Equality for Economic Sustainability in the Digital Era," *Quality & Quantity*, 2026, 1–24.

is restricted. Digital financial services solve this problem through mobile networks and digital means to access remote communities. Farmers and rural households do not have to travel long distances to receive payments, credit, and insurance, which saves money and time. Digital financial inclusion helps in economic resilience in BRI economies. Digital financial services enable people and businesses to keep on with their transactions even when physical access is limited, such as during economic shocks, natural catastrophes, or health emergency situations. Electronic payment systems serve to keep the economy going and as a quicker method of recovery assistance. This strength is especially valuable in the areas that are vulnerable to both economic and environmental damage.

4 The Role of Fintech Innovations in DSR

4.1 Financial Inclusion and Digital Access

Fintech innovations have played an essential role in enhancing financial inclusion by offering digital-first financial services to groups of the population who were previously not accessible to formal banking systems.[33] Digital Financial Inclusion and Fintech Innovations in BRI Economies represents a set of innovations that allow unbanked and underbanked people, in particular, in the developing parts of Africa and Asia, to have secure, affordable, and convenient access to financial services without the need to go to traditional bank branches.

Fintech applications, most specifically mobile-first applications, including digital wallets, mobile banking apps, and agency-based applications, fill this void by providing convenient financial services directly on smartphones or feature phones. Fintech-led digital access also enhances access to marginalized populations, including women, informal employees, and small business owners, who are affected by socio-economic and structural obstacles to traditional banking.[34] This enables people and micro-entrepreneurs who were formerly locked out and would not have otherwise accessed loans, insurance, and investment instruments to participate in the economy and entrepreneurship. The popularization of this type of mobile-based financial services in BRI economies is transforming the financial system by reducing the reliance on traditional banking infrastructure and promoting inclusive and technology-based economic growth.

---

[33] Amrik Singh and Lalit Mohan Sharma, "Fintech and Financial Inclusion: Transforming Underserved Access to Financial Services," *International Journal of Tourism and Hotel Management* 5, no. 2 (2023): 07–11.

[34] Poonam Prakash Dhawale, "Empowering Underserved Communities Through Fintech-Driven Inclusion," *International Research on Sustainability and Innovation: A Multidisciplinary Approach to Global Development*, 2025, 139.

4.2 Cross-Border Trade Facilitation

Digital innovations as an engine of modern global trade are basically deconstructing the historic barriers to global trade.[35] With the application of blockchain and improved payment architecture, the financial sector has now been in a position to make cross-border transactions that are far faster, more secure, and less costly than the old means of banking. These distributed registers give an unalterable account of commerce, which eradicates the necessity of numerous intermediaries and radically decreases the administrative strain that used to afflict large-scale shipping and logistics. These are technical advancements, which are planned in the development of the Digital Silk Road (DSR) and the mechanization of Digital Financial Inclusion and Fintech Innovations in BRI Economies. The digital bridges that China and its partner countries in Central Asia, Africa, and Southeast Asia are building with huge fiber-optic and satellite networks are enhanced by these modernized systems of payment. The DSR assists in the establishment of a free trade zone where trade transactions are settled by stablecoins or Central Bank Digital Currencies (CBDCs).[36] Such alignment guarantees that the contemporary Silk Road is not just a route for physical cargo, but a very well-coordinated digital ecosystem. The introduction of transparent digital standards enhances the stability of the modern DSR since antique merchants required the guarantee of a safe route and a shared sense of worth to move merchandise across thousands of miles. The digital bridges of the new Silk Road will be not only a channel of information, as these cryptographic and financial tools and physical infrastructure will provide a cohesive and enforceable economic system.

4.3 Supply Chain and SME Finance

By offering Micro, Small, and Medium Enterprises (MSMEs) tailored credit solutions that were almost impossible to access in traditional banking systems, Fintech solutions are revolutionizing access to finance.[37] In the Digital Financial Inclusion and Fintech Innovations in BRI Economies, digital systems apply transaction histories, online business data, and other data to determine creditworthiness, enabling MSMEs to access loans, working capital, and other supply chain financing without any issues. MSMEs form the foundation of the local economies, although they are

---

[35] Zong Liang, "Innovation in Globalization Theory and Reconstruction of International Trade Rules," in *The Innovation of Economic Theory in China: Theoretical Perspectives* (Springer, 2026).

[36] Jamil Afzal, "Decentralized Currencies and Digital Economy: Stability and Implications of Digital Currency," in *Exploring the New Horizons of International Law Concerning Globalization of Economy* (Springer, 2026).

[37] J. Madegowda, "Traditional vs. Contemporary Financing Models for MSMEs and Startups: A Comparative Study," in *Empowering Inclusive Innovation* (Routledge, 2026).

always faced with the challenge of accessing formal finance.[38] Lack of collateral, lack of financial records, and the nature of small operations can result in traditional banks thinking of such businesses as risky. Fintech solutions solve these holes by employing the use of digital tools, which include e-invoicing, mobile transaction data, and purchase order information to form a consistent profile of the financial behavior of a business. By doing this, it will enable the lenders to understand the credit risk more precisely and make loans to suit the needs of the small business. Another critical area where fintech platforms have a significant influence is supply chain finance. Due to the late payments of the bigger clients or suppliers, MSMEs usually have a low cash flow. Digital financing solutions help these businesses to access early payment, invoice discounting, and working capital loans using automated services.

4.4 Green Finance and Sustainability

Green finance is one of the areas where fintech innovations are becoming more and more significant in ensuring sustainable development.[39] Green fintech uses digital technologies to offer investments, loans, and financial services to support environmentally friendly projects along the BRI lines.[40] These programs make capital available to all and promote responsible business and environmentally friendly development. Some of the environmental issues that affect many of the BRI economies include air and water pollution, deforestation, and unsustainable industrial practices. Green fintech platforms can solve these problems by providing digital platforms that allocate funds to renewable energy initiatives, energy-saving infrastructure, and sustainable businesses. Investors are able to monitor the environmental impact of investment projects they fund through digital monitoring and reporting systems, which ensure accountability and transparency in sustainable financing. Digital platforms can also be used to create green credit products that would focus on MSMEs and local communities. These products may comprise loans to install solar energy, energy-saving manufacturing machinery, and sustainable farming. Through low-interest credit or incentives-based credit offered via fintech systems, these measures render the sustainable practices economically feasible to the smaller businesses that would not otherwise receive green funding.

[38] K. Rajamani et al., "Access to Finance: Challenges Faced by Micro, Small, and Medium Enterprises in India," *Engineering Economics* 33, no. 1 (2022): 73–85.

[39] Maxwell Chukwudi Udeagha and Edwin Muchapondwa, "Striving for the United Nations (UN) Sustainable Development Goals (SDGs) in BRICS Economies: The Role of Green Finance, Fintech, and Natural Resource Rent," *Sustainable Development* 31, no. 5 (2023): 3657–72.

[40] Bo Dai et al., "Policy Pathways through FinTech and Green Finance for Low-Carbon Energy Transition in BRICS Nations," *Energy Strategy Reviews* 57 (2025): 101603.

4.5 *Industrial and Digital Upgrading*

Industrial and digital upgrading in BRI economies focus on fintech and digital technologies, which have become the driving force of efficiency, innovation, and technological progress.[41] Artificial intelligence (AI), blockchain, and big data analytics find applications not only in finance but also in the entire process of manufacturing, logistics, and supply chains, which are fulfilled in the overall objectives of the Digital Silk Road initiative. AI can be used to help firms optimize their manufacturing processes, forecast demand, and maintain stocks at the most precise level.[42] This enhanced efficiency in terms of lower costs of production, lower delivery time, and competitiveness in the local and global markets. The blockchain technology improves the industrial and supply chain systems with transparency, traceability, and security of transactions. The blockchain also enables the real-time monitoring of the whereabouts of goods, establishing the origin of goods, and a secure digital contract in the manufacturing and trade, which reduces conflicts and delays. Big data analytics is also accelerating the digitalization process since it provides information regarding consumer behavior, market trends, and operational performance. These insights can be used by governments and private businesses in BRI economies to adopt smart manufacturing, allocate resources, and strategically plan infrastructure investments.

5 Fintech Innovations in China and Role Model

5.1 *Mobile Payments and Super-Apps*

Mobile payments and super-app ecosystems have turned out to be the staple of China fintech and have played a crucial role in enhancing digital financial inclusion and transforming consumer behavior.[43] In the framework of Digital Financial Inclusion and Fintech Innovations in BRI Economies, the examples of Alipay (Ant Group) and WeChat Pay (Tencent Financial Technology) are the digital platforms where integrated services can be provided and offer easy access to payments, banking, and

[41] Wang Xiaobin et al., "Natural Resources, Trade and Fintech in the Era of Digitalization: A Study of Economies Involved in Belt and Road Initiative," *Resources Policy* 93 (2024): 105082.

[42] Uche Nweje and Moyosore Taiwo, "Leveraging Artificial Intelligence for Predictive Supply Chain Management, Focus on How AI-Driven Tools Are Revolutionizing Demand Forecasting and Inventory Optimization," *International Journal of Science and Research Archive* 14, no. 1 (2025): 230–50.

[43] Haojun Chen, "The Age of Super-Apps: Insights From China's Evolving," *Regulation, Emerging Risk, and Ethics in FinTech and AI*, 2025, 163.

lifestyle management in both urban and rural areas.[44,45] Alipay and WeChat Pay have gone way beyond conventional banking to provide features that cover peer-to-peer payments, bill payments, utility payments, online shopping, wealth management, insurance, and even microloans, all of them all in a single mobile application.[46] These super-apps provide a broad range of financial and business operations without necessarily accessing physical banks, and financial access has become more inclusive of historically underserved groups of the population, such as rural residents, migrant workers, and small business owners.

Mobile payment integration with lifestyle services empowers user engagement and financial literacy. As an example, Alipay offers saving, investment, and credit rating services, whereas WeChat Pay combines social and business services that stimulate the regular use of digital payments. These super-apps reduce the barriers to entry of new users, decrease cash use, and streamline daily financial operations by combining several financial services in a single platform. Small businesses and e-commerce in China are also carried out through mobile payment platforms. Digital payments can be accepted by merchants of any size with little infrastructure, decreasing the costs of transactions and enhancing cash flow. To SMEs and entrepreneurs, the merging of payments and credit scoring, with online marketplaces into one are simplifying financial management and advancing business.

5.2 AI-Driven Credit Scoring and Lending

In China, AI and big data are changing credit scoring and lending, dramatically increasing financial access to underserved people and small enterprises.[47] In the context of BRI Economies, Du Xiaoman Financial, 360 DigiTech, and Lufax are companies that use AI-based models and all-encompassing data analytics to offer rapid, effective, and unsecured loans to consumers and micro, small, and medium enterprises (MSMEs) who would otherwise be subject to formal credit restrictions.[48,49,50] Such fintech systems collect and process a range of digital data, such

44 Ding Ding et al., "From Ant Financial to Alibaba's Rural Taobao Strategy–How Fintech Is Transforming Social Inclusion," in *Handbook of Blockchain, Digital Finance, and Inclusion, Volume 1* (Elsevier, 2018).

45 Kathryn Pan, *Ant Group's Transformative Impact on China's Financial Industry*, 2025.

46 Max Parasol, "China's Digital Yuan: Reining in Alipay and WeChat Pay," *Banking & Finance Law Review* 37, no. 2 (2022): 265–303.

47 Nir Kshetri, "Big Data's Role in Expanding Access to Financial Services in China," *International Journal of Information Management* 36, no. 3 (2016): 297–308.

48 Miaojun Bai et al., "Gradient Boosting Survival Tree with Applications in Credit Scoring," *Journal of the Operational Research Society* 73, no. 1 (2022): 39–55.

49 Julan Du et al., *Shadow Banking Activities in Non-Financial Firms: Evidence from China* (SSRN, 2016).

50 Xinyi Guo et al., "China Ping an Insurance Co., Ltd. as an Example of Effective Cooperation Between Company, Society and Government," 2020, 387–90.

as transaction history, mobile payment history, e-commerce activity history, social media behavior, utility payments, and so on, to create precise credit profiles. AI algorithms can evaluate the risk in real-time, which saves the necessity of conventional collateral and the long process of approvals.[51] This will enable MSMEs and people with no formal financial records to take loans that would otherwise be inaccessible. In the case of SMEs, AI-based lending assists in working capital management, supply chain, and business growth. Fast loan acquisition and release allow companies to react promptly to market needs, sustain cash flow, and invest in production or technological upgrades. Individual consumers get personal loans, microloans, and installment credit, which are used to fund such things as emergencies, education, or even business.

5.3 AI-Based Insurance Tech (Insurtech)

The Chinese insurance industry is changing with artificial intelligence (AI), which is allowing the industry to be more efficient, transparent, and accessible.[52] AI-based insurance technology, or insurtech, is assisting firms like ZhongAn Insurance, Ping An Insurance, and Cheche Technology to offer innovative solutions in the underwriting, claims-processing, and risk-assessment of people and businesses that were underserved.[53,54,55] The algorithms of AI can also enable insurers to handle claims virtually in seconds, which saves a lot of time and costs on administration that were imposed on conventional insurance systems.[56] Another important use of AI in insurtech is digital underwriting.[57] Using big data, such as demographic data, behavior, and historical claims, the AI systems are able to evaluate risks with precision and provide customized insurance products. This will make it easy to have micro-insurance and short-term policies that suit low-income groups, MSMEs, and

---

[51] Chandra Shikhi Kodete, "A Real Time AI System for Automated Financial Technology Payment Detection and Risk Reduction," *International Journal of Scientific Research in Computer Science Engineering and Information Technology* 7 (2021): 685–710.

[52] Wang Wentao, "Modern Digital Technology in China's Insurance Industry," *Вестник Томского Государственного Университета. Экономика*, no. 55 (2021): 148–65.

[53] Oliver Ralph and Don Weinland, "ZhongAn Launches Insurtech Concept," *The Financial Times*, 2017, 14–14.

[54] Xinyi Guo et al., "China Ping an Insurance Co., Ltd. as an Example of Effective Cooperation Between Company, Society and Government," 2020, 387–90.

[55] Iván Sosa and Óscar Montes, "Understanding the InsurTech Dynamics in the Transformation of the Insurance Sector," *Risk Management and Insurance Review* 25, no. 1 (2022): 35–68.

[56] Anat Lior, "Insuring AI: The Role of Insurance in Artificial Intelligence Regulation," *Harv. JL & Tech.* 35 (2021): 467.

[57] Ramnath Balasubramanian et al., "Rewriting the Rules: Digital and AI-Powered Underwriting in Life Insurance," *McKinsey & Company, July* 31 (2020).

rural dwellers. Such accessibility increases financial inclusion since it provides insurance coverage to groups of people who have not been in a position to obtain formal insurance services.

5.4 Blockchain and Supply Chain Finance

Supply chain finance has been becoming more popular in the use of blockchain technology to improve transparency, security, and efficiency of financial transactions.[58] Examples of companies that operate within the framework of Digital Financial Inclusion and Fintech Innovations in BRI Economies include Qulian Technology and Linklogis.[59,60] The former uses blockchain-based solutions to automate supply chain management, enhance invoice financing, and offer secure credit access to businesses traditionally underserved by traditional banks. Blockchain makes it possible to create an immutable and decentralized registry of all transactions along the supply chain in real time. This makes sure that suppliers, manufacturers, distributors, and financial institutions have access to correct and tamper-free information on the shipments, invoices, and payments. Blockchain proves its worth in the field of invoice financing. Organizations are able to computerize their invoices and send them to blockchain-based solutions to have them verified and financed. Banking institutions are able to check the authenticity and the status of invoices in real time without consulting the paperwork or having to go through intermediaries.

5.5 Digital Wealth Management

Digital wealth management has emerged as a foundation of the Chinese fintech industry, providing users and individual investors with convenient, cheap, and easy access to the management and growth of their finances. Platforms such as Yu'eBao (Tianhong Asset Management/Ant Group) have transformed the traditional money market funds by implementing them directly into mobile payment wallets, enabling users to invest and manage their wealth directly through digital means.[61,62] Yu'eBao allows people to invest even very small sums of money right out of their mobile wallets, without the hassle of issuing formal brokerage accounts or high initial capital.

---

[58] Lingling Guo et al., "A Blockchain and IoT-Based Lightweight Framework for Enabling Information Transparency in Supply Chain Finance," *Digital Communications and Networks* 8, no. 4 (2022): 576–87.

[59] Xiangfeng Chen et al., "Linklogis: A Supply Chain Fintech Solution Provider," *FUDAN*, 2023, 1–15.

[60] Liang Cai et al., "Blockchain in China," *Communications of the ACM* 64, no. 11 (2021): 88–93.

[61] KRISHNA G. PALEPU et al., *Ant Group (A)*, 2021.

[62] Wei Wang and Lin Li, "Digital Payment, Money Market Fund and Investment Behavior," *Pacific-Basin Finance Journal* 85 (2024): 102348.

In the connection of investment accounts to popular applications such as Alipay, the user can transfer money in seconds, automatically reinvest earnings, and track their investments in real-time. This is a democratization of access to investment opportunities that promotes financial participation by low-income earners, first-time investors, and users in rural or underserved areas.

5.6 *Virtual Banking*

Virtual banking is one of the significant changes within the Chinese financial environment, providing a branchless and entirely digital approach to banking services that increase financial access to underserved communities.[63] An example of 100% digital banks that do not need any physical presence would be WeBank (Tencent-backed) and XW Bank (Xiaomi-backed), which use technology to provide banking services with efficiency and inclusivity.[64,65] These virtual banks offer all types of financial products and services, such as opening accounts, deposits, withdrawals, transfers, lending, and management of wealth, all via mobile applications. The customers are able to take care of their finances solely via the internet, which means that they do not have to travel to brick-and-mortar banks, which is useful especially to rural populations and businesses in remote areas within the BRIs' economies. Credit checks, fraud detection, and customized financial advice are performed with advanced algorithms, thus making decisions quick and reducing operational costs. Other fintech applications, including digital wallets, mobile payments, and investment platforms, also have an easy time integrating with virtual banks, forming a connected financial ecosystem. Such assimilation makes the users more convenient and encourages the daily utilization of digital financial services. Biometric authentication and encryption are security provisions that guarantee that the funds and personal data of the customers stay safe, which fosters confidence in the complete digitalization of the banking models.

---

[63] Shaoyi Liao et al., "The Adoption of Virtual Banking: An Empirical Study," *International Journal of Information Management* 19, no. 1 (1999): 63–74.

[64] Tomasz Dziawgo, *Big Tech Influence on China Financial Sector*, 2021.

[65] Chuhan Zhang and Xiuting Li, "Unveiling the Technological Dynamics of Banking Systems: A Network Analysis of Chinese and Global Banking Innovation," *Systems* 13, no. 5 (2025): 323.

5.7 *Regulatory Technology (RegTech)*

Regulatory technology or RegTech has become a vital element in the Chinese fintech ecosystem and offers innovative digital solutions to assist financial institutions and fintech firms in meeting increasingly complicated regulatory demands.[66] Companies like Baiwang Cloud offer automated compliance, taxation, reporting, and risk management tools that allow companies to operate efficiently and take into account legal standards. RegTech platforms are AI-based, big data analytics, and cloud computing that track transactions in the financial sector in real time, identify anomalies, and create automated reports to the regulatory bodies. This will ease the administrative load on banks, fintech providers, and other financial service providers and improve transparency and accountability. RegTech reduces human error through automation of compliance processes and minimizes operations costs and regulatory compliance with the timing of regulatory changes, which is essential in the fast-changing financial markets. RegTech improves the stability of the entire digital financial ecosystem because it creates a framework that enables risk management, detecting fraud, and regulatory compliance. It allows fintech businesses to develop and grow their activities without undermining the confidence of regulators, investors, and consumers, which will contribute to secure and inclusive financial access in the BRI economies.

5.8 *Fintech Infrastructure and AI Services*

Fintech infrastructure and AI-based services have emerged in China as the essential institutions of digital financial ecosystems, which provide the technological platform of existing financial institutions and new fintech firms. The example of such companies as 4Paradigm and ABC Technology introduces innovative cloud-based computing systems and data processing techniques relying on AI that allow providing safe, effective, and scalable financial management.[67] Such environments allow the banks, online lenders, and payment providers to process high volumes of transactional and customer data in real time.

---

[66] Ya Bu et al., "Effective Regulations of FinTech Innovations: The Case of China," *Economics of Innovation and New Technology* 31, no. 8 (2022): 751–69.

[67] Jossy George et al., *Cognitive Cloud Computing: Building Intelligent Systems for Tomorrow* (CRC Press, 2025).

6 Legal and Regulatory Frameworks for Digital Financial Inclusion

Regulations and laws play a pivotal role in digital financial inclusion development. These frameworks define the regulations under which financial institutions, fintech, and other service providers are provided. The Belt and Road Initiative (BRI) should provide the economies with an appropriate legal and regulatory ecosystem that would support innovation, consumer protection, and financial stability. Unless there are effective and balanced regulations, digital financial services may fail to develop or expose the users to a lot of danger. One of the main objectives of the regulation of digital finance is to protect consumers. With the growth of digital financial services, consumers are exposed to fraud, false information, undisclosed charges, and misuse of personal information. The regulations help protect the consumers by making sure that consumers are treated fairly, with terms and conditions that are clear and that they are charged transparently. The consumer protection laws also ensure that the users have a system of making complaints and settling disputes in case of difficulties. Another area of concern as far as regulation is concerned is financial stability. Financial services on the digital front have high volumes of transactions and data and may pose systematic risks if they are not effectively controlled.[68] Fintech activities are regulated by regulators in BRI economies to avoid the risks of over-lending, money laundering, and cyber threats. Prudential rules assist in making sure that banks and technology companies in the finance department work safely and responsibly. One of the major parts of the regulatory frameworks of digital financial inclusion is licensing and authorization requirements.

The laws are set by governments and regulators on who is allowed to provide digital financial services and on what terms. The licensing conditions assist the authorities in ensuring that the service providers meet the minimum standards concerning capital, governance, and risk management. Regulators in most BRI countries have also come up with special licenses for fintech companies to promote innovation, and yet still provide supervision. Digital payments should be regulated, especially in BRI economies. E-payment systems are common in all daily transactions and in transfers within the government. Some of the issues addressed by regulations include security of transactions, the settlement system, and interoperability. Elucidated payment policies facilitate trust and reliability in financial services online to promote further usage among users. Data protection and privacy policies are the key to digital financial inclusion. Digital financial services are dependent on personal and financial data. Unless there are robust laws on data protection, users will lose confidence in online applications. A lot of the BRI countries are formulating/enhancing data protection laws to make sure that individual information is gathered, stored, and utilized in a judicial manner. These laws assist in ensuring that no one misuses the data obtained and that the privacy rights of users are not violated.

---

[68] Ross P. Buckley et al., "The Dark Side of Digital Financial Transformation: The New Risks of Fintech and the Rise of Techrisk," *UNSW Law Research Paper*, nos. 19–89 (2019).

The digital financial inclusion is also influenced by the anti-money laundering (AML) and counter-terrorism financing (CTF) regulations.[69] Digital platforms easily become susceptible to criminal activities unless they are regulated. AML and CTF regulations oblige financial service providers and fintech companies to check the identity of the customers, as well as monitor payments.[70] Although these regulations are needed to maintain security, too strict requirements can disqualify low-income users who do not have formal identification. Regulators of the BRI economies are confronted by the issue of security versus inclusion. A regulatory sandbox is a significant instrument in a number of BRI countries. A regulatory sandbox is an opportunity that gives fintech firms a chance to pilot new products and services under controlled conditions and regulatory oversight. This will stimulate innovation as the regulators get to know the risks emerging. Sandboxes help build inclusive fintech by lowering regulatory and uncertainties to startups. Central banks play a very important role in the regulation of digital financial inclusion. The Central banks regulate payment systems, control financial institutions, as well as overseeing monetary stability. Most BRI economies have been proactive by central banks in encouraging digital finance by issuing policy principles, digital payment programs, and regulating the activities of fintech. Digital identity systems are another key area of digital money; some central banks are also examining them as part of wider financial inclusion policies. Legal framework's Digital identity systems are also a keyway of accessing digital financial services. The digital identification aids in validating user identities and aids in secure transactions.

7 Addressing the Barriers to Digital Financial Inclusion

Although there is a booming digital financial services industry, several challenges still hinder digital financial inclusion in Belt and Road Initiative (BRI) economies. These obstacles include economic, technological, social, and institutional barriers. They need to be addressed so that the digital financial systems can be inclusive, accessible, and beneficial to all classes of the population.

7.1 Digital and Financial Illiteracy

The greatest challenge to the success of the regional economic integration process is ignorance of how to utilize the digital platforms, and research shows that a good

---

[69] William Gaviyau and Athenia Bongani Sibindi, "Global Anti-Money Laundering and Combating Terrorism Financing Regulatory Framework: A Critique," *Journal of Risk and Financial Management* 16, no. 7 (2023): 313.

[70] Muhammad Nawaz Shahid, "Role of Digital Public Infrastructure (DPI) in Strengthening AML/KYC for Developing Economies," *International Journal of Law and Legal Advancement* 2, no. 1 (2026): 13–22.

number of users are ill-equipped with the skills to operate new e-payment systems. Within the present context of the BRI, this "Knowledge Gap" has already turned into a structural bottleneck of the Digital Silk Road. Technology has been introduced at a high rate that is not matched with the cognitive preparation of the workforce, creating a digital divide in which the means to earn wealth are available, but the knowledge on how to use them safely is lacking.

7.2 *Infrastructure and Access Issues*

The availability of physical hardware is the fundamental pillar of the operational success of Digital Financial Services (DFS); nevertheless, the lack of internet connectivity, low access to smartphones, and insufficient technology infrastructure in rural or developing locations are the key factors of the financial equity inhibitors. This "Infrastructure Gap" has been transformed, within the Digital Silk Road strategic framework, from a mere absence of cables into a complex "Energy-Fintech Paradox". Moreover, a Hardware-Software Mismatch is becoming more and more characteristic of the crisis of smartphone penetration. Being the Fintech giants of China, like Ant Group and Tencent, their apps demand high-performance RAM and sophisticated biometric sensors to ensure the safety of authentication. Nevertheless, the secondary markets of most BRI countries are flooded with legacy, low-memory devices that cannot execute these bulky encryption protocols. This results in a Device-Poverty Trap in which the poor can be seen digitally but not technologically.

7.3 *Affordability and Costs*

The universal connectivity is often endangered by the deeply rooted segregations within society, and women are especially disadvantaged, with lower literacy rates and less access to mobile access. In the conceptual model of the DSR, this Gender Gap is a Structural Asymmetry in which technological export is not correlated with social evolution. Rationally, when the main point of entry of the digital economy is the smartphone, which is dominated by a male head of household, the digital identity of the woman is just a sub-unit of a larger family, which essentially deprives her of financial agency and privacy.

7.4 *Lack of Trust and Security Concerns*

On the one hand, the use of digital tools is essentially the cession of anonymity, but the threat of fraud, money laundering, and privacy issues in the field of personal data places a rational barrier of Trust Deficit to participation. It is not a psychological issue in the architecture of the DSR, but a Systematic Risk Problem. In the process of a user in a BRI economy switching from a cash-based, or rather, an invisible economy, to a digital, or rather, a visible economy, he or she is essentially exchanging physical security with digital insecurity. The conceptual crisis in this case is that Digital Financial Inclusion (DFI) is in need of a degree of institutional trust, and many developing BRI countries, historically, have not yet developed. Unless the user is confident in the state or the platform provider with their data, the "Digital Ledger" is not viewed as an empowerment tool, but as an instrument of surveillance or a target to cyber-predators. A fintech should be fast and frictionless (low-KYC) to make it inclusive, and it should be rigorous and high-friction to ensure that it is secure against money laundering (AML) and fraud. This friction is the point of break in the system in most BRI regions. The export of Chinese AI-based biometric authentication (face and fingerprint scanning) can be used as an example, which is a high-tech solution to identity theft, but also raises an alarm of "Data Sovereignty". Theoretically, when the data is stored on centralized servers that are not within the home country of the user, the Lack of Trust is a geopolitical threat.

7.5 *Preference for Cash*

The next main rival of fintech in most emerging markets is not other applications, but the very banknote. Such a strong dependence on cash, together with the intangible and impersonal quality of digital platforms, poses an enormous adoption challenge. Cash is not merely a value but an instrument of instant, faceless, and irreversible payment that does not need electricity, information, or the sanction of a third party within the boundaries of the Belt and Road Initiative. To a small-scale trader, moving to a digital wallet would be like selling a physical item and replacing it with a promise on a screen, a mental leap that many people are not sufficiently prepared to make yet. Such an attitude of Cash-First develops a Functional Disconnect within the digital corridor. To fill this divide, attention is turning to Phygital (Physical + Digital) Solutions. Instead of trying to kill cash overnight, new models of fintech are integrating local agents of cash-in/cash-out, like local kiosks, to bring a human interface to the digital world.

8 Conclusion

One aspect of economic development in BRI economies is digital financial inclusion. It also provides a gateway for persons and businesses previously excluded from the formal financial system, enabling them to access the required financial services. These services include payments, investments, insurance, savings, and loans. The mobile money services and digital banking have helped millions of individuals who previously had no access to banking services to get into the financial system of a BRI country. They should come up with laws and regulations that would make digital finance inclusion a risk-free, sustainable, and viable concept. The legislation safeguards the consumer's financial health and promotes good competition amongst the service providers. Such issues as data privacy, cybersecurity, licensing, and anti-money laundering are considered in adequate regulatory frameworks. In the meantime, the balancing point between innovation and the safety of the user ought to be discovered by the regulators. Adaptive policies and regulatory sandboxes have been established to be useful in facilitating fintech innovation and risk management. Digital financial inclusion in BRI economies is related to a variety of challenges despite having positive sides. The factors that may make people incapable of using digital financial services are the lack of digital infrastructure, low digital literacy rates, low rates of trust, and high costs.

Chapter 8
Green Digital Economy and Sustainable Legal Development

Abstract The green digital economy has emerged as a complementary strategy in the effort to ensure sustainable growth. It is a combination of digital technologies and environmentally responsible economic practices that allows practicing more efficiently, low-carbon, and resource-conscious. Quick economic growth without proper regard for the environmental and social effects may cause long-term risks, which may involve depletion of resources, pollution, social disturbance, and financial inefficiency. Sustainable legal development offers a platform upon which these risks can be handled so that economic growth can be achieved with regard to environmental conservation and social accountability. It entails setting, enacting, and enforcing laws, regulations, and policies that advance responsible practices in the economic, societal, and environmental aspects. Sustainable legal frameworks in BRI economies facilitate the setting of standards in areas of environmental protection, corporate responsibility, social inclusion, and financial integrity. Findings of this chapter reveal that through the implementation of digital solutions, the countries will be able to minimize the ecological footprint of economic operations, bring green investments, and promote innovation without losing their competitiveness in global markets.

Keywords Green Digital Economy · Green Finance · Green Computing and IT Sustainability · Green FinTech · Digital Twins for Manufacturing

1 Defining Sustainable Development and Green Digital Economy

The concept of sustainable development is multidimensional because it aims at balancing economic growth, social well-being, and protection of the environment.[1] It has become a world agenda towards the end of the twentieth century and was formally an agreement with the adoption of the United Nations Sustainable Development

[1] Elena Mezentseva et al., "The Impact of Sustainable Development on Economic Growth: Balancing Environmental, Social and Economic Factors," *Reliability: Theory & Applications* 19, no. SI 6 (81) (2024): 1269–74.

J. Afzal and Y. Chen, *Legal Framework of Digital Economy and Digital Trade Under the Belt and Road Initiative*, https://doi.org/10.1007/978-981-92-4444-7_8

Goals (SDGs).[2,3] Simply, sustainable development focuses on the ability to fulfill the needs of the current generations without affecting the capability of future generations to fulfill their needs. This strategy involves the incorporation of environmental stewardship, social equity, and economic efficiency into the planning, policymaking, and implementation of projects. Sustainable development enhances resilience, inclusiveness, and sound management of resources in various sectors by laying emphasis on long-term outcomes, as opposed to short-term gains. Economic sustainability entails providing a stable and inclusive growth that brings about employment, higher productivity, and higher living standards with minimal negative impact on the environment and society.[4] It focuses on resource efficiency, responsible investment, and innovation in order to initiate progress. The social sustainability is based on equity, inclusiveness, and human development, whereby the poor people and communities can access basic services, education, and medical care, and have opportunities to participate in economic activities.[5] Environmental sustainability means safeguarding the natural ecosystems, maintaining biodiversity, lessening pollution, and mitigating the effects of climate change by ensuring the prudent use of energy, water, land, and other natural resources.[6,7] These three dimensions are mutually dependent, and sound development policies imply the need to balance between economic, social, and environmental goals.

The green digital economy is based on these values by introducing digital technologies to the economic operations in a responsible approach to the environment.[8] It is a contemporary development strategy that incorporates digital innovation and the concept of sustainability. Artificial intelligence, big data analytics, blockchain, cloud computing, and the Internet of Things (IoT) are digital tools that help to monitor, decide, and manage resources in such a manner that they cause fewer environmental effects and increased efficiency. As an illustration, AI algorithms can optimize energy use in urban and industrial locations, whereas IoT-based sensors are able to scan the quality of water, air pollution, or waste management systems in real time. The blockchain technology will improve the transparency of supply chains, whereby

[2] Naveen Kumar Arora and Isha Mishra, "United Nations Sustainable Development Goals 2030 and Environmental Sustainability: Race against Time," *Environmental Sustainability* 2, no. 4 (2019): 339–42.

[3] Lars Carlsen and Rainer Bruggemann, "The 17 United Nations' Sustainable Development Goals: A Status by 2020," *International Journal of Sustainable Development & World Ecology* 29, no. 3 (2022): 219–29.

[4] Peter N. Hess, *Economic Growth and Sustainable Development* (Routledge, 2016).

[5] Preethi Nanjundan et al., "Social Inclusion and Sustainability," *Global Nexus Handbook* 3 (2026): 965–74.

[6] Deepak Kumar Garg, "Environmental Challenges and Sustainable Development," *Journal of Global Values* 14 (2023): 203–10.

[7] Jamil Afzal et al., "Effects of Dam on Temperature, Humidity and Precipitation of Surrounding Area: A Case Study of Gomal Zam Dam in Pakistan," *Environmental Science and Pollution Research* 30, no. 6 (2023): 14592–603.

[8] Serhii Arefiev et al., "The Use of Digital Technologies to Ensure Environmental Safety in the Context of the Green Economy Development," *Revista de La Universidad Del Zulia* 15, no. 42 (2024): 353–69.

goods are manufactured and transported in a manner that is ecologically friendly.[9] The green digital economy, therefore, offers the technical capabilities as well as the strategic platform to execute the sustainable practices adequately.[10] Green finance is a major element of the green digital economy, which connects both investment and sustainability objectives.[11] It is the process of steering financial tools into projects with a good resultant environment or social factors, including renewable energy, energy efficiency, sustainable agriculture, and low-carbon infrastructure. Digital solutions enable green finance when it comes to accessing information, lowering transaction costs, and allowing transparent tracking of investments.[12] Economies would upgrade financial tools and digital innovation to promote environmentally friendly behaviors and economic growth.

Innovation in the business model, industrial practices, and energy systems is also promoted by the green digital economy. Digital solutions in the traditional sectors turn them into a more sustainable system, such as smart grids, the integration of renewable energy, precision agriculture, and low-carbon manufacturing. Digital technologies can help companies to consume less power, manage supply chains, and enhance environmental performance.[13] Meanwhile, the digital platforms provide a more effective means of communication with consumers, investors, and communities, which facilitates transparency and responsibility in environmental and social practices. The green digital economy and sustainable development are two concepts that are tightly connected.[14] Sustainable practices are introduced through the tools of digital technologies, and the principles of sustainability determine the responsible use of the technology. They combine to generate possibilities of low-carbon development, resource effectiveness, and social integration. This integration is especially applicable to large-scale setups that touch on multiple nations, and one of them is the Belt and Road Initiative. The alignment of legal regulations, technologies, and sustainability goals can be used to ensure that economic projects do not produce lasting negative effects on the environment and the community. Policies,

---

[9] Mobashar Mubarik et al., "Impact of Blockchain Technology on Green Supply Chain Practices: Evidence from Emerging Economy," *Management of Environmental Quality: An International Journal* 32, no. 5 (2021): 1023–39.

[10] Yanlin Liu et al., "The Impact of Technological Innovation on the Green Digital Economy and Development Strategies," *Plos One* 19, no. 4 (2024): e0301051.

[11] Chengbo Fu et al., "Advancing Green Finance: A Review of Sustainable Development," *Digital Economy and Sustainable Development* 1, no. 1 (2023): 20.

[12] Gregor Dorfleitner and Diana Braun, "Fintech, Digitalization and Blockchain: Possible Applications for Green Finance," in *The Rise of Green Finance in Europe: Opportunities and Challenges for Issuers, Investors and Marketplaces* (Springer, 2019).

[13] Manu Sharma et al., "The Impact of Environmental Dynamism on Low-carbon Practices and Digital Supply Chain Networks to Enhance Sustainable Performance: An Empirical Analysis," *Business Strategy and the Environment* 31, no. 4 (2022): 1776–88.

[14] AB Savchenko and TL Borodina, "Green and Digital Economy for Sustainable Development of Urban Areas," *Regional Research of Russia* 10, no. 4 (2020): 583–92.

legal framework, and technological systems that are congruent with these priorities bring investments, spur innovation, and raise credibility.[15]

2 Types and Applications of Green Digital Economy

2.1 Green Computing and IT Sustainability

The development of the environmentally friendly digital ecosystems, for Sustainable Legal Development and Green Digital Economy in BRI, is based on the idea of green computing and IT sustainability.[16,17] It is a concept that is concerned with designing and running computing systems, hardware, and software in a way that lowers the amount of energy used and the carbon footprint of the information technology infrastructure. In BRI economies, where the levels of digitalization are growing at a high pace along with industrial and economic progress, the implementation of green computing practices is the only thing that guarantees that technological development meets the goals of sustainable development. The practices of green IT focus on efficient servers, data centers, and network devices based on energy.[18] The use of low-power hardware, ensuring the optimal utilization of servers, and the application of virtualization technology will allow financial institutions, fintech platforms, and other digital businesses to significantly decrease their electricity consumption and maintain high-performance computing. Sustainability is also achieved through cloud services by having multiple organizations share infrastructure and thus reducing unnecessary energy consumption and promoting more intelligent use of resources.[19]

Green computing within the green digital economy offers a sustainable financial and legal framework by offering green digital platforms.[20] As an example, the use of digital payment with the help of fintech companies, AI-based lending, or blockchain-based supply chains can integrate green IT infrastructure and minimize the energy needs of activities. This coincides with regulatory and policy initiatives in the BRI

[15] Jean-Eric Aubert, *Promoting Innovation in Developing Countries: A Conceptual Framework*, vol. 3554 (World Bank Publications, 2005).

[16] Jianping Yu et al., "Enhancing Sustainable Development through Digital Economy and Natural Resource Management in One Belt One Road Countries," *Technology in Society* 81 (2025): 102812.

[17] Shahid Mahmood et al., "Green Finance, Sustainable Infrastructure, and Green Technology Innovation: Pathways to Achieving Sustainable Development Goals in the Belt and Road Initiative," *Environmental Research Communications* 6, no. 10 (2024): 105036.

[18] Adya Mishra, "Energy Efficient Infrastructure Green Data Centers: The New Metrics for IT Framework," *International Journal For r Multidisciplinary Research* 4 (2022): 1–12.

[19] Rajkumar Buyya et al., "Energy-efficiency and Sustainability in New Generation Cloud Computing: A Vision and Directions for Integrated Management of Data Centre Resources and Workloads," *Software: Practice and Experience* 54, no. 1 (2024): 24–38.

[20] Abhiram Reddy Bommareddy, "Towards Sustainable Federal Financial IT: Green Computing Practices In Data Centers And Cloud Platforms," *International Journal of Environmental Sciences* 11, no. 24s (n.d.): 2025.

economies that promote environmentally friendly business practices and, at the same time, ensure that they can meet the energy efficiency conditions. The other advantageous aspect of green IT sustainability is the alleviation of the environmental effects of data-intensive applications, including digital banking and AI services, and big data analytics.[21] As these services expand to provide financial inclusion, industrial upgrading, and intercountry trade between BRI countries, it is important to make sure that these services are small in their energy footprint so that ecological balance is observed in the long-term. The idea behind the use of energy-efficient methods of incorporating computing into the digital ecosystems is that technological advancement shall not undermine the environmental integrity, and this will be included in the overall goals of a green digital economy. Green computing practices are also a supplement to sustainable legal development in the sense that it provides the technological foundation to implement the environmental law, to check carbon emissions, and to facilitate the economic policies that are friendly towards the environment.[22] Focusing on energy-efficient IT infrastructure, BRI economies will be able to develop digital transformation and enhance environmental responsibility, lower operational expenses, and enhance the sustainability of financial and industrial systems.

2.2 *Smart Energy Management*

Smart energy management is one of the most important pillars of the Sustainable Legal Development and a Green Digital Economy in BRI.[23] It implies the application of the newest technologies, such as artificial intelligence (AI), the Internet of Things (IoT), and data analytics, to make the process of energy production, distribution, and consumption more efficient. The economies of the BRIs will be in a position to reduce the use of fossil fuels, improve energy efficiency, and facilitate the economic growth that can be ecologically friendly with the combination of renewable energy systems and smart grids. The intelligent energy management is based on smart grids. These grids track the electricity flows in real-time and identify inefficiencies using sensors, IoT devices, and AI algorithms, and adjust the supply and demand dynamically. Smart grids reduce carbon emissions and maintain a constant flow of power by using renewable sources of power such as solar, wind, and hydropower. The financial institutions, industrial centers, and cities can find smart grid integration useful because

[21] Izabela Rojek et al., "The Impact of Data Analytics Based on Internet of Things, Edge Computing, and Artificial Intelligence on Energy Efficiency in Smart Environment," *Applied Sciences* 16, no. 1 (2025): 225.

[22] Akoh Atadoga et al., "Advancing Green Computing: Practices, Strategies, and Impact in Modern Software Development for Environmental Sustainability," *World Journal of Advanced Engineering Technology and Sciences* 11, no. 1 (2024): 220–30.

[23] Liwen Zuo and Yuheng Ren, "How Renewable Energy Consumption and Digitalization Contribute to Environmental Sustainability: Evidence from One Belt One Road Countries," *Journal of Environmental Management* 380 (2025): 124379.

it will make them manage the cost of running energy operations more efficiently without contravening green policies and environmental laws.

The establishment of the green digital economy is directly associated with smart energy management that provides realistic suggestions to the policy makers and regulators.[24] The information about the energy usage, which is collected by the IoT devices and analytics platforms, can be utilized to develop a sustainable legal framework in such a way that the governments would be able to implement the energy efficiency standards, promote the use of renewable energy, and control compliance with environmental regulations. This will make sure that technological improvements are coherent with the long-range goals of sustainability, economic resilience, and climate responsibility of BRI economies.

2.3 *Precision Agriculture and Farming*

Precision agriculture and smart farming may be regarded as the new practice of sustainable agriculture in the framework of Sustainable Legal Development and Green Digital Economy in BRI.[25,26] With the help of digital technologies, such as IoT sensors, drones, satellite imagery, and AI analytics, farmers would be able to monitor the health of products, the condition of soil, and water consumption in real-time and make data-driven decisions that will maximize productivity and minimize the impact on the environment. The sensors on the fields through IoT are able to collect precise data on soil moisture, nutrient status, and temperature. This knowledge will help the farmers apply water, fertilizers, and pesticides when and where they are needed and, therefore, will significantly minimize the level of wastage and the chances of runoff that can contaminate water sources. Drones with multispectral cameras and GPS may survey extensive areas of the land in a brief time frame and pinpoint the stressed crops, pests, or irrigation mistakes. AIs analyze these datasets to propose the optimal planting times, irrigation time, and input allocation to achieve an efficient and sustainable utilization of resources.

Precision agriculture is environmentally friendly, and it reduces the production cost, increases the crop yield, and improves the profitability of the farms.[27] In BRI economies, particularly the water-sensitive or soil-degraded regions, the technologies can give farmers a chance to store agricultural production and save natural resources

[24] Priyanka Mishra and Ghanshyam Singh, "Energy Management Systems in Sustainable Smart Cities Based on the Internet of Energy: A Technical Review," *Energies* 16, no. 19 (2023): 6903.

[25] Lirong Xing et al., "Advancing Coupling Coordination: Bridging China's Digital Economy and Green Agriculture for Sustainable Rural Development," *Information Technology for Development* 31, no. 4 (2025): 1017–38.

[26] Xiaowen Dai et al., "Technological Revolution in the Field: Green Development of Chinese Agriculture Driven by Digital Information Technology (DIT)," *Agriculture* 13, no. 1 (2023): 199.

[27] Sewnet Getahun et al., "Application of Precision Agriculture Technologies for Sustainable Crop Production and Environmental Sustainability: A Systematic Review," *The Scientific World Journal* 2024, no. 1 (2024): 2126734.

as well. A combination of smart irrigation systems and automated machinery will make farming a digital, sustainable, and climate-resilient business that will enable farmers to be extremely efficient with the minimum amount of human interaction. This is also in line with the green digital economy because agricultural practices enabled by data support the monitoring of the environment, conservation of resources, and compliance with sustainability regulations. The combined agricultural information can help governments and other regulatory bodies in BRI countries to track water and fertilizer utilization, enforce green agricultural production, and provide incentives to embrace green farming.

2.4 Circular Economy Platforms

Digital tools assist in building robust platforms of the circular economy that are oriented on recovery, sharing, and resale of resources, instead of the traditional model of consumption. These platforms can identify the lifecycle of the materials through IoT sensors and data analytics tools powered by AI, thus allowing the manipulation of waste reduction to be accurate and the inputs of recycling to be optimized. This online management enables the design of products that have a long-life cycle and rework the raw materials that are in landfills back into the manufacturing cycle, hence building a more sustainable and environmentally friendly industrial base. Such technical innovations are tactical extensions of the development of the Digital Silk Road (DSR) and the mechanical core of Digital Financial Inclusion and Fintech Innovations in BRI Economies. The digital bridges that China and its allies in Central Asia, Africa, and Southeast Asia are establishing are reinforced with these new resource-sharing networks as they install giant fiber-optic networks and satellites. The DSR, with the assistance of blockchain-based monitoring of recycled resources, allows establishing a green trade area, where small and medium-sized companies (SMEs) can operate in an equal-efficiency environment as large companies. This is in order to ensure that the modern Silk Road is not only a path where physical products move around, but a very well-organized virtual environment as far as sustainable development is concerned.

After a direct tradition of the ingenuity of the ancient Silk Road, where the obsession, recycling, and proper safeguarding of cloth, metal, and animal harnesses decided the success of the road, modern circular platforms constitute the twenty-first century form of an efficient trade guild. The ancient traders required sustainable logistics that could help them to deliver products over thousands of miles without depleting their very limited resources; in the same manner, the present DSR sustainable nature is justified with the appearance of such transparent material standards. The adoption of these cryptographic and environmental instruments and physical infrastructure will ensure that the digital bridges of the new Silk Road are not only a platform through which data travels but are anchored on a cohesive and enforceable economic framework. This compliance of technical harmony by the state renders the Silk

Road a strong ecosystem where the connectivity is controlled by a shared lexicon of effectiveness, safety, and signed trust.

2.5 Green FinTech and Impact Investing

Green FinTech and impact investing may be regarded as an emerging force of the Sustainable Legal Development and Green Digital Economy in BRI that enables individuals and businesses to coordinate financial activities with the environmental sustainability goals.[28,29] The digital apps and fintech (Treecard or Tomorrow) allow the user to calculate their own carbon footprint, invest in environmentally friendly projects, and engage in the low-carbon economic development without losing financial benefits. Such platforms are financial services and environmental impact measurements. As an example, users will be able to monitor the carbon emissions of their daily expenditure and make a good decision to decrease their impact on the environment. The integration of payment systems and investment portfolios with sustainable projects provides fintech apps with the opportunity to change the routine financial processes into opportunities to become environmentally responsible.[30] The renewable energy projects, green bonds, sustainable agriculture, and reforestation programs can be invested in and would allow users to directly participate in the green economy.[31]

AI and data analytics have the potential to enhance the user experience of green fintech websites, whereby users may receive customized recommendations on sustainable investments and optimization of portfolios based on the environmental, social, and governance (ESG) criteria.[32] The user can learn about the environmental cost of their own financial decisions in real-time, and aggregated data may be used

---

[28] Yi Li et al., "Navigating the Path to Environmental Sustainability: Exploring the Role of Fintech, Natural Resources and Green Energy in Belt and Road Countries," *Resources Policy* 88 (2024): 104485.

[29] Eugenia Macchiavello and Michele Siri, "Sustainable Finance and Fintech: Can Technology Contribute to Achieving Environmental Goals? A Preliminary Assessment of 'Green Fintech' and 'Sustainable Digital Finance,'" *European Company and Financial Law Review* 19, no. 1 (2022): 128–74.

[30] Oluwafemi Elias et al., "The Evolution of Green Fintech: Leveraging AI and IoT for Sustainable Financial Services and Smart Contract Implementation," *World Journal of Advanced Research and Reviews* 23, no. 1 (2024): 2710–23.

[31] Yiyi Ning et al., "Green Bond as a New Determinant of Sustainable Green Financing, Energy Efficiency Investment, and Economic Growth: A Global Perspective," *Environmental Science and Pollution Research* 30, no. 22 (2023): 61324–39.

[32] S. Gupta et al., "Sustainable Digital Banking: Exploring the Role of Fintech in Promoting Green Finance and Sustainable Development Goals," *Journal of Information Systems Engineering & Management* 10, no. 3 (2025): 547–57.

by platforms to learn trends and see how much they have achieved their sustainability objectives. This kind of approach creates awareness, encourages responsible consumption, and mobilizes the mobilization of private funds towards climate-friendly activities. Another way in which Green Fintech contributes to sustainable legal development is by providing transparent and auditable follow-up on investment flows. These digital tools will give governments and regulators in BRI economies a chance to monitor compliance with green finance policies, encourage investments that are environmentally friendly, and report on the performance of countries/regions in terms of carbon reduction targets.

2.6 Intelligent Transportation and Logistics

The optimization of the transportation networks will occur with the introduction of IoT and AI analytics, real-time monitoring of data, to reduce traffic jams, optimize energy consumption, and the introduction of electric vehicles (EVs) and environmentally friendly public transport. Traffic systems, roads, and vehicles have IoT sensors that continuously gather information about the traffic flow, the position of the vehicle, and energy consumption.[33] Smart transportation also contributes to the green digital economy and sustainable law systems by providing practical visions to the authorities. Aggregated and real-time transportation information can assist governments to charge emissions and developing urban development and shared mobility. Such integration will ensure that technological innovations in the transport industry are aligned with the environmental standards and sustainability targets in the BRI economies. As IoT, AI, and data analytics are introduced to the transport and logistics infrastructure of countries, BRI will achieve two goals simultaneously, which are the reduction of greenhouse gas emissions and the increase in the efficiency of mobility. This strategy will increase the productivity of the economy, improve environmental custodianship, and add to the overarching vision of a digitally enabled, sustainable, and low-carbon transportation ecosystem.

2.7 Digital Twins for Manufacturing

Digital twins can be used as a high-fidelity virtual foundation of industrial optimization to allow manufacturers to create fine-grained real-time simulations of physical

[33] Auwal Alhassan Musa et al., "Sustainable Traffic Management for Smart Cities Using Internet-of-Things-Oriented Intelligent Transportation Systems (ITS): Challenges and Recommendations," *Sustainability* 15, no. 13 (2023): 9859.

production systems.[34] The ability of these virtual models to simulate complex workflows by integrating fixed data streams delivered by IoT sensors and then applying advanced analytics to identify potential bottlenecks before they can manifest themselves in the real-world environment. This forecasting capability will ensure that production cycles are always optimized in order to minimize wastage of materials and better use of resources, which will respond more quickly to market shifts. When these virtual architectures are located as the central component of the Digital Silk Road (DSR), they provide the technical particularity that is required in the case of Digital Financial Inclusion and Fintech Innovations in BRI Economies. Such simulation and monitoring devices and physical basis will ensure that the digital bridges of the contemporary Silk Road will not be just a data conduit but also will be supported by a single and binding economic structured framework.

2.8 Digital Sobriety

Among the measures of the Sustainable Legal Development and Green Digital Economy in BRI, there is the introduction of digital sobriety that is targeted at reducing the environmental impact of technology because of moderate digital consumption.[35] It promotes an intentional attitude, where digital systems are made more sustainable by people, companies, and organizations, reducing unreasonable internet use, digital streamlining, and energy-efficient means of operation. Digital sobriety is a decrease in energy-intensive activities such as massive streaming, on-demand cloud storage, and re-transfers of data. Such activities are manageable to minimize the amount of electricity consumed by data centres, network infrastructures, and personal devices, and lower the carbon emissions. Organizations can help this by simplifying software operations, balancing server loads, and scheduling high-demand computational operations when there is no peak energy load. Policymakers have the opportunity to encourage a more energy-conscious digital practice, define efficiency standards of hardware and software, and offer incentives to companies that can transition to more environmentally friendly digital practices. The use of digital energy is also reported in a transparent manner, which is another way of supporting compliance and accountability. Through digital sobriety, the BRI countries will be in a position to balance the additional technological advancement and environmental sustainability.[36]

[34] Yangjun Sun et al., "A Modular Multi-Granularity Simulation Modelling Method for Manufacturing Systems Oriented towards Digital Twins," *International Journal of Production Research*, 2025, 1–21.

[35] Sainan Zhao et al., "Dynamic Influence of Digital and Technological Advancement on Sustainable Economic Growth in Belt and Road Initiative (BRI) Countries," *Sustainability* 14, no. 23 (2022): 15782.

[36] Xiaoping Wu and Muhammad Bilawal Khaskheli, "Systems Thinking of Marine Policies in Promoting Environmental Law, Sustainability, and Digital Technologies: Social Challenges in Belt and Road Initiative Countries," *Systems* 12, no. 10 (2024): 400.

3 The Need for Sustainable Legal Development

Sustainable legal development offers grounds to mitigate the dangers and ensure growth is achieved without compromising the environment, being socially responsible, and having a stable economy in the long run.[37] China has a clear policy to protect the natural environment; however, sustainable development in the BRI is still a matter of concern in environmental management.[38] Projects related to infrastructure and industries may lead to deforestation, air and water pollution, destruction of biodiversity, and an increase in carbon emissions. Good legal systems offer clear guidelines towards environmental impact assessment, management of natural resources, and adherence to international environmental treaties.[39] The regulatory systems provide responsibility to the developers and investors, who have to build in an eco-friendly way in the planning, execution, and running of the project. Legal controls also make sure that there is long-term monitoring and reporting, which would assist in the maintenance of the ecological balance as well as reduce the adverse impacts on the local communities. Environmental regulation is closely related to social considerations.[40] The BRI projects may interfere with communities that are dependent on land, water, and natural resources as a source of livelihood.[41] The usual risks in the absence of social safeguards include displacement, loss of jobs, and disruption of social networks. Laws, which embrace the rights to consultation, fair compensation, and participation by communities, encourage inclusive development.[42,43] They empower the populations that are affected to take part in the processes of decision-making, protect the vulnerable populations, and minimize the conflicts among the stakeholders. These laws enhance social solidarity, and development programs are shared in the benefits.

Various nations that are members of BRI initiatives usually have diverse legal systems, standards, and enforcement practices. Scattered regulations can cause

---

[37] Marie-Claire Cordonier Segger and Damilola S. Olawuyi, *Sustainable Development Law: Principles, Practices, and Prospects* (Oxford University Press, 2025).

[38] Kun-min Zhang and Zong-guo Wen, "Review and Challenges of Policies of Environmental Protection and Sustainable Development in China," *Journal of Environmental Management* 88, no. 4 (2008): 1249–61.

[39] Jamil Afzal and Aftab Haider, "Environmental and Resource Protection Law by Ke Zhou, Luozhi Yi, Xinjian Su and Youhai Sun," *International Journal of Law and Legal Advancement* 1, no. 2 (2025).

[40] Ibrar Ahmad and Jamil Afzal, "Human Rights Approach for Climate Justice–Verein Klimaseniorinnen Schweiz and Others v. Switzerland," *Studies in Social Justice* 19, no. 1 (2025): 163–70.

[41] Zhao Xu et al., "Availability and Access to Livelihood Capital Assets for Development of Sustainable Livelihood Strategies of Fishermen: A Case Study of Manchar Lake Pakistan," *Heliyon* 9, no. 12 (2023).

[42] Ifzal Ahmad and M. Rezaul Islam, "Empowerment and Participation: Key Strategies for Inclusive Development," in *Building Strong Communities: Ethical Approaches to Inclusive Development* (Emerald Publishing Limited, 2024).

[43] Jamil Afzal and Chen Yongmei, "Federal and Provincial Legislation Regarding 'Right to Information' for Good Governance in Pakistan," *Discover Global Society* 1, no. 1 (2023): 12.

conflicts, inefficiencies, and corruption, which can compromise the results of a project. Unified legal systems bring about clarity on duties, implementation of standard operating procedures, and ease in cross-border coordination.[44] Legal systems fostering transparency, accountability, and predictability increase collaboration between governments and investors as well as communities. Another important dimension that is seriously dealt with by the legal development is financial integrity. The hyper-investment in infrastructure, energy, and digital technologies implies a significant financial stream that can be easily mismanaged or indulged in acts of malpractice. Financial reporting, auditing, anti-corruption, and responsible investment are some of the mechanisms of law that help in ensuring resources are used efficiently. Sustainable finance regulations embark on the implementation of environmental and socially responsible investment practices, which guide capital to invest in projects that facilitate low-carbon infrastructure, renewable energy, and sustainable development goals.[45] The whole legal framework of BRI projects is emphasized by the introduction of digital technologies into it. The digital systems facilitate logistics, energy management, environmental monitoring, and data-driven decision making. Most BRI projects include collaboration with international financial experts, development agencies, and multinational corporations, all of which comply with the environment, social, and governance standards. These standards in the legal systems enhance project credibility, attract sustainable investment, and mitigate environmental and social risks.

4 Green Investment Principles (GIP)

The Green Investment Principle (GIP) is a systematic roadmap for promoting investments that are environmentally friendly. It encourages the financial institutions and investors to invest in low-carbon, resource-efficient, and climate-resilient projects to ensure economic growth.[46] The GIP was co-developed by the Green Finance Committee of the Chinese Society of Finance and Banking and the Green Finance Initiative of the Corporation of the City of London that demonstrates a collaborative approach of the Chinese and international stakeholders.[47] Other players and multi-lateral support networks with regard to integrating environmental concerns in investment practices are the Principles for Responsible Investment (PRI), the Belt and Road Bankers Roundtable, the Green Belt and Road Investors Alliance, the

[44] Emmanuel Guillermo Carreño Bernal, "Harmonization of Cross-Border Contract Law: Legal Solutions in a Globalized World," *Journal of Policy and Society* 2, no. 2 (2024).

[45] Raghu Raman et al., "Innovations and Barriers in Sustainable and Green Finance for Advancing Sustainable Development Goals," *Frontiers in Environmental Science* 12 (2025): 1513204.

[46] Wenting Cheng, "The Green Investment Principles: From a Nodal Governance Perspective," *International Environmental Agreements: Politics, Law and Economics* 23, no. 3 (2023): 373–93.

[47] Christoph Nedopil, "Green Finance for Soft Power: An Analysis of China's Green Policy Signals and Investments in the Belt and Road Initiative," *Environmental Policy and Governance* 32, no. 2 (2022): 85–97.

World Economic Forum (WEF), and the Paulson Institute. The principles were first introduced in London in November 2018. GIP received foreign intervention soon after it was introduced. By the date of signing the framework, April 25, 2019, 27 financial institutions had signed the framework. As of June 2021, 39 signatories and 11 supporting organizations in 14 countries and regions had joined, which means that the interest in environmentally responsible investment along the BRI is quite extensive.

Principle 1: Embedding Sustainability into Corporate Governance
The establishment of a new standard of institutional control, the environmental, social, and governance (ESG) factors, will ensure that sustainability is inculcated in the very material of the company's approach. Organizations in the modern world are actively incorporating these metrics in their risk management and day-to-day decision-making processes, rather than treating them as a post hoc problem. This transition enables the leadership to foresee the effects of climate changes or social changes before they strike the balance sheet, designing a new business model in which the long-term stability is more valued than short-term profits. This transformation to open governance is the layer of trust in the DSR, because it will engage Digital Financial Inclusion and Fintech Innovations in BRI Economies. The success of these digital bridges is not only due to the high-speed cables but also to shared ethics, since the digital networks of such massive proportions are to be deployed in Central Asia and Africa. By embracing such patterns of governance, they create a safe pathway for investment through which the local startups and small businesses can prove to be trustworthy to the international markets. This will ensure that the DSR is not a data road only, but a holistic ecosystem where all the stakeholders collaborate to create a modernized and verifiable system of sustainability guidelines.

Principle 2: Understanding Environmental, Social, and Governance Risks
Principle 2 of GIP focuses on the need to identify, appraise, and control Environmental, Social, and Governance (ESG) risks on a systematic basis across the life cycle of projects. This concept acknowledges the idea that investment choices should transcend economic gain to encompass the overall effect of initiatives on ecosystems, communities, and institutional governance frameworks. When it comes to the environmental sphere, risk assessment includes the investigation of possible sources of pollution, resource depletion, and greenhouse gas emissions, and the assessment of the project's susceptibility to climate change. The investors are asked to think about the way in which the projects can lead to the degradation of the environment or how the natural hazards can reduce the sustainability of the projects in the long run. Risk assessment should be done properly to make sure that the project is designed and operated to incorporate the measures in terms of emission control, introduction of renewable energy, and sustainable use of resources. Social risk assessment concentrates on the effects that projects may have on the local communities and stakeholders. These involve the assessment of livelihood, health, social equity, labor standards, and community involvement effects.

Environmental impact assessment (EIA), social impact assessment (SIA), and environmental reporting mechanisms can be used to facilitate good monitoring and alleviation of risks. Through the emphasis on ESG risk management, BRI investors and institutions can be able to ensure that their projects provide sustainable development results, reduce the negative externalities, and generate long-term value to both stakeholders and the environment. This strategy also enhances adherence to the overall goals of the Green Investment Principles, which support responsible and resilient investment practices in the BRI region.

Principle 3: Disclosing Environmental Information
The open disclosure of environmental data means that the ecological footprint of any company is no longer an imponderable phenomenon, which gives a provable benchmark on corporate responsibility. Those organisations that declare energy consumption, Greenhouse Gas (GHG) emissions, and the production of individual pollutants in a structured manner go beyond the misty sustainability statements, into hard, data-rich disclosure. Through matching such disclosures with the internationally applied standards, including the Task Force on Climate-related Financial Disclosures (TCFD), cross-border comparisons on performance can also be made by investors and regulators using the internationally consistent green balance sheet. The companies are pushed into the reporting process by this kind of mechanical treatment, which makes them internalize the costs of their environmental impact and turns the raw data into a strategic resource for risk mitigation and resource efficiency. These reporting standards will be included in DSR and will be a high-trust environment that will underlie Digital Financial Inclusion and Fintech Innovations in BRI Economies.

Principle 4: Enhancing Communication with Stakeholders
The fourth principle of the Green Investment Principles (GIP) highlights that all interested stakeholders must actively be involved in the operations. This principle is based on the necessity of regular communication with the governments, local communities, NGOs, and other stakeholders to justify socially responsible and environmentally sustainable investment. Stakeholder engagement involves the establishment of organized channels of communication where issues, expectations, and feedback can be managed within the lifecycle of the project. This may be in the form of open consultations, local meetings, and joint workshops in the planning, implementation, and operational stages of the project. This sort of interaction enables investors to comprehend social, cultural, and environmental backgrounds and modify strategies to eliminate risks and negative effects. Formation of dispute resolution mechanisms is one of the primary components of this principle. They may be grievance redress systems, a mediation platform, or digital reporting whereby the stakeholders may report a conflict or issue to the project managers or regulators. The adoption of these systems guarantees the timely resolution of issues to avoid their growth and the delays of the project.

Principle 5: Utilizing Green Financial Instruments
Principle 5 of GIP focuses on the strategic application of green financial instruments to direct investments to sustainable infrastructure and environmentally responsible

projects. This principle recognizes that the traditional sources of funding might not be sufficient to fund the capital requirements of low-carbon, resource-efficient, and climate-resilient development. By issuing green bonds, green funds, and other special instruments, investors can transform financial flows in accordance with the sustainability targets in order to be able to control environmental risks. Green bonds are simply debt securities that are issued to fund capital with only positive environmental projects, i.e., renewable energy plants, energy-efficient buildings, sustainable transport systems, and pollution reduction projects. Individuals who invest in green bonds are assured of fixed income, and at the same time, the capital is invested in environmentally friendly purposes. They are accountable and provide confidence to the accountable parties because they provide transparency by reporting requirements to track the environmental performance of the funded projects.

The other way in which the application of green financial instruments in the concept of BRI has supported the cross-border cooperation is the fact that an international investor can be incorporated in the funding of infrastructure projects without undermining the attainment of the international environmental standards. The issuance, monitoring, and evaluation of these instruments are governed by the regulatory frameworks and standardized reporting under the GIP, which ensures that investments are significant towards the Sustainable Development Goals. By using green financial instruments in the project finance process, BRI investors can raise capital most efficiently, lower the environmental risks, and finance the large-scale sustainable infrastructure projects that will also contribute to the development of low-carbon economies.

Principle 6: Adopting Green Supply Chain Management

Green Investment Principles principle 6 is concerned with the introduction of sustainable practices across the entire supply chain. It persuades the investors, the developers, and contractors to take into consideration the environmental aspects in the procurement, production, logistics, and delivery processes so as to align the entire supply chain with environmental sustainability. Green supply chain management will be adopted, starting with the selection and assessment of suppliers. Corporations are being motivated to focus on the suppliers that adhere to the environmentally responsible measures that include minimization of waste, minimization of emissions, utilization of renewable energy, or sources of raw material in friendly forms. The criteria of the environmental performance can be put in the contract, because such partners will comply with the accepted green standards and certifications. BRI projects will also make sure that not only the individual company is taking care of the environment, but the entire system of suppliers and contractors.

Principle 7: Building Capacity through Collective Action

The 7th principle of the GIP is that governments, financial institutions, investors, and other stakeholders must collaborate to improve expertise and capacity in sustainable and green investment. This principle underlines the fact that capacity building is not an isolated task, but it is more effective when the actors are collaborating in an effort to exchange knowledge, best practices, and develop human capital to support the projects that are eco-friendly. Knowledge sharing is one of the main elements of this principle. It is also recommended that international forums, workshops, and working groups be organized where international experience on different regions and sectors is exchanged by the institutions and investors. The members will be in a position to adopt new financial structures, risk analysis techniques, and sustainable project design techniques that suit their home markets through the experience of successful green investment. International collaboration is also helpful in harmonizing standards and regulatory practices among the BRI economies. Through multilateral platforms, institutions will be able to embrace similar ESG requirements, reporting systems, and green finance models. The convergence assists in reducing fragmentation, encourages cross-border investment, and ensures that sustainable projects are comparable across jurisdictions.

5 Policy and Regulatory Support for Green Finance

BRI projects usually entail cross-border investment, necessitating uniform standards of the environment and financial aspects in the participating countries.[48] The adherence to international standards of the Green Bond Principles, the Climate Bonds Initiative, and the United Nations Sustainable Development Goals is a source of information regarding the best practices and reporting and verification of rules. Most central banks within BRI economies have formulated principles of green lending, whereby banks are supposed to set aside a given percentage of credit to be issued to projects (environmentally friendly) only. The prudential regulations are modified in order to appreciate green investment on a long-term basis, whereby the banks are able to consider both environmental and financial gains. Proponents of green projects are offering incentives to the private sector by way of reduced capital requirements, preferential interest rates, and risk-sharing mechanisms. These steps provide positive environments for the growth of green finance in various fields. Green finance is enhanced when there is international collaboration and standardization.

One of the important ways of implementing the policies of green finance is through public–private partnerships. Governments give regulatory advice, incentives, and partial funding, whereas the private ventures make up the investment capital, technical expertise, and project management skills. The establishment of renewable energy projects, energy-efficient infrastructures, and sustainable industrial practices is also implemented with the help of partnerships between the public financial institutions, commercial banks, and multinational companies, as well as local enterprises. The joint efforts of public and private stakeholders would make sure that the green finance initiatives not only meet the economic goals and targets but also attain the environmental goals and targets at a minimal risk and maximum

[48] Yaolin Zhang, "Developing Cross-Border Blockchain Financial Transactions under the Belt and Road Initiative," *The Chinese Journal of Comparative Law* 8, no. 1 (2020): 143–76.

social impact. Stakeholders can evaluate the outcomes of projects through regulatory disclosure requirements on environmental performance, financial impact, and adherence to ESG standards. External checking and auditing make it credible and improve investor confidence. Constant monitoring and assessment help policymakers to amend rules, perfect policies, and identify areas that should be improved.

5.1 Top-Level Guidance

The Opinions on Promoting the Green Development of the Belt and Road and the Guidance on Promoting Investment and Financing to Address Climate Change (2020) are some of the initial legal tools that define that China is determined to integrate environmental sustainability and digital governance into the Silk Road system.[49,50,51] These guidance documents are not just the financial guidelines, but they are the legal and regulatory foundations to attaining sustainable digital-green development in the BRI participating countries. The 2020 guidance documents give financial institutions binding environmental expectations, which are mandatory in nature as opposed to voluntary recommendations. These are the policies that expressly prioritize the mainstream of green development principles in all five connectivity pillars of the BRI: policy coordination, infrastructure connectivity, free trade, financial integration, and people-to-people connections. The financial institutions are required to enhance environmental and social risk management, undertake stringent environmental impact assessment of overseas projects, and include environmental protection in the investment decision-making process. This legal basis solves a very important problem: the majority of BRI countries possess different environmental management capabilities and regulations, and by defining the Chinese environmental standards as the benchmark, such pieces of guidance can encourage legal harmonization along the Silk Road Economic Belt and the 21st Century Maritime Silk Road.

Another peculiarity of the Chinese green BRI strategy is the combination of digital technologies with legal compliance systems.[52,53] The guidance documents openly encourage the development of the Belt and Road Ecological Big Data Service Platform and digital environmental monitoring systems. The element of the digital

49 Cheng Cuiyun and Ge Chazhong, "Green Development Assessment for Countries along the Belt and Road," *Journal of Environmental Management* 263 (2020): 110344.

50 Govinda R. Timilsina, "Financing Climate Change Adaptation: International Initiatives," *Sustainability* 13, no. 12 (2021): 6515.

51 Kevin Hernandez, *Achieving Complex Development Goals along China's Digital Silk Road*, 2019.

52 Xiaoping Wu and Muhammad Bilawal Khaskheli, "Systems Thinking of Marine Policies in Promoting Environmental Law, Sustainability, and Digital Technologies: Social Challenges in Belt and Road Initiative Countries," *Systems* 12, no. 10 (2024): 400.

53 Jamil Afzal and Ibrar Ahmad, "The ITLOS Advisory Opinion on Climate Change and Marine Pollution: Some Reflections," *Environmental Policy and Law* 55, nos. 2–3 (2025): 68–75.

economy helps the legal sustainability directly, as it establishes transparent and traceable environmental compliance systems. Financial institutions and enterprises can prove compliance with environmental regulations in real-time with the help of digital signatures, e-contracts, and blockchain-based verification systems. One of the most important innovations of the 2020 guidance is the connection between financial accessibility and legal compliance. The documents urge financial institutions to implement stringent environmental screening policies and incorporate Environmental, Social, and Governance (ESG) concepts in lending policies. This makes a great incentive scheme: the projects that comply with the green standards of China and international environmental regulations will receive preferential funding in the form of green bonds and sustainable investment vehicles. The guidance defines various levels of legal tools, such as soft law through voluntary green finance principles and industry standards, contractual requirements in bilateral investment treaties (BITs) and multilateral environmental agreements (MEAs), and regulatory frameworks that operationalize the environmental impact assessment and mitigation requirements. These 2020 guidance documents are the operationalization of the vision of a "Green Silk Road" as part of the broader context of the Silk Road Initiative.

5.2 Green Development Guidance for Projects

The key institutional organization that has been established to create an overall green development guidance to BRI projects on the Silk Road Economic Belt and the 21st Century Maritime Silk Road is the BRI International Green Development Coalition (BRIGC), which was initiated in April 2019 as one of the key deliverables of the Second Belt and Road Forum.[54] The Coalition unites the environmental experience of several partners to make sure that the Belt and Road can create long-term, environmentally friendly development in favor of the 2030 Agenda of Sustainable Development, entrenching the ecological civilization of Xi Jinping at the core of the modern Silk Road. By December 2021, 152 partners were part of the Coalition, including 26 environmental ministries of United Nations Member States and other United Nations bodies and agencies such as the United Nations Environment Programme and the United Nations Industrial Development Organization, demonstrating a very global approach to greening this flagship development undertaken by China.[55,56] The BRIGC is an open, inclusive, and voluntary global network, to which sustainable development and especially environmental sustainability are applied in the five priorities of the Belt and Road Initiative: policy coordination, facilities connectivity, unimpeded trade, financial integration, and people-to-people

---

[54] MEE China, *BRI International Green Development Coalition (BRIGC)*, 2020.

[55] North Africa, "Other United Nations Bodies," *Organization*, 2020.

[56] Swati Prabhu, *European Union's Connectivity Agenda: Forging Partnerships for Environmental Governance* (Springer, 2025).

bonds, thus making sure that the environmental considerations permeate all levels of Silk Road connection and cooperation.

One of the most important accomplishments of the BRIGC work is the creation of the Green Development Guidance of the BRI projects, which was initially presented in the form of a baseline study report in 2020, and which presupposes a complete reorganization of the conceptualization and regulation of development projects along the Silk Road. The proposed guidance framework suggests a new system of classification called the "traffic light system," according to which the projects are classified into a positive and negative list according to their environmental performance. The framework is a twist to the conventional environmental assessment approaches because it explicitly applies development aspects in addition to ecological standards, rendering it more culturally and economically relatable to BRI participating countries spanning Central Asia, East Africa, and Southeast Asia.

The green development assessment framework is also significantly strengthened by the development of various digital tools that will contribute to better access and operational performance in the large geographical scope of the Silk Road Initiative. Such tools are the Whole Process Green Assessment Framework of BRI Projects, the Environmental Risk Screening Tool (ERST), the Climate and Environment Risk Assessment Toolbox (CERAT), and the Belt and Road Ecological Big Data Service Platform, which are all embodiments of digital governance operation in the green digital economy vision of the Silk Road.[57,58] These online tools have ensured that the BRI overseas investment accessibility on environmental and climate risk and impact assessment is significantly increased, and at the same time, advance the management efficiency and operability.

5.3 Regulatory Focus

The legal framework that regulates environmental protection in the Belt and Road is basically based on the collaboration of various Chinese state authorities that collaborate to create uniform implementation of strict environmental regulations for Silk Road projects. The institutional implementation body to convert high-level green development commitments into operational requirements to bind Chinese financial institutions and enterprises that conduct investments along the Silk Road Economic Belt and the 21st Century Maritime Silk Road include the People's Bank of China (PBOC), the Ministry of Ecology and Environment (MEE), and the National Financial Regulatory Administration (NFRA). These regulatory authorities have come up with several departmental normative documents that direct the financial institutions

[57] Taoan Ge, "A Conceptual Framework for Assessing Social and Environmental Impacts of Belt and Road Initiative and Just Energy Transition," *Frontiers in Sustainable Food Systems* 6 (2022): 982086.

[58] A. Gialletti et al., *Climate Risk Toolbox: Guiding Material for Climate Risk Screening* (Food & Agriculture Org., 2025).

in enabling low-carbon development and climate mitigation of BRI countries, whilst also avoiding and addressing climate risks. Through the development of such regulatory frameworks, the Chinese authorities have developed a multi-layered regulatory framework, providing that environmental protection is not reliant upon the voluntary corporate compliance but is, in fact, instilled within the mandatory regulatory requirements that financial institutions must comply with to sustain their operating license and regulatory status.

One of the pillars of this regulatory strategy is the fact that Chinese companies and financial institutions that engage in BRI projects are required to rigorously follow the host country environmental laws and regulations and at the same time, they are also encouraged to take the higher international environmental standards or the more stringent environmental standards by China where these standards are higher than those of the host country. This dual-standard solution solves a serious governance issue: although the weaker environmental regulating structures of many developing countries along the Silk Road than Chinese or international best practices, the unilateral imposition of Chinese standards may be seen as meddling with the sovereignty of the host country or as creating competition disadvantages to local host country enterprises. The regulatory framework, by setting up a hierarchy that gives host country law primacy but fosters voluntary adoption of higher standards, will generate incentive structures that would foster the achievement of environmental excellence without compromising the principle of non-interference that defines the approach of China to development cooperation. The PBOC has been more prolific in this regard, publishing the Guidelines on Green Credit and instituting the Statistical System of Green Credit, which lists eleven categories of green industry and expressly specifies that overseas projects that are adopting international practices or international standards should be treated under the classification of green credit. This regulatory framework directly relates desirable financing terms, such as access to green bonds and preferential interest rates, to proven adherence to either international or stringent local environmental standards, which form strong economic incentives to Chinese enterprises to perform better than minimum environmental standards.

5.4 Regional Growth

One of the most influential changes in the process of establishing a sustainable legal framework in the course of the Silk Road Initiative is the spread of green finance regulations throughout the countries of the Belt and Road. By 2019, more than 30 countries taking part in the Belt and Road Initiative had implemented green finance policies, which reflects a drastic pace of institutionalization of the environmental financial regulation throughout the Silk Road Economic Belt and the 21st Century

Maritime Silk Road.[59,60] This accelerated regionalization is an indication of the significant impact that the green finance system in China has had on the involved countries, developing a demonstration effect in which countries along the Silk Road will note the dedication of China towards green development and increasingly adjust their own financial regulatory frameworks to similar levels of environmental conservation. The pace and scope of this regulatory implementation are impressive considering the diversity of BRI members, as they are comprised of lower-middle-income countries with immature financial systems and middle-income economies with well-developed capital markets, indicating that green finance frameworks are flexible enough to support different degrees of financial sophistication without conflicting with their environmental goals. This regionalized green financing drive is a paradigm shift of development finance along the Silk Road from a paradigm where environmental concerns are central to the financial decision-making process to one where ecological sustainability is the core of the very fabric of development finance.

The green finance market in China has become the leading force that has triggered this convergence in the region, and the level of green finance in China and its trends in 2023–2024 prove both the maturity of domestic systems and their expansion into the Belt and Road environment. China has established one of the most extensive green finance networks in the world, including green bonds, green credit, green insurance, and green funds, with advanced policies enabling the system, including directives of the central bank, financial regulators, and integrated implementation systems throughout the various governmental agencies.[61,62] The magnitude of the green finance market in China has been increasing exponentially, with green bonds issued by Chinese companies amounting to large sums that put China high in the ranks of sustainable finance innovation globally. Most importantly, this domestic Chinese green finance infrastructure has facilitated Chinese financial institutions to act as the conduit channeling green finance principles and practices to BRI countries, as more Chinese banks and insurance companies in foreign countries are implementing domestic green finance principles and standards in their BRI project portfolios. Playing a key role in this process have been the Industrial and Commercial Bank of China (ICBC) as well as other large Chinese banks, which have issued green bonds specifically allocated to Belt and Road projects and have also put in place green credit assessment frameworks on overseas investments. Through its positioning as the leader of green finance in the region, China has successfully set itself as a normative setpoint on what it means to have appropriate green financial governance, which in turn has affected the formation of policies in the Silk Road network.

---

[59] Jasmine Siu Lee Lam et al., "The 21st-Century Maritime Silk Road: Challenges and Opportunities for Transport Management and Practice," *Transport Reviews* 38, no. 4 (2018): 413–15.

[60] Fanny M. Cheung and Ying-yi Hong, *Green Finance, Sustainable Development and the Belt and Road Initiative* (Routledge London, 2021).

[61] Green Finance Task Force, "Establishing China's Green Financial System," *People's Bank of China & United Nations Environment Programme: Beijing, China*, 2015.

[62] Lin Lin and Yanrong Hong, "Developing a Green Bonds Market: Lessons from China," *European Business Organization Law Review* 23, no. 1 (2022): 143–85.

The facilitative role of China has been supplemented and enhanced by the international financial institutions working within the Belt and Road framework by creating multilateral coordination mechanisms of green finance. In 2018, major Chinese, French, Hong Kong, Pakistani, Singaporean, the United Arab Emirates, and the United Kingdom financial institutions, together with the United Kingdom, released the Belt and Road Initiative Green Finance Index.[63,64] The index is a benchmarking tool, which enables BRI countries to evaluate how their progress in green finance has been compared against others, which provides competitive pressure to countries to develop their systems of green finance regulation to enhance their index scores. Equally, Green Investment Principles of Belt and Road Development, which were signed by 27 financial institutions in the Second BRI Forum in April 2019, pledged binding obligations to incorporate sustainability in corporate governance, comprehend environmental and social governance risks, and apply green financial instruments.[65] Such multilateral mechanisms have made green finance not only a bilateral issue between China and each of the host countries but a regionalized network of entrapments, standards, and accountability systems that together contribute to green development along the Silk Road. The integration of various financial institutions, such as the Asian Infrastructure Investment Bank, the New Development Bank, and other regional development banks, has ensured that principles of green finance are enforced uniformly across various investment channels to avoid regulatory arbitrage and to provide consistent environmental expectations of businesses operating along Silk Roads.

6 International Initiatives and Partnerships of the Green Digital Economy

6.1 Green Digital Action Hub (GDA Hub)

The Green Digital Action Hub (GDA Hub), declared at COP30 in 2025 with headquarters in Brazil, is a major shift in the international governance regimes of sustainable development by establishing a specific space of global scaling of green digital

[63] Donald J. Lewis et al., "Dynamic Synergies between China's Belt and Road Initiative and the UN's Sustainable Development Goals," *Journal of International Business Policy* 4, no. 1 (2021): 58.

[64] Jennifer A. Hillman et al., *China's Belt and Road: Implications for the United States* (Council on Foreign Relations New York, 2021).

[65] China Council for International Cooperation on Environment and Development (CCICED) Secretariat, "Enhancing Environmental Management for BRI Projects to Boost Green BRI and 2030 Agenda for Sustainable Development," in *Green Recovery with Resilience and High Quality Development: CCICED Annual Policy Report 2021* (Springer, 2023).

technologies.[66] The GDA Hub is based on the COP29 Declaration on Green Digital Action that was signed by 82 states and creates a binding obligation to ensure digital transformation is in line with climate goals and environmental sustainability ambitions.[67] This multilateral program is to contribute to the acceleration of green technology and the environmental footprint of technology production, deployment, and operation because the digital economy is currently expanding rapidly and has already posed new environmental challenges, as well as the ability to find solutions. The founding of the GDA Hub is an indication of the increasing global understanding that climate action and digital transformation should be combined and not be pursued as two areas of policy, a value that has gained more and more centrality in the climate frameworks of the United Nations and national development policies.

The creation of the GDA Hub in Brazil, a nation with high potential renewable energy resources and a future leader in sustainable development, has a certain symbolic and strategic importance in the development of the Silk Road Initiative. As the Belt and Road Initiative is no longer caught in the early phase of infrastructure construction and enters a new stage of development with a new focus on green and digital collaboration, the advent of platforms such as the GDA Hub opens the possibility of aligning the regional structure of the Silk Road with the global systems of governance in sustainable development. Countries participating in the COP29 discussions led by China and Belt and Road have actively taken part in the COP29 deliberations that resulted in the Green Digital Action declaration, positioning the GDA Hub not as an independent or competing framework but as an amplifier and an extension of the green and digital promises of the Silk Road itself. The 2023 publication of the BRI 10-year vision and action plan, which made it clear that green development and digital cooperation were the main priorities of the next decade of Belt and Road work, has established a compatibility between the strategic priorities of the Silk Road and the goals of the GDA Hub.[68,69]

[66] Lilian Eldin, *Digital Capacity Building for Climate Empowerment: Evaluating Post-COP29 Implementation and Gaps in ACE Delivery*, 2025.

[67] Aynur Sadikhzada and Sarvar Gurbanov, "Closing the Climate Finance Gap: Strategies and Recommendations in the Context of COP29," *Available at SSRN 5255829*, 2025.

[68] Jing Gu, "Building Partnerships for Sustainable Development: Case Study of Laos, the BRI, and the SDGs," *Asian Review of Political Economy* 3, no. 1 (2024): 5.

[69] Vanxay Sayavong, "Chinese Belt and Road Initiative (BRI) and the Sustainable Development in Lao PDR," in *Belt and Road Initiative and South Asia* (Routledge, 2023).

6.2 International Telecommunication Union (ITU)—Green Digital Action

The specialized agency of the United Nations on information and communication technologies, the International Telecommunication Union (ITU), plays a central institutional role in ensuring that global efforts are coordinated to ensure that the development of digital technology is aligned with the Sustainable Development Goals.[70] The ITU, as a UN agency with 193 member states, represents governments, private sector institutions, and academic institutions, and takes the lead in multistakeholder initiatives that bring together both technology organizations and governments, as well as civil society actors, to fast-track the convergence of digital technologies and sustainable development goals. The Green Digital Action initiative by the ITU acknowledges the inseparable nature of the growth of digital infrastructure and ecological sustainability, and it is established that the unprecedented pace of the spread of information and communication technologies (ICTs) across the global economy should be planned in terms of reducing environmental footprints and maximizing beneficial effects on climate mitigation and sustainable development.

The Green Digital Action of the ITU is a complex of dimensions of sustainable digital transformation that can be directly applied to the context of Belt and Road development.[71] ITU determines environmental performance criteria of telecommunications infrastructure, such as data centers, mobile networks, and satellite networks, such that the digital infrastructure on which economic activity relies is used to its full energy efficiency and as much as possible with renewable energy sources. These technical standards respond to a fundamental issue in the Silk Road situation: as the Digital Silk Road becomes a ubiquitous telecommunications network across Asia, Africa, and other parts of the world, the aggregate energy use of the digital infrastructure may be a major contributor to national carbon footprint unless consciously designed with sustainability requirements. The ITU facilitates the transfer of technology and capacity building in the management of digital infrastructures, which means that developing countries along the Silk Road can prevent technological lock-in to outdated or energy-intensive telecommunications infrastructure but move directly to the state-of-the-art green digital infrastructure through the project design.

The factual implementation of Green Digital Action by ITU is especially noteworthy to the countries of the Silk Road that engage in the deployment of digital infrastructure projects. The technical standards of ITU on secure internet servers, network efficiency, and data center sustainability have a direct impact on how countries build their digital infrastructure. The number of secure internet servers, according to the Silk Road e-commerce cooperation initiative, is used as a proxy measure of the level of digital infrastructure development, and the ITU offers the international standards framework through which these critical infrastructure elements

[70] Ileana Citaristi, "International Telecommunication Union—Itu," in *The Europa Directory of International Organizations 2022* (Routledge, 2022).

[71] Sen Gong et al., *The Impact of the Belt and Road Initiative Investment in Digital Connectivity and Information and Communication Technologies on Achieving the SDGs*, 2019.

are implemented. In establishing that nations must focus on green data center design, renewable energy, and network optimization, the ITU will make sure that, as BRI countries grow their digital infrastructure to accommodate e-commerce, smart cities, and digital finance projects, they do so in an environmental sustainability paradigm and not in a high-carbon digital infrastructure that would need to be retrofitted or replaced in the future.

6.3 European Green Digital Coalition (EGDC)

The European Green Digital Coalition (EGDC) is an important initiative within the European Union supported by the European Commission for accelerating green digital innovation in Europe.[72] The EGDC acts as a multi-stakeholder commitment mechanism where businesses, research institutions, and civil society organizations make formal commitments to develop and deploy green digital solutions to lower emissions from energy-intensive industries such as energy generation and distribution, transportation infrastructure, and construction. The EGDC embodies the EU's commitment to sustainability, as established in the European Green Deal and the "Fit for 55" package, by formalizing the use of digital innovation in achieving Europe's broader sustainability goals through individual corporate actions and technological advances at the sector level.[73] The EGDC provides a de facto design option to mobilize private sector innovativeness toward achieving climate goals through frameworks for transparent commitments, technical support for implementation, and creating market demand signals that reward companies that create green digital products. As a coalition based on cooperation and collaboration, the structure of the EGDC recognizes the necessity of cooperation among many various participants with varying levels of ability, incentive, or constraint in order to reduce emissions across the complex economic sectors in which they operate.

The Silk Road, while providing a framework for cooperative agreement for regional development and infrastructure connection from China to Africa and then into the EU, is comparable in its intent to the European Union's Global Gateway and the European Green Digital Coalition (EGDC) initiatives that describe a European institutional approach to sustainable infrastructure development and to the development of green technologies. The European Commission has framed the Global Gateway as a response to the Belt and Road Initiative (BRI) and has made it clear that any infrastructure projects funded by the EU will adhere to democratic principles, good governance, environmental sustainability, and strong labor standards. In contrast, the EU believes/Belt and Road Initiative places much less emphasis on these

[72] Bettina Bahn-Walkowiak et al., *Eco-Innovation and Digitalisation: Case Studies, Environmental and Policy Lessons from EU Member States for the EU Green Deal and the Circular Economy: EIO Biennial Report 2020*, 2021.

[73] Sebastian Oberthür and Kati Kulovesi, "Accelerating the EU's Climate Transformation: The European Green Deal's Fit for 55 Package Unpacked," *Review of European, Comparative & International Environmental Law* 34, no. 1 (2025): 7–22.

values and much more on how quickly and how much financial support is provided. The EGDC and Silk Road are not viewed in opposition to each other nor in competition but represent opportunities for complementary interests and synergies created by the ongoing development of global green digital transformation initiatives: The Technical Standards and Models of Green Innovation, developed by EGDC Members, can be scaled up and implemented through the Silk Road; In turn, financial resources of the Silk Road can assist EGDC member companies with their expansion into emerging markets.

6.4 OECD—Inclusive, Green and Digital Transformation

As a leading global organization that establishes the economic co-operators within the United States of America and other developed/developing nations, the Organisation for Economic Co-operation and Development (OECD) sets out to define the policy standards as they relate to green innovation, green governance, and green best practices around the world and as part of its contribution to Sustainable Development beyond 2022. The OECD's principal role in the provision of global green digital governance is to create a policy framework that defines the parameters by which individual nations can create standards for green technology and adopt AI/ digital solutions that are environmentally sustainable to solve the global environmental challenge of the enormous environmental impact of the digital infrastructure and tools that form the basis of the global economy. The OECD understands that as Digital Infrastructure continues to expand due to the development of the Silk Road and other economic development programs in various parts of the world, there is a growing energy demand. Therefore, environmental sustainability includes both: (a) Utilising digital technology to solve sustainability challenges; (b) Redesigning digital technologies from a fundamental standpoint to reduce their overall impact on the environment. The OECD's work on standardisation is important for the Silk Road Initiative because it gives BRI countries and Chinese businesses the tools, they need to make sure that Digital Silk Road infrastructure projects meet internationally recognised green technology standards.

6.5 Global Green Growth Institute (GGGI)

Global Green Growth Institute (GGGI) takes a unique institutional role in the global green development governance.[74] As a multilateral international institution with membership across developed economies, emerging markets, and developing

[74] Jill Kosch O'Donnell, "The Global Green Growth Institute: On a Mission to Prove Green Growth," *New York: Council of Foreign Relations*, 2012.

countries, by using the policy frameworks and technical standards of the organizations to provide practical, country-level implementation assistance that allows countries to adopt and implement green digital strategies. The GGGI has its mandate towards promoting inclusive green growth, economic development that is not only expanding economies, but also creating jobs and ensuring environmental integrity, and also providing technical assistance, capacity building, knowledge sharing, and institutional strengthening in partner countries.

The fact that GGGI supports the adoption of green digital strategies in the Silk Road countries specifically targets the implementation gaps that would hinder the conversion of the commitment of BRI to green development into tangible project results. Although the Belt and Road Initiative has released detailed green development frameworks and pledged to factor in environmental sustainability in all BRI projects, the effectiveness of these promises is hampered because many countries involved in this initiative do not have the institutional capacity, technical skills, and policy frameworks to translate their promises into action. The GGGI bridges this capacity gap by engaging in direct partnership with governments of the Silk Road countries to come up with country-specific green digital strategies that are responsive to the economic structure of the country, its level of development, and its environmental challenges. As an illustration, GGGI technical assistance assists energy-dependent developing nations to develop strategies to incorporate renewable energy and smart grid technologies into infrastructure development; assists manufacturing-oriented nations to develop digital solutions to combat industrial waste and energy use; assists agricultural countries to implement digital solutions to develop climate-smart farming and resource efficiency. The GGGI also makes sure that the Silk Road countries can find a way to develop green digitally, which will not contradict their development needs, but instead strengthen them by adapting the green digital strategies to the country-specific situation.

6.6 ERIA Digital Innovation and Sustainable Economy Centre (E-DISC)

The Economic Research Institute of ASEAN and East Asia (ERIA) has developed the Digital Innovation and Sustainable Economy Centre (E-DISC) as a center for translating international frameworks of green digital governance and adapting them. ERIA itself was created to promote regional economic integration and collaboration in East Asia and specifically ASEAN as the institutional center around which wider East Asian cooperation is structured through mechanisms such as ASEAN Plus Three, the East Asia Summit, and the Regional Comprehensive Economic Partnership (RCEP). The strategic significance of ASEAN as a part of the Belt and Road Initiative and the world digital economy, in general, makes the creation and functional concentration of E-DISC of particular importance to comprehend how the international green digital governance architecture operates at the regional level.

The relation between the work of E-DISC and the Belt and Road Initiative is direct and multiple and is based on the fact that China is a large ERIA member and designer of the Silk Road, and in these areas, ERIA research and E-DISC policy recommendations directly affect the development of the Digital Silk Road cooperation design and implementation by China and ASEAN countries. It is specifically the Silk Road e-commerce cooperation initiative that has developed e-commerce cooperation frameworks between China and 36 BRI countries, with a specific focus on ASEAN, that have created platforms and mechanisms through which E-DISC research on sustainable and responsible adoption of digital e-commerce can be used to design and govern projects.[75] The China-ASEAN Information Harbor is a large-scale Digital Silk Road project that creates digital infrastructure and platforms that facilitate trade, investment, and economic collaboration between China and ASEAN, which offers a concrete implementation mechanism on which E-DISC policy recommendations about sustainable digital infrastructure can be implemented.[76,77] Moreover, China-ASEAN cooperation frameworks such as the bilateral forum, ASEAN Regional Forum, and East Asia Summit discourses of the digital economy and green development are increasingly bringing E-DISC research and recommendations into policy-making processes, establishing institutional channels through which E-DISC work enters Belt and Road digital development decision-making.

7 Legal Challenges to Achieving a Green Digital Economy

Through the legal and regulatory environment, technological and financial ability are the factors shaping the transition to a green digital economy across the BRI countries. The large-scale application of sustainable practices and digital innovation would need well-defined, harmonized, and enforceable legal frameworks. Nevertheless, various challenges appear because of the lack of uniformity in legal systems, inconsistent implementation, gaps in governance in the digital sphere, and dynamic regulatory demands. These issues may stall the progress, risk, and restrict the success of green digital projects. Among the main obstacles, one may single out the difference in environmental laws and regulations in BRI countries. Every nation has come up with specific legal provisions to govern environmental protection, the utilization of resources, and emission regulation. Some nations have strongly developed environmental laws that have strict enforcement measures, whereas others may either have weak laws or lack the capacity to enforce the laws. In certain BRI countries, digital finance regulations are under development, and the control systems might

[75] David Gordon and Meia Nouwens, *The Digital Silk Road: China's Technological Rise and the Geopolitics of Cyberspace* (Taylor & Francis, 2022).

[76] Hilmy Prilliadi, *Harnessing AI for ASEAN's Future: Governance, Adoption, and Sustainability under the DEFA* (2025).

[77] Zhou Taidong and Xue Qi, "The Digital Silk Road and Southeast Asian Countries," *The Fourth Industrial Revolution and the Future of Work: Implications for Asian Development Cooperation. Ed. by Anthea Mulakala. Sejong-Si: KDI School of Public Policy and Management*, 2020, 132–64.

be inadequate. This might lead to poor distribution of funds, greenwashing, or no proper monitoring, which undermines the credibility of green finance programs and puts off investor involvement. The coordination across borders is especially complicated in the case of the BRI. Large projects, such as infrastructure projects and digital projects, may feature various jurisdictions that have different legal and regulatory frameworks. It is challenging to harmonize environmental, financial, and technological regulations across borders because of the differences in political, economic and institutional aspects. Controversies can emerge on the issues of accountability on environmental impacts, sharing of information, and adherence to the standards of sustainability. In the absence of good legal provisions that will coordinate and solve disputes across borders, there is a likelihood of delays, higher costs, and lower sustainability results of the projects. Another influential barrier is the enforcement capacity. The lack of institutional capacity, training, and monitoring tools may hinder the effective implementation of those rules even when the countries have established environmental and digital regulations. Projects can be undertaken without meeting the standards required, or non-observation of violations can be ignored, as there are no inspection, reporting, and punishment systems. Enhancing the enforcement of regulations, developing the capacity of institutions, and incorporating digital surveillance can play a crucial role in maintaining adherence to sustainability goals.

8 Conclusion

Green digital projects realization shows how technology and finance could maintain sustainable urban development, industrial efficiency, and smart transport systems. The examples of practical uses of digital tools in the realization of environmental goals include such topics as renewable energy projects, smart city projects, and industrial digitalization. Through a mixture of monitoring technologies, predictive analytics, and automated systems, energy, water, waste, and emissions can be managed in real-time. Green digital initiatives mainly rely on legal and regulatory frameworks. Clear environmental regulations, information privacy, intellectual property, and digital finance policies provide the parameters, duties, and responsibilities needed to achieve sustainable development. Similarity in regulations among the member countries of BRI would promote transnational collaboration and minimize the contradictions and foster the realization of massive projects. Enhancing enforcement, filling digital governance gaps, and encouraging citizen involvement further encourage initiatives to have desirable environmental and social outcomes.

Chapter 9
Prospective Legal Framework for Digital Economy and Digital Trade

Abstract This chapter discusses the need and possibility of defining a shared legal framework of the digital economy and digital trade. This section examines the international law contribution to develop a consistent digital framework based on the existing global and regional agreements to determine the best practices and the legal principles to apply to the BRI context. It identifies the central elements of an ordinary legal framework, with data control, the support of digital trade, consumer protection, cybersecurity, and intellectual property. The findings of this chapter suggest creating a common system of digital dispute resolution that is provided by the BRI and facilitated by technology-supported processes, joint involvement of stakeholders, and a combination of mediation and negotiation procedures. It presents policy-based solutions on the alignment of national regulations, the creation of a BRI-specific digital trade deal, institutional capacity building, and technical support.

Keywords Common legal framework · Electronic transaction recognition · Data governance · Paperless trade · Technology neutrality · Online protection

1 Introduction

The world economy is experiencing a drastic overhaul that is being driven by digital technologies.[1] The international law presents significant benchmarks upon which digital legal frameworks is developed.[2] The concepts of electronic commerce, digital contracts, and dispute resolution have been added to institutions like the World Trade Organization (WTO), the United Nations Commission on International Trade Law

[1] Erik Brynjolfsson and Andrew McAfee, *Race against the Machine: How the Digital Revolution Is Accelerating Innovation, Driving Productivity, and Irreversibly Transforming Employment and the Economy* (Brynjolfsson and McAfee, 2011).

[2] Jamil Afzal, "Best Practice of Digital Laws and Digital Justice," in *Implementation of Digital Law as a Legal Tool in the Current Digital Era* (Springer, 2024).

J. Afzal and Y. Chen, *Legal Framework of Digital Economy and Digital Trade Under the Belt and Road Initiative*, https://doi.org/10.1007/978-981-92-4444-7_9

(UNCITRAL), and other regional trade agreements.[3,4] These global frameworks, however, tend not to have certain provisions that are specific to the varying economic and regulatory realities of BRI countries. Consequently, the necessity to have a BRI-specific approach, which will be based on the international norms but flexible enough to follow the national differences.

The other major problem in the digital economy is the solution of a digital trade dispute.[5] Conventional dispute resolution procedures are slow, expensive, and incompatible with the rapidly changing digital transaction.[6] Disagreements between jurisdictions, issues in enforcement, and a cross-border problem of online actions also contribute to the fact that resolving the issue of disputes online is a more complicated task.[7] This chapter attempts to explore the potential to establish a universal definition of law in the digital economy and the digital trade in the BRI. It discusses why such a framework is required, how international law can be used to design it, and what major elements it should contain. Establishing an international legal framework of digital economy/digital trade can be a measure that enforces economic integration, sustainable development, and the subsequent long-term success of the Belt and Road Initiative in the digital age.

[3] William F. Fox, *International Commercial Agreements and Electronic Commerce* (Kluwer Law International BV, 2018).

[4] Jie Zheng, *Online Resolution of E-Commerce Disputes* (Springer, 2020).

[5] Ahmed Arafa Abdelrehim Hammad et al., "Digital Economy Barriers to Trade Regulation Status, Challenges, and China's Response," *International Journal of Social Sciences Perspectives* 8, no. 2 (2021): 41–49.

[6] Bhupinder Singh, "Unleashing Alternative Dispute Resolution (ADR) in Resolving Complex Legal-Technical Issues Arising in Cyberspace Lensing e-Commerce and Intellectual Property: Proliferation of e-Commerce Digital Economy," *Revista Brasileira de Alternative Dispute Resolution-Brazilian Journal of Alternative Dispute Resolution-RBADR* 5, no. 10 (2023): 81–105.

[7] Amaresh Patel et al., "Online Dispute Resolution Mechanism as an Effective Tool for Resolving Cross-Border Consumer Disputes in the Era of e-Commerce," *International Journal of Law and Management*, 2025.

2 The Need for a Common Legal Framework

2.1 *Enhancing Legal Certainty and Reducing Complexity*

2.1.1 Harmonization of Rules

The companies that conduct cross-border digital transactions must simultaneously interpret and adhere to several legal regimes, which adds to the operational expenses of the business and subjects them to legal ambiguity.[8] Lack of uniform legal frameworks makes basic features of digital trade, such as the enforceability of electronic contracts, the recognition of digital signatures, and the cross-border validity of digital identities, more complicated.[9] These inconsistencies diminish the trust in online transactions and create challenges in the process of seamless integration of the global market. Another example of how legal standards should be harmonized is the introduction of interoperable digital payment systems and cross-border fintech platforms, since these technologies are based on the necessity to treat digital transactions and financial information in the same way.

The regulatory divergence may be especially problematic in the context of data governance.[10] Such jurisdictions are those that have strict policies on data localization in which the data must be located within the national boundaries, and there are those jurisdictions in which there is free movement of data with limited restrictions. Such a discrepancy compels multinational companies to build disjointed data management systems, which adds to expenses and lowers productivity. Big tech companies have reacted by setting up regionally specific data centers in order to meet the regulations of the specific regions, which is financially unaffordable to smaller businesses. Similarly, the difference in privacy legislation, e.g., stringent data protection legislation in one country, and relatively liberal frameworks in another, creates compliance imbalances, complicating cross-border business. The uncertainty in the law has an impact on investment decisions and the creation of the digital infrastructure as well.[11,12] Cross-border digital services are less likely to be invested in by the firms when the regulatory requirements are unclear or subject to change. Long-term investment in

---

[8] Anita Ama Sakumaa Yanney, "Cross-Border Financial Regulation and Its Influence on Multinational Business Operations, Tax Structures and Investment Flows," *World Journal of Advanced Research and Reviews* 26, no. 3 (2025): 597–620.

[9] Mohammad Saeed Abdallah ALsheyab, "Legal Analysis of the Merits of Electronic Transferable Records: Toward Cross-Border Trade Digitalization," *International Journal of Law and Management* 67, no. 1 (2025): 145–63.

[10] Douglas W. Arner et al., "The Transnational Data Governance Problem," *Berkeley Technology Law Journal* 37, no. 2 (2022): 623–700.

[11] Robert J. Kauffman et al., "Technology Investment Decision-Making under Uncertainty," *Information Technology and Management* 16, no. 2 (2015): 153–72.

[12] Manole Decebal Bogdan, "The Law of the Digital Economy a Reality for Legal Relations in the Future-New International Investment Protection," *International Investment Law Journal* 3, no. 2 (2023): 146–55.

cloud computing, digital logistics, and data-driven services will be encouraged by the availability of predictable and uniform legal regulations.

2.1.2 Electronic Transaction Recognition

As a precondition for the effective functioning of the digital economy, electronic transactions have been pointed out, particularly in the replacement of time-consuming and paper-based administrative operations with an efficient technology-based solution.[13] The electronic contracts, digital signatures, and trust services such as e-seals and e-invoicing systems are making cross-border trade reliant; however, due to the differences in the regulatory systems, not all are legally enforceable across jurisdictions.[14] The inconsistency creates doubts as to the enforceability of digital agreements, and in the vast majority of cases, it necessitates parallel paper documentation to digitalization, weakening the efficiencies of digitalization. By creating a common recognition of these electronic instruments, the transactions made in a particular jurisdiction can be recognized in another one and be legally enabled in that jurisdiction, thus avoiding these duplications and greatly lowering the administrative delays. Such recognition may be reflected in the convenience of trade operations, as viewed through real-life developments. Implementation of electronic invoicing systems in other economies has assisted in reducing the processing time, lessening human errors, and enhancing financial reporting transparency.

2.1.3 Predictability

Digital trade cannot operate effectively when the legal validity of its fundamental instruments is not clear across borders.[15] Digital signatures, electronic contracts, and trust services have emerged as the core of commercial transactions, but they are still not fully recognized, and businesses are compelled to use hybrid solutions to execute contracts electronically and validate them with paper-based documents. Such a two-tier system is inefficient and creates delays in the transaction process and recreates inefficiencies that digitalization is supposed to remove. Transborder legal recognition, therefore, is not a procedural change, but a structural change to enable all-digital trade environments.

---

[13] Oyebola Okunogbe and Fabrizio Santoro, "Increasing Tax Collection in African Countries: The Role of Information Technology," *Journal of African Economies* 32, no. Supplement_1 (2023): i57–83.

[14] Riham Mohamed Soliman, *Private Sector's Perceptions and Adoption of the e-Invoicing System in Egypt*, 2024.

[15] Usman Ahmed, "The Importance of Cross-Border Regulatory Cooperation in an Era of Digital Trade," *World Trade Review* 18, no. S1 (2019): S99–120.

2.2 *Facilitating Cross-Border Data Flows with Trust*

2.2.1 Data Governance

The ability to move the information between the countries without any loss is the main key to the further development of digital trade.[16] Data is not only the medium of exchange but the major financial asset that facilitates the functioning of the platform and the application of algorithms to make decisions.[17] Cross-border data transfer limits, particularly under tighter localization requirements, create structural inefficiencies by forcing businesses to support more infrastructure and to separate their data management systems. In the meantime, uncontrolled data transfer lacks control mechanisms, and it is about the privacy, security, and the misuse of valuable data. One common legal solution to this conflict is to move to a model of data-free movement with trust, where cross-border data flow is achieved, and the standards of data protection and accountability become enforceable. The control of data under such a system is aimed at coming up with minimum principles that guarantee that data may flow across borders without impacting its integrity and confidentiality.[18] This includes finding a balance between the most important regulations, e.g., consent procedures, restrictions on data processing, storage conditions, and breach reporting. National differences in dealing with these matters have brought about compliance asymmetries, under which companies have to change their data treatment practices based on the jurisdiction in which they are operating. To provide an example, some jurisdictions have a stringent privacy regime, where stringency over the transfer of data is high, but other jurisdictions employ models that are less stringent and oriented toward innovation and digital progress. These differences render it challenging to perform cross-border performances and create confusion when determining the legal data flows.

2.2.2 Prohibiting Protectionism

The redundant data localization has a number of practical problems. The companies have to construct backup data centers, duplicate IT infrastructure, and enact jurisdiction-based compliance policies that add expenses and decrease rapid digital

[16] Ikrom Ahmedov, "The Impact of Digital Economy on International Trade," *European Journal of Business and Management Research* 5, no. 4 (2020).

[17] Srinivas Rao Rao Challa, "Advancements in Digital Brokerage and Algorithmic Trading: The Evolution of Investment Platforms in a Data Driven Financial Ecosystem," *Advances in Consumer Research* 2 (2025): 238–49.

[18] W. Gregory Voss, "Cross-Border Data Flows, the GDPR, and Data Governance," *Wash. Int'l LJ* 29 (2019): 485.

innovation.[19] This has been especially heavy for small and medium-sized companies, which are not able to absorb the financial and administrative costs of having region-specific data storage. Multinational technology platforms have not been left out either because it has to cope with the disjointed data governance systems in order to remain within the spectrum of different national needs, which limits the effectiveness of operations across the globe. Other than the effect on the economy, over-localization may be employed to increase the level of cybersecurity threat.[20] An emphasis on data within local systems may unwittingly create single points of weakness in the business, and international cooperation in threat detection and cyber incident response is hampered.

2.2.3 Standardizing Privacy

The advent of the digital economy has shown the vast differences in how various jurisdictions and mixed-up business affairs have approached personal data and privacy, and the absence of equal consumer protection. The different privacy regimes, in which certain regions have rigid laws and regulations, and others have a relatively loose structure, pose a challenge to the global business of digital enterprises. This disaggregation not only increases the cost of compliance but also poses a threat to lower consumer trust in digital services. The uniformity of privacy with the common law system introduces uniformity of internationally established standards of data gathering, data processing, data storing, and data sharing in a manner that safeguards consumers and makes digital business across international borders easy.[21] A coherent vision about privacy maintains the core regulatory issues about informed consent, data minimization, transparency, and accountability. Business-provided compliance processes can be extended to various jurisdictions due to the predictability provided by the rules of personal information handling, and the associated administrative and operational load of compliance with the different national standards can be avoided.

[19] Evans Kofi Agbeno, "Algorithmic Sovereignty: Regulating Artificial Intelligence and Data Colonialism under the African Continental Free Trade Area (AfCFTA) Framework," *International Journal of Humanities, Management, Engineering, Education and Legal Studies*, 2025, 42–83.

[20] Joshua D. Blume, "Reading the Trade Tea Leaves: A Comparative Analysis of Potential United States WTO-GATS Claims Against Privacy, Localization, and Cybersecurity Laws," *Geo. J. Int'l L.* 49 (2017): 801.

[21] Michael L. Rustad and Thomas H. Koenig, "Towards a Global Data Privacy Standard," *Fla. L. Rev.* 71 (2019): 365.

2.3 *Promoting Digital Trade and Economic Growth*

2.3.1 Ban on Customs Duties

The practical advantage of duty-free digital flows is seen in the experience of international trade frameworks.[22] In the societies that have signed the moratorium of the World Trade Organization, there has been more involvement of SMEs in e-commerce across borders, more exportation of digital services, and more foreign investment in digital infrastructure.[23] On the other hand, the jurisdictions that levy digital tariffs tend to experience reduced growth in digital exports, less adoption of platforms, and increased business and consumer costs. Such effects are particularly acute in the sectors depending on real-time data delivery, such as cloud computing, online media, and software-as-a-service offerings, where the delays in operations directly impact the service quality and competitiveness. Duty-free treatment allows firms to invest in innovation as well, instead of following the regulations.[24] Companies can invest in research and development, new technologies, and digital infrastructure, and encourage the creation of new products and services that can enhance competitiveness in the world.

2.3.2 Paperless Trade

Digitalization of the paper-based processes into the digital documentation systems is turning into one of the keys to the modernization of international trade. Trade documents, such as bills of lading, customs declarations, and invoices, were traditionally slow supply chains, added verification issues, and presented opportunities for fraud or misconduct. Paperless trade takes advantage of safe electronic systems to facilitate the process of document making, transfer, and authentication so that stakeholders can access validated records immediately and lessen reliance on the physical process.[25] It has been proven to be an effective approach through the use of electronic bills of lading (e-B/L). Such electronic applications enable the ownership, transferring, and verification of cargo to be done electronically, thus removing the delays incurred when couriering original copies and the possibility of disputes over documents. The system of e-invoicing also contributes to a well-run process of relations between

---

[22] Shamel Azmeh et al., "The International Trade Regime and the Quest for Free Digital Trade," *International Studies Review* 22, no. 3 (2020): 671–92.

[23] Sina Mirzaye and Muhammad Mohiuddin, "Digital Transformation in International Trade: Opportunities, Challenges, and Policy Implications," *Journal of Risk and Financial Management* 18, no. 8 (2025): 421.

[24] Scott Veitch, "Duty Free," in *Law, Obligation, Community* (Routledge, 2018).

[25] Mohammad Saeed Abdallah ALsheyab, "Legal Analysis of the Merits of Electronic Transferable Records: Toward Cross-Border Trade Digitalization," *International Journal of Law and Management* 67, no. 1 (2025): 145–63.

exporters, importers, and the regulatory bodies, accelerating the process of customs clearance and improving the process of financial reconciliation.

2.3.3 Technology Neutrality

The speed of digital innovation underlines the need to have regulatory systems that do not restrict the development of technology. Technology neutrality allows legislations to focus on the outcomes they desire, including security, privacy, and enforceability, but does not care which tools to use to achieve such outcomes because technology is neutral to the tools used to achieve such outcomes.[26,27] Technology-neutral frameworks enable firms to be flexible in their operations to test and adopt innovative solutions.[28] Such a solution minimizes the chance of legal ambiguity in situations where companies implement new technologies or modernize existing ones and maintain enforceability and accountability. In terms of policy, the global coordination is also improved by neutrality. Regulators can also coordinate rules across jurisdictions without creating conflicting technical requirements by not creating technology-specific requirements. This ensures easy cross-border interoperability where multinational businesses can implement various solutions that can meet the international standards.

2.4 Ensuring Consumer Trust and Safety

2.4.1 Online Protection

The digital economy needs consumer trust since the dealings are not typically a face-to-face exchange and are cross-jurisdictional.[29] Online markets are expected to have equal or greater protections as the offline markets to eliminate fraudulent activities, as well as safeguard personal and financial information.[30] The existence of a homogenous legal framework creates a clear set of consumer rights, offers a standard on transparency, and sets binding policies to fight fraud, unauthorized access to data, and misrepresentation. To reduce the risk of a scam and maximize involvement, online platforms have taken precautionary measures, such as secure rates of

[26] Mireille Hildebrandt and Laura Tielemans, "Data Protection by Design and Technology Neutral Law," *Computer Law & Security Review* 29, no. 5 (2013): 509–21.

[27] Brad A. Greenberg, "Rethinking Technology Neutrality," *Minn. L. Rev.* 100 (2015): 1495.

[28] Essi Puhakainen and Karin Elisabeth Väyrynen, *The Benefits and Challenges of Technology Neutral Regulation–a Scoping Review*, 2021.

[29] Amy J. Schmitz, "There's an App for That: Developing Online Dispute Resolution to Empower Economic Development," *Notre Dame JL Ethics & Pub. Pol'y* 32 (2018): 1.

[30] Emmanuel Damilare Balogun et al., "A Risk Intelligence Framework for Detecting and Preventing Financial Fraud in Digital Marketplaces," *Iconic Research and Engineering Journals* 4, no. 08 (2021): 134–49.

payment, checking user identity, and digital receipts. The dispute resolution systems offer convenient and ready solutions to the consumers and track complaints. By harmonizing these protections among countries, the consumers would have protection in every country, and the businesses would be in a predictable legal environment, which would make it easy to conduct business internationally. The synchronization of the laws also enhances the monitoring of e-commerce. Trustworthy consumer guarantees have a direct impact on market participation.

2.4.2 Cybersecurity

The proliferation of the digital economy has put individuals at risk of cybersecurity on a mass scale, and the protection of critical infrastructure and transactional systems has turned into a global concern. Interruptions in business operations that are classified as cyberattacks involve data breaches, ransomware, and Distributed Denial-of-Service (DDoS) attacks that, to a larger extent, kill the confidence in online business.[31] To build resilience against such threats, a legal and technical strategy is necessary, as digital transactions and services are cross-border dependent and need to be interconnected with networks, cloud providers, and third-party service providers. International collaboration is the key to successful cybersecurity measures. A standardised legal framework will also lead to intergovernmental co-ordination and regulation, and stakeholders in the private sector will be in a position to share information very quickly, conduct joint evaluation of threats and response in case of incidents.

2.5 Addressing Regulatory Gaps and Geopolitical Challenges

2.5.1 Preventing Fragmentation

It is also possible to have fragmented regulation of international digital trade, and national standards are becoming an impediment to efficient trade.[32] The US focuses on lax, innovation-friendly laws that are conducive to flexibility and speed in embracing new technologies, but the European Union has stringent regulations of data protection, privacy, and consumer protection.[33] The Chinese strategy, especially its Digital Silk Road project, is a hybrid of infrastructure development and export of interoperable standards in other nations to coordinate the data control, digital

---

[31] Olumide Olugbenga Malomo, *Cybersecurity Through a Blockchain Enabled Federated Cloud Framework*, 2018.

[32] Felicity Deane et al., "Trade in the Digital Age: Agreements to Mitigate Fragmentation," *Asian Journal of International Law* 14, no. 1 (2024): 154–79.

[33] Erik Longo and Filippo Bagni, "From Legal Experimentation to Regulatory Sandboxes: The EU's Pioneering Approach to Digital Innovation and Regulation," in *White Paper on Regulatory Sandboxes for AI and Cybersecurity* (Nessuno, 2025).

payments, and cybersecurity between the states.[34,35] These divergent plans may end up creating incompatible systems, which will make compliance difficult and sluggish when making international digital transactions. Some of the areas where regulatory fragmentation can be observed are the cross-border data flows, electronic contracts recognition, and cybersecurity requirements. To fill such gaps, globally acceptable principles to aid interoperability without compromising the national policy goals are necessary.

2.5.2 Inclusivity

The digital economy should be based on inclusivity, and developing economies and marginalized populations should have the opportunity to benefit from the cross-border digital trade. Such rules and standardized frameworks are important to minimize the structural barriers, allowing countries with new digital infrastructure to act at the same level as developed economies.[36] Without these structures, the current availability of technology, regulatory skills, and digital literacy disparities can be a source of the digital divide, limited economic opportunities between businesses and consumers in less wealthy regions.

3 The Role of International Law in Shaping a Common Framework

It is true that the international law has many principles that project the premise of carrying out economic activities across borders despite the relative novelty of digital technologies. These principles help states to cooperate, reduce legal ambiguity and address the relations between the legal systems. The international law can also be useful when considering the Belt and Road Initiative (BRI) to come up with a unified digital platform to operate beyond the borders of multiple nations.[37,38] One of the most significant contributions of international law is consistency and

[34] Andrew Mazen Dahdal and Adel Abdel Ghafar, "The Digital Silk Road:'Tech-Diplomacy' as a Paradigm for Understanding Technological Adoption and Emerging Digital Regulations in MENA," *Asian Journal of Law and Society* 12, no. 2 (2025): 163–88.

[35] Alex He, *The Digital Silk Road and China's Influence on Standard Setting* (CIGI Papers, 2022).

[36] Revd Dr Chukwunonso Joseph Nosike, "Digitalization in Developing Countries: Opportunities and Challenges," *Nigerian Journal of Arts and Humanities (NJAH)* 4, no. 1 (2024).

[37] Poomintr Sooksripaisarnkit and Sai Ramani Garimella, *China's One Belt One Road Initiative and Private International Law* (Routledge London, 2018).

[38] Chi He, "The Belt and Road Initiative as Global Public Good: Implications for International Law," in *Normative Readings of the Belt and Road Initiative: Road to New Paradigms* (Springer, 2018).

predictability of the trade between different countries.[39] The basic principles, non-discrimination, transparency, and fair treatment have been established by the international trade law, the World Trade Organization (WTO).[40] Even though most WTO rules were developed even before the digital economy emerged, they possess principles that can be applied today in digital trading, and can be utilized as a guide in the creation of digital legal systems in the BRI. WTO is now more interested in electronic commerce, which is manifested in deliberations and collaborations among member states. These projects are based on such issues as digital facilitation of trade, paperless trade, cross-border information. The other international law institution that is relevant is the United Nations Commission on International Trade Law (UNCITRAL).[41] UNCITRAL has developed model laws and other bodies of law which aim to harmonise commercial legislation in the various countries. The Model Law on Electronic Commerce and the Model Law on Electronic Signatures are tools that provide viable recommendation on how to regulate electronic transactions as well as electronic contracts.[42,43,44] These model laws are particularly applicable to countries of BRI as they do not have strict lines of thinking and can be adjusted to other systems of law.

BRI countries can use the standards of UNCITRAL to harmonize the national laws without sacrificing the sovereignty of their legal systems. The soft law and international standards are also another way in which international law plays a role in digital frameworks. Soft law comprises rules, principles, and good practices that are created by international organizations and professional bodies. Even though they are not legally authoritative, they usually influence the policies and the method of regulation of nations. The digital context that soft law is relevant to includes data protection, cybersecurity, and digital governance, where overall legal rigidity is decreasing with fast-changing technology.[45] In the case of the BRI, soft law enables nations to collaborate and coordinate their policies without necessarily signing treaties. International agreements on trade (regional and bilateral) are also indicative of the influence that international law can have over digital regulation. A good number of recent trade agreements comprise digital trade, electronic trade, and flow of data chapters. Some of the issues covered by such agreements include electronic authentication, consumer protection when conducting online transactions, and collaboration on cybersecurity. Although there are other regional arrangements that BRI countries are involved with,

---

[39] Babadjanova Nazokat, "The Role of International Trade Law in Promoting Global Economic Stability," *Shokh Library* 1, no. 13 (2025).

[40] Tamara Kortukova and Lilia Nevara, "Features of the Principle of Non-Discrimination in International Trade and Economic Law," *Legal Horizons*, 2023, 41.

[41] Maria Gabriela Sarmiento and Katia Fach Gómez, "The United Nations Commission on International Trade Law (UNCITRAL)," *The International Law of Economic Integration, Oxford University Press, DRAFT PRE-PRINT, Forthcoming*, 2023.

[42] Alan Davidson, *The Law of Electronic Commerce* (Cambridge University Press, 2009).

[43] Stephen Mason, "Electronic Signatures in Practice," *J. High Tech. L.* 6 (2006): 148.

[44] Stephen Mason, *Electronic Signatures in Law* (University of London press, 2016).

[45] Ryan Hagemann et al., "Soft Law for Hard Problems: The Governance of Emerging Technologies in an Uncertain Future," *Colo. Tech. LJ* 17 (2018): 37.

the lessons learnt in the arrangements offer valuable insights into the creation of a wider digital framework within the BRI.

The digital economy also applies to the international human rights law.[46] Digital technologies have an impact on such basic rights as confidentiality, the right to free speech, and the right to information.[47,48] The existence of international human rights instruments sets some fundamental principles that should be used to determine how states should regulate online activities.[49] Indicatively, the global human rights are slowly taking control of data protection and privacy policies. An implementation of these principles into digital legal frameworks in the BRI context may be useful in order to make economic development based on digital trade balanced with preserving individual rights. International law is another area that has contributed to resolving disputes. Cross-border commercial disputes have models that are set by international legal mechanisms, including arbitration and mediation.[50] The processes are useful, particularly in the digital economy, when the standard court system may be faced with a problem of jurisdiction and procedure. The international law practices on alternative dispute resolution can be applied in creating digital dispute resolution in the BRI and make it efficient and more accessible. The international law also fosters cooperation and building of capacity among states. The various international legal norms focus on technical support, knowledge exchange, and institutionalization, particularly in developing nations. As the levels of digital readiness between the countries of the BRI are varied, cooperating on the international level guided by the law may assist in achieving a more equal digital development.

[46] Cristina Elena Popa Tache, "Between Human Rights and the Digital Economy," *Pandectele Romane*, 2022, 65.

[47] Riduan Siagian et al., "Human Rights in the Digital Era: Online Privacy, Freedom of Speech, and Personal Data Protection," *Journal of Digital Learning and Distance Education* 2, no. 4 (2023): 548–58.

[48] Jamil Afzal and Chen Yongmei, "Federal and Provincial Legislation Regarding 'Right to Information' for Good Governance in Pakistan," *Discover Global Society* 1, no. 1 (2023): 12.

[49] Christina Angelopoulos et al., *Study of Fundamental Rights Limitations for Online Enforcement through Self-Regulation*, 2015.

[50] Ely Nursamsiah et al., "International Commercial Mediation: Towards a Harmonized Legal Framework for Cross-Border Business Dispute Resolution," *Journal Evidence of Law* 4, no. 3 (2025): 1164–72.

4 Current Legal Frameworks and Initiatives

4.1 *Key Legal Frameworks and Mechanisms*

4.1.1 Dispute Resolution Hubs

The Belt and Road Initiative is complicated by the number of different legal frameworks, ways of doing business, and regulations in different countries involved in the project. China has implemented unique mechanisms in order to overcome these challenges so as to offer a structured dispute resolution and legal certainty to investors and contractors. China International Commercial Court (CICC), which was constituted in 2018, is one of the main centers of dispute resolution based on international-level commercial contracts, infrastructure projects, and foreign investment.[51] In addition to the CICC, countries of the BRI are now more dependent on the international arbitration systems to resolve cross-border disputes. The arbitration centers, which include the Shanghai International Arbitration Center (SHIAC) and the China International Economic and Trade Arbitration Commission (CIETAC), are neutral centers where disputes are resolved, multi-jurisdictional contractual arrangements are accommodated, and awards are enforced in international conventions.[52,53] Such mechanisms enable investors and contractors to work with certainty to reduce the legal ambiguities of the varying national courts of law and the interpretation of various regulations.

4.1.2 Hybrid Clauses

The traditional methods of dispute resolution, such as arbitration or litigation alone, are not usually sufficient since they are time-consuming, costly, and can disrupt the colossal infrastructural or technological development. The hybrid clauses have turned out to be a sophisticated solution; the combined advantages of mediation and enforceability of arbitration are combined to provide a flexible and structured way of solving conflicts. Hybrid clauses usually provide that the first step to resolve a dispute is through mediation, which is handled by neutral experts, or panels of experts in the industry concerned.[54] This step is concerned with communication, getting to know each other and during the initial phase, finding out contract ambiguities or differences in operation. Mediation gives the stakeholders a chance to seek innovative mutually

[51] Sima Nzang and Julio Cesar Obiang, "Judicial Innovation and Global Governance: The Strategic Role of China International Commercial Court in Advancing the Belt and Road Initiative, The Case of Xian International Commercial Court," *ScienceOpen Preprints*, 2026.

[52] Ricardo E. Ugarte and Stephanie Wu, "International Arbitration in China: 2023 in Review," *Journal of International Arbitration* 41, no. 5 (2024).

[53] Chapter I. General Provisions, *China International Economic and Trade Arbitration Commission CIETAC Arbitration Rules*, n.d.

[54] Carrie Menkel-Meadow, *Hybrid and Mixed Dispute Resolution Processes: Integrities of Process Pluralism* (Edward Elgar Publishing, 2020).

beneficial solutions without necessarily going to a formal adjudication.[55] In the event that the mediation process does not yield a solution, disputes can escalate into arbitration whereby solutions are legally binding and enforceable in the international systems such as the New York Convention. This single design reduces the possibility of long-term conflicts and preserves the business strategic partnerships which are of the ultimate importance to further BRI projects. The effectiveness of hybrid clauses is manifested in the practical implementation of the hybrid clauses in the BRI projects. Hybrid clauses in large infrastructure projects, transboundary railways, energy and telecommunication network pipelines have been used to solve technical conflicts in a timely fashion, milestone payments delays and variation in construction standards. An example is the use of mediation to deal with local regulatory interpretations, labor conflicts, and logistical bottlenecks in transnational railway contracts between China and Southeast Asia. Further arbitration guaranteed binding results in case of technical disagreement in the future, which would guarantee investors with certainty and project momentum. Technology is also incorporated in hybrid clauses in order to increase efficiency in dispute resolution. Online mediation, online transfer of evidence, and electronic arbitration hearings are becoming a frequent occurrence online. Evidence management systems and smart contract frameworks based on blockchain have the potential to automatically record compliance milestones and initiate dispute resolution processes, reducing human error and enhancing transparency. Such technology integration can be very helpful in BRI projects where the parties involved may be located across numerous time zones and legal jurisdictions. The hybrid clauses have strategic value that goes to the regulatory and geopolitical considerations.[56] Civil law, common law, or hybrid legal traditions that may have different procedural norms are common between countries with BRI projects. As the standardized contracts include the use of hybrid clauses, the Chinese authorities and the countries engage in a predictable framework that reconciles these differences to create reduced legal uncertainty and limit the legal risks that are associated with conflict of jurisdiction.

4.1.3 Standardized Cooperation Documents

Standardized cooperation documents, especially Memoranda of Understanding (MoUs), are elements of strategy, which are used to coordinate cross-border cooperation.[57] These documents establish a common governance framework, detailing institutional roles, performance metrics, and procedural guidelines that are needed

[55] Oksana Melenko, "Mediation as an Alternative Form of Dispute Resolution: Comparative-Legal Analysis," *European Journal of Law and Public Administration* 7, no. 2 (2020): 46–63.

[56] Stephen Minas, "Conflicting Connectivities: Legal Considerations for Negotiating Geotechnological Rivalry," *Iustinianus Primus L. Rev.* 16 (2025): 147.

[57] A. Carvajal, "A Comparative Study of Commitment of Collaboration (COC) and Memorandum of Understanding (MOU) as Instruments in Driving Successful Partnerships in ASEAN Member Countries," *Int. J. Open-Access, Interdiscipl. New Educ. Discoveries ETCOR Educ. Res. Center (iJOINED ETCOR)* 20, no. 3 (2023): 503–20496.

in multi-country, complex projects. MoUs facilitate the modular design of projects by defining a level of shared terms between countries. This allows BRI efforts to be tailored to fit local regulatory environments, without reduction of primary areas of operation. For example, technical standards, terms, and ecological requirements in the transnational projects of railway and energy corridors between China and Central and South Asian countries are drafted in the form of MoUs. This standardization ensures less negotiation complexity, quicker project start, and offers a more consistent structure of continued oversight and responsibility. Besides the transparency of operations, standardized cooperation documents are risk management instruments and alignment of policies. They make key terminologies on environmental sustainability, adherence to international standards in investment, and dispute resolution mechanisms, in a manner that host-country laws and Chinese objectives in investment are synergized. Such a two-fold alignment reduces legal ambiguity as well as avoids project delays, which are bound to occur due to jurisdiction or contract differences.

4.2 Key Initiatives and Strategic Priorities

4.2.1 Six Corridors, Six Routes, and Multiple Countries and Ports

BRI is a strategic connectivity oriented in different regions through its six corridors, six routes, and a multi-country and ports framework, which provides a blueprint in terms of infrastructure connectivity.[58] The coordination between countries is operationalized through the implementation of such strategic corridors. In one instance, China Pakistan Economic Corridor (CPEC) is in the form of highway networks, energy grid, and port projects that will connect inland production centers with the Gwadar port, to ensure goods and energy flow.[59] Similarly, the China-Central Asia-West Asia Corridor enhances the overland connectivity through rail and pipeline networks that facilitate exports of energy, industrial trade, and cross-border investments.[60] Sea projects such as building ports in Sri Lanka, Djibouti, and Greece support regional trade centers, which are strategic points that complement the terrestrial routes.[61] The strategic framework also determines the prioritization of investment and risk management. The BRI creates a model that can be replicated in other regions by organizing the development of infrastructure around clearly defined corridors and connecting various countries and ports. The framework not only enables the

[58] Galen Murton and Tom Narins, "Corridors, Chokepoints and the Contradictions of the Belt and Road Initiative," *Area Development and Policy* 9, no. 4 (2024): 445–65.

[59] Jamil Afzal et al., "Completion of the Ten Years of the China-Pakistan Economic Corridor (CPEC) and Its Economical Goals," *Inverge Journal of Social Sciences* 2, no. 4 (2023): 23–29.

[60] Wang Jinbo, "The China–Central Asia–West Asia Economic Corridor," in *The Routledge Handbook of the Belt and Road* (Routledge, 2022).

[61] Xiaoxiao Zhu, *The Architecture of the Belt and Road Initiative-Feasibility Study on Sustainable Development of Free Trade Zone Made by BRI*, 2022.

free flow of goods, energy, and services but also establishes consistency between the financial, regulatory, and operational mechanisms across borders, thereby increasing predictability and investor confidence.

4.2.2 Digital and Tech Partnerships

The Digital Silk Road project within the Belt and Road system is an indication of a change in the physical infrastructure to the connectivity that is knowledge and technology based. This methodology is unlike the traditional transport and energy corridors since the focus is on the incorporation of digital networks and the cross-border e-commerce ecosystems and smart city infrastructures to make the region more competitive and economically modernized. The centre of such collaborations is the development of digital platforms that are interoperable to facilitate easy trade, financial transactions, and the sharing of information. The implementation of AI-driven traffic management, digital energy management, and real-time environmental management in smart city pilots in Malaysia and Kazakhstan is one of such areas, which are directly connected to the regional trade centers and urban planning policies.

4.2.3 Sustainable Development Goals (SDGs)

The BRI projects are being measured using global sustainability measures (including the Sustainable Development Goals). Unlike the conventional developmental approaches where speed and scale are key, SDG-consistent projects look at the multi-dimensional effect, balancing between the economic development and the environmental protection, social inclusiveness, and a robust infrastructure. Such a strategic orientation makes BRI investments a tool for long-term sustainable development and not just short-term economic benefits. Realistically, SDGs adherence is achieved through special environmental and social interventions that are added to each project. The development plans in Southeast Asia are based on smart water management, energy-saving buildings, and community-oriented public spaces directly aligned with SDG 6 (Clean Water and Sanitation), SDG 11 (Sustainable Cities and Communities), and SDG 13 (Climate Action).[62] Similar focus on solar, wind, and hydro-electric capacity development in energy infrastructure projects will support SDG 7 (Affordable and Clean Energy) and help cut the carbon intensity of regional development.[63,64] Sustainability performance is associated with financial mechanisms that provide incentives to enterprises and governments to comply with the international

[62] Angelina Kissiwaa Twum et al., "Advancing Renewable Energy Strategies towards Sustainable Development Goal 13: Insights from Belt and Road Initiative (BRI) Countries," *Environment, Development and Sustainability*, 2024, 1–32.

[63] Guansu Wang et al., "Analysis of ASEAN Water Resource Policies in the Context of Belt and Road Initiative: A Perspective on Sustainable Development Goal 6 (SDG6)," 2023, 119–37.

[64] Wang et al., "Analysis of ASEAN Water Resource Policies in the Context of Belt and Road Initiative: A Perspective on Sustainable Development Goal 6 (SDG6)."

environmental standards and local regulatory demands. This will make the public and the private actors take into consideration the larger socio-environmental impacts of the investment decision-making processes, which will enhance accountability and transparency.

4.2.4 Regional Cooperation Agreements

The regional cooperation agreements play an important role in boosting the BRI by offering systematic mechanisms of facilitation of trade, harmonisation of policies, and integration of economies.[65] One strategy that can be employed to harmonize tariff regimes, facilitate the customs process, and reduce regulatory barriers among the member states is the free trade agreements, such as the China-ASEAN Free Trade Agreement (CAFTA).[66] Such agreements guarantee predictable business environments and allow businesses to plan investments, simplify supply chains, and cross-border trade more effectively and efficiently with reduced risk. Through regional cooperation agreements, the BRI not only increases economic connectivity but also offers an organized, policy-based platform of sustainable and inclusive development.

5 Challenges in Implementing a Digital Dispute Resolution Mechanism (DDRM)

Digital trade introduces a new form of disputes that cannot be compared to the classical commercial disputes. Such disputes may include electronic agreements, inter-country data transfer, online resources, or online payment systems. The establishment of the Digital Dispute Resolution Mechanism (DDRM) in the Belt and Road Initiative is associated with a number of legal, technical, and institutional challenges, which impact both the national systems and the collaboration across borders.[67] In case a conflict engages parties of various nations, conflicting laws may result in uncertainty of jurisdiction, and it may be hard to know which rules to use and how decisions would be implemented. Digital trade can be characterized by services, platforms, or data that can be spread across several countries. Although a dispute may be settled in a particular jurisdiction, the issue of enforcement in a different country may not be easy. All BRI countries do not yet have systems in place to identify or execute foreign arbitration or mediation awards in digital disputes. This ambiguity exposes companies operating in international digital commerce to risk and may prevent them from using online platforms.

[65] David Vines, "The BRI and RCEP: Ensuring Cooperation in the Liberalisation of Trade in Asia," *Economic and Political Studies* 6, no. 3 (2018): 338–48.

[66] Fei Nie et al., "Agricultural Trade Liberalization and Domestic Fertilizer Use: Evidence from China-ASEAN Free Trade Agreement," *Ecological Economics* 195 (2022): 107341.

[67] Ana Chitoroaga, *Dispute Resolution Mechanism in the Belt and Road Initiative*, n.d.

The integration of digital specialists into the dispute resolution processes presupposes the availability of proficient professionals in different jurisdictions, which is challenging to organize and may make the process of dispute resolution more time- and cost-intensive. The barriers are also accessibility and cost. Digital dispute resolution platforms bridge the gap between parties all over the world, and smaller businesses and individuals could not realize how to use them. Expenses on appeals, employing professionals, or maneuvering through unfamiliar jurisprudence may be prohibitive. Economic differences among BRI countries complicate the process of making certain that digital dispute mechanisms can be available to a large number of actors.

6 Legal Challenges and Trends

6.1 Conflict of Law

Chinese companies involved in infrastructural, energy, and digital projects in Central Asia, Southeast Asia, and the Middle East face civil law, common law, and Islamic law.[68,69] These variations impact the enforcement of contracts, sharing of liabilities, compliance with regulations, and dispute resolution, and need a keen alignment of law in order to ensure the continuation of operations. Likewise, CPEC contracts should strike a balance between the Chinese corporate governance and Pakistani procurement and labor regulations, and international financing needs.[70] The China-Central Asia-West Asia Railway Network faces the same issues, having to strike a balance between the Civil law of Kazakhstan and Uzbekistan and international investment standards.[71] The Middle East projects are a mixture of Sharia- compliant financing models and Chinese contractual experiences, where there is a need to align

[68] Aftab Haider et al., "Can Islamic Law and Secular Law Coexist Without Conflict," *Al-Istinbath: Jurnal Hukum Islam* 10, no. 2 (2025): 485–512.

[69] Andrew Mazen Dahdal and Adel Abdel Ghafar, "The Digital Silk Road: 'Tech-Diplomacy' as a Paradigm for Understanding Technological Adoption and Emerging Digital Regulations in MENA," *Asian Journal of Law and Society* 12, no. 2 (2025): 163–88.

[70] Dr Saeed Shafqat and Saba Shahid, *China Pakistan Economic Corridor: Demands, Dividends and Directions* (Centre for Public Policy and Governance, 2018).

[71] Roza Nurgozhayeva, "Rule-Making, Rule-Taking or Rule-Rejecting under the Belt and Road Initiative: A Central Asian Perspective," *The Chinese Journal of Comparative Law* 8, no. 1 (2020): 250–78.

both of them legally to prevent conflicts.[72,73] To reduce the ambiguity of jurisdiction, mixed legal systems are employed.

6.2 Debt Management

Debt sustainability is a serious issue of concern, especially in developing countries with low financial stability.[74] Structured debt frameworks are used by Chinese financial institutions, multilateral development banks, and host-country agencies to reduce risks in financing infrastructure on a large scale.[75] The Gwadar Port in Pakistan and the Standard Gauge Railway in Kenya are examples of projects that are challenging to manage in terms of debt. Borrower countries have to manage long-term repayment of loans with national economic concerns, and the lenders have mechanisms that make projects viable. Some of the debt structuring methods are staggered repayment schedules, concessional financing, revenue-linked repayment, and public–private arrangements. These methods spread financial risk among the stakeholders and minimize the chances of fiscal distress that may affect the completion of the project. Sustainable debt management entails monitoring and assessment.[76] The lending decisions are based on the financial performance indicators, macroeconomic risk analysis, and scenario planning, and these inform the contingency measures. Investment contracts usually contain in their terms and conditions fiscal transparency, audit compliance, and debt service coverage ratios, so that the lenders and host governments are in agreement on the repayment terms. BRI projects are faced with numerous challenges in operation due to varying legal and regulatory environments. The infrastructure and digital investments have to adhere to the laws of the host country, such as environmental regulations, labor standards, and investment restrictions, as well as to Chinese

[72] Ramadhani Mashaka Shabani, "Shari'ah-Compliant Financing Mechanisms for Belt and Road Initiative: Mitigating Debt Trap Risks," *AL-ARBAH: Journal of Islamic Finance and Banking* 6, no. 1 (2024): 17–34.

[73] J. Chu and Aishath Muneeza, "Belt and Road Initiative and Islamic Financing: The Case in Public Private Partnership Infrastructure Financing," *International Journal of Management and Applied Research* 6, no. 1 (2019): 24–40.

[74] Shakira Mustapha and Annalisa Prizzon, "Debt Sustainability and Debt Management in Developing Countries," *Economic and Private Sector Professional Evidence and Applied Knowledge Service Topic Guide. London: Overseas Development Institute*, 2015.

[75] Ammar Malik et al., "Banking on the Belt and Road: Insights from a New Global Dataset of 13,427 Chinese Development Projects," *Williamsburg, VA: AidData at William & Mary*, 2021, 23–36.

[76] Most Asikha Aktar et al., "Fair Debts Management for Sustainable Development," in *Reduced Inequalities* (Springer, 2021).

standards of corporate governance and international standards of contracts.[77,78] The misalignment in regulations may slow down the project schedules, raise the project costs, and cause uncertainty to investors. Digital compliance platforms and real-time reporting systems can be used to monitor operations across borders using national and international standards. The automatic process of tracking allows approvals and reporting requirements, assisting in balancing out that projects meet the requirements of the regulation and reducing the administrative bottlenecks.

6.3 Regulatory Alignment

Green BRI projects are the projects that act at the crossroad of the laws of the countries, the international goals of sustainability, and the Chinese investment policies.[79] The example of projects in Central Asia demonstrates that multi-layered regulatory integration is needed. The solar and hydroelectric projects in Kazakhstan and Uzbekistan are intended to comply with the national requirements of the environmental impact assessment and the Chinese Green BRI requirements of emissions, efficiency of resources, and ecosystem protection. The construction techniques are aligned with the local labor regulations, offering occupational safety and reasonable payment, and using energy-efficient technologies and environmentally sensitive materials. These two compliance systems make regulatory requirements operational strategies as opposed to bureaucratic checkpoints. Combined Chinese project managers and host-country officials show environmental performance, observe labor conditions, and give advice to improve it constantly, through joint supervisory committees. Uniform compliance systems, which have been designed to fit in particular corridors, can be used as effective mechanisms to harmonize the disparities in reporting systems, enforcement practices, and monitoring requirements. State-of-the-art digital systems help to conduct real-time monitoring, and IoT-based sensors and AI-enhanced analytics can monitor the levels of pollution, energy consumption, and safety indicators at the project locations.

---

[77] Shumin Wang et al., "Management Economic Systems and Governance to Reduce Potential Risks in Digital Silk Road Investments: Legal Cooperation between Hainan Free Trade Port and Ethiopia," *Systems* 12, no. 8 (2024): 305.

[78] Mike Morris, *Chinese Firms and Adherence to Global Environmental, Social and Governance (ESG) Standards in Developing Countries: Is There Potential to Create Common Ground?*, no. 18/2023 (IDOS Discussion Paper, 2023).

[79] Christoph Nedopil Wang, "China Belt and Road Initiative (BRI) Investment Report 2021," *Green BRI Center, International Institute of Green Finance (IIGF)* 9, no. 5 (2022).

7 Effective Digital Dispute Resolution System (EDDRS)

The Belt and Road Initiative requires an Efficient Digital Dispute Resolution System (EDDRS) to facilitate trust, stability, and legal confidence in digital trade. With the use of digital transactions, the use of cross-border platforms, online services, and electronic contracts, the traditional dispute resolution systems are commonly unable to resolve the speed and complexity of the digital conflicts.[80] In reaction to these realities, the BRI needs a dispute resolution model that is adaptable, affordable, and able to function within a wide range of legal and technological settings. Among them, one of the proposals is to create a single digital dispute resolution scheme within the BRI. This framework would not supplant legal systems of countries, but it would coexist with them, and it would offer some procedural standards and principles. There would be a common framework that would assist in minimizing uncertainty for businesses since there would be clear information as to how digital disputes are handled and resolved when the involved parties are in various jurisdictions. The following are the key components of the proposed Effective Digital Dispute Resolution System (EDDRS) within BRI.

7.1 The Tech Component

7.1.1 Secure Case Management System (CMS)

Secure Case Management System (CMS) offers the technological foundation for efficient, transparent, and responsible dispute resolution in the context of the Belt and Road Initiative. The CMS is a computerized system that combines various features, such as the possibility to file complaints, evidence, monitor the latest situation on the ground in real-time, automatically inform, and process the archival sources. The allotted ticket numbers to a particular case form a traceable workflow that increases responsibility and eliminates administrative bottlenecks that are inherent to paper-based legal procedures.

7.1.2 AI-Enabled Tools

The adoption of Artificial Intelligence (AI) in digital case management platforms comes with revolutionary possibilities of dispute resolution and administration in BRI projects. AI applications facilitate user interfaces, enhance the efficiency of the processes, and intelligently assist in multi-jurisdictional legal systems. Chatbots

[80] Amaresh Patel et al., "Online Dispute Resolution Mechanism as an Effective Tool for Resolving Cross-Border Consumer Disputes in the Era of e-Commerce," *International Journal of Law and Management*, 2025.

help a user to go through the complicated filing process, provide step-by-step instructions, explain the requirements of the documents, and respond to jurisdiction-related questions in real time.[81] Natural Language Processing (NLP) allows cross-border accessibility by means of instant translation and contextual interpretation of the case documents so that stakeholders with different linguistic backgrounds can effectively communicate with the system.[82] The feature is critical in projects in BRI countries, such as projects in infrastructure between China, Kazakhstan, and Pakistan, where stakeholders may speak many languages, such as Mandarin, Russian, and Urdu. Machine Learning (ML) algorithms can be used in the decision-making process because they categorize evidence, identify trends in the types of disputes, and suggest the possible settlement ranges, relying on the historical data and similar cases.

7.1.3 Document Management and Authentication

The digital technologies provided the opportunity to change the legal infrastructure of the Belt and Road Initiative (BRI) projects to manage the complex cross-border processes effectively, transparently, and safely. Digital Case Management Systems (CMS) are centralized dispute and administrative lifecycle digital systems, automating platforms and centralizing complaints registration, evidence submission, tracking progress, and procedural management. Each case is tracked using a special identifier, and sensitive information is safeguarded using a role-based access control and end-to-end encryption that disallows inter-jurisdictional. The system is also designed in such a manner that it can be adapted to different legal systems, like the civil law in Central Asia, the common law in Southeast Asia, and the Sharia-compliant systems in the Middle East, without negatively contributing to the efficiency of the operations of the system. Adding to the CMS, AI-based solutions provide predictive analytics and smart directions, in which machine learning algorithms categorize evidence, identify trends, and offer possible settlement ranges, based on previous data and regional law. The other required part of the infrastructure is the secure document management and authentication, which is based on the audit-trails built on the blockchain, encrypted submissions, and digital signatures to ensure the integrity and legal admissibility of electronic records. Such procedures minimize the chances of mistakes in the procedures, fraud, and build confidence among the international partners.

---

[81] Dignesh Kumar Khatri et al., "AI Chatbots in SAP FICO: Simplifying Transactions," *Innovative Research Thoughts* 8, no. 3 (2022): 294–306.

[82] Sayed Mahbub Hasan Amiri, "Beyond Language Barriers: Multilingual NLP and Voice Recognition for Global Connectivity," *International Journal of Science and Research Archive* 15 (2025): 406–19.

7.2 *The Legal Component*

7.2.1 Hybrid ADR Structure

The legal aspect of BRI projects focuses on a multi-layered and flexible system of dispute resolution, amongst efficiency, enforceability, and cross-border applicability. The Hybrid Alternative Dispute Resolution (ADR) models are founded on sequential and flexible models that include negotiation, mediation, and arbitration models that allow the parties to resolve the conflict at the first stage yet retain the possibility of having a binding adjudication in case of failure to reach a consensus.[83,84] The tiered model begins with direct negotiation, where the stakeholders are urged to clear up the contractual needs and expectations without any formalization. In case of any outstanding differences, structured mediation is usually carried out by third-party facilitators, who are neutral and who moderate the discussions, identify solutions that are agreeable to all, and offer procedural proposals that are jurisdiction-specific and culturally sensitive. In cases where negotiation and mediation fail to bring about a solution, binding arbitration gives binding results. Professionals with experience in international investment, infrastructure, and regulatory requirements in the industry can also be included in the arbitration panels. This is particularly helpful where the project will involve more than one BRI country with different legal systems.

7.2.2 Legally Binding Outcomes

The ultimate success of dispute resolution mechanisms regarding the Belt and Road Initiative is based on the enforceability of settlements and arbitral awards. Formal, legally binding results offer a governed and globally acknowledged avenue to make sure that negotiated agreements or arbitration findings are as binding as official court decisions, reducing the risk of non-cooperation, time loss, and withdrawal.[85,86] This is of special concern when it comes to multi-jurisdictional infrastructure, energy, and digital projects, where the stakeholders may be subject to different legal frameworks, such as civil law in Central Asia, common law in Southeast Asia, or Sharia-compliant law in the Middle East. In addition, legally binding results are imperative in enhancing investor confidence and ensuring sustainable cross-border trade and investment. The

---

[83] Rusli Subrata et al., "Hybrid Dispute Resolution in Administrative Law: Toward an Integrated Model for Government Conflict Management," *International Journal of Public Administration*, 2025, 137–62.

[84] Aparna Sreekumar, "Hybrid ADR Mechanisms," *Edulogic International Journal for Multi Disciplinary Research P-ISSN: 3051-2395 E-ISSN: 3051-2409* 1, no. 01 (2025): 87–106.

[85] Anne Peters, "International Dispute Settlement: A Network of Cooperational Duties," *European Journal of International Law* 14, no. 1 (2003): 1–34.

[86] Jamieson Kirkwood, "Characterization (and Registration) of a 'BRI Dispute,'" *Asian Journal of International Law* 14, no. 2 (2024): 324–57.

confidence that the agreements will be accepted and implemented in various jurisdictions will attract the involvement of both the stakeholders in the private and the public sectors, who would otherwise not participate because of the perceived legal ambiguity.

7.2.3 Clear Rules of Procedure

An effective governance and dispute resolution mechanism relies on a set of procedural rules, which should be well-defined and thorough to address the needs of a complex and multi-jurisdictional system.[87] The simple principle is to make procedural rules clearly available and understandable to all stakeholders, such as state institutions, private investors, and digital enterprises.[88] Complex or unclear processes tend to deter involvement and result in operational inefficiencies. An efficient procedural structure minimizes the confusion and allows the stakeholders to participate in cross-border economic and digital processes related to the Silk Road framework. This will be vital, especially to smaller organizations that might not have highly developed legal facilities but are actively participating in emerging digital trade networks. Transparency enhances the legitimacy of procedural systems through the visibility and understanding of all the stages of the process. Well-documented regulations enable the participants to know what to expect at every stage, consider possible scenarios, and work out informed approaches. In the Digital Silk Road, where digital transactions and the exchange of data are a common occurrence, transparency reduces uncertainty and boosts trust. It also restricts the chances of making discretionary decision-making, as every action is governed by pre-fixed standards.

7.2.4 Neutral Third-Party Selection

The choice of an impartial third party is an important element in the credibility and efficiency of any dispute resolution system, especially those that are technologically orientated and cross-border.[89] Neutrality plays a vital role in achieving fairness, eliminating the factor of bias, and undermining the entire process.[90] A transparent and efficient process of appointing mediators or arbitrators ensures that no one questions the individuals who will mediate or judge the case. There will be an open process of

[87] Ahmad Arzlee Hassan et al., "Mediation Procedural Rules and Their Application in the Malaysian Construction Industry: A Doctrinal Legal Research," *Journal of Construction in Developing Countries* 30, no. 2 (2025): 247–67.

[88] Bram Klievink et al., "The Collaborative Realization of Public Values and Business Goals: Governance and Infrastructure of Public–Private Information Platforms," *Government Information Quarterly* 33, no. 1 (2016): 67–79.

[89] Kumar Bal Govind Singh, "Online Dispute Resolution in Cross-Border Disputes: A Comprehensive Analysis," *Available at SSRN 4643682*, 2023.

[90] Stephen Macdonald and Briony Birdi, "The Concept of Neutrality: A New Approach," *Journal of Documentation* 76, no. 1 (2020): 333–53.

selection that will be initiated with clear eligibility and appointment criteria. These requirements are usually in the form of professional qualifications, related legal or technical knowledge, previous experience in dealing with similar disputes, and knowledge of digital technologies. The lack of conflict of interest and independence of the disputing entities supports the neutrality through the systems. There must be safeguards in the choice process, such as disclosure requirements, so that potential mediators or arbitrators can disclose any past relationships or interests that may lead to biased judgment.

7.3 The Security Component

7.3.1 Confidentiality and Privacy

Security is one of the fundamental principles in establishing the modern system of dispute resolution and governance, particularly in interrelated digital environments.[91] The necessity to guarantee confidentiality and privacy is not only a technical one but a legal and institutional one that is the foundation of the trust between the stakeholders in different jurisdictions. Another basic principle in maintaining integrity in the processes of dispute resolution is confidentiality.[92] Any data that is communicated in the course of proceedings, such as contractual, financial, technical, and strategic communications, should be protected against unauthorized access. The sensitivity of information in the context of the Digital Silk Road is extremely high when the conflicts of the area in which the latter is often associated with the digital infrastructure, e-commerce platforms, and data-driven services. The protection of privacy is not only in the procedural framework, but also in adherence to international data protection standards and regulations. The systems being in line with international norms, such as the General Data Protection Regulation (GDPR), provide a logical approach to addressing personal and sensitive data. Adherence to these regulatory frameworks ensures that the information about users is collected, processed, and stored in a legal and ethical way. The adoption of the standards under the framework of the Silk Road, where various countries may be at various stages of maturity of their data protection, will facilitate the harmonization of various countries and facilitate their cross-border cooperation.

[91] Fahimeh Abedi et al., "Developing Regulatory Standards for the Concept of Security in Online Dispute Resolution Systems," *Computer Law & Security Review* 35, no. 5 (2019): 105328.

[92] Abdolhossein Shiravi and Mohammad Javad Abdollahi, "Privacy and Confidentiality in Alternative Dispute Resolution Methods," *Journal of Economic & Management Perspectives* 11, no. 3 (2017): 835–44.

7.3.2 Neutrality and Fairness

The principles of impartiality and fairness are also significant when it comes to designing the new system of dispute resolution.[93,94] The question of whether these systems can remain unbiased as they increasingly assume more and more functions of artificial intelligence and human decision-makers would take the traditional meaning of neutrality further, making sure that technology and institutional actors are not biased. You need to have a system in place that ensures that there is neutrality to maintain legitimacy, protect the interests of the stakeholders, and facilitate equitable contribution of the different jurisdictions. Human mediators and arbitrators also play an important role in creating equity. Organized appointment systems, code of ethics, and supervision systems without conflicts of interest should ensure their impartiality. The professional standards, disclosure requirements, and institutional monitoring can help to guarantee that the mediators are independent and not under the influence of others. When cross-border disputes occur under the Digital Silk Road, and there can be a vast difference in economic resources or legal acumen of the parties involved, the role of a neutral mediator is especially relevant in striking a balance between the two sides.

7.3.3 Accessibility and Inclusivity

The success of digital dispute resolution systems lies in their access and inclusiveness. Such programs connect spheres of various technological progress, linguistic diversity, and socio-economic conditions.[95] We need to create platforms that would suit all the participants, individuals with disabilities and those with language or digital literacy barriers, in order to make them equally active and to broaden the range of such systems. One important element of access is in the technical architecture of digital platforms. The interfaces must be built in accordance with the principles of the universal design, such that the users with visual, aural, cognitive, or motor disabilities would be able to use the system without any complications.

---

[93] Lisa Blomgren Amsler et al., "Dispute System Design and Bias in Dispute Resolution," *SMUL Rev.* 70 (2017): 913.

[94] Fahimeh Abedi et al., "Universal Standards for the Concept of Fairness in Online Dispute Resolution in B2C E-Disputes," *Ohio St. J. on Disp. Resol.* 34 (2019): 357.

[95] Andreas T. Hirblinger, *Digital Inclusion in Peacemaking: A Strategic Perspective*, 2020.

7.4 *Implementation and Operational Elements*

7.4.1 Stakeholder Engagement and Education

As the Digital Silk Road is the location where the representatives of other languages should be found, the site must have multilingual facilities and good translation software. They can assist localized interfaces and culturally peculiar forms of communication to make people realize the procedural requirements and clarify their position. This will minimize chances of misinterpretation and enhance the general fairness of the process. The level of online familiarity amongst the users is also quite divergent. The vast majority of the subjects may not be familiar with advanced web platforms, and, therefore, the intuitive layout should take first place. The websites should be oriented on ease of use with simple directions to follow, step by step, and instinctively. Interactive instructions and dynamic support services could be used to make the users more confident and competent when using the system. The assistive and adaptive technologies promote user engagement.[96] The features that make people with various needs more productive in their activities are speech recognition, automated captioning, and interactive help systems. Such tools provide a more flexible environment that responds to the users instead of having the users respond to the system. Support mechanisms that are established within institutions can help to make the experience more inclusive. Multilingual support centers, technical support teams, and real-time customer support are avenues to address issues that users encounter in the process in a timely fashion. This will minimize frustration and promote further involvement, especially by those who are new to digital dispute resolution.

7.4.2 Feedback Mechanism

The use of structured feedback should be a characteristic attribute of a contemporary online dispute resolution (ODR) platform. Feedback systems ensure a base of continual enhancement and efficiency since they offer users the opportunity to share their experience and critique the process. These mechanisms can be employed to make sure that the platform can adjust to the real-life problems, requirements of the stakeholders, and even the technological developments. The feedback system must be accessible, user-friendly, and must be a part of the workflow in the platform where individuals would leave feedback immediately after they are done with a dispute resolution session. The participants can assess the usability, the clarity of instructions, responsiveness, performance of the mediators, and the neutrality of the results. Instead of relying on unstructured feedback and data, collecting the data in a structured format ensures that the collected data is usable and can be objectively analyzed to reveal the trends, areas of concern, and areas of improvement that are prevalent.

---

[96] Paula Kelly et al., "Design for Enabling Technologies. A Framework to Empower Multi-Level User Engagement," 2018, 65–74.

7.4.3 Support and Technical Assistance

Digital dispute resolution platforms rely heavily on effective support and technical assistance to succeed. A special help-desk system will be provided to make sure that every participant, irrespective of his/her technical skills or knowledge of online processes, will be able to use the platform effectively and participate in the dispute resolving activities to the full extent. This assistance not only helps in engaging the user but also helps to build trust in the reliability and accessibility of the system. The help-desk services should be provided in real-time to the users in different ways, like live chat, email, and phone services, so that the user can never leave their problems unresolved as they arise. Platforms can consist of tutorials, frequently asked questions, and screen-by-screen tutorials to train participants on how platforms work and what they need to know. They are particularly applicable where the response is the first time or in a less experienced region of the digital dispute resolution systems. The provision of multilingual resources also ensures that those users who have other language backgrounds will be in a position to access support.

8 Common Legal Framework for Digital Economy and Trade

Developing a shared legal framework of the digital economy and digital trade will be important in facilitating cross-border collaboration, economic integration, and technological advancement of the Belt and Road Initiative. With digital trade bridging markets in Asia, Europe, and Africa, among others, national laws may cause confusion, extra costs associated with compliance, and legal uncertainties. An integrated law could be used to minimize the fragmentation and assist in inclusive and sustainable digital growth among the BRI countries. Suggestions made include encouraging harmonization of the law over time, as opposed to instant uniformity.

8.1 Harmonizing Laws and Policies

Harmonization does not mean that all the BRI countries should have the same laws. Rather, it aims at harmonizing major principles and standards, and flexibility in domestic priorities.[97] Global nations are able to reach a consensus on shared definitions, minimum protection, and basic rules that govern digital trade. As an illustration, an agreement on the use of electronic contracts and digital signatures can be used to ensure that legal agreements pursued online can be accepted in different jurisdictions. Harmonization is also based on policy coordination. Governments can collaborate

[97] Julio Cesar Obiang Sima Nzang and Ying Ying Wang, "Harmonizing Legal Diversity: The Role of Soft Law and Model Rules in Belt and Road Dispute Prevention," *ScienceOpen Preprints*, 2026.

to harmonize digital economy policies, regulatory mechanisms, and implementation strategies. Constant communication of regulators assists in detecting inconsistencies and the areas where the most alignment can be achieved. The BRI system supports this cooperation by regional forums, working groups, or policy coordination platforms. Another feasible harmonization tool is model laws and guidelines. BRI countries can progressively coordinate their regulations by coming up with non-binding legal templates or best-practice guidelines without enforcing strict commitments. These tools offer the ability of the lawmakers to localize international standards to local settings without sacrificing regional consistency. Standardized laws and policies enable a business to have a better idea of what to expect and minimize the costs of compliance. They also improve the predictability of the law, which promotes investment and innovation in digital markets in BRI countries.

8.2 *Unified Digital Trade Agreement*

With the increased use of digital trade among BRI countries, the variation in national laws causes uncertainty for businesses and investors. The digital trade agreement based on BRI can deal with these issues by establishing common rules and principles that facilitate collaboration without going against national laws. Although nations are justified in their anxieties about data safety and privacy, unified regulations can be used to enable the legal flow of data required to run digital commerce. The agreement would foster the privacy of data and enable any required protection of the national interests and national security. The accord can also tackle the equitable treatment of online platforms and digital service providers. Non-discrimination, market access, and so on are the principles that assist in establishing a level playing field in businesses across borders. Flexibility provisions enable the countries at various digital levels to implement commitments at a slow pace. Mechanisms of institutional cooperation may aid in the implementation of the agreement. Consultations, information exchange, and technical cooperation on a regular basis are useful to ensure that the rules are not outdated with the changes in technology. A BRI digital trade agreement has the capability of establishing a legal benchmark that promotes uniform regulations and diminishes the legal aspect of cross-border digital trade.

8.3 *Institutional Capacity for Digital Trade*

The development and regulation of digital trade in the Belt and Road Initiative requires the development of institutional capacity. The digital trade business is associated with the intricate legal, technological, and regulatory challenges that demand properly equipped institutions and qualified experts. A lack of expertise, loosely enforced or poorly coordinated regulatory bodies, are problems in some of the BRI countries. The initial steps to strengthening institutional capacity include training and education. Regulators, judges, government officials, and legal practitioners ought to have a clear understanding of the concepts of the digital economy, such as electronic commerce, data governance, cybersecurity, and platform regulation. To improve digital trade laws, they should be given specialized training that will help them to draft, interpret, and apply digital trade laws. Another factor that is important is the need to institutionalize coordination. Trade across different regulatory jurisdictions is a common phenomenon in digital trade, including trade, telecommunications, finance, and data protection. Regulatory overlap and inconsistency can be avoided through cooperation between the institutions and the roles of each.

9 Conclusion

One of the crucial issues in establishing a shared legal system of digital economy and trade in the Belt and Road Initiative is the need to ensure proper enforcement. Although alignment of laws and standards can be used to curb the effectiveness of a framework, inconsistent application or non-application may reduce its effectiveness even in cases where the countries have adopted the aligned laws and standards. Digital transactions that cross borders have a tendency to involve more than one jurisdiction, and it is not easy to enforce decisions, contracts, or dispute resolutions across jurisdictions. The improvement of collaboration among national regulatory bodies can be one of the methods of making enforcement stronger. Compliance can be enhanced by sharing information, coordinating investigations, and being aware of the decisions made in other jurisdictions. The fact that the digital contracts, arbitration awards, and mediation outcomes may be mutually recognized enables businesses to get legal certainty even in the case of operating in several countries. It is also helpful to create effective enforcement procedures in the digital trade system.

Chapter 10
Potential Legal and Geopolitical Implications of the Digital Silk Road: Power, Influence, and Global Governance

Abstract Digital Silk Road is a revolutionary feature of the Belt and Road Initiative, which integrates both real infrastructure and highly technological digital networks and makes the region and the world more connected. It is not limited to the conventional trade and infrastructure projects since it incorporates the technologies of fiber-optic cables, 5G networks, satellite communications, cloud computing, e-commerce platforms, and smart city systems. Such changes enable the involved nations to increase digital trade, innovation, and technological collaboration, as well as transform strategic and legislative relations at regional and global levels. This chapter focuses on the Digital Silk Road as a legal and geopolitical initiative, and not just a technological or even a commercial effort. The chapter discusses the effect of the development of digital infrastructure under the Digital Silk Road on state sovereignty, control, and geopolitical location. Findings of this study reveal that telecommunication, e-commerce, and satellite investments contribute to making China a force in creating technological and regulatory standards of the digital economy. Other than domestic laws, China sets regulatory principles for the international community alongside the DSR participating countries. The participating nations can implement these principles in order to harmonize their national rules with the international rules, minimize conflicts, and achieve legal predictability in e-commerce.

Keywords Geopolitical implications of BRI · Legal implications of BRI · Responsible AI and governance · Legal tech evolution · Digital evidence authentication

J. Afzal and Y. Chen, *Legal Framework of Digital Economy and Digital Trade Under the Belt and Road Initiative*, https://doi.org/10.1007/978-981-92-4444-7_10

1 Introduction

Digital Silk Road (DSR) aims at increasing the level of regional and global connectivity through the creation of digital infrastructure, such as fiber-optic networks, satellite systems, cloud computing, e-commerce platforms, and smart technologies.[1] The DSR has been an essential part of global trade, economic growth, and technology through connecting nations through physical and digital networks. The Digital Silk Road, in addition to its economic impact, has geopolitical and legislative consequences.[2] Digital connectivity provides countries with access to regional and global markets, exposure to sophisticated technologies, and enhances strategic impact on the geopolitical front.[3] The balancing of the legal approaches and compliance with national sovereignty is a key issue in supporting digital trade and cooperation. The DSR also indicates changes in legal and regulatory power in the world. Digital leaders with advanced technology, data management, and data infrastructure may influence international markets by developing rules, standards, and norms.[4] This process connects the power of the law to the power of geopolitics because countries that possess the technological advantage can influence international structures of governance indirectly.[5] Simultaneously, the increasing cross-border network integration underscores the necessity of a multilateral dialogue, cooperation, and shared governance mechanisms to establish fairness, transparency, and stability in the digital trade.

The DSR allows countries to build legal presence and formulate regulatory frameworks and globalization patterns of the digital economy by integrating infrastructure building and digital connectivity. In this case, legal power means not only the capacity to establish and implement domestic laws, but also the possibility to affect international rules, norms, and practices according to which digital trade and technological collaboration across borders are regulated.

China encourages a paradigm of digital governance, which is in line with the national regulations and technological standards, through investments in digital

[1] Fakhar Hussain et al., "The Digital Rise and Its Economic Implications for China through the Digital Silk Road under the Belt and Road Initiative," *Asian Journal of Comparative Politics* 9, no. 2 (2024): 238–53.

[2] David Gordon and Meia Nouwens, *The Digital Silk Road: China's Technological Rise and the Geopolitics of Cyberspace* (Taylor & Francis, 2022).

[3] Bilal Ahmed, "Cross-Border Connectivity: Strengthening Economic Ties and Regional Integration," *Journal of Regional Connectivity and Development* 3, no. 1 (2024): 70–84.

[4] Andrei Shelepov, "The Influence of the G20's Digitalization Leadership on Development Conditions and Governance of the Digital Economy," *International Organisations Research Journal* 17, no. 1 (2022).

[5] Ivan V. Danilin, "The Impact of Digital Technologies on Leadership in Global Processes: From Platforms to Markets?," *MGIMO Review of International Relations* 13, no. 1 (2020): 100–116.

infrastructures, telecommunication, satellite, and e-commerce systems.[6,7] Countries that are involved in the DSR usually borrow some elements of these legal and regulatory frameworks to ease the investment, interoperability, and connectivity. This is the means by which China can influence the development of international law indirectly when countries involved in this process adopt these standards into their own legal systems.[8] The DSR also allows the involved nations to build their own legal capacity in the regional and international arenas. The interaction of the countries, that are active in the development of digital infrastructures and law will enable the countries to play a role in the development of regional standards and cooperative agreements. The balancing countries can potentially influence the digital trade, data protection, cybersecurity, and intellectual property standards by negotiating multilaterally, addressing regional digital policy issues, and setting the standards.

2 New Trends in Digital Laws

2.1 Artificial Intelligence Regulation and Ethics

2.1.1 AI Act Compliance

One of the technologies created through the Digital Silk Road is artificial intelligence, which brings the Digital Silk Road to the forefront in the field of cross-border logistics, e-commerce, intelligent control of infrastructure, and digital governance systems.[9] Its implementation, however, is a complicated regulatory and ethical issue, especially in such cases as transnational practices in which different legal traditions, potential of technology, and social norms overlap. The international established laws on AI, such as the AI Act of the European Union, offer a systematic method of the reduction in the number of applications with high risk and encourage ethical use of AI technologies.[10,11] Firms that take part in the Digital Silk Road

---

[6] Shumin Wang et al., "Management Economic Systems and Governance to Reduce Potential Risks in Digital Silk Road Investments: Legal Cooperation between Hainan Free Trade Port and Ethiopia," *Systems* 12, no. 8 (2024): 305.

[7] Genia Kostka, "Digital Governance in China," in *Handbook on Local Governance in China* (Edward Elgar Publishing, 2023).

[8] Pitman B. Potter, "China and the International Legal System: Challenges of Participation," *The China Quarterly* 191 (2007): 699–715.

[9] Nariman Aliyev, "Artificial Intelligence in Digital Silk Road: Driving Innovation and Economic Transformation," *Euroasia Journal of Social Sciences & Humanities* 12, no. 1 (2025): 95–102.

[10] Junaid Butt, "Analytical Study of the World's First EU Artificial Intelligence (AI) Act," *International Journal of Research Publication and Reviews* 5, no. 3 (2024): 7343–64.

[11] Sandra Wachter, "Limitations and Loopholes in the EU AI Act and AI Liability Directives: What This Means for the European Union, the United States, and Beyond," *Yale JL & Tech.* 26 (2023): 671.

projects are forced to make their AI applications capable to meeting local and international legal requirements. A second implication of the AI Act on transparency is the explainability of outputs of the algorithms, that can enable stakeholders to understand the way AI-informed decisions are reached. This is particularly necessary in cross-border transactions along the Digital Silk Road, investor, regulatory agencies, and end-users demand accountability on automated systems that influence the trade flows, the supply chain logistics, or the financial transactions. Ethical considerations are not limited to compliance with the regulations, but they are wider and have more extended mandates, such as restricting biases, safeguarding human rights, and preventing abuse. Multi-jurisdictional projects, such as China-Southeast Asia or Europe links, have diverse cultural, legal, and ethical demands because of the divergent cultural, legal ethical demands, flexible structures that accommodate the local expectations but adhere to global standards of equity and responsibility.

2.1.2 Responsible AI and Governance

The use of artificial intelligence in the Digital Silk Road is transforming trade, the management of infrastructure, and the provision of digital services, but it presents major legal and ethical issues.[12] The concept of responsible AI governance has become a pressing issue, and companies and legal teams have developed structural models to allow AI systems to be transparent, fair, and safe in various jurisdictions.[13] The concept of governance is becoming part of AI lifecycle management, which is designed, deployed, and monitored as opposed to being a subsequent compliance metric.[14] Detection and mitigation of bias is an essential part of these frameworks. The risk with AI systems taking data on different countries is that they may generate results unintentionally biased towards some groups, resulting in unfair treatment or inefficiencies in their work.[15] In response to this, organizations are doing so by introducing continuous auditing and dataset review, model logic review, and decision output review as a way of preventing discriminatory patterns. This transparency is essential to cross-border affairs along the Digital Silk Road, as stakeholders must be convinced that automated decision-making is based on objective and verifiable factors as opposed to black box algorithms. Ethical governance goes hand in hand with security and data protection. The sensitive cross-border data is the basis of the AI system, and a properly developed cybersecurity and data integrity is invaluable. Technical and ethical safeguards are supplemented with accountability mechanisms.

---

[12] Bora Ly, "Challenge and Perspective for Digital Silk Road," *Cogent Business & Management* 7, no. 1 (2020): 1804180.

[13] Jalil Ahmad, "Global AI Governance Assessment for AI-Generated Content for a Globalized Digital World," *International Journal of Law and Legal Advancement* 2, no. 1 (2026): 4–12.

[14] Guru Bhaskar Reddy Duggireddy, "Integrated Data and AI Governance Framework: A Lifecycle Approach to Responsible AI Implementation," *Journal of Computer Science and Technology Studies* 7, no. 7 (2025): 771–77.

[15] Alfonso Min, "Artificial Intelligence and Bias: Challenges, Implications, and Remedies," *Journal of Social Research* 2, no. 11 (2023).

2.1.3 AI-Related Intellectual Property (IP) Disputes

The meaning of the personal and sensitive data is quickly changing in global regulatory frameworks, as the digital operations across borders become more complex along the Digital Silk Road.[16] The traditional concept of personal information (names, addresses, or financial identifiers) is also being extended to biometric information, genetic information, and even neural or behavioral information. Additionally, the existing rules are broadening the definition of inferences using user interactions, predictive analytics, and AI-generated insights to sensitive data, expanding the scope of legal liability of companies that operate within more than one jurisdiction.[17] This expansion has a significant influence on multinational enterprises and technology providers, who have a role in the digital infrastructure of the Silk Road. Organizations need to establish more protective measures to ensure that such derived data can be stored, processed, and shared as per the laws of privacy established in the area to avoid legal and reputational risks. Firms involved in cross-border initiatives along the Digital Silk Road will have to revise their data classification systems, accordingly, making sure that AI and data analytics platforms afford the utmost level of protection to enlarged groups of sensitive data.

2.1.4 AI "Hallucination" Liability

Artificial intelligence is shaping the Digital Silk Road, and it is affecting the supply chain management, monitoring digital trade, and infrastructure. Though AI improves efficiency and decision-making, it also presents legal, ethical, and operational issues that require governance in detail.[18,19] Institutions are placing systems to make AI operate in a fair, transparent, and secure manner to satisfy the regulatory and cultural demands of various jurisdictions. Prevention of bias is one of the main issues. To counter this, organizations perform continuous data sets, algorithmic logic, and output auditing. Unintended biases can be detected and resolved before the implementation of AI by the independent oversight and scenario-based testing, so that all operations can be made with balanced and fair decisions.

---

[16] Gulbakyt Bolatbekkyzy, "Legal Issues of Cross-Border Data Transfer in the Era of Digital Government," *Journal of Digital Technologies and Law* 2, no. 2 (2024): 286–307.

[17] Vikrant Sopan Yadav and Abhijeet Dhere, "AI Agents and Legal Intricacies: A Comprehensive Literature Review," 2025, 28–45.

[18] Junaid Sattar Butt, "The Impact of Artificial Intelligence (AI) on the Efficiency of Administrative Decision Making Including Ethical & Legal Considerations and Comparative Study about Countries Already Incorporated AI for Administrative Decisions.," *Acta Universitatis Danubius. Juridica* 19, no. 3 (2023): 7–25.

[19] Axel Walz and Kay Firth-Butterfield, "Implementing Ethics into Artificial Intelligence: A Contribution, from a Legal Perspective, to the Development of an AI Governance Regime," *Duke L. & Tech. Rev.* 18 (2019): 176.

2.2 Data Protection and Privacy

The blistering development of the Digital Silk Road has emphasized the urgent need to have strong data protection and privacy systems. The companies cannot use the standard compliance models as was the case in the early stages of global digital trade. Rather, they are confronted with a disjointed international privacy situation, with national and regional laws creating different and even conflicting duties. This fragmentation has released operational complexity and strategic consideration to organizations that must be involved in multi-jurisdictional digital endeavors. Data privacy in the United States is highly regulated, and the state has made a move to regulate data privacy by creating state laws like the California Consumer Privacy Act (CCPA) and the Virginia Consumer Data Protection Act, which have given stringent regulations on how data is processed, consent, and user rights.[20,21] The companies that exist on the Digital Silk Road must negotiate these state-based structures, as well as deal with cross-border data flows, which must have a fine-tuned legal strategy and technical architecture.

The proposed Digital Personal Data Protection Act and the new regulatory guidance places the organization to have the duty of localized data storage, strict control over consent management, and responsibility over data processing. Such regulations in the context of business ventures participating in the Silk Road initiatives that involve regional-based adjustments in data governance frameworks particularly in cross-border AI and cloud-based business. New data privacy laws in Africa, such as in Nigeria (Data Protection Regulation) and South Africa (Protection of Personal Information Act (POPIA)) only add to the situation, and multinational companies must develop their own compliance programs to comply with local laws and regulations and stay afloat economically.[22,23] The difference in enforcement schemes, understanding of personal data, and punishment frameworks among territories further stipulates why flexible, dynamic approaches to privacy are desirable, as opposed to enforcing a uniform compliance scheme and a blanket approach to regulations.

---

[20] Rob Bonta, "California Consumer Privacy Act (CCPA)," *Retrieved from State of California Department of Justice:* https://Oag.ca.Gov/Privacy/Ccpa, 2022, 4–40.

[21] Bryce Clayton Newell et al., "Regulating the Data Market: The Material Scope of American Consumer Data Privacy Law," *U. Pa. J. Int'l L.* 45 (2023): 1055.

[22] Olumide Babalola, "Data Protection Legal Regime and Data Governance in Africa: An Overview," *Data Governance and Policy in Africa*, 2023, 71–96.

[23] Victoria Udoh and David Ademola Olajide, "Data Protection in Nigeria: A Review of the Nigerian Data Protection Regulation 2019 and the Need for Nigeria to Sign the African Convention on Data Protection," *Available at SSRN 3766819*, 2021.

2.3 *Legal Tech Evolution*

2.3.1 Agentic AI in Workflow

The AI-based systems are changing to the next level of communication to stop mere automation and transform the legal sphere into a totally different sphere.[24] The basic document review or generative chatbots are being replaced by autonomous AI agents, which are capable of handling a multi-step legal procedure.[25] End-to-end processes, such as contract analysis, monitoring regulatory compliance, and e-discovery, can be handled by these agents with a minimum of human input. The shift to agentic AI enables law firms and corporate legal departments to handle more complex cases more efficiently, to minimize areas of operational bottlenecks, and to achieve a greater degree of precision in document processing. The repetitive or routine tasks are no longer limited to the AI implementation in the legal processes.[26] Current systems are able to process high amounts of cross-border agreements, isolate key terms, and find risks of non-compliance in a variety of jurisdictions, which is especially applicable to the Digital Silk Road. Such AI agents can spot inconsistencies, predict potential disagreements, and even suggest mitigation measures with a combination of natural language processing and machine learning, which are, in effect, proactive legal assistants. The other significant innovation is that AI is compatible with the already existing legal management systems. The AI agents can easily incorporated into document management systems, e-filing systems, and knowledge databases, forming an automated and ubiquitous workflow, accelerating the process of decision-making.[27] Such a kind of integration minimizes human error, provides uniformity of regulatory standards, and scalability of operations, particularly in multinational enterprises operating in a complex cross-border legal environment crossing the Digital Silk Road.

2.3.2 Digital Evidence Authentication

As deepfakes, AI-generated media, and advanced editing of content continue to grow, the legal world is encountering more challenges in the authenticity of digital

---

[24] Francesco Contini, "Artificial Intelligence and the Transformation of Humans, Law and Technology Interactions in Judicial Proceedings," *Law, Tech. & Hum.* 2 (2020): 4.

[25] Sara Migliorini, "'More than Words': A Legal Approach to the Risks of Commercial Chatbots Powered by Generative Artificial Intelligence," *European Journal of Risk Regulation* 15, no. 3 (2024): 719–36.

[26] Chay Brooks et al., "Artificial Intelligence in the Legal Sector: Pressures and Challenges of Transformation," *Cambridge Journal of Regions, Economy and Society* 13, no. 1 (2020): 135–52.

[27] Md Nazrul Islam Khan, "Legal Documentation and Case Management: A Systematic Review of Digitization Trends and Cybersecurity Challenges in Legal Support Roles," *Review of Applied Science and Technology* 2, no. 01 (2023): 01–25.

evidence than ever before.[28,29] There is a growing trend of courts and other regulatory bodies to identify whether videos and images, as well as audio and text, have been manipulated, forged, or synthesized. This has turned digital authentication of evidence into a high-stakes litigation and compliance field, particularly in cross-border business disputes enabled by platforms on the Digital Silk Road. The current evidence verification methods integrate cryptographic time stamping, blockchain provenance, and forensic analysis based on AI. Metadata inconsistencies, artifacts of manipulation, and provenance of each digital asset are examined, allowing legal departments to create a chain of custody that can withstand courtroom questioning. These technologies make sure that evidence used in court is not only real but also can be traced to the source, which will reduce the chances of fraud or misrepresentation. It is further complicated when evidence becomes inter-border. Legal teams have to manoeuvre between these differing regulations and, at the same time, make sure the verification procedures are in line with the legal framework of the sending and receiving countries. It has resulted in the acceptance of consistent worldwide standards of digital evidence management, which facilitates uninterrupted authentication of multinational litigation.

2.3.3 Blockchain and Smart Contracts

The development of blockchain technology is causing a change in the perception of the legal systems towards digital agreements.[30] Self-enforcing protocols, or smart contracts, are pushing the traditional idea of enforceability to its limits, and regulators and courts need to develop new paradigms so that technological autonomy and legal accountability are both enforced. In the Digital Silk Road, in which the transactions between jurisdictions are concerned, ensuring that the smart contracts comply with the needs of domestic and foreign laws has become a strategic issue for multinational companies. The laws have evolved to emphasize transparency of code, tracking of execution, and audit trails in order to make it dependable. Smart contracts are no longer viewed as automated tools but are increasingly being considered as legally binding tools that may be reviewed, corrected, or arbitrated in the case of a dispute.[31] Firms are also shifting towards dual-layered governance, which includes

[28] Jamil Afzal, "Comparative Review on Acceptance of Digital Evidence within the Legal Frameworks of Pakistan and China," *International Journal of Law and Legal Advancement* 1, no. 1 (2025).

[29] David Chukwuebuka MKPO, "Is Truth And Integrity Of Justice On Trial In The Age Of Artificial Intelligence (Ai)? Re-Assessing Digital Evidence in the Context of Ai-Generated Evidence Such As Deepfakes," *International Review of Law and Jurisprudence (IRLJ)* 7, no. 1 (2025).

[30] Daniel Bennet et al., "Blockchain Technology: Revolutionizing Transactions in the Digital Age," *ADI Journal on Recent Innovation* 5, no. 2 (2024): 192–99.

[31] Reyan Hameed Arain, "Colonial Shadows and Digital Era: Reforming the Arbitrary and Draconian Justice System of Pakistan," *International Journal of Law and Legal Advancement* 1, no. 2 (2025).

legal controls on blockchain networks, enabling automated execution of contracts, however, without conflict with applicable statutory provisions.

2.4 *Digital Economy and Transactions*

The introduction of transnational digital trade, particularly the Digital Silk Road, has ensured that there are effective enforcement mechanisms in the e-marketplaces. The change in law through the EU Digital Services Act (DSA) and UK Digital Markets, Competition, and Consumer (DMCC) Act provides regulators with the ability to counteract deceptive practices, anti-competitive behaviour, and exploitative digital design patterns known as dark patterns.[32,33] Such laws signify a shift towards active surveillance as opposed to a passive one, and that the digital platforms should be operated in an open, fair, and accountable way. Enforcement is not a simple compliance. Regulators are also paying attention to the accountability of algorithms, assessing the impact of recommendation engines, pricing algorithms, and review management systems on consumer behavior. Artificial improvement of product ratings, controlling how visible the competitors' listing appears, or creating interfaces that create a false impression of the user being in an unwanted purchase, is a practice that is receiving a growing share of legal scrutiny. Those companies unable to abide by may face huge fines, restrictions on their operations, or, as part of remedial actions, be forced to undertake measures that ensure the implementation of cross-border e-commerce laws, especially in countries that have enforced these laws. The new trends presuppose that the regulatory technology (RegTech) solutions will be more central.[34] Marketplaces can validate compliance claims and proactively reduce risks with tools that can provide continuous auditing, blockchain-based verification of transaction validity, and behavioral analytics based on AI. The inventions are especially applicable to the operators of Digital Silk Roads when large quantities of cross-border activities require scalable, automated, and legally binding oversight systems.

---

[32] Emely von Platen, "With or without Efficiency Defence? Analysing the Role of Efficiency Defence in Traditional Ex-Post Enforcement, the EU Digital Markets Act & the UK Digital Markets, Competition and Consumers Act," *NEL Rev.* 10 (2024): 22.

[33] Miroslava Marinova, "The UK's Digital Market Regulation: The Need for a Proportionality Principle in the CMA's New Framework," *Journal of European Competition Law & Practice* 15, no. 7 (2024): 491–97.

[34] Daniel Broby et al., "Towards Secure and Intelligent Regulatory Technology (Regtech): A Research Agenda," *Technology and Regulation* 2022 (2022): 88–99.

3 Geopolitical Implications of the Digital Silk Road

3.1 Technological Dependence and Influence

The combination of Chinese digital infrastructure in Belt and Road countries has formed a new level of technological impact.[35] Besides conventional investment in network infrastructure or hardware, this dependency brings operational and informational leverage to the digital infrastructure of recipient countries. Huawei, ZTE, and Alibaba companies offer not only telecommunications and cloud platforms but also frameworks according to which data management, communications, and AI-enhanced services are managed.[36] Such a structure places the provider country in a position to have long-term strategic leverage in the technological, economic, and even policy spheres. Dependence on technology results in dynamic operational control.[37] The countries that rely on external cloud-based systems, AI-based logistics, or management platforms of smart cities tend to exist within frameworks that are supported by third-party providers. Such an arrangement may provide the provider country with indirect control over the efficiency of operations, system upgrades, and a collective intelligence of sensitive industries, and establish a lever without being too obvious.

Another aspect of influence is ecosystem shaping. The tendency of recipient countries that adopt foreign technology is to conform to proprietary standards, regulatory protocol, and development methodology that are externally defined. This location generates path dependency, in which it is costly or complex to perform domestic substitutes. The national digital infrastructure is slowly overlaying the foreign-designed infrastructure, and the presence of the initial supplier of the technology in different industries, including finance, healthcare, and transport, is being extended strategically. This dependency is enhanced by the geopolitical consequences of data governance. Digital networks that are being created in high-tech generate a lot of information, such as industrial processes, governmental processes, and services to its citizens.[38] Indirect understanding of the network and pattern of operations is provided by the architectural design and metadata, even in situations where access of foreigners is restricted by contract. This type of informational asymmetry offers

---

35 Sainan Zhao et al., "Dynamic Influence of Digital and Technological Advancement on Sustainable Economic Growth in Belt and Road Initiative (BRI) Countries," *Sustainability* 14, no. 23 (2022): 15782.

36 Adnan Shahid et al., "Large-Scale AI in Telecom: Charting the Roadmap for Innovation, Scalability, and Enhanced Digital Experiences," *arXiv Preprint arXiv:2503.04184*, 2025.

37 K. J. Ju et al., "Causal Relationship between Supply Chain Dynamic Capabilities, Technological Innovation, and Operational Performance," *Management and Production Engineering Review* 7 (2016).

38 Michael E. Milakovich, *Digital Governance: New Technologies for Improving Public Service and Participation* (Routledge, 2012).

the provider country an opportunity to forecast economic trends, monitor the performance of the system, and manipulate the behavior of the stakeholders in the host countries.

3.2 *Surveillance and Governance Export*

Digital Silk Road allows the cross-border export and import of cutting-edge surveillance technologies, which places China as a significant exporter of digital governance solutions.[39] The initiative goes beyond just providing technology to partner nations by facilitating the implementation of these tools, which incorporate elements of regulatory philosophy, operational control, and monitoring practices into the infrastructures of recipient countries.[40] This exportation of instruments of governance is an excellent method of fostering the alignment of overseas digital policy with Chinese ideals of information management and security systems. Such systems offer the recipient countries a chance to enjoy advanced monitoring opportunities, which can facilitate the real-time collection and analysis of personal, commercial, and public sector data. Even though such technologies facilitate better law enforcement and control the administrations, they create a certain reliance on foreign technology experience, program maintenance, and exclusive algorithms, which enhance the influence of the provider on the operations and regulatory decision-making. The Digital Silk Road is therefore not only an outlet to technology but also an avenue of influencing the practices of national governance according to the Chinese norms.

3.3 *Standard Setting and AI Standards*

The Digital Silk Road is a powerful mechanism to regulate the technological situation in the world, particularly in such a strategic sphere as artificial intelligence, 5G networks, Internet of Things (IoT), and cloud computing infrastructure. Besides the simple implementation of hardware, the strategy of Beijing is on the establishment of norms, protocols, and interoperable structures that define how digital systems operate in the global market. These criteria are embedded in the infrastructural work, software platform, and AI systems being provided to partner countries, and they are in fact exporting a form of governance that integrates technical, regulatory, and operational ideals. The recipient countries, especially in Africa, Southeast Asia, and Latin America, are usually constrained in their budgets and have a pressing need to digitalize their ways at a high rate. The DSR offers affordable, pre-assembled, and

[39] Kevin Hernandez, *Achieving Complex Development Goals along China's Digital Silk Road*, 2019.

[40] Mihail C. Roco, "Possibilities for Global Governance of Converging Technologies," *Journal of Nanoparticle Research* 10, no. 1 (2008): 11–29.

technological solutions, which enable governments to bypass the usual infrastructure development processes. Although this speeds up the digitalization of the economy, it also presents China with a special chance to influence the design of these digital ecosystems, such as protocol design or network security standards. The integration of Chinese standards into AI algorithms, 5G implementation, and smart cities gradually brings the technological systems of these countries to the priorities of Beijing, which generates a long-term effect that is carried over into the policymaking process, the design of regulators, and operational decisions.

3.4 Security Vulnerabilities

The high use of Chinese digital infrastructure by the Belt and Road countries has brought about complicated security issues to both recipient nations and their foreign collaborators. Employing new technologies can become areas of vulnerability that, in uncontrollable cases, can be used by criminal organizations or can be exploited to exert geopolitical power.[41] These weaknesses do not just confine themselves to more traditional types of cyber threats, but also encompass the integrity of the supply chains, manipulation of firmware, and systematic dependencies in operations. Some of the countermeasures by the Western-oriented countries and alliances have been triggered by this growing Chinese domination of key sectors.[42,43] Only a few of the initiatives, which are introduced to make sure that digital ecosystems are not exploited, are the G7 Partnership for Global Infrastructure and Investment (PGII), the shared technological projects of the Quad countries, and the shared structures of the EU and the U.S. These strategies are to build resilient, interoperable, and secure infrastructure with other external technologies and governance models to minimize the dependence on a single external provider without slowing down the pace of modernization objectives.

[41] Molly Cook-Kwenda, "Tech-Enabled Global Cybercrime: Exploitation by Transnational Criminal Organizations (TCOS)," *Iconic Research and Engineering Journals* 8, no. 3 (2024): 55–101.

[42] Stephen Aris and Aglaya Snetkov, "'Global Alternatives, Regional Stability and Common Causes': The International Politics of the Shanghai Cooperation Organization and Its Relationship to the West," *Eurasian Geography and Economics* 54, no. 2 (2013): 202–26.

[43] Murat Güneylioğlu, "Globalization, Deglobalization, and the US-China Competition: The Balance between Geopolitics and Geoeconomics," *Türk Sosyal Bilimler Araştırmaları Dergisi* 8, no. 2 (2023): 89–113.

4 Legal Implications of the Digital Silk Road

4.1 Export of Digital Authoritarianism

The Digital Silk Road enables the export of China's model of a state-centred system of internet regulation, also known as the China Solution, to other nations.[44,45] This framework puts emphasis on cyber sovereignty, in which governments are given extensive control over the territories on the internet within their jurisdictions. The mechanisms, technologies, and structures involved are made available to the countries involved to enable them to monitor the content, selectively censor, and manage user identities effectively, altering the working and regulatory landscape of their digital worlds. In contrast to the traditional models of internet governance based on the ideas of openness and interoperability, the model supported by DSR promotes the centralized governance of the flows of information over the internet. With the aggregation of surveillance platforms, AI-based content moderation and identity verification systems, states will be able to precisely regulate communications, social media interactions, and online shopping. Through such abilities, governments can enforce local discourses, suppress opposition, and restrict online anonymity without affecting the outward appearance of a digital infrastructure. Exportation of these systems is not totally technological; it also proposes normative structures of governance. The adoption of the DSR-enabling tools by countries tends to enact their own policies that align with the Chinese demands in digital ethics, laws, and regulations on cybersecurity and legal systems for managing content. Over the long-term, such alignment culminates in institutionalized practices that capture the Chinese way of doing things and bring about a long-term shift in the notion of conceptualizing and exercising digital sovereignty.

4.2 Regulatory Harmonization and Standards

The Digital Silk Road plays a strategic role; China exercises both technological and regulatory influence on the world, not only in the form of infrastructure, but also in the form of legal and policy structures of the countries involved. Through offering superior solutions in 5G telecommunications, artificial intelligence, biometric systems, and facial recognition technologies, China essentially sets the technical standards that

---

[44] Ernst-Ulrich Petersmann, "International Settlement of Trade and Investment Disputes over Chinese 'Silk Road Projects' inside the European Union," in *A Legal Analysis of the Belt and Road Initiative: Towards a New Silk Road?* (Springer, 2020).

[45] Francine Hug, "Domestic E-Commerce Promotion through State-Managed Liberalisation," in *China's Free Trade Agreement Strategies: Securing the Chinese Developmental State and Socialist Market Economy* (Springer, 2024).

guide the regulatory standards in Southeast Asia, Africa, and the Middle East.[46,47] These norms tend to be incorporated into local law to establish a structural fit between domestic law and Chinese norms. The Chinese have a strategic advantage in creating normative convergence. Through the influence of law-making, as well as the implementation of technology, China makes sure that recipient countries implement policies that will benefit its digital ecosystem.

4.3 Legal Fragmentation

The introduction of the DSR-conformant systems to the countries will most likely bring in the Chinese cybersecurity, data governance, and AI regulation frameworks. Western practices are also very different in these rules and contain the General Data Protection Regulation (GDPR) of the EU or industry-specific cybersecurity rules in the United States, each with conflicting duties on multinational technology operators. This separation equates to convoluted compliance environments for multinational technology firms. As well as the regulations in the host countries, which should also be modified to DSR, the products, software updates, and working procedures will have to be modified to Western or international standards. This twofold need adds to the cost of operation and the risk of lawsuits and complicates the administration, especially in cases where it is concerned with businesses using AI-based services, cross-border cloud services, and critical infrastructure management.

4.4 Dispute Resolution

The Digital Silk Road highlights the necessity of flexible, technology-conscious, and globally integrated dispute resolution measures, where digital modernization and digital infrastructural development do not proceed faster than dispute resolution mechanisms. Good structures need to be able to balance the technological advances, business needs, and regulatory measures, and establish robust mechanisms for handling conflicts in a fast-changing digital economy.

---

[46] Mohamed Id Bouhou and Yongmei Chen, "The Application of Laws Related to International Trade in Africa: Conflict and the Possibility of Unification," *International Journal of Law and Legal Advancement* 1, no. 2 (2025).

[47] Andrew Mazen Dahdal and Adel Abdel Ghafar, "The Digital Silk Road: 'Tech-Diplomacy' as a Paradigm for Understanding Technological Adoption and Emerging Digital Regulations in MENA," *Asian Journal of Law and Society* 12, no. 2 (2025): 163–88.

5 Geopolitical Competition of Digital Governance

Geopolitical and legal competition among countries (the global north and the global south) has increased due to the growth of the Digital Silk Road, and it is reshaping the structure and implementation of digital governance across borders. In the framework of the DSR, the issue of governance cannot be viewed merely as a technical or administrative one, yet governance can be identified as a strategic means by which nations project power, gain economic benefits, and safeguard their national interest. This competition is a symptom of larger tussles over world power, where countries are competing to have control over the policy and regulation of the world that is becoming more and more digitalized. The concept of digital governance brings up geopolitical competition due to the strategic importance of digital infrastructure.[48] The controversy surrounding compliance, liability, and enforcement shows that the competition in the field of governance is not limited to investment in infrastructure but also to such areas as the law and enforcement of rules. Geopolitical and legal competition is also focused on intellectual property rights (IPR). The power to regulate software, digital platforms, algorithms, and new technologies enables nations to exert pressure over IP regimes of the world. The legal systems that regulate patents, licensing, and technological innovation ascertain the nation or companies that can dominate the markets, regulate innovation, and exercise rights worldwide. Signing bilateral and multilateral deals enables countries to have legal reach as well as create a competitive environment for online technologies. The digitalization of governance is strengthening regional competition through positioning it in the greater economic and strategic efforts.

6 Global Legal Governance and the Digital Silk Road

Global legal governance is defined as the systems, rules, and institutions that help international cooperation as well as govern activities that cut across national boundaries. The DSR works with such systems of governance by influencing standards, shaping regulations, and providing avenues of multilateral coordination. The application of the international legal framework and the integration of international, regional, and domestic laws help to emphasize the significance of managing the complex interactions between the digital and the real world.[49,50] The regulation of cross-border

---

[48] Kieron O'hara and Wendy Hall, *Four Internets: The Geopolitics of Digital Governance*, 2018.

[49] Nsisong Louis Eyo-Udo et al., "International Trade Law in the Modern World: A Review of Evolving Practices and Agreements," *International Journal of Multidisciplinary Research and Growth Evaluation*, 2025.

[50] Zaid Rehman, "Beyond Borders: International Law and Global Governance in the Digital Age," *Journal of Accounting & Business Archive Review* 1, no. 1 (2023): 1–12.

digital trade is one of the key elements of global legal regulation in the DSR context. The online banking services, e-commerce platforms, and cloud computing services are becoming the core of international trade. The regulation in this area assumes that regulations to control the sphere should be transparent, reliable, and fair in terms of online transactions.[51] In order to trade and invest, the countries that are the parties in the DSR are usually forced to harmonize the laws in their home countries with international ones. These standards are on electronic contracts, digital signatures, consumer protection, and dispute resolution systems. Conformity of local laws to those of the international standards will facilitate cross-border transactions and limit uncertainty in the law among businesses and investors. The technical capacity of countries allows directing such legal frameworks, which affect the process of partners putting in place protection measures, risk management, and incident response.

7 Future Scenario of the Digital Silk Road

The Digital Silk Road is still growing, and it defines the ways in which digital infrastructure, trade networks, and governance systems of the member countries interact. In the future, DSR will be interfered with by the changing legislation, technology, and geopolitics. Different scenarios can be expected, with the way countries establish regulations, policy coordination, and trade between national interest and international cooperation. Knowledge of these possible situations is paramount to policymakers, companies, and international organizations who are willing to join or control the expanding digital network.

Among the possible scenarios is the reinforcement of the legal harmonization among the participating countries. With the rise in digital trade and interconnectivity across borders, pressure to implement uniform laws and regulations of e-commerce, data protection, cybersecurity, and intellectual property may be on the rise. The DSR countries may use domestic rules to match the global standards and Chinese technical standards and make digital transactions easier and less ambiguous. Legal harmonization can also facilitate such regional integration where nations are able to work together more efficiently in matters relating to dispute resolution, monitoring of compliance, and management of infrastructure. The DSR in this case acts as a network of nations that have harmonized legal systems promoting commerce, innovation, and advancement of technologies.

The other situation is the emergence of regional clusters of influence in accordance with the technological leadership and regulatory models. Countries that can establish sufficient amounts of digital infrastructure and control opportunities can become champions of clusters within the general DSR network. This situation highlights the

[51] Ian Brown and Christopher T. Marsden, *Regulating Code: Good Governance and Better Regulation in the Information Age* (MIT Press, 2023).

significance of foreign policy, political acumen, and intergovernmental cooperation to plan the future of the DSR. The Digital Silk Road will not be any less than the interaction of economic growth, legal power, and geopolitical power. The project will offer investment, transfer of technology, and cooperation in the region. The future of the Digital Silk Road will depend on an alignment of laws and technological leadership, as well as the negotiation approach of the involved countries.

Bibliography

Aaronson, Susan Ariel. "Data Is Different, and That's Why the World Needs a New Approach to Governing Cross-Border Data Flows." *Digital Policy, Regulation and Governance* 21, no. 5 (2019): 441–60.

Abdelrehim Hammad, Ahmed Arafa, Asif Khan, and Nishan-E. Soomro. "Digital Economy Barriers to Trade Regulation Status, Challenges, and China's Response." *International Journal of Social Sciences Perspectives* 8, no. 2 (2021): 41–49.

Abdieva, Yrys. "Organization for Economic Cooperation and Development (OECD)." In *The Palgrave Encyclopedia of Global Security Studies*. Springer, 2023.

Abedi, Fahimeh, John Zeleznikow, and Chris Brien. "Developing Regulatory Standards for the Concept of Security in Online Dispute Resolution Systems." *Computer Law & Security Review* 35, no. 5 (2019): 105328.

Abedi, Fahimeh, John Zeleznikow, and Chris Brien. "Universal Standards for the Concept of Fairness in Online Dispute Resolution in B2C E-Disputes." *Ohio St. J. on Disp. Resol.* 34 (2019): 357.

Abiodun, Kehinde. "Digital Infrastructure & Sustainable Data Centers Investment in Africa: Role of Tier III & Tier IV." *Int. J. Multidiscip. Res. Growth Eval* 6 (2025): 1878–88.

Aboul-Dahab, Karim Mohamed. "The Virtual Silk Road between China and the Arab States." *Asian Journal of Middle Eastern and Islamic Studies* 15, no. 1 (2021): 51–65.

Adebiyi, Olubukola Omolara. "Taxation in the Digital Age: An Examination of the Necessity, Feasibility, and Implications of Taxing Virtual Infrastructures." *Asian Journal of Economics, Business and Accounting* 23, no. 23 (2023): 13–35.

Africa, North. "Other United Nations Bodies." *Organization*, 2020.

Afzal, J., N. Mathlouthi, MS Rahal, C. Yongmei, A. Haider, and MA Afzal. *Statistical Analysis of Foreign Investment Using Neutrosophic Interval Based Approach. Neutrosophic Sets and Systems, 79 (1), 14.* 2025.

Afzal, Jamil. "Best Practice of Digital Laws and Digital Justice." In *Implementation of Digital Law as a Legal Tool in the Current Digital Era*. Springer, 2024.

Afzal, Jamil. "Comparative Review on Acceptance of Digital Evidence within the Legal Frameworks of Pakistan and China." *International Journal of Law and Legal Advancement* 1, no. 1 (2025).

Afzal, Jamil. "Decentralized Currencies and Digital Economy: Stability and Implications of Digital Currency." In *Exploring the New Horizons of International Law Concerning Globalization of Economy*. Springer, 2026.

Afzal, Jamil. *Exploring the New Horizons of International Law Concerning Globalization of Economy*. Springer Nature, 2026.

Afzal, Jamil. *Implementation of Digital Law as a Legal Tool in the Current Digital Era*. Springer, 2024.

J. Afzal and Y. Chen, *Legal Framework of Digital Economy and Digital Trade Under the Belt and Road Initiative*, https://doi.org/10.1007/978-981-92-4444-7

Afzal, Jamil. "Legal Challenges Regarding Digital Operations." In *Implementation of Digital Law as a Legal Tool in the Current Digital Era*. Springer, 2024.

Afzal, Jamil. "Nomenclature of the Digital Economy and Contemporary Theory of Digitalization." In *Exploring the New Horizons of International Law Concerning Globalization of Economy*. Springer, 2026.

Afzal, Jamil. "Theory of Digitalization: Contemporary Theory of Digitalization." *International Journal of Discovery in Social Sciences* 2, no. 1 (2026).

Afzal, Jamil, and Muhammad Adeel Afzal. "Leveraging ICT for Social Sustainability in Pakistan through the Mediating Role of Gender Empowerment and Institutional Support." *Quality & Quantity*, 2026, 1–25.

Afzal, Jamil, Muhammad Adeel Afzal, and Catherine Hume. "Analyzing the Role of Foreign Direct Investment, Human Welfare, and Gender Equality for Economic Sustainability in the Digital Era." *Quality & Quantity*, 2026, 1–24.

Afzal, Jamil, Muhammad Adeel Afzal, and Zuhaib Nishtar. "Completion of the Ten Years of the China-Pakistan Economic Corridor (CPEC) and Its Economical Goals." *Inverge Journal of Social Sciences* 2, no. 4 (2023): 23–29.

Afzal, Jamil, and Ibrar Ahmad. "The ITLOS Advisory Opinion on Climate Change and Marine Pollution: Some Reflections." *Environmental Policy and Law* 55, nos. 2–3 (2025): 68–75.

Afzal, Jamil, and Aftab Haider. "Environmental and Resource Protection Law by Ke Zhou, Luozhi Yi, Xinjian Su and Youhai Sun." *International Journal of Law and Legal Advancement* 1, no. 2 (2025).

Afzal, Jamil, Zhou Yihong, Maria Qayum, Usama Afzal, and Muhammad Aslam. "Effects of Dam on Temperature, Humidity and Precipitation of Surrounding Area: A Case Study of Gomal Zam Dam in Pakistan." *Environmental Science and Pollution Research* 30, no. 6 (2023): 14592–603.

Afzal, Jamil, and Chen Yongmei. "Federal and Provincial Legislation Regarding 'Right to Information' for Good Governance in Pakistan." *Discover Global Society* 1, no. 1 (2023): 12.

Agbeno, Evans Kofi. "Algorithmic Sovereignty: Regulating Artificial Intelligence and Data Colonialism under the African Continental Free Trade Area (AfCFTA) Framework." *International Journal of Humanities, Management, Engineering, Education and Legal Studies*, 2025, 42–83.

Aguilar, Eddy S. Astudillo. "Waking the Sleeping Lion: The China-Ecuador FTA and Its Implications." *Global Trade and Customs Journal* 19, no. 11/12 (2024).

Ahmad, Ibrar, and Jamil Afzal. "Human Rights Approach for Climate Justice–Verein Klimaseniorinnen Schweiz and Others v. Switzerland." *Studies in Social Justice* 19, no. 1 (2025): 163–70.

Ahmad, Ibrar, Aftab Haider, and Jamil Afzal. "The Geopolitical and Economic Impact of BRICS on the Middle East." *FWU Journal of Social Sciences* 18, no. 4 (2024): 80–95.

Ahmad, Ifzal, and M. Rezaul Islam. "Empowerment and Participation: Key Strategies for Inclusive Development." In *Building Strong Communities: Ethical Approaches to Inclusive Development*. Emerald Publishing Limited, 2024.

Ahmad, Jalil. "Global AI Governance Assessment for AI-Generated Content for a Globalized Digital World." *International Journal of Law and Legal Advancement* 2, no. 1 (2026): 4–12.

Ahmed, Bilal. "Cross-Border Connectivity: Strengthening Economic Ties and Regional Integration." *Journal of Regional Connectivity and Development* 3, no. 1 (2024): 70–84.

Ahmed, Usman. "The Importance of Cross-Border Regulatory Cooperation in an Era of Digital Trade." *World Trade Review* 18, no. S1 (2019): S99–120.

Ahmedov, Ikrom. "The Impact of Digital Economy on International Trade." *European Journal of Business and Management Research* 5, no. 4 (2020).

Akbar, Faisal, Junaid Hussain, Muhammad Babar Usman, and Jamil Afzal. "The Impact of Financial Scams on Consumer Trust in the Banking Sector: A Qualitative Analysis." *International Journal of Discovery in Social Sciences* 1, no. 1 (2025).

Aktar, Most Asikha, Mu'ath Hesham Metlaq Al-Azzam, and Md Mahmudul Alam. "Fair Debts Management for Sustainable Development." In *Reduced Inequalities*. Springer, 2021.

Al Kez, Dlzar, Aoife M. Foley, David Laverty, Dylan Furszyfer Del Rio, and Benjamin Sovacool. "Exploring the Sustainability Challenges Facing Digitalization and Internet Data Centers." *Journal of Cleaner Production* 371 (2022): 133633.

Aladwan, Zaid. "The Implementation of the Fraud Exception Rule: A Comparative Study." *Journal of Financial Crime* 27, no. 3 (2020): 977–93.

Alam, Tanweer, Mohammad Ayoub Khan, Natheer K. Gharaibeh, and Malik Khlaif Gharaibeh. "Big Data for Smart Cities: A Case Study of NEOM City, Saudi Arabia." In *Smart Cities: A Data Analytics Perspective*. Springer, 2020.

Alami, Ilias. "Foreign Investment Screening Mechanisms and Emergent Geographies of (Post) Globalization." *Dialogues in Human Geography*, 2024, 20438206241278733.

Albalawee, Nasir. "E-Contracting within Jordan's Legal Framework." *Pakistan Journal of Criminology* 16, no. 1 (2024).

Albalooshia, Sultan Ahmed, Md Ahsan, and Mohammad Habibur Rahman. "Deployment of 5G Technology in the United Arab Emirates: Perspectives and Insights." *Kamu Yönetimi ve Politikaları Dergisi* 2, no. 1 (2021): 35–53.

Alexander, Nadja, and Alvin Leu Jun Kang. "Das Neue ODR-Rahmenwerk Der APEC Als Wegbereiter Für Internationale Online-Streitbeilegung." *Zeitschrift Für Konfliktmanagement* 25, no. 6 (2022).

Aliyev, Nariman. "Artificial Intelligence in Digital Silk Road: Driving Innovation and Economic Transformation." *Euroasia Journal of Social Sciences & Humanities* 12, no. 1 (2025): 95–102.

Al-khawatreh, Abdulaziz, and Ahmad Imad Yusuf Mefleh Al-Ghoiwari. "Modern Technologies in Enhancing the Oversight of Money Laundering Crimes and Their Social Impact." In *Artificial Intelligence for Sustainable Innovation Management and Risk Management: A Systems (and Network) Perspective*. Springer, 2026.

AllahRakha, Naeem. "Rethinking Digital Borders to Address Jurisdiction and Governance in the Global Digital Economy." *Int. J. Law Policy* 2, no. 1 (2024).

Almulhim, Abdulaziz I., and Tan Yigitcanlar. "Understanding Smart Governance of Sustainable Cities: A Review and Multidimensional Framework." *Smart Cities* 8, no. 4 (2025): 113.

ALsheyab, Mohammad Saeed Abdallah. "Legal Analysis of the Merits of Electronic Transferable Records: Toward Cross-Border Trade Digitalization." *International Journal of Law and Management* 67, no. 1 (2025): 145–63.

Al-Surmi, Abdulrahman, Mahdi Bashiri, and Ioannis Koliousis. "AI Based Decision Making: Combining Strategies to Improve Operational Performance." *International Journal of Production Research* 60, no. 14 (2022): 4464–86.

Ambalov, Vitaly, and Irina Heim. "Investments in the Digital Silk Road." In *Kazakhstan's Diversification from the Natural Resources Sector: Strategic and Economic Opportunities*. Springer, 2020.

Amiri, Sayed Mahbub Hasan. "Beyond Language Barriers: Multilingual NLP and Voice Recognition for Global Connectivity." *International Journal of Science and Research Archive* 15 (2025): 406–19.

Ammer, Mohammed Abdullah, and Abdisamat Sattarov. "Enhancing Investors' Decision-Making through Financial Risk Management: Role of Corporate Governance and Financial Communication Transparency." *Decision Making: Applications in Management and Engineering* 8, no. 2 (2025): 376–94.

Andersen, Lars Erslev. *One Belt One Road' and China's Westward Pivot: Past, Present and Future*. 2017.

Angelopoulos, Christina, Annabel Brody, Wouter Hins, et al. *Study of Fundamental Rights Limitations for Online Enforcement through Self-Regulation*. 2015.

Anh, Nguyen Thi Lan, and Mai Ngan Ha. "Legal Challenges to the Belt and Road Initiative." In *Critical Reflections on China's Belt & Road Initiative*. Springer, 2020.

Ansari, Sarmad, and Muhammad Tayyeb. "Saudi Vision 2030 and Liquidity Constraints: Evaluating Financing Requirements, Aramco Dependency, and Geopolitical Risks to Sustainable GDP Growth." *Social Science Review Archives* 4, no. 1 (2026): 3435–53.

Antov, Momchil. "Challenges to Customs Imposed by the New European Union Value-Added Tax Rules on Cross-Border E-Commerce–the Case of Bulgaria." *World Customs Journal* 17, no. 1 (2023): 33–53.

Arain, Reyan Hameed. "Colonial Shadows and Digital Era: Reforming the Arbitrary and Draconian Justice System of Pakistan." *International Journal of Law and Legal Advancement* 1, no. 2 (2025).

Arefiev, Serhii, Iryna Zhyhlei, Yuliia Pereguda, Nataliia Kryvokulska, and Mariya Lushchyk. "The Use of Digital Technologies to Ensure Environmental Safety in the Context of the Green Economy Development." *Revista de La Universidad Del Zulia* 15, no. 42 (2024): 353–69.

Aris, Stephen, and Aglaya Snetkov. "'Global Alternatives, Regional Stability and Common Causes': The International Politics of the Shanghai Cooperation Organization and Its Relationship to the West." *Eurasian Geography and Economics* 54, no. 2 (2013): 202–26.

Arner, Douglas W., Ross P. Buckley, and Dirk A. Zetzsche. "Fintech for Financial Inclusion: A Framework for Digital Financial Transformation." *UNSW Law Research Paper*, nos. 18–87 (2018).

Arner, Douglas W., Giuliano G. Castellano, and Ēriks K. Selga. "The Transnational Data Governance Problem." *Berkeley Technology Law Journal* 37, no. 2 (2022): 623–700.

Arora, Naveen Kumar, and Isha Mishra. "United Nations Sustainable Development Goals 2030 and Environmental Sustainability: Race against Time." *Environmental Sustainability* 2, no. 4 (2019): 339–42.

Arzo, Sisay Tadesse, Dimitrios Sikeridis, Michael Devetsikiotis, et al. "Essential Technologies and Concepts for Massive Space Exploration: Challenges and Opportunities." *IEEE Transactions on Aerospace and Electronic Systems* 59, no. 1 (2022): 3–29.

Ashraf, Junaid, Liangqing Luo, and Muhammad Khalid Anser. "Do BRI Policy and Institutional Quality Influence Economic Growth and Environmental Quality? An Empirical Analysis from South Asian Countries Affiliated with the Belt and Road Initiative." *Environmental Science and Pollution Research* 29, no. 6 (2022): 8438–51.

Aslan, Ömer, Semih Serkant Aktuğ, Merve Ozkan-Okay, Abdullah Asim Yilmaz, and Erdal Akin. "A Comprehensive Review of Cyber Security Vulnerabilities, Threats, Attacks, and Solutions." *Electronics* 12, no. 6 (2023): 1333.

Aslaner, Milad. *Cybersecurity Strategies and Best Practices: A Comprehensive Guide to Mastering Enterprise Cyber Defense Tactics and Techniques*. Packt Publishing Ltd, 2024.

Atadoga, Akoh, Uchenna Joseph Umoga, Oluwaseun Augustine Lottu, and Enoch Oluwademilade Sodiya. "Advancing Green Computing: Practices, Strategies, and Impact in Modern Software Development for Environmental Sustainability." *World Journal of Advanced Engineering Technology and Sciences* 11, no. 1 (2024): 220–30.

Attah, Rita Uchenna, I. Gil-Ozoudeh, BMP Garba, and Obinna Iwuanyanwu. "Leveraging Geographic Information Systems and Data Analytics for Enhanced Public Sector Decision-Making and Urban Planning." *Magna Sci Adv Res Rev* 12, no. 2 (2024): 152–63.

Aubert, Jean-Eric. *Promoting Innovation in Developing Countries: A Conceptual Framework*. Vol. 3554. World Bank Publications, 2005.

Avi-Yonah, Reuven, Young Ran Kim, and Karen Sam. "A New Framework for Digital Taxation." *Harv. Int'l LJ* 63 (2022): 279.

Awaisheh, Sadam Mohammad. "From Paper to Pixels: The Legal Status and Challenges of Electronic Writing in Administrative Contracts. A Comparative Study of Current Legal Systems." *Electronic Government, an International Journal* 21, no. 2 (2025): 210–26.

Awotunde, Joseph Bamidele, Emmanuel Abidemi Adeniyi, Roseline Oluwaseun Ogundokun, and Femi Emmanuel Ayo. "Application of Big Data with Fintech in Financial Services." In *Fintech with Artificial Intelligence, Big Data, and Blockchain*. Springer, 2021.

Ayodele, Odilile. "Digital Infrastructure: Creating the Backbone for Development." In *The Quest for Unity*. Routledge, 2024.

Azmeh, Shamel, Christopher Foster, and Jaime Echavarri. "The International Trade Regime and the Quest for Free Digital Trade." *International Studies Review* 22, no. 3 (2020): 671–92.

Baark, Erik. *Powering China's Digital Future: Strategies and Challenges*. 2022.

Babalola, Olumide. "Data Protection Legal Regime and Data Governance in Africa: An Overview." *Data Governance and Policy in Africa*, 2023, 71–96.

Bahn-Walkowiak, Bettina, Chiara Magrini, Holger Berg, et al. *Eco-Innovation and Digitalisation: Case Studies, Environmental and Policy Lessons from EU Member States for the EU Green Deal and the Circular Economy: EIO Biennial Report 2020*. 2021.

Bai, Miaojun, Yan Zheng, and Yun Shen. "Gradient Boosting Survival Tree with Applications in Credit Scoring." *Journal of the Operational Research Society* 73, no. 1 (2022): 39–55.

Balaji, K. "E-Government and E-Governance: Driving Digital Transformation in Public Administration." *Public Governance Practices in the Age of AI*, 2025, 23–44.

Balasubramanian, Ramnath, Ari Chester, and Nick Milinkovich. "Rewriting the Rules: Digital and AI-Powered Underwriting in Life Insurance." *McKinsey & Company, July* 31 (2020).

Balbi, Gabriele, and Andreas Fickers. *History of the International Telecommunication Union (ITU): Transnational Techno-Diplomacy from the Telegraph to the Internet*. Vol. 1. Walter de Gruyter GmbH & Co KG, 2020.

Balogun, Emmanuel Damilare, Kolade Olusola Ogunsola, and Adebanji Samuel. "A Risk Intelligence Framework for Detecting and Preventing Financial Fraud in Digital Marketplaces." *Iconic Research and Engineering Journals* 4, no. 08 (2021): 134–49.

Basu, Subhajit. "E-government and Developing Countries: An Overview." *International Review of Law, Computers & Technology* 18, no. 1 (2004): 109–32.

Batura, Olga. "Liberalisation and Regulation of International Trade in Telecommunications Services Through the WTO." In *Universal Service in WTO and EU Law: Liberalisation and Social Regulation in Telecommunications*. Springer, 2015.

Bayramov, Agha, and Fabio Indeo. "Uzbekistan, and Turkmenistan." *European Union Governance in Central Asia: A Sectoral Approach*, 2024.

Beaumier, Guillaume, Kevin Kalomeni, Malcolm Campbell-Verduyn, et al. "Global Regulations for a Digital Economy: Between New and Old Challenges." *Global Policy* 11, no. 4 (2020): 515–22.

Bechara, Fabio Ramazzini, and Samara Bueno Schuch. "Cybersecurity and Global Regulatory Challenges." *Journal of Financial Crime* 28, no. 2 (2021): 359–74.

Belli, Luca, Water B. Gaspar, and Shilpa Singh Jaswant. "Data Sovereignty and Data Transfers as Fundamental Elements of Digital Transformation: Lessons from the BRICS Countries." *Computer Law & Security Review* 54 (2024): 106017.

Benlian, Alexander, William J. Kettinger, Ali Sunyaev, Till J. Winkler, and Guest Editors. "The Transformative Value of Cloud Computing: A Decoupling, Platformization, and Recombination Theoretical Framework." *Journal of Management Information Systems* 35, no. 3 (2018): 719–39.

Bennet, Daniel, Lily Maria, Yulia Putri Ayu Sanjaya, and Achani Rahmania Az Zahra. "Blockchain Technology: Revolutionizing Transactions in the Digital Age." *ADI Journal on Recent Innovation* 5, no. 2 (2024): 192–99.

Berman, Paul Schiff. "The Globalization of Jurisdiction." *U. Pa. L. Rev.* 151 (2002): 311.

Bernal, Emmanuel Guillermo Carreño. "Harmonization of Cross-Border Contract Law: Legal Solutions in a Globalized World." *Journal of Policy and Society* 2, no. 2 (2024).

Bettini, Giovanni, Giovanna Gioli, and Romain Felli. "Clouded Skies: How Digital Technologies Could Reshape 'Loss and Damage' from Climate Change." *Wiley Interdisciplinary Reviews: Climate Change* 11, no. 4 (2020): e650.

Bird, Richard M., and Eric M. Zolt. "Tax Policy in Emerging Countries." *Environment and Planning C: Government and Policy* 26, no. 1 (2008): 73–86.

Blanchard, Jean-Marc F., and Colin Flint. "The Geopolitics of China's Maritime Silk Road Initiative." *Geopolitics* 22, no. 2 (2017): 223–45.

Blanchard, Jean-Marc F., and Bas Hooijmaaijers. "Connecting into the Social Sustainability Effects of Infrastructure through China's Digital Silk Road: Issues, Indices, and Indications." *Sustainability* 13, no. 22 (2021): 12739.

Blomgren Amsler, Lisa, Alexander B. Avtgis, and M. Scott Jackman. "Dispute System Design and Bias in Dispute Resolution." *SMUL Rev.* 70 (2017): 913.

Blume, Joshua D. "Reading the Trade Tea Leaves: A Comparative Analysis of Potential United States WTO-GATS Claims Against Privacy, Localization, and Cybersecurity Laws." *Geo. J. Int'l L.* 49 (2017): 801.

Blythe, Stephen Errol. *An E-Commerce Law For The World: The Model Electronic Transactions Act: The Model Electronic Transactions Act.* Xlibris Corporation, 2012.

Bogdan, Manole Decebal. "The Law of the Digital Economy a Reality for Legal Relations in the Future-New International Investment Protection." *International Investment Law Journal* 3, no. 2 (2023): 146–55.

Boikova, Tatyana, Sandija Zeverte-Rivza, Peteris Rivza, and Baiba Rivza. "The Determinants and Effects of Competitiveness: The Role of Digitalization in the European Economies." *Sustainability* 13, no. 21 (2021): 11689.

Bolatbekkyzy, Gulbakyt. "Legal Issues of Cross-Border Data Transfer in the Era of Digital Government." *Journal of Digital Technologies and Law* 2, no. 2 (2024): 286–307.

Bommareddy, Abhiram Reddy. "Towards Sustainable Federal Financial IT: Green Computing Practices In Data Centers And Cloud Platforms." *International Journal of Environmental Sciences* 11, no. 24s (n.d.): 2025.

Bonardi, Giulia. *Outbound Data Transfer from China: Implications for National Security and Foreign Businesses*. 2023.

Bonta, Rob. "California Consumer Privacy Act (CCPA)." *Retrieved from State of California Department of Justice:* https://Oag.ca.Gov/Privacy/Ccpa, 2022, 4–40.

Botta, Marco, and Klaus Wiedemann. "The Interaction of EU Competition, Consumer, and Data Protection Law in the Digital Economy: The Regulatory Dilemma in the Facebook Odyssey." *The Antitrust Bulletin* 64, no. 3 (2019): 428–46.

Bottis, Maria, Fereniki Panagopoulou-Koutnatzi, Anastasia Michailaki, and Maria Nikita. "The Right to Access Information under the GDPR." *International Journal of Technology Policy and Law* 3, no. 2 (2019): 131–42.

Bouhou, Mohamed Id, and Yongmei Chen. "The Application of Laws Related to International Trade in Africa: Conflict and the Possibility of Unification." *International Journal of Law and Legal Advancement* 1, no. 2 (2025).

Bourreau, Marc, and Tommaso Valletti. "Enabling Digital Financial Inclusion through Improvements in Competition and Interoperability: What Works and What Doesn't." *CGD Policy Paper* 65 (2015): 1–30.

Bradford, Anu. *Digital Empires: The Global Battle to Regulate Technology*. Oxford University Press, 2023.

Bradford, Anu. "The False Choice between Digital Regulation and Innovation." *Nw. UL Rev.* 119 (2024): 377.

Brenner, Barbara. "Transformative Sustainable Business Models in the Light of the Digital Imperative—A Global Business Economics Perspective." *Sustainability* 10, no. 12 (2018): 4428.

Broby, Daniel, Angela Daly, and David Legg. "Towards Secure And Intelligent Regulatory Technology (Regtech):: A Research Agenda." *Technology And Regulation* 2022 (2022): 88–99.

Brooks, Chay, Cristian Gherhes, and Tim Vorley. "Artificial Intelligence in the Legal Sector: Pressures and Challenges of Transformation." *Cambridge Journal of Regions, Economy and Society* 13, no. 1 (2020): 135–52.

Brown, Ian, and Christopher T. Marsden. *Regulating Code: Good Governance and Better Regulation in the Information Age*. MIT Press, 2023.

Brunetti, Federico, Dominik T. Matt, Angelo Bonfanti, Alberto De Longhi, Giulio Pedrini, and Guido Orzes. "Digital Transformation Challenges: Strategies Emerging from a Multi-Stakeholder Approach." *The TQM Journal* 32, no. 4 (2020): 697–724.

Brynjolfsson, Erik, and Avinash Collis. "How Should We Measure the Digital Economy." *Harvard Business Review* 97, no. 6 (2019): 140–48.

Brynjolfsson, Erik, and Andrew McAfee. *Race against the Machine: How the Digital Revolution Is Accelerating Innovation, Driving Productivity, and Irreversibly Transforming Employment and the Economy*. Brynjolfsson and McAfee, 2011.

Bu, Ya, Hui Li, and Xiaoqing Wu. "Effective Regulations of FinTech Innovations: The Case of China." *Economics of Innovation and New Technology* 31, no. 8 (2022): 751–69.

Buckley, Ross P., Douglas W. Arner, Dirk A. Zetzsche, and Eriks Selga. "The Dark Side of Digital Financial Transformation: The New Risks of Fintech and the Rise of Techrisk." *UNSW Law Research Paper*, nos. 19–89 (2019).

Buckley, Ross P., Douglas W. Arner, Dirk A. Zetzsche, and Robin Veidt. "Sustainability, FinTech and Financial Inclusion." *A Research Agenda for Financial Inclusion and Microfinance*, 2019.

Burk, Bernard A., and David McGowan. "Big but Brittle: Economic Perspectives on the Future of the Law Firm in the New Economy." *Colum. Bus. L. Rev.*, 2011, 1.

Butt, Junaid. "Analytical Study of the World's First EU Artificial Intelligence (AI) Act." *International Journal of Research Publication and Reviews* 5, no. 3 (2024): 7343–64.

Butt, Junaid Sattar. "The Impact of Artificial Intelligence (AI) on the Efficiency of Administrative Decision Making Including Ethical & Legal Considerations and Comparative Study about Countries Already Incorporated AI for Administrative Decisions." *Acta Universitatis Danubius. Juridica* 19, no. 3 (2023): 7–25.

Buyya, Rajkumar, Shashikant Ilager, and Patricia Arroba. "Energy-efficiency and Sustainability in New Generation Cloud Computing: A Vision and Directions for Integrated Management of Data Centre Resources and Workloads." *Software: Practice and Experience* 54, no. 1 (2024): 24–38.

Cai, Liang, Yi Sun, Zibin Zheng, Jiang Xiao, and Weiwei Qiu. "Blockchain in China." *Communications of the ACM* 64, no. 11 (2021): 88–93.

Calzada, Igor. "Citizens' Data Privacy in China: The State of the Art of the Personal Information Protection Law (PIPL)." *Smart Cities* 5, no. 3 (2022): 1129–50.

Camilleri, Mark Anthony. "The Use of Data-Driven Technologies for Customer-Centric Marketing." *International Journal of Big Data Management* 1, no. 1 (2020): 50–63.

Canton, Helen. "United Nations Office on Drugs and Crime—UNODC." In *The Europa Directory of International Organizations 2021*. Routledge, 2021.

Cao, Liang, Dewan An, Chunfang Cao, and Xiang Gao. "Artificial Intelligence Empowering the Construction of the China–Cambodia Community of Shared Future: Mechanisms and Collaborative Pathways." *Advances in Social Behavior Research* 17, no. 1 (2026): 105–22.

Carlsen, Lars, and Rainer Bruggemann. "The 17 United Nations' Sustainable Development Goals: A Status by 2020." *International Journal of Sustainable Development & World Ecology* 29, no. 3 (2022): 219–29.

Carvajal, A. "A Comparative Study of Commitment of Collaboration (COC) and Memorandum of Understanding (MOU) as Instruments in Driving Successful Partnerships in ASEAN Member Countries." *Int. J. Open-Access, Interdiscipl. New Educ. Discoveries ETCOR Educ. Res. Center (iJOINED ETCOR)* 20, no. 3 (2023): 503–20496.

Chaisse, Julien, and Jamieson Kirkwood. "Smart Courts, Smart Contracts, and the Future of Online Dispute Resolution." *Stan. J. Blockchain L. & Pol'y* 5 (2022): 62.

Challa, Srinivas Rao Rao. "Advancements in Digital Brokerage and Algorithmic Trading: The Evolution of Investment Platforms in a Data Driven Financial Ecosystem." *Advances in Consumer Research* 2 (2025): 238–49.

Challapalli, Surendra. "Benefits and Constraints Associated with the Harmonization of Financial Regulations: An Overview." *Asian Journal of Economics, Business and Accounting* 23, no. 15 (2023): 49–56.

Chander, Anupam, and Haochen Sun. *Data Sovereignty: From the Digital Silk Road to the Return of the State*. Oxford University Press, 2023.

Chang, Yanling, Eleftherios Iakovou, and Weidong Shi. "Blockchain in Global Supply Chains and Cross Border Trade: A Critical Synthesis of the State-of-the-Art, Challenges and Opportunities." *International Journal of Production Research* 58, no. 7 (2020): 2082–99.

Chen, Haojun. “The Age of Super-Apps: Insights From China’s Evolving.” *Regulation, Emerging Risk, and Ethics in FinTech and AI*, 2025, 163.

Chen, Jihong, and Jiabin Sun. “Understanding the Chinese Data Security Law.” *International Cybersecurity Law Review* 2, no. 2 (2021): 209–21.

Chen, Meng. “Developing China’s Approaches to Regulate Cross-Border Data Transfer: Relaxation and Integration.” *Computer Law & Security Review* 54 (2024): 105997.

Chen, Wei, Haipeng Zhang, Zhipeng Tang, and Zhaoyuan Yu. “Assessing the Structural Connectivity of International Trade Networks along the ‘Belt and Road.’” *Plos One* 18, no. 3 (2023): e0282596.

Chen, Xiangfeng, Chenyu Wang, and Jieyou Zhang. “Linklogis: A Supply Chain Fintech Solution Provider.” *FUDAN*, 2023, 1–15.

Chen, Xin, Jose Miguel Alonso-Trabanco, and Haiping Zhang. “Emerging Digital Currency Statecraft with Chinese Characteristics: Chinese Expectations About the Influence of the e-CNY on RMB Internationalization.” In *The Geoeconomics of the International Monetary Order: Money and Power in the 21st Century*. Springer, 2025.

Chen, Xin wei. “The Legal Protection of” Silk Road E-Commerce”: Challenges, Approaches, and Solutions.” *International Journal of Law and Politics Studies* 7, no. 3 (2025): 01–14.

Chen, Xinxiang, Jiaqing Gao, and Wenda Tan. “ICT in China: A Strong Force to Boost Economic and Social Development.” In *Perspectives and Policies on ICT in Society: An IFIP TC9 (Computers and Society) Handbook*. Springer, 2005.

Cheng, Wenting. “The Green Investment Principles: From a Nodal Governance Perspective.” *International Environmental Agreements: Politics, Law and Economics* 23, no. 3 (2023): 373–93.

Cheng, Xuanmei, Fangting Ge, Anna Min Du, and Weiji Wang. “Digital Economy, Energy Trade, and the Path to Sustainability: A G7 Perspective.” *International Review of Financial Analysis* 109 (2026): 104807.

Cheng, Ziying. *China’s Influence on Laos’ Infrastructure Investment and Lao People’s Views on It-the Case Study of China-Laos Railway*. 2022.

Cheryl, Barr-Kumarakulasinghe, and Boon-Kwee Ng. “Protecting the Unprotected Consumer Data in Internet of Things: Current Scenario of Data Governance in Malaysia.” *Sustainability* 14, no. 16 (2022): 9893.

Cheung, Fanny M., and Ying-yi Hong. *Green Finance, Sustainable Development and the Belt and Road Initiative*. Routledge London, 2021.

China Council for International Cooperation on Environment and Development (CCICED) Secretariat. “Enhancing Environmental Management for BRI Projects to Boost Green BRI and 2030 Agenda for Sustainable Development.” In *Green Recovery with Resilience and High Quality Development: CCICED Annual Policy Report 2021*. Springer, 2023.

China, MEE. *BRI International Green Development Coalition (BRIGC)*. 2020.

Chinese Academy of Cyberspace Studies. “Development of the World’s Information Infrastructure.” In *World Internet Development Report 2017: Translated by Peng Ping*. Springer, 2018.

Chinoracký, Roman, and Tatiana Čorejová. “Impact of Digital Technologies on Labor Market and the Transport Sector.” *Transportation Research Procedia* 40 (2019): 994–1001.

Chitoroaga, Ana. *Dispute Resolution Mechanism in the Belt and Road Initiative*. n.d.

Chu, J., and Aishath Muneeza. “Belt and Road Initiative and Islamic Financing: The Case in Public Private Partnership Infrastructure Financing.” *International Journal of Management and Applied Research* 6, no. 1 (2019): 24–40.

Chung, Alex, and Ying Yu. “Delivering Justice in the Digital Economy.” *Digitalization and Artificial Intelligence in Courts: Opportunities and Challenges*, 2025, 157.

Ciborek, Przemysław. “China’s Global Initiatives: Challenges and Prospects.” *New Chinese Initiatives for a Changing Global Security*, 2023, 91–110.

Citaristi, Ileana. “International Telecommunication Union—Itu.” In *The Europa Directory of International Organizations 2022*. Routledge, 2022.

Cohen, Bret, Britanie Hall, and Charlie Wood. "Data Localization Laws and Their Impact on Privacy, Data Security and the Global Economy." *Antitrust* 32 (2017): 107.

Cohen, Julie E. "Law for the Platform Economy." *UCdL Rev.* 51 (2017): 133.

Contini, Francesco. "Artificial Intelligence and the Transformation of Humans, Law and Technology Interactions in Judicial Proceedings." *Law, Tech. & Hum.* 2 (2020): 4.

Cook-Kwenda, Molly. "Tech-Enabled Global Cybercrime: Exploitation by Transnational Criminal Organizations (TCOS)." *Iconic Research and Engineering Journals* 8, no. 3 (2024): 55–101.

Cordes, Ashley. *From the Gold Rush to the Cryptocurrency Code Rush?: Communication of Currencies in Native American Communities*. University of Oregon, 2019.

Correa, Carlos María. *Trade Related Aspects of Intellectual Property Rights: A Commentary on the TRIPS Agreement*. Oxford University Press, 2020.

Cortés, Pablo. "Embedding Alternative Dispute Resolution in the Civil Justice System: A Taxonomy for ADR Referrals and a Digital Pathway to Increase the Uptake of ADR." *Legal Studies* 43, no. 2 (2023): 312–30.

Cowhey, Peter F., and Jonathan D. Aronson. *Digital DNA: Disruption and the Challenges for Global Governance*. Oxford University Press, 2017.

Creemers, Rogier. "Cybersecurity Law and Regulation in China: Securing the Smart State." *China Law and Society Review* 6, no. 2 (2023): 111–45.

Cremades, Bernardo M., and Ignacio Madalena. "Parallel Proceedings in International Arbitration." *Arbitration International* 24, no. 4 (2008): 507–40.

Cuiyun, Cheng, and Ge Chazhong. "Green Development Assessment for Countries along the Belt and Road." *Journal of Environmental Management* 263 (2020): 110344.

Cutolo, Donato, and Martin Kenney. "Platform-Dependent Entrepreneurs: Power Asymmetries, Risks, and Strategies in the Platform Economy." *Academy of Management Perspectives* 35, no. 4 (2021): 584–605.

Dahdal, Andrew Mazen, and Adel Abdel Ghafar. "The Digital Silk Road:'Tech-Diplomacy' as a Paradigm for Understanding Technological Adoption and Emerging Digital Regulations in MENA." *Asian Journal of Law and Society* 12, no. 2 (2025): 163–88.

Dahlman, Carl. "Technology, Globalization, and International Competitiveness: Challenges for Developing Countries." *Industrial Development for the 21st Century: Sustainable Development Perspectives*, 2007, 29–83.

Dai, Bo, Jian Zhang, and Nasir Hussain. "Policy Pathways through FinTech and Green Finance for Low-Carbon Energy Transition in BRICS Nations." *Energy Strategy Reviews* 57 (2025): 101603.

Dai, Xiaowen, Yi Chen, Chunyan Zhang, Yanqiu He, and Jiajia Li. "Technological Revolution in the Field: Green Development of Chinese Agriculture Driven by Digital Information Technology (DIT)." *Agriculture* 13, no. 1 (2023): 199.

Dailami, Mansoor, and Mansoor Dailami. *Sovereign Debt Distress and Corporate Spillover Impacts*. World Bank, 2010.

Danilin, Ivan V. "The Impact of Digital Technologies on Leadership in Global Processes: From Platforms to Markets?" *MGIMO Review of International Relations* 13, no. 1 (2020): 100–116.

Davidson, Alan. *The Law of Electronic Commerce*. Cambridge University Press, 2009.

Deane, Felicity, Emily Woolmer, and Kieran TRANTER. "Trade in the Digital Age: Agreements to Mitigate Fragmentation." *Asian Journal of International Law* 14, no. 1 (2024): 154–79.

Delautre, Guillaume. "The Distribution of Value Added among Firms and Countries: The Case of the ICT Manufacturing Sector." *ILO Research Department Working Paper* 16 (2017): 18.

Denysenko, Mykola. "Management Technologies for Enhancing Integrated Processes in the Customs and Logistics Services Sector." *Вісник Київського Національного Університету Технологій Та Дизайну. Серія Економічні Науки*, 2020.

Devadason, Evelyn S. "Rethinking Trade Policy in Malaysia." *Post-Pandemic Economic and Social Development: Recovery, Challenges, and Policy in Malaysia*, 2024.

Dhawale, Poonam Prakash. "Empowering Underserved Communities Through Fintech-Driven Inclusion." *International Research on Sustainability and Innovation: A Multidisciplinary Approach to Global Development*, 2025, 139.

Ding, Ding, Guan Chong, David LEE Kuo Chuen, and Tan Lee Cheng. "From Ant Financial to Alibaba's Rural Taobao Strategy–How Fintech Is Transforming Social Inclusion." In *Handbook of Blockchain, Digital Finance, and Inclusion, Volume 1*. Elsevier, 2018.

Domazet, Ivana, and Milena Lazić. "Information and Communication Technologies as a Driver of the Digital Economy." *Glasnik Srpskog Geografskog Društva*, 2017, 11–19.

Domorenok, Ekaterina, Paolo Graziano, and Laura Polverari. "Introduction: Policy Integration and Institutional Capacity: Theoretical, Conceptual and Empirical Challenges." *Policy and Society* 40, no. 1 (2021): 1–18.

Dong, Shi, Khushnood Abbas, Meixi Li, and Joarder Kamruzzaman. "Blockchain Technology and Application: An Overview." *PeerJ Computer Science* 9 (2023): e1705.

Donoghue, Jane. "The Rise of Digital Justice: Courtroom Technology, Public Participation and Access to Justice." *The Modern Law Review* 80, no. 6 (2017): 995–1025.

Dorfleitner, Gregor, and Diana Braun. "Fintech, Digitalization and Blockchain: Possible Applications for Green Finance." In *The Rise of Green Finance in Europe: Opportunities and Challenges for Issuers, Investors and Marketplaces*. Springer, 2019.

Du, Julan, Chang Li, and Yongqin Wang. *Shadow Banking Activities in Non-Financial Firms: Evidence from China*. SSRN, 2016.

Duggireddy, Guru Bhaskar Reddy. "Integrated Data and AI Governance Framework: A Lifecycle Approach to Responsible AI Implementation." *Journal of Computer Science and Technology Studies* 7, no. 7 (2025): 771–77.

Dupont, Vincent, Diana Pietrzak, and Boris Verbrugge. "A Step in the Right Direction, or More of the Same? A Systematic Review of the Impact of Human Rights Due Diligence Legislation." *Human Rights Review* 25, no. 2 (2024): 131–54.

Dziawgo, Tomasz. *Big Tech Influence on China Financial Sector*. 2021.

Ebabu, Engidaw Abriham, Haichun Yu, and Zou Weikang. "Opportunities and Challenges in Cross-Border e-Commerce: Strategic Management within the Legal Context of BRI Countries-A Systematic Literature Synthesis and Future Research Directions." *Technology Analysis & Strategic Management*, 2025, 1–20.

Ebabu, Engidaw Abriham, Haichun Yu, Zou Weikang, Huang Yixiong, and Ayele Addis Ambelu. "Navigating Sustainable Digital Transformation in South-South Cross-Border E-Commerce: Insights on Cultural Adaptation, Green Marketing Strategy, and Inclusive Business Model Innovation." *International Review of Economics & Finance*, 2026, 104907.

Eguegu, Ovigwe. "The Digital Silk Road: Connecting Africa with New Norms of Digital Development." *Asia Policy* 17, no. 3 (2022): 30–39.

El Amri, Mohamed Cherif, Mustafa Omar Mohammed, and Ayman Mohamad Bakr. "Enhancing Financial Inclusion Using FinTech-Based Payment System." In *Islamic FinTech: Insights and Solutions*. Springer, 2021.

Eldin, Lilian. *Digital Capacity Building for Climate Empowerment: Evaluating Post-COP29 Implementation and Gaps in ACE Delivery*. 2025.

Elias, Oluwafemi, Opeyemi Joseph Awotunde, Oladiipo Ishola Oladepo, et al. "The Evolution of Green Fintech: Leveraging AI and IoT for Sustainable Financial Services and Smart Contract Implementation." *World Journal of Advanced Research and Reviews* 23, no. 1 (2024): 2710–23.

Enaifoghe, Andrew. "Bridging the Digital Divide in the South African Public Sector: Assessing Digital Literacy Gaps and Capacity-Building Strategies." In *Digital Equity and Literacy*. IntechOpen, 2025.

Erie, Matthew S., and Thomas Streinz. "The Beijing Effect: China's Digital Silk Road as Transnational Data Governance." *NYUJ Int'l L. & Pol.* 54 (2021): 1.

Eyo-Udo, Nsisong Louis, Charles Elachi Apeh, Bernadette Bristol-Alagbariya, Chioma Ann Udeh, and Chikezie Paul-Mikki Ewim. "International Trade Law in the Modern World: A

Review of Evolving Practices and Agreements." *International Journal of Multidisciplinary Research and Growth Evaluation*, 2025.

Fadler, Martin, and Christine Legner. "Data Ownership Revisited: Clarifying Data Accountabilities in Times of Big Data and Analytics." *Journal of Business Analytics* 5, no. 1 (2022): 123–39.

Fan, Yinghui, Haiyan Zheng, Romeo Salvo Ebonite, Werson Role De Asis, and RA Juanatas. "Overview and Developmental Analysis of China's Technical and Vocational Education and Training." *International Journal of Innovative Research and Scientific Studies* 7, no. 1 (2024): 251–60.

Fan, Zhencheng, Zheng Yan, and Shiping Wen. "Deep Learning and Artificial Intelligence in Sustainability: A Review of SDGs, Renewable Energy, and Environmental Health." *Sustainability* 15, no. 18 (2023): 13493.

Fasnacht, Daniel. "Banking 4.0: Digital Ecosystems and Super-Apps." In *Theories of Change: Change Leadership Tools, Models and Applications for Investing in Sustainable Development*. Springer, 2021.

Ferracane, Martina Francesca. "Data Flows and National Security: A Conceptual Framework to Assess Restrictions on Data Flows under GATS Security Exception." *Digital Policy, Regulation and Governance* 21, no. 1 (2019): 44–70.

Flew, Terry, Fiona Martin, and Nicolas Suzor. "Internet Regulation as Media Policy: Rethinking the Question of Digital Communication Platform Governance." *Journal of Digital Media & Policy* 10, no. 1 (2019): 33–50.

Force, Green Finance Task. "Establishing China's Green Financial System." *People's Bank of China & United Nations Environment Programme: Beijing, China*, 2015.

Fowowe, Olumide Olumayowa, Chinalulum Micheal Nnajiofor, and Eigbedion Aimanose Phyllis. *The Role of FinTech in Expanding Access to Finance for Underserved Communities: A Policy-Focused Study Linking Digital Financial Services to Economic Inclusion*. 2025.

Fox, William F. *International Commercial Agreements and Electronic Commerce*. Kluwer Law International BV, 2018.

Fu, Chengbo, Lei Lu, and Mansoor Pirabi. "Advancing Green Finance: A Review of Sustainable Development." *Digital Economy and Sustainable Development* 1, no. 1 (2023): 20.

Fu, Xiaolan, Pervez Ghauri, Nwamaka Ogbonna, and Xiaoqiang Xing. "Platform-Based Business Model and Entrepreneurs from Base of the Pyramid." *Technovation* 119 (2023): 102451.

Fuchs, Daniel, Daniel Sprick, and Marianne von Blomberg. "China and the Standardization of Digital Technologies–Introduction to the Special Issue." *China Law and Society Review* 10, no. 2 (2025): 75–80.

Gabriel, Henry D. "The UNCITRAL Model Law on Electronic Transferable Records." *Uniform Law Review* 24, no. 2 (2019): 261–80.

Gallagher, Kevin P. *The China Triangle: Latin America's China Boom and the Fate of the Washington Consensus*. Oxford University Press, 2016.

GAO, Henry S. *The Joint Statement on E-Commerce: Is This Glass Half Empty or Half Full?* 2024.

Garg, Deepak Kumar. "Environmental Challenges and Sustainable Development." *Journal of Global Values* 14 (2023): 203–10.

Gaviyau, William, and Athenia Bongani Sibindi. "Global Anti-Money Laundering and Combating Terrorism Financing Regulatory Framework: A Critique." *Journal of Risk and Financial Management* 16, no. 7 (2023): 313.

Ge, Taoan. "A Conceptual Framework for Assessing Social and Environmental Impacts of Belt and Road Initiative and Just Energy Transition." *Frontiers in Sustainable Food Systems* 6 (2022): 982086.

George, A. Shaji, T. Baskar, and P. Balaji Srikaanth. "Cyber Threats to Critical Infrastructure: Assessing Vulnerabilities across Key Sectors." *Partners Universal International Innovation Journal* 2, no. 1 (2024): 51–75.

George, Jossy, Kamal Upreti, Ramesh Chandra Poonia, Ankit Gautam, and Danish Nadeem. *Cognitive Cloud Computing: Building Intelligent Systems for Tomorrow*. CRC Press, 2025.

Getahun, Sewnet, Habtamu Kefale, and Yohannes Gelaye. "Application of Precision Agriculture Technologies for Sustainable Crop Production and Environmental Sustainability: A Systematic Review." *The Scientific World Journal* 2024, no. 1 (2024): 2126734.

Ghiasy, Richard, and Rajeshwari Krishnamurthy. "China's Digital Silk Road." *Institute of Peach and Conflict Studies, Leiden Asia Center* 26 (2020).

Gialletti, A., J. Alvar-Beltrán, A. Setti, T. Allen, R. Soldan, and L. Neretin. *Climate Risk Toolbox: Guiding Material for Climate Risk Screening*. Food & Agriculture Org., 2025.

Glaser, Bonnie S. *Made in China 2025 and the Future of American Industry*. Center for Strategic and International Studies (CSIS), 2022.

Goh, Allison. "Digital Readiness Index for Arbitration Institutions: Challenges and Implications for Dispute Resolution under the Belt and Road Initiative." *Journal of International Arbitration* 38, no. 2 (2021).

Goldenfein, Jake, and Andrea Leiter. "Legal Engineering on the Blockchain: 'Smart Contracts' as Legal Conduct." *Law and Critique* 29, no. 2 (2018): 141–49.

Gomez, Edmund Terence. "State-Business Relations and Public-Public Partnerships: China's State-Owned Enterprises in Southeast Asia." *Malaysian Journal of Economic Studies* 61, no. 1 (2024): 141–57.

Gong, Sen, Jing Gu, and Fei Teng. *The Impact of the Belt and Road Initiative Investment in Digital Connectivity and Information and Communication Technologies on Achieving the SDGs*. 2019.

Gordon, David, and Meia Nouwens. *The Digital Silk Road: China's Technological Rise and the Geopolitics of Cyberspace*. Taylor & Francis, 2022.

Greenberg, Brad A. "Rethinking Technology Neutrality." *Minn. L. Rev.* 100 (2015): 1495.

Greenleaf, Graham. "Five Years of the APEC Privacy Framework: Failure or Promise?" *Computer Law & Security Review* 25, no. 1 (2009): 28–43.

Grgić, Mladen. *Chinese Infrastructure Diplomacy in the Balkans: Beijing 'Sponsored' Consensus*. Taylor & Francis, 2025.

Gu, Jing. "Building Partnerships for Sustainable Development: Case Study of Laos, the BRI, and the SDGs." *Asian Review of Political Economy* 3, no. 1 (2024): 5.

Guillén, Arturo, and Ivan Cortés Torres. "Changes in the World Geopolitical Order and the Reconfiguration of Productive Systems: The Mexican Case." *Agrarian South: Journal of Political Economy* 14, no. 1 (2025): 26–59.

Gulia, Jatish. "Cross-Border Data Transfers: International Cooperation and Conflicts." *Legal Lock J.* 4 (2024): 263.

Güneylioğlu, Murat. "Globalization, Deglobalization, and the US-China Competition: The Balance between Geopolitics and Geoeconomics." *Türk Sosyal Bilimler Araştırmaları Dergisi* 8, no. 2 (2023): 89–113.

Guo, Cheng. "China's Digital Silk Road in the Age of the Digital Economy: Political Analysis." *Вестник Российского Университета Дружбы Народов. Серия: Международные Отношения* 22, no. 2 (2022): 271–87.

Guo, Lingling, Jingjing Chen, Shihan Li, Yafei Li, and Jinzhi Lu. "A Blockchain and IoT-Based Lightweight Framework for Enabling Information Transparency in Supply Chain Finance." *Digital Communications and Networks* 8, no. 4 (2022): 576–87.

Guo, Meirong. "Internet Court's Challenges and Future in China." *Computer Law & Security Review* 40 (2021): 105522.

Guo, Yuxia, Huiying Mao, Heping Ding, et al. "Data-Driven Coordinated Development of the Digital Economy and Logistics Industry." *Sustainability* 14, no. 14 (2022): 8963.

Gupta, Mukul, Deepa Gupta, and Priti Rai. "Digital Payment Systems and Financial Inclusion: Examine How Digital Payment Systems, Such as Mobile Wallets and Digital Currencies, Can Improve Financial Inclusion by Providing Access to Banking Services for the Unbanked and Underbanked Population." 2023, 725–37.

Gupta, S., RR Modi, D. Das, and P. Sahu. "Sustainable Digital Banking: Exploring the Role of Fintech in Promoting Green Finance and Sustainable Development Goals." *Journal of Information Systems Engineering & Management* 10, no. 3 (2025): 547–57.

Gyamerah, Samuel, Zheng He, Enock Mintah Ampaw, Dennis Asante, and Lydia Asare-Kyire. "The Belt and Road Initiative and East African Small and Medium-Sized Enterprises: Benefits, Drivers and Particular Sectors." *International Journal of Emerging Markets* 18, no. 2 (2023): 463–82.

Ha, Huong, and CK Peter Chuah. "Digital Economy in Southeast Asia: Challenges, Opportunities and Future Development." *Southeast Asia: A Multidisciplinary Journal* 23, no. 1 (2023): 19–35.

Hadfield, Gillian K., and Iva Bozovic. "Scaffolding: Using Formal Contracts to Support Informal Relations in Support of Innovation." *Wis. L. Rev.*, 2016, 981.

Hagemann, Ryan, Jennifer Huddleston Skees, and Adam Thierer. "Soft Law for Hard Problems: The Governance of Emerging Technologies in an Uncertain Future." *Colo. Tech. LJ* 17 (2018): 37.

Hager, LM. "Development Law Capacity Building: Training Legal Professionals for Development." *International Sustainable Development Law-Volume II*, 2010, 258.

Haider, Aftab, Naim Mathlouthi, Mohamed Saer Rahal, and Jamil Afzal. "Can Islamic Law and Secular Law Coexist Without Conflict." *Al-Istinbath: Jurnal Hukum Islam* 10, no. 2 (2025): 485–512.

Hassan, Ahmad Arzlee, Mohd Suhaimi Mohd-Danuri, Umi Kalsum Zolkafli, Muhammad Hadi Mustafa, and Sharifah Nur Aina Syed Alwee. "Mediation Procedural Rules and Their Application in the Malaysian Construction Industry: A Doctrinal Legal Research." *Journal of Construction in Developing Countries* 30, no. 2 (2025): 247–67.

He, Alex. *The Digital Silk Road and China's Influence on Standard Setting*. CIGI Papers, 2022.

He, Chi. "The Belt and Road Initiative as Global Public Good: Implications for International Law." In *Normative Readings of the Belt and Road Initiative: Road to New Paradigms*. Springer, 2018.

He, Dong. "Digitalization of Cross-Border Payments." *China Economic Journal* 14, no. 1 (2021): 26–38.

He, Yujia. "Chinese Digital Platform Companies' Expansion in the Belt and Road Countries." In *China's Digital Expansion in the Global South*. Routledge, 2024.

Hernandez, Kevin. *Achieving Complex Development Goals along China's Digital Silk Road*. 2019.

Hess, Peter N. *Economic Growth and Sustainable Development*. Routledge, 2016.

Hildebrandt, Mireille, and Laura Tielemans. "Data Protection by Design and Technology Neutral Law." *Computer Law & Security Review* 29, no. 5 (2013): 509–21.

Hillman, Jennifer A., David Sacks, Jacob J. Lew, and Gary Roughead. *China's Belt and Road: Implications for the United States*. Council on Foreign Relations New York, 2021.

Hillman, Jonathan E. *The Digital Silk Road: China's Quest to Wire the World and Win the Future*. Profile Books, 2021.

Himmer, Michal, and Zdeněk Rod. "Chinese Debt Trap Diplomacy: Reality or Myth?" *Journal of the Indian Ocean Region* 18, no. 3 (2022): 250–72.

Hirblinger, Andreas T. *Digital Inclusion in Peacemaking: A Strategic Perspective*. 2020.

Hoang, Kimberly Kay. "Risky Investments: How Local and Foreign Investors Finesse Corruption-Rife Emerging Markets." *American Sociological Review* 83, no. 4 (2018): 657–85.

Hoffmann, Stacie, Dominique Lazanski, and Emily Taylor. "Standardising the Splinternet: How China's Technical Standards Could Fragment the Internet." *Journal of Cyber Policy* 5, no. 2 (2020): 239–64.

Hongfei, Yue. "National Report on E-Commerce Development in China." *Inclusive and Sustainable Industrial Development Working Paper Series WP17* 6 (2017).

Hu, Bo, Peng Zhou, and LP Zhang. "A Digital Business Model for Accelerating Distributed Renewable Energy Expansion in Rural China." *Applied Energy* 316 (2022): 119084.

Hu, Haisheng, and Jernej Pikalo. "Fragmented Governance in the Belt and Road Initiative: Aligning Policy with SDGs 8 and 9." *Global Policy* 16, no. 5 (2025): 1004–20.

Huadong, Guo. "Steps to the Digital Silk Road." *Nature* 554, no. 7690 (2018): 25–27.

Huang, Wenny, and Yoshihisa Hayakawa. "The APEC Collaborative Framework for Online Dispute Resolution (ODR) of Cross-Border B2B Disputes: An Overview and Analysis (Part 1)." *Dispute Resolution International*, no. 100 (2025).

Huang, Yiping, and Xun Wang. "Digital Connectivity in China and Asia: The Case of Mobile Payments." *New Dimensions of Connectivity in the Asia-Pacific*, 2021, 203.

Hufbauer, Gary, and Steven Globerman. *The United States-Mexico-Canada Agreement: Overview and Outlook*. Fraser Institute Vancouver, 2018.

Hug, Francine. "Domestic E-Commerce Promotion through State-Managed Liberalisation." In *China's Free Trade Agreement Strategies: Securing the Chinese Developmental State and Socialist Market Economy*. Springer, 2024.

Huifang, Tian. "Green Investment Principles for the Belt and Road." In *The Routledge Handbook of the Belt and Road*. Routledge, 2022.

Hussain, Fakhar, Zakar Hussain, Muhammad Ikramullah Khan, and Ali Imran. "The Digital Rise and Its Economic Implications for China through the Digital Silk Road under the Belt and Road Initiative." *Asian Journal of Comparative Politics* 9, no. 2 (2024): 238–53.

Hussain, Fakhar, Ali Imran, Zakar Hussain, and Muhammad Ikramullah Khan. "Infrastructure Development for the Digital Silk Road (DSR) and Its Implications for China under the Belt and Road Initiative." *Asia-Pacific Social Science Review* 23, no. 4 (2023): 7.

Ibor, Ayei, Mark Hooper, Carsten Maple, Jon Crowcroft, and Gregory Epiphaniou. "Considerations for Trustworthy Cross-Border Interoperability of Digital Identity Systems in Developing Countries." *AI & Society* 40, no. 4 (2025): 2729–50.

Iftikhar, Huma, Luo Guang, and Atta Ullah. "A Multi-Dimensional FinTech Composite Integrating Infrastructure, Access, Usage, Knowledge Transfer, and Governance-by-Technology: The Role of Digital Silk Road Policy in BRI Economies." *Technology in Society*, 2025, 103162.

Ilawagbon, Osas-Osayomwanbor, and Adesoye Isiaka Mustapha. "The Role of E-Administration in Enhancing Time Efficiency in Public Service Delivery: A Case Study of the Federal Civil Service of Nigeria Post-COVID-19." *ICONIC Research and Engineering Journals, 7 (12), 445* 457 (2024).

Inamdar, Tipusultan Alarsaheb. "Digital Divide: Analysing the Impact of Unequal Access to Technology On Social Mobility." *Janus* 16, no. 2 (2025).

Innovations, TechComp. "Managing Digital Economic Corridors: International Cooperation and Regional Integration in the Digital Age." *TechComp Innovations: Journal of Computer Science and Technology*, 2025.

Jackson, Steven J. "Speed, Time, Infrastructure." *The Sociology of Speed: Digital, Organizational, and Social Temporalities* 169 (2017).

James, Jeffrey. "Confronting the Scarcity of Digital Skills among the Poor in Developing Countries." *Development Policy Review* 39, no. 2 (2021): 324–39.

Jiang, Hong, and Johann Peter Murmann. "The Rise of China's Digital Economy: An Overview." *Management and Organization Review* 18, no. 4 (2022): 790–802.

Jinbo, Wang. "The China–Central Asia–West Asia Economic Corridor." In *The Routledge Handbook of the Belt and Road*. Routledge, 2022.

Jing, Yijia, and Danyao Li. "Private Roles in Enhancing Multi-Level Governance: China's 'Internet+' National Strategy." *Public Policy and Administration* 34, no. 2 (2019): 144–64.

Jones, Lee, and Shahar Hameiri. "Debunking the Myth of 'Debt-Trap Diplomacy.'" *Chatham House* 19, no. 2020 (2020): 657–71.

Joseph, KJ, Liyan Zhang, and Rajesh Many. "Information Technology Agreement of WTO: Call for a Revisit." *Centre for WTO Studies Working Paper No* 9 (2013).

Joshi, Vasant C. "Changing Dimensions of Financial Services and Banking Regulation." *Springer Books*, 2025.

Ju, K. J., Byeonghwa Park, and Taikyoo Kim. "Causal Relationship between Supply Chain Dynamic Capabilities, Technological Innovation, and Operational Performance." *Management and Production Engineering Review* 7 (2016).

Kachyke, Aiymgul. *The Use of Information Technologies in the European Union's Special Regulations on Cross-Border Civil Procedure: Regulations on the Order for Payment, Small Claims, Service of Documents and Taking of Evidence*. 2026.

Kahn, Asif, and Ximei Wu. "Impact of Digital Economy on Intellectual Property Law." *J. Pol. & L.* 13 (2020): 117.

Kalogiannidis, Stavros. "Economic Cooperative Models: Agricultural Cooperatives in Greece and the Need to Modernize Their Operation for the Sustainable Development of Local Societies." *International Journal of Academic Research in Business and Social Sciences* 10, no. 11 (2020): 452–68.

Kam, Ming-Ting Oceanus. "A Comparative Analysis of Customer Data Privacy Protection under the European Union's General Data Protection Regulation and the People's Republic of China's Personal Information Protection Law." *Beijing L. Rev.* 16 (2025): 1721.

Kamal, Mostafa, and Tarek Aziz Bablu. "Mobile Applications Empowering Smallholder Farmers: A Review of the Impact on Agricultural Development." *International Journal of Social Analytics* 8 (2023): 36–50.

Kamasa, Frasminggi, and Riva'atul Adaniah Wahab. "China Technological Transformation: A Case Study of Telecommunications Equipment Industry." *Buletin Pos Dan Telekomunikasi*, 2021, 59–80.

Kasunda, Jani Grey. "The Digital Silk Road in a Cash-Limited Society: A Critical Analysis of Chinese Fintech Expansion and Its Impact on Financial Sovereignty in Malawi." *Journal of Economic Development, Innovation and Policy* 2, no. 1 (2026): 34–52.

Kauffman, Robert J., Jun Liu, and Dan Ma. "Technology Investment Decision-Making under Uncertainty." *Information Technology and Management* 16, no. 2 (2015): 153–72.

Kavitha, D., B. Uma Maheswari, and R. Sujatha. "Super Apps: The Natural Progression in Fin-Tech." *Fintech and Cryptocurrency*, 2023, 383–412.

Kaya, Serkan, and Muhammad Danyal Khan. "Online Dispute Resolution in Pakistan: Challenges and Opportunities." *Journal of Nusantara Studies (JONUS)* 7, no. 2 (2022): 103–19.

Kayyali, Mustafa. "Digital Literacy in Higher Education: Preparing Students for the Workforce of the Future." *International Journal of Information Science and Computing* 11, no. 1 (2024): 53–73.

Kelly, Paula, Matteo Zallio, Bruna Duarte, and Damon Berry. "Design for Enabling Technologies. A Framework to Empower Multi-Level User Engagement." 2018, 65–74.

Kelsey, Jane. *Opportunities and Challenges for ASEAN and East Asia from the Regional Comprehensive Economic Partnership on E-Commerce*. Economic Research Institute for ASEAN and East Asia, 2022.

Kennedy, Scott, and Christopher K. Johnson. *Perfecting China, Inc.: China's 13th Five-Year Plan*. Bloomsbury Publishing USA, 2016.

Khan, Asif. "Rules on Digital Trade in the Light of WTO Agreements." *PhD Law Dissertation, School of Law, Zhengzhou University China*, 2023.

Khan, Bilal, Rabia Hussain, and Zaenal Arifin Sahabuddin. *Global Digital Risk Governance and Cyber Sovereignty: Implications for Coordinated Infrastructure Defense*. 2024.

Khan, Md Nazrul Islam. "Legal Documentation and Case Management: A Systematic Review of Digitization Trends and Cybersecurity Challenges in Legal Support Roles." *Review of Applied Science and Technology* 2, no. 01 (2023): 01–25.

Khan, Muhammad Khalil, Imran Ali Sandano, Cornelius B. Pratt, and Tahir Farid. "China's Belt and Road Initiative: A Global Model for an Evolving Approach to Sustainable Regional Development." *Sustainability* 10, no. 11 (2018): 4234.

Khatri, Dignesh Kumar, Anshika Aggarwal, and P. Goel. "AI Chatbots in SAP FICO: Simplifying Transactions." *Innovative Research Thoughts* 8, no. 3 (2022): 294–306.

Kim, Kyungha. "Assessing the Impact of Mobile Money on Improving the Financial Inclusion of Nairobi Women." *Journal of Gender Studies* 31, no. 3 (2022): 306–22.

Kim, Phillip H., and Mingxiang Li. "Seeking Assurances When Taking Action: Legal Systems, Social Trust, and Starting Businesses in Emerging Economies." *Organization Studies* 35, no. 3 (2014): 359–91.

Kirkwood, Jamieson. "Characterization (and Registration) of a 'BRI Dispute.'" *Asian Journal of International Law* 14, no. 2 (2024): 324–57.

Klievink, Bram, Nitesh Bharosa, and Yao-Hua Tan. "The Collaborative Realization of Public Values and Business Goals: Governance and Infrastructure of Public–Private Information Platforms." *Government Information Quarterly* 33, no. 1 (2016): 67–79.

Koch, Stefan, and Duygu Inanc. "Mass Customization for Financial Services: An Empirical Study of Adoption and Usage Behavior." *Journal of Services Marketing* 29, no. 3 (2015): 235–43.

Kodete, Chandra Shikhi. "A Real Time AI System for Automated Financial Technology Payment Detection and Risk Reduction." *International Journal of Scientific Research in Computer Science Engineering and Information Technology* 7 (2021): 685–710.

Kokuytseva, Tatiana V., Irina A. Rodionova, and Vesna Damnjanovic. "Preconditions for the Transition of Developed and Developing Countries to the Cyber Economy through the Process of Digital Modernization." In *The Cyber Economy: Opportunities and Challenges for Artificial Intelligence in the Digital Workplace*. Springer, 2019.

Kolb, Marina. "The Memorandum of Understanding." In *The European Union and the Council of Europe*. Springer, 2013.

Kormelink, Joost Groot. *Responsible Innovation: Ethics, Safety and Technology*. TU Delft OPEN Publishing, 2019.

Kortukova, Tamara, and Lilia Nevara. "Features of the Principle of Non-Discrimination in International Trade and Economic Law." *Legal Horizons*, 2023, 41.

Kostka, Genia. "Digital Governance in China." In *Handbook on Local Governance in China*. Edward Elgar Publishing, 2023.

Kowalski, Bartosz. "V. Serbia-China Relations: The Security Dimension." *Publishing Series IEŚ Policy Papers Number 6/2022*, n.d., 59.

Kshetri, Nir. "Big Data's Role in Expanding Access to Financial Services in China." *International Journal of Information Management* 36, no. 3 (2016): 297–308.

Kudaibergenova, Diana T., and Marlene Laruelle. "Making Sense of the January 2022 Protests in Kazakhstan: Failing Legitimacy, Culture of Protests, and Elite Readjustments." *Post-Soviet Affairs* 38, no. 6 (2022): 441–59.

Kulsoom, Sara, and Pritam Banerjee. *Realising The Hong Kong Ministerial Vision: Towards Deeper Mode 1 Liberalisation in Trade in Services*. 2025.

Kumar, J. Suresh. "E Commerce and Intellectual Property Resolving Disputes in the Digital Marketplace." *Vidyavardhaka First Grade College, Mysuru, Karnataka*, 2023.

Kuner, Christopher. "Data and Extraterritoriality." In *Research Handbook on Extraterritoriality in International Law*. Edward Elgar Publishing, 2023.

Kuon, Vannsy, Haknoukrith Han, and Heidi Dahles. "Cambodia." In *Risk and Tourism Marketing in Asia*. Routledge, 2026.

Kyeyune, Gorrettie Nakyeyune, and Joseph Mpeera Ntayi. "Empowering Rural Communities: The Role of Financial Literacy and Management in Sustainable Development." *Frontiers in Human Dynamics* 6 (2025): 1424126.

Laffont, Jean-Jacques, and Jean Tirole. *Competition in Telecommunications*. MIT Press, 2001.

Łągiewska, Magdalena. "Chinese Approach to Online Dispute Resolution." *Budúcnosť Práva–Právo Budúcnosti II.*, 2022, 47.

Łągiewska, Magdalena. "Legal Aspects of the Digital Silk Road: Trends and Challenges." *Routledge Handbook of Chinese and Eurasian International Relations*, 2024, 405–16.

Lam, Jasmine Siu Lee, Kevin Patrick Brendan Cullinane, and Paul Tae-Woo Lee. "The 21st-Century Maritime Silk Road: Challenges and Opportunities for Transport Management and Practice." *Transport Reviews* 38, no. 4 (2018): 413–15.

Larionova, Marina, and Andrey Shelepov. "Emerging Regulation for the Digital Economy: Challenges and Opportunities for Multilateral Global Governance." *International Organisations Research Journal* 16, no. 1 (2021): 29–63.

Leal-Arcas, Rafael. "China and the Regional Comprehensive Economic Partnership." *Journal of Global Policy and Governance* 2, no. 2 (2013): 287–304.

Lele, Ajey, and Kritika Roy. *Analysing China's Digital and Space Belt and Road Initiative*. Institute for Defence Studies and Analysis, 2019.

Leong, Kelvin, and Anna Sung. "FinTech (Financial Technology): What Is It and How to Use Technologies to Create Business Value in Fintech Way?" *International Journal of Innovation, Management and Technology* 9, no. 2 (2018): 74–78.

Lescrauwaet, Lyytinen, Hekkert Wagner, Cheng Yoon, and Sovacool Shukla. *Law and Economics*. 2022.

Lewis, Donald J., Xiaohua Yang, Diana Moise, and Stephen John Roddy. "Dynamic Synergies between China's Belt and Road Initiative and the UN's Sustainable Development Goals." *Journal of International Business Policy* 4, no. 1 (2021): 58.

Li, Jiatao, Ari Van Assche, Lee Li, and Gongming Qian. "Foreign Direct Investment along the Belt and Road: A Political Economy Perspective." *Journal of International Business Studies* 53, no. 5 (2022): 902–19.

Li, Lin. "Data Sovereignty and National Security: Governance Challenges and Pathways in the Digital Age." *Global Review of Humanities, Arts, and Society* 1, no. 1 (2025): 49–58.

Li, Rui, Shuaiyong Zheng, Ershen Wang, et al. "Advances in BeiDou Navigation Satellite System (BDS) and Satellite Navigation Augmentation Technologies." *Satellite Navigation* 1, no. 1 (2020): 12.

Li, Wenlong, and Jiahong Chen. "From Brussels Effect to Gravity Assists: Understanding the Evolution of the GDPR-Inspired Personal Information Protection Law in China." *Computer Law & Security Review* 54 (2024): 105994.

Li, Xiaolong, Jiyin Li, Chunhui Yuan, Songliang Guo, and Zhen Wang. "Digital Infrastructure." In *Development Practice of Digital Business Environment in China*. Springer, 2022.

Li, Yi, Christy Ying Ni Liu, Ut Lao, and Jiangtong Dang. "Navigating the Path to Environmental Sustainability: Exploring the Role of Fintech, Natural Resources and Green Energy in Belt and Road Countries." *Resources Policy* 88 (2024): 104485.

Li, Yuanyuan. "Research on Huawei Mobile Phone Marketing Strategy Based on Market Segmentation Theory." 2019, 293–300.

Li, Ziru, Gunwoong Lee, TS Raghu, and Zhan Shi. "Impact of the General Data Protection Regulation on the Global Mobile App Market: Digital Trade Implications of Data Protection and Privacy Regulations." *Information Systems Research* 36, no. 2 (2025): 669–89.

Liang, Lin, and Yan Li. "How Does Government Support Promote Digital Economy Development in China? The Mediating Role of Regional Innovation Ecosystem Resilience." *Technological Forecasting and Social Change* 188 (2023): 122328.

Liang, Yingying, Liangliang Guo, Jianlu Li, Shuang Zhang, and Xiangyun Fei. "The Impact of Trade Facilitation on Cross-Border E-Commerce Transactions: Analysis Based on the Marine and Land Cross-Border Logistical Practices between China and Countries along the 'Belt and Road.'" *Water* 13, no. 24 (2021): 3567.

Liang, Zong. "Innovation in Globalization Theory and Reconstruction of International Trade Rules." In *The Innovation of Economic Theory in China: Theoretical Perspectives*. Springer, 2026.

Liao, Shaoyi, Yuan Pu Shao, Huaiqing Wang, and Ada Chen. "The Adoption of Virtual Banking: An Empirical Study." *International Journal of Information Management* 19, no. 1 (1999): 63–74.

Lin, Jian, Wilfred Yang Wang, and Ping Sun. *Chinese Platforms: A Critical Introduction*. John Wiley & Sons, 2025.

Lin, Lin, and Yanrong Hong. "Developing a Green Bonds Market: Lessons from China." *European Business Organization Law Review* 23, no. 1 (2022): 143–85.

Lin, Yang. "E-Commerce and Online Dispute Resolution in Hong Kong: The Case of eBRAM." *Amicus Curiae* 4 (2022): 542.

Linkov, Igor, Benjamin D. Trump, Kelsey Poinsatte-Jones, and Marie-Valentine Florin. "Governance Strategies for a Sustainable Digital World." *Sustainability* 10, no. 2 (2018): 440.

Lior, Anat. "Insuring AI: The Role of Insurance in Artificial Intelligence Regulation." *Harv. JL & Tech.* 35 (2021): 467.

Liu, Lizhi. "The Rise of Data Politics: Digital China and the World." *Studies in Comparative International Development* 56, no. 1 (2021): 45–67.

Liu, Xinru. *The Silk Road in World History*. Oxford University Press, 2010.

Liu, Yanlin, Yaoguang Yang, Xiyue Zhang, and Yaohui Yang. "The Impact of Technological Innovation on the Green Digital Economy and Development Strategies." *Plos One* 19, no. 4 (2024): e0301051.

Longo, Erik, and Filippo Bagni. "From Legal Experimentation to Regulatory Sandboxes: The EU's Pioneering Approach to Digital Innovation and Regulation." In *White Paper on Regulatory Sandboxes for AI and Cybersecurity*. Nessuno, 2025.

Loo, Becky PY, and Yu Loong Ngan. "Developing Mobile Telecommunications to Narrow Digital Divide in Developing Countries? Some Lessons from China." *Telecommunications Policy* 36, nos. 10–11 (2012): 888–900.

Lum, Thomas. *China's Assistance and Government-Sponsored Investment Activities in Africa, Latin America, and Southeast Asia*. 2009.

Luo, Tian Yang, and Yu Qin Zhu. "Pathways for the Digital Economy to Drive Urban-Rural Integration in Guangxi, China." *GAS J. Econ. Bus. Manag* 1 (2024): 162–74.

Ly, Bora. "Challenge and Perspective for Digital Silk Road." *Cogent Business & Management* 7, no. 1 (2020): 1804180.

Ma, Quan. "Leadership and Innovation in the Digital Economy." *Academic Journal of Business & Management* 5, no. 10 (2023): 146–50.

Ma, Wei, Haiyang Nian, Yue Zheng, and Rong Ma. "Inhibit or Promote: Assessing the Impact of Digital Economy on Poverty Reduction in the Belt and Road Initiative Countries." *Applied Spatial Analysis and Policy* 18, no. 4 (2025): 132.

Ma, Winston. *China's Mobile Economy: Opportunities in the Largest and Fastest Information Consumption Boom*. John Wiley & Sons, 2016.

Macchiavello, Eugenia, and Michele Siri. "Sustainable Finance and Fintech: Can Technology Contribute to Achieving Environmental Goals? A Preliminary Assessment of 'Green Fintech' and 'Sustainable Digital Finance.'" *European Company and Financial Law Review* 19, no. 1 (2022): 128–74.

Macdonald, Stephen, and Briony Birdi. "The Concept of Neutrality: A New Approach." *Journal of Documentation* 76, no. 1 (2020): 333–53.

Madegowda, J. "Traditional vs. Contemporary Financing Models for MSMEs and Startups: A Comparative Study." In *Empowering Inclusive Innovation*. Routledge, 2026.

Mahmood, Shahid, Huaping Sun, Asifa Iqbal, Amel Ali Alhussan, and El-Sayed M. El-kenawy. "Green Finance, Sustainable Infrastructure, and Green Technology Innovation: Pathways to Achieving Sustainable Development Goals in the Belt and Road Initiative." *Environmental Research Communications* 6, no. 10 (2024): 105036.

Mahmoud Selwawy Mansy, Muhammed. "The Impact of IPR in Protecting And Enhancing Digital Economy." *Journal of Intellectual Property and Innovation Management* 5, no. 4 (2022): 189–216.

Majumdar, Shouvik Kishore, Angana Parashar Sarma, and Srishti Majumdar. "E-Commerce and Digital Connectivity: Unleashing the Potential for Greater India–ASEAN Integration." *Journal of Asian Economic Integration* 2, no. 1 (2020): 62–81.

Malhotra, Rashmi, and DK Malhotra. "The Impact of Technology, Big Data, and Analytics: The Evolving Data-Driven Model of Innovation in the Finance Industry." *Journal of Financial Data Science* 5, no. 3 (2023).

Malik, Ammar, Bradley Parks, Brooke Russell, et al. “Banking on the Belt and Road: Insights from a New Global Dataset of 13,427 Chinese Development Projects.” *Williamsburg, VA: AidData at William & Mary*, 2021, 23–36.
Malomo, Olumide Olugbenga. *Cybersecurity Through a Blockchain Enabled Federated Cloud Framework*. 2018.
Mania, Karolina. “Online Dispute Resolution: The Future of Justice.” *International Comparative Jurisprudence* 1, no. 1 (2015): 76–86.
Manners-Bell, John, Thomas Cullen, and Cathy Roberson. *Logistics and Supply Chains in Emerging Markets*. Kogan Page Publishers, 2014.
Mansell, Robin, and Jean-Christophe Plantin. “Imagining 5G Networks: Infrastructure and Public Accountability.” *International Journal of Communication* 16 (2022): 19–19.
Marinova, Miroslava. “The UK’s Digital Market Regulation: The Need for a Proportionality Principle in the CMA’s New Framework.” *Journal of European Competition Law & Practice* 15, no. 7 (2024): 491–97.
Mariscal, Judith. “Digital Divide in a Developing Country.” *Telecommunications Policy* 29, nos. 5–6 (2005): 409–28.
Masenya, Tlou Maggie. “Digital Literacy Skills as Prerequisite for Teaching and Learning in Higher Education Institutions.” *Mousaion* 39, no. 2 (2021).
Mason, Stephen. *Electronic Signatures in Law*. University of London press, 2016.
Mason, Stephen. “Electronic Signatures in Practice.” *J. High Tech. L.* 6 (2006): 148.
Massalha, Mona Omar Ali. *China’s Digital Silk Road Impact on the Gulf Cooperation Council’s Information and Communication Technology Sector Growth Amid Sino American Competition* 2025 .رسالة دكتوراة.
Matinmikko, Marja, Matti Latva-aho, Petri Ahokangas, and Veikko Seppänen. “On Regulations for 5G: Micro Licensing for Locally Operated Networks.” *Telecommunications Policy* 42, no. 8 (2018): 622–35.
Matyushenko, Igor, Serhii Hlibko, Olena Khanova, Anastasiia Rudych, and Larysa Grygorova-Berenda. “Assessment of the Digital Gap in Developing Countries.” *L. & Innovative Soc’y*, 2024, 130.
Mbise, Theo, Sainabou Taal, Michael Roberts, and Frans Lammersen. *Digital Connectivity & E-Commerce: Overview of Financing Flows and Examples of Aid for Trade Support*. 2018.
Medina, Lisset, Marcelo Cano-Kollmann, and Isabel Alvarez. “International Connectivity in the Generation of Information and Communication Technology (ICT) in Spain.” *Competitiveness Review: An International Business Journal* 30, no. 3 (2020): 355–71.
Meissner, Dirk. “Public-Private Partnership Models for Science, Technology, and Innovation Cooperation.” *Journal of the Knowledge Economy* 10, no. 4 (2019): 1341–61.
Melashchenko, Nikita. *Data Barriers to International Trade*. 2022.
Melenko, Oksana. “Mediation as an Alternative Form of Dispute Resolution: Comparative-Legal Analysis.” *European Journal of Law and Public Administration* 7, no. 2 (2020): 46–63.
Melkumyan, Anahit, and Maria Sahakyan. “Digital Technologies and Labour Market Development in the Republic of Armenia.” *Management Research and Practice* 14, no. 2 (2022): 37–45.
Meltzer, Joshua Paul. “The I Nternet, Cross-Border Data Flows and International Trade.” *Asia & the Pacific Policy Studies* 2, no. 1 (2015): 90–102.
Mendes, Carmen Amado, and Xuheng Wang. “The Belt and Road Initiative in Global Governance: Impact on the International World Order.” In *The Palgrave Handbook of Globalization with Chinese Characteristics: The Case of the Belt and Road Initiative*. Springer, 2023.
Menkel-Meadow, Carrie. *Hybrid and Mixed Dispute Resolution Processes: Integrities of Process Pluralism*. Edward Elgar Publishing, 2020.
Mercurio, Bryan, and Ronald Yu. *Regulating Cross-Border Data Flows: Issues, Challenges and Impact*. Anthem Press, 2022.

Mezentseva, Elena, Malika Baysaeva, and Nurulla Fayzullaev. "The Impact of Sustainable Development on Economic Growth: Balancing Environmental, Social and Economic Factors." *Reliability: Theory & Applications* 19, no. SI 6 (81) (2024): 1269–74.

Mhlongo, Siyabonga, Khanyisile Mbatha, Boitumelo Ramatsetse, and Reuben Dlamini. "Challenges, Opportunities, and Prospects of Adopting and Using Smart Digital Technologies in Learning Environments: An Iterative Review." *Heliyon* 9, no. 6 (2023).

Migliorini, Sara. "'More than Words': A Legal Approach to the Risks of Commercial Chatbots Powered by Generative Artificial Intelligence." *European Journal of Risk Regulation* 15, no. 3 (2024): 719–36.

Milakovich, Michael E. *Digital Governance: New Technologies for Improving Public Service and Participation*. Routledge, 2012.

Min, Alfonso. "Artificial Intelligence and Bias: Challenges, Implications, and Remedies." *Journal of Social Research* 2, no. 11 (2023).

Minarni, Eni. "Impact of Digital Payment Systems on Financial Inclusion and Small Business Growth in Developing Economies." *International Journal of Innovation and Thinking* 2, no. 1 (2025): 1–12.

Minas, Stephen. "Conflicting Connectivities: Legal Considerations for Negotiating Geotechnological Rivalry." *Iustinianus Primus L. Rev.* 16 (2025): 147.

Mirzaye, Sina, and Muhammad Mohiuddin. "Digital Transformation in International Trade: Opportunities, Challenges, and Policy Implications." *Journal of Risk and Financial Management* 18, no. 8 (2025): 421.

Mishra, Adya. "Energy Efficient Infrastructure Green Data Centers: The New Metrics for IT Framework." *International Journal For r Multidisciplinary Research* 4 (2022): 1–12.

Mishra, Priyanka, and Ghanshyam Singh. "Energy Management Systems in Sustainable Smart Cities Based on the Internet of Energy: A Technical Review." *Energies* 16, no. 19 (2023): 6903.

MKPO, David Chukwuebuka. "Is Truth And Integrity Of Justice On Trial In The Age Of Artificial Intelligence (Ai)? Re-Assessing Digital Evidence In The Context Of Ai-Generated Evidence Such As Deepfakes." *International Review Of Law And Jurisprudence (IRLJ)* 7, no. 1 (2025).

Mogielnicki, Robert. "The Intersection of Digital Development Trajectories." *Routledge Handbook on China–Middle East Relations*, 2021.

Mohamed, Id Bouhou, and Ikram Ben Ali Kaddour. "Protection for Working Women: Comparative Study of Moroccan and Chinese Regulations." *International Journal of Discovery in Social Sciences* 2, no. 1 (2026).

Morris, Mike. *Chinese Firms and Adherence to Global Environmental, Social and Governance (ESG) Standards in Developing Countries: Is There Potential to Create Common Ground?* no. 18/2023. IDOS Discussion Paper, 2023.

Mubarik, Mobashar, Raja Zuraidah Raja Mohd Rasi, Muhammad Faraz Mubarak, and Rashid Ashraf. "Impact of Blockchain Technology on Green Supply Chain Practices: Evidence from Emerging Economy." *Management of Environmental Quality: An International Journal* 32, no. 5 (2021): 1023–39.

Muhammad, Abdulgaffar, Micah Ezekiel Elton Mike, Mohammed Bello Idris, Aisha Ahmad Ishaq, and Auwal Kabir Abdullah. "The Belt and Road Initiative: Implications for Infrastructure Development and Economic Integration in Eurasia." *J Environ Sci Econ* 2, no. 2 (2023).

Murton, Galen, and Tom Narins. "Corridors, Chokepoints and the Contradictions of the Belt and Road Initiative." *Area Development and Policy* 9, no. 4 (2024): 445–65.

Musa, Auwal Alhassan, Salim Idris Malami, Fayez Alanazi, Wassef Ounaies, Mohammed Alshammari, and Sadi Ibrahim Haruna. "Sustainable Traffic Management for Smart Cities Using Internet-of-Things-Oriented Intelligent Transportation Systems (ITS): Challenges and Recommendations." *Sustainability* 15, no. 13 (2023): 9859.

Musoni, Melody, Poorva Karkare, Chloe Teevan, and Ennatu Domingo. "Global Approaches to Digital Sovereignty: Competing Definitions and Contrasting Policy." *Maastricht: ECDPM*, 2023.

Mustapha, Shakira, and Annalisa Prizzon. "Debt Sustainability and Debt Management in Developing Countries." *Economic and Private Sector Professional Evidence and Applied Knowledge Service Topic Guide. London: Overseas Development Institute*, 2015.

Mwaniki, Dennis, Michael Kinyanjui, and Romanus Opiyo. "Towards Smart Economic Development in Nairobi: Evaluating Smart City Economy Impacts and Opportunities and Challenges for Smart Growth." *Smart Economy in Smart Cities: International Collaborative Research: Ottawa, St. Louis, Stuttgart, Bologna, Cape Town, Nairobi, Dakar, Lagos, New Delhi, Varanasi, Vijayawada, Kozhikode, Hong Kong*, 2016, 749–90.

N., Kamalesh. "Analysis of UNCITRAL Model Law Provision on E-Commerce with Respect to Indian Perspective." *Part 1 Indian J. Integrated Rsch. L.* 2 (2022): 1.

Nanjundan, Preethi, Lijo Thomas, Indu PV, and Saeid Eslamian. "Social Inclusion and Sustainability." *Global Nexus Handbook* 3 (2026): 965–74.

Narula, Rajneesh. *Globalization and Technology: Interdependence, Innovation Systems and Industrial Policy*. John Wiley & Sons, 2014.

Nazokat, Babadjanova. "The Role of International Trade Law in Promoting Global Economic Stability." *Shokh Library* 1, no. 13 (2025).

Nedopil, Christoph. "Green Finance for Soft Power: An Analysis of China's Green Policy Signals and Investments in the Belt and Road Initiative." *Environmental Policy and Governance* 32, no. 2 (2022): 85–97.

Newell, Bryce Clayton, Nadezhda Purtova, Young Eun Moon, and Hugh J. Paterson III. "Regulating the Data Market: The Material Scope of American Consumer Data Privacy Law." *U. Pa. J. Int'l L.* 45 (2023): 1055.

Ni, Mengmeng. *Policy Approaches and Entrepreneurial Responses in Strategic Industries: Comparing Innovation Ecosystems in China and the United States*. 2025.

Nie, Fei, Jian Li, Xiang Bi, and Gucheng Li. "Agricultural Trade Liberalization and Domestic Fertilizer Use: Evidence from China-ASEAN Free Trade Agreement." *Ecological Economics* 195 (2022): 107341.

Nie, Wenjuan. "China's State-Owned Enterprises: Instruments of Its Foreign Strategy?" *Journal of Contemporary China* 31, no. 135 (2022): 383–97.

Ning, Yiyi, Jacob Cherian, Muhammad Safdar Sial, Susana Álvarez-Otero, Ubaldo Comite, and Malik Zia-Ud-Din. "Green Bond as a New Determinant of Sustainable Green Financing, Energy Efficiency Investment, and Economic Growth: A Global Perspective." *Environmental Science and Pollution Research* 30, no. 22 (2023): 61324–39.

Nirmani, IAP. "Barriers to Digital Participation in Developing Countries: Identifying Technological, Social, and Cultural Obstacles to Community Involvement." *GSC Advanced Research and Reviews* 23, no. 2 (2025): 061–071.

Nolan, Peter, and Jin Zhang. "The Challenge of Globalization for Large Chinese Firms." *World Development* 30, no. 12 (2002): 2089–107.

Nosike, Revd Dr Chukwunonso Joseph. "Digitalization in Developing Countries: Opportunities and Challenges." *Nigerian Journal of Arts and Humanities (NJAH)* 4, no. 1 (2024).

Nuccio, Massimiliano, and Marco Guerzoni. "Big Data: Hell or Heaven? Digital Platforms and Market Power in the Data-Driven Economy." *Competition & Change* 23, no. 3 (2019): 312–28.

Nurgozhayeva, Roza. "Rule-Making, Rule-Taking or Rule-Rejecting under the Belt and Road Initiative: A Central Asian Perspective." *The Chinese Journal of Comparative Law* 8, no. 1 (2020): 250–78.

Nursamsiah, Ely, Yuhelson Yuhelson, and Supaphorn Akkapin. "International Commercial Mediation: Towards a Harmonized Legal Framework for Cross-Border Business Dispute Resolution." *Journal Evidence of Law* 4, no. 3 (2025): 1164–72.

Nwachukwu, Priscilla Samuel, Onyeka Kelvin Chima, and Chinelo Harriet Okolo. *Marketing Financial Products in Emerging Economies: Global Strategies, Effectiveness, and a Conceptual Customer-Centric Banking Model*. 2023.

Nweje, Uche, and Moyosore Taiwo. "Leveraging Artificial Intelligence for Predictive Supply Chain Management, Focus on How AI-Driven Tools Are Revolutionizing Demand Forecasting and Inventory Optimization." *International Journal of Science and Research Archive* 14, no. 1 (2025): 230–50.

NZANG, SIMA, and JULIO CESAR OBIANG. "Judicial Innovation and Global Governance: The Strategic Role of China International Commercial Court in Advancing the Belt and Road Initiative, The Case of Xian International Commercial Court." *ScienceOpen Preprints*, 2026.

Nzuva, Silas Mutie. "Smart Contracts Implementation, Applications, Benefits, and Limitations." *Journal of Information Engineering and Applications*, 2019.

Öberg, Christina, and Gary Graham. "How Smart Cities Will Change Supply Chain Management: A Technical Viewpoint." *Production Planning & Control* 27, no. 6 (2016): 529–38.

Oberthür, Sebastian, and Kati Kulovesi. "Accelerating the EU's Climate Transformation: The European Green Deal's Fit for 55 Package Unpacked." *Review of European, Comparative & International Environmental Law* 34, no. 1 (2025): 7–22.

O'Donnell, Jill Kosch. "The Global Green Growth Institute: On a Mission to Prove Green Growth." *New York: Council of Foreign Relations*, 2012.

O'hara, Kieron, and Wendy Hall. *Four Internets: The Geopolitics of Digital Governance*. 2018.

Okano-Heijmans, Maaike, and Wilhelm Vosse. "Promoting Open and Inclusive Connectivity: The Case for Digital Development Cooperation." *Research in Globalization* 3 (2021): 100061.

Okunogbe, Oyebola, and Fabrizio Santoro. "Increasing Tax Collection in African Countries: The Role of Information Technology." *Journal of African Economies* 32, no. Supplement_1 (2023): i57–83.

Oraegbunam, Ikenga KE, and Chiugo Onwuatuegwu. "Addressing the Challenges in the Contemporary International Trading System: The Limitations of General Agreements on Tariffs Trade (Gatt) and General Agreements on Trade in Services (GATS)." *IJOCLLEP* 5 (2023): 64.

Oreglia, Elisa, Hongyi Ren, and Chia-Chi Liao. "The Puzzle of the Digital Silk Road." *Digital Silk Road in Central Asia: Present and Future* 1 (2021).

Oreglia, Elisa, and Weidi Zheng. "The Digital Silk Road between National Rhetoric and Provincial Ambitions." *The China Quarterly* 261 (2025): 183–95.

Osuji, Vivian Chilee, Omoize Fatimetu Dako, and Chizoba Michael Okafor. "Seamless Integration of Digital Supply-Chain Platforms with Commercial Banking to Enhance Working Capital Efficiency for SMEs." *Journal Not Specified*, 2023.

Palepu, Krishna G., Feng Zhu, Susie L. MA, and Kerry Herman. *Ant Group (A)*. 2021.

Pan, Kathryn. *Ant Group's Transformative Impact on China's Financial Industry*. 2025.

Parasol, Max. "China's Digital Yuan: Reining in Alipay and WeChat Pay." *Banking & Finance Law Review* 37, no. 2 (2022): 265–303.

Parzyan, Anahit. "China's Digital Silk Road: Empowering Capabilities for Digital Leadership in Eurasia." In *China and Eurasian Powers in a Multipolar World Order 2.0*. Routledge, 2023.

Patel, Amaresh, Radha Ranjan, Rahul Kumar Kumar, Namisha Ojha, and Aarti Patel. "Online Dispute Resolution Mechanism as an Effective Tool for Resolving Cross-Border Consumer Disputes in the Era of e-Commerce." *International Journal of Law and Management*, 2025.

Paudel, Pramila. "Connecting Asia: The Rise of China's Digital Silk Road in ASEAN Countries." *Realism: Law Review* 3, no. 2 (2025): 70–94.

Paudel, Pramila. "Divergent Digital Paths: A Comparative Study of Regulatory Frameworks and Participation in the Digital Silk Road between China and Nepal." *International Journal of Law and Legal Advancement* 1, no. 2 (2025).

Pazarbasioglu, Ceyla, Alfonso Garcia Mora, Mahesh Uttamchandani, Harish Natarajan, Erik Feyen, and Mathew Saal. "Digital Financial Services." *World Bank* 54, no. 1 (2020): 1–54.

Peng, Shuhong, Jing Qian, Xiuwei Xing, Jing Wang, Aliya Adeli, and Shujie Wei. "Technological Cooperation for Sustainable Development under the Belt and Road Initiative and the Sustainable Development Goals: Opportunities and Challenges." *Sustainability* 17, no. 2 (2025): 657.

Peters, Anne. "International Dispute Settlement: A Network of Cooperational Duties." *European Journal of International Law* 14, no. 1 (2003): 1–34.

Peters, Michael A. "Digital Trade, Digital Economy and the Digital Economy Partnership Agreement (DEPA)." *Educational Philosophy and Theory* 55, no. 7 (2023): 747–55.

Petersmann, Ernst-Ulrich. "International Settlement of Trade and Investment Disputes over Chinese 'Silk Road Projects' inside the European Union." In *A Legal Analysis of the Belt and Road Initiative: Towards a New Silk Road?* Springer, 2020.

Philip, Lorna, and Fiona Williams. "Remote Rural Home Based Businesses and Digital Inequalities: Understanding Needs and Expectations in a Digitally Underserved Community." *Journal of Rural Studies* 68 (2019): 306–18.

Platen, Emely von. "With or without Efficiency Defence? Analysing the Role of Efficiency Defence in Traditional Ex-Post Enforcement, the EU Digital Markets Act & the UK Digital Markets, Competition and Consumers Act." *NEL Rev.* 10 (2024): 22.

Pollio, Andrea. *Silicon Elsewhere*. University of California Press, 2026.

Pongsiri, Nutavoot. "Regulation and Public-private Partnerships." *International Journal of Public Sector Management* 15, no. 6 (2002): 487–95.

Popkova, Elena G., Paola De Bernardi, Yuliya G. Tyurina, and Bruno S. Sergi. "A Theory of Digital Technology Advancement to Address the Grand Challenges of Sustainable Development." *Technology in Society* 68 (2022): 101831.

Portrait, A. "The Cyberspace Administration of China." *The Emergence of China's Smart State*, 2023, 9.

Potter, Pitman B. "China and the International Legal System: Challenges of Participation." *The China Quarterly* 191 (2007): 699–715.

Prabhu, Swati. *European Union's Connectivity Agenda: Forging Partnerships for Environmental Governance*. Springer, 2025.

Prakash, Anita. "Connecting the Connectivity Plans in Asia and beyond: International Cooperation for Expanded Supply Chains and Resilient Growth." *The Comprehensive Asia Development Plan 3.0 (CADP 3.0): Towards an Integrated, Innovative, Inclusive, and Sustainable Economy*, 2022, 100.

Prilliadi, Hilmy. *Harnessing AI for ASEAN's Future: Governance, Adoption, and Sustainability under the DEFA*. 2025.

Provisions, Chapter I. General. *China International Economic and Trade Arbitration Commission CIETAC Arbitration Rules*. n.d.

Pugh, Michael. "Employment, Labour Rights and Social Resistance." In *Whose Peace? Critical Perspectives on the Political Economy of Peacebuilding*. Springer, 2008.

Puhakainen, Essi, and Karin Elisabeth Väyrynen. *The Benefits and Challenges of Technology Neutral Regulation–a Scoping Review*. 2021.

Qiang, Christine Zhen-Wei. *China's Information Revolution: Managing the Economic and Social Transformation*. World Bank Publications, 2007.

Qiu, Yumin, Hongquan Chen, Zhaohan Sheng, and Shuping Cheng. "Governance of Institutional Complexity in Megaproject Organizations." *International Journal of Project Management* 37, no. 3 (2019): 425–43.

Qudus, Lawal. "Cybersecurity Governance: Strengthening Policy Frameworks to Address Global Cybercrime and Data Privacy Challenges." *International Journal of Science and Research Archive* 14, no. 1 (2025): 1146–63.

Rachmawati, Rini, Nur Mohammad Farda, R. Rijanta, and Bowo Setiyono. "The Advantages and Analysis of the Location of Branchless Banking in Urban and Rural Areas in Yogyakarta Special Region, Indonesia." *Journal of Urban and Regional Analysis* 11, no. 1 (2019): 53–68.

Raghuram, Sumita, N. Sharon Hill, Jennifer L. Gibbs, and Likoebe M. Maruping. "Virtual Work: Bridging Research Clusters." *Academy of Management Annals* 13, no. 1 (2019): 308–41.

Rahman, Irsan, Mohamad Hidayat Muhtar, Novita M. Mongdong, Rahmat Setiawan, Beni Setiawan, and Henry Kristian Siburian. "Harmonization of Digital Laws and Adaptation Strategies in Indonesia Focusing on E-Commerce and Digital Transactions." *Innovative: Journal Of Social Science Research* 4, no. 1 (2024): 4314–27.

Rahman, Mahfuzur, Moshfique Uddin, and George Lodorfos. "Barriers to Enter in Foreign Markets: Evidence from SMEs in Emerging Market." *International Marketing Review* 34, no. 1 (2017): 68–86.

Rainey, Daniel, Mohamed S. Abdel Abdel Wahab, and Ethan Katsh. *Online Dispute Resolution-Theory and Practice: A Treatise on Technology and Dispute Resolution*. 2021.

Rajamani, K., N. Akbar Jan, AK Subramani, and A. Nirmal Raj. "Access to Finance: Challenges Faced by Micro, Small, and Medium Enterprises in India." *Engineering Economics* 33, no. 1 (2022): 73–85.

Ralph, Oliver, and Don Weinland. "ZhongAn Launches Insurtech Concept." *The Financial Times*, 2017, 14–14.

Raman, Raghu, Suparna Ray, Dayana Das, and Prema Nedungadi. "Innovations and Barriers in Sustainable and Green Finance for Advancing Sustainable Development Goals." *Frontiers in Environmental Science* 12 (2025): 1513204.

Rashid, Md Harun Ur, Afzal Ahmad, Muhammad Saleh Abdullah, Monir Ahmmed, and Serajul Islam. "Doing Business and Tax Evasion: Evidence from Asian Countries." *Sage Open* 12, no. 4 (2022): 21582440221131280.

Raviteja, Nalabothu. "Financial Technology (Fintech) and Banking Industry Transformation: A Symbiotic Evolution into the Digital Era." *Transactions* 1, no. 2 (2024): 23–29.

Rehman, Zaid. "Beyond Borders: International Law and Global Governance in the Digital Age." *Journal of Accounting & Business Archive Review* 1, no. 1 (2023): 1–12.

Ren, Jing. *Stumbling into the Digital Era: How Can Electronic Bills of Lading Achieve Functional and Legal Equivalence to Paper Bills of Lading?* 2023.

Roco, Mihail C. "Possibilities for Global Governance of Converging Technologies." *Journal of Nanoparticle Research* 10, no. 1 (2008): 11–29.

Rojek, Izabela, Piotr Prokopowicz, Maciej Piechowiak, Piotr Kotlarz, Nataša Náprstková, and Dariusz Mikołajewski. "The Impact of Data Analytics Based on Internet of Things, Edge Computing, and Artificial Intelligence on Energy Efficiency in Smart Environment." *Applied Sciences* 16, no. 1 (2025): 225.

Rusakova, Ekaterina P., and Evgenia E. Frolova. "Digital Disputes in the New Legal Reality." *RUDN Journal of Law* 26, no. 3 (2022): 695–704.

Rustad, Michael L., and Thomas H. Koenig. "Towards a Global Data Privacy Standard." *Fla. L. Rev.* 71 (2019): 365.

Sadikhzada, Aynur, and Sarvar Gurbanov. "Closing the Climate Finance Gap: Strategies and Recommendations in the Context of COP29." *Available at SSRN 5255829*, 2025.

Santaniello, Mauro. "Attributes of Digital Sovereignty: A Conceptual Framework." *Geopolitics* 31, no. 2 (2026): 788–809.

Sapovadia, Vrajlal. "Financial Inclusion, Digital Currency, and Mobile Technology." In *Handbook of Blockchain, Digital Finance, and Inclusion, Volume 2*. Elsevier, 2018.

Sarmiento, Maria Gabriela, and Katia Fach Gómez. "The United Nations Commission on International Trade Law (UNCITRAL)." *The International Law of Economic Integration, Oxford University Press, DRAFT PRE-PRINT, Forthcoming*, 2023.

Savchenko, AB, and TL Borodina. "Green and Digital Economy for Sustainable Development of Urban Areas." *Regional Research of Russia* 10, no. 4 (2020): 583–92.

Sayavong, Vanxay. "Chinese Belt and Road Initiative (BRI) and the Sustainable Development in Lao PDR." In *Belt and Road Initiative and South Asia*. Routledge, 2023.

Sazmand, Bahareh. "China and Global South: BRI in Southeast Asia." In *Implications, Prospects, and Challenges in China's Global South Strategy*. IGI Global Scientific Publishing, 2025.

Schmitz, Amy J. "There's an App for That: Developing Online Dispute Resolution to Empower Economic Development." *Notre Dame JL Ethics & Pub. Pol'y* 32 (2018): 1.

Segger, Marie-Claire Cordonier, and Damilola S. Olawuyi. *Sustainable Development Law: Principles, Practices, and Prospects*. Oxford University Press, 2025.

Sekhri, Desh Gaurav, and NITI OSD. "Designing the Future of Dispute Resolution: The ODR Policy Plan for India." *Message Posted To*, 2020.

Selby, John. "Data Localization Laws: Trade Barriers or Legitimate Responses to Cybersecurity Risks, or Both?" *International Journal of Law and Information Technology* 25, no. 3 (2017): 213–32.

Sen, Gong, and Li Bingqin. *The Digital Silk Road and the Sustainable Development Goals*. 2019.

Serrano, Will. "Digital Systems in Smart City and Infrastructure: Digital as a Service." *Smart Cities* 1, no. 1 (2018): 134–54.

Shabani, Ramadhani Mashaka. "Shari'ah-Compliant Financing Mechanisms for Belt and Road Initiative: Mitigating Debt Trap Risks." *AL-ARBAH: Journal of Islamic Finance and Banking* 6, no. 1 (2024): 17–34.

Shafqat, Dr Saeed, and Saba Shahid. *China Pakistan Economic Corridor: Demands, Dividends and Directions*. Centre for Public Policy and Governance, 2018.

Shah, Wasi Ul Hassan, Bo Wang, and Rizwana Yasmeen. "Evaluating the Role of Banking Efficiency, Institutions and Financial Development for Sustainable Development: Implications for Belt and Road Initiative (BRI)." *Plos One* 18, no. 10 (2023): e0290780.

Shahbaz, Adrian. "The Digital Silk Road and Normative Values." *Adelphi Series* 60, nos. 487–489 (2020): 107–30.

Shahid, Adnan, Adrian Kliks, Ahmed Al-Tahmeesschi, et al. "Large-Scale AI in Telecom: Charting the Roadmap for Innovation, Scalability, and Enhanced Digital Experiences." *arXiv Preprint* arXiv:2503.04184, 2025.

Shahid, Muhammad Nawaz. "Role of Digital Public Infrastructure (DPI) in Strengthening AML/KYC for Developing Economies." *International Journal of Law and Legal Advancement* 2, no. 1 (2026): 13–22.

Shahzad, Aamir, Hamza Rashid, and Syed Mudasser Abbas. "The Belt and Road Initiative: Catalyzing Human Capital Development and Technological Innovation for Sustainable Growth." *China Quarterly of International Strategic Studies* 9, nos. 01–04 (2023): 361–80.

Shan, Wenhua, and Yunya Feng. "The China International Commercial Court: Towards an Integrated Dispute Resolution System." *Asia Pacific Law Review* 29, no. 1 (2021): 107–28.

Shandilya, Shishir Kumar, Agni Datta, Yash Kartik, and Atulya Nagar. "Navigating the Regulatory Landscape." In *Digital Resilience: Navigating Disruption and Safeguarding Data Privacy*. Springer, 2024.

Sharma, Aadit, Bolaji Iyanu Adekunle, Jeffrey Chidera Ogeawuchi, Abraham Ayodeji Abayomi, and Omoniyi Onifade. "Governance Challenges in Cross-Border Fintech Operations: Policy, Compliance, and Cyber Risk Management in the Digital Age." *IRE Journals* 4, no. 9 (2021): 1–8.

Sharma, Manu, Anil Kumar, Sunil Luthra, Sudhanshu Joshi, and Arvind Upadhyay. "The Impact of Environmental Dynamism on Low-carbon Practices and Digital Supply Chain Networks to Enhance Sustainable Performance: An Empirical Analysis." *Business Strategy and the Environment* 31, no. 4 (2022): 1776–88.

Shelepov, Andrei. "The Influence of the G20's Digitalization Leadership on Development Conditions and Governance of the Digital Economy." *International Organisations Research Journal* 17, no. 1 (2022).

Shen, Hong. "Building a Digital Silk Road? Situating the Internet in China's Belt and Road Initiative." *International Journal of Communication* 12 (2018): 19–19.

Shen, Xin Yue. *Chinese ICT on the Digital Silk Road: A Case Study of Infrastructure Building in Pakistan*. 2020.

Sheng, Li. "The World Trade Organization and the Digital Economy Partnership Agreement: Analog Trade Rules in a Digital Era." In *Big Tech Firms and International Relations: The Role of the Nation-State in New Forms of Power*. Springer, 2022.

Shi, Changqing, Tania Sourdin, and Bin Li. "The Smart Court-A New Pathway to Justice in China?" 12 (2021): 1.

Shi, Jingxia, and Fenghua Li. "Aligning the BRI with Sustainable Development: A Regulatory Framework and Its Implementation." *Journal of World Trade* 57, no. 6 (2023).

Shiravi, Abdolhossein, and Mohammad Javad Abdollahi. "Privacy and Confidentiality in Alternative Dispute Resolution Methods." *Journal of Economic & Management Perspectives* 11, no. 3 (2017): 835–44.

Shivayogi, Sheela Kakanur. "Data Classification Methodologies and Implementation." *Journal of Computer Science and Technology Studies* 7, no. 5 (2025): 202–10.

Shlapak, Alla, Olha Yatsenko, Tetiana Tananaiko, and Lesia Lyskova. "Institutional Provision of Tariff and Non-Tariff Regulation of Cross-Border Trade." *Economics. Ecology. Socium*, no. 7 (2023): 1–23.

Shofawati, Atina. "The Role of Digital Finance to Strengthen Financial Inclusion and the Growth of SME in Indonesia." *KnE Social Sciences*, 2019, 389–407.

Shoukat, Daniyal. "Resolving Civil-Commercial Disputes through Mediation in Pakistan: Legal Framework, Sector-Specific Application, and Digital Trends." *Journal for Social Science Archives* 3, no. 2 (2025): 10–59075.

Siagian, Riduan, Leonard Siahaan, and Muhammad Ichwan Hamzah. "Human Rights in the Digital Era: Online Privacy, Freedom of Speech, and Personal Data Protection." *Journal of Digital Learning and Distance Education* 2, no. 4 (2023): 548–58.

Sima Nzang, Julio Cesar Obiang, and Ying Ying Wang. "Harmonizing Legal Diversity: The Role of Soft Law and Model Rules in Belt and Road Dispute Prevention." *ScienceOpen Preprints*, 2026.

Singh, Amrik, and Lalit Mohan Sharma. "Fintech and Financial Inclusion: Transforming Underserved Access to Financial Services." *International Journal of Tourism and Hotel Management* 5, no. 2 (2023): 07–11.

Singh, Bhupinder. "Unleashing Alternative Dispute Resolution (ADR) in Resolving Complex Legal-Technical Issues Arising in Cyberspace Lensing e-Commerce and Intellectual Property: Proliferation of e-Commerce Digital Economy." *Revista Brasileira de Alternative Dispute Resolution-Brazilian Journal of Alternative Dispute Resolution-RBADR* 5, no. 10 (2023): 81–105.

Singh, Kumar Bal Govind. "Online Dispute Resolution in Cross-Border Disputes: A Comprehensive Analysis." *Available at SSRN 4643682*, 2023.

Sinitsyn, Sergei A., Maria O. Diakonova, and Tatyana I. Chursina. "Smart Contracts in the Digital Economy: Contractual Regulation and Dispute Resolution." In *Smart Technologies for the Digitisation of Industry: Entrepreneurial Environment*. Springer, 2021.

Siqi, Chen, Ramalinggam Rajamanickam, Nazura Abdul Manap, and Zamre Mohd Zahir. "Application of Blockchain Technology in Cross-Border Telecommunications Network Fraud to Ensure China's Judicial Justice." *Jurnal IUS Kajian Hukum Dan Keadilan* 12, no. 3 (2024): 472–86.

Smedinghoff, Thomas J. "Is It Legal? Will It Be Trusted? What Are the Rules?--Enabling Electronic Identity Management Under the New UNCITRAL Model Law." *Enabling Electronic Identity Management Under the New UNCITRAL Model Law (April 15, 2024)*, 2024.

Söderholm, Patrik. "The Green Economy Transition: The Challenges of Technological Change for Sustainability." *Sustainable Earth* 3, no. 1 (2020): 6.

Soliman, Riham Mohamed. *Private Sector's Perceptions and Adoption of the e-Invoicing System in Egypt*. 2024.

Song, Jiaqi. *Reforming Mechanisms for Investment Dispute Settlement under the 21st Century Maritime Silk Road Initiative: With Special Reference to Disputed Maritime Areas*. 2025.

Song, Xiaoling, Xuan Qin, and XiaoMeng Feng. "Creating Financial Inclusion in 'Belt and Road' Countries in Europe, Asia and Africa: Regulation, Technology and Financial Literacy." *Journal of Financial Regulation and Compliance* 32, no. 4 (2024): 445–61.

Song, Zhouying, Shuyun Che, and Yu Yang. "The Trade Network of the Belt and Road Initiative and Its Topological Relationship to the Global Trade Network." *Journal of Geographical Sciences* 28, no. 9 (2018): 1249–62.

Sooksripaisarnkit, Poomintr, and Sai Ramani Garimella. *China's One Belt One Road Initiative and Private International Law*. Routledge London, 2018.
Sosa, Iván, and Óscar Montes. "Understanding the InsurTech Dynamics in the Transformation of the Insurance Sector." *Risk Management and Insurance Review* 25, no. 1 (2022): 35–68.
Sreekumar, Aparna. "Hybrid ADR Mechanisms." *Edulogic International Journal for Multi Disciplinary Research P-ISSN: 3051–2395 E-ISSN: 3051–2409* 1, no. 01 (2025): 87–106.
Stucke, Maurice E., and Ariel Ezrachi. "How Digital Assistants Can Harm Our Economy, Privacy, and Democracy." *Berkeley Technology Law Journal* 32, no. 3 (2017): 1239–300.
Subrahmanyam, Satya. "Capacity Building and Skill Development in Rural Manufacturing." In *Rural Social Entrepreneurship Development: Network-Based Manufacturing System Model*. IGI Global Scientific Publishing, 2025.
Subrata, Rusli, Firdaus Arifin, and Ihsanul Maarif. "Hybrid Dispute Resolution in Administrative Law: Toward an Integrated Model for Government Conflict Management." *International Journal of Public Administration*, 2025, 137–62.
Sugianto, Fajar, Ellora Sukardi, and Tomy Michael. "Comparison of Legal Consumer Protection Systems in E-Commerce Transactions To Support Digital Economic Growth in Indonesia." *Dalat University Journal of Science*, 2022, 39–51.
Suh, Jeongmeen, and Jaeyoun Roh. "The Effects of Digital Trade Policies on Digital Trade." *The World Economy* 46, no. 8 (2023): 2383–407.
Sullivan, Clare. "EU GDPR or APEC CBPR? A Comparative Analysis of the Approach of the EU and APEC to Cross Border Data Transfers and Protection of Personal Data in the IoT Era." *Computer Law & Security Review* 35, no. 4 (2019): 380–97.
Sun, Pengfei. "Media, Education, and Healthcare." In *Unleashing the Power of 5GtoB in Industries*. Springer, 2021.
Sun, Xiangzhuang. "A Chinese Approach to International Commercial Dispute Resolution: The China International Commercial Court." *The Chinese Journal of Comparative Law* 8, no. 1 (2020): 45–54.
Sun, Yangjun, Zhuorui Fu, and Ning Zhao. "A Modular Multi-Granularity Simulation Modelling Method for Manufacturing Systems Oriented towards Digital Twins." *International Journal of Production Research*, 2025, 1–21.
Svantesson, Dan. "Data Localisation Trends and Challenges: Considerations for the Review of the Privacy Guidelines." *OECD Digital Economy Papers*, no. 301 (2020).
Syamsuri, Liza Mahavianti, and Whildan Pakartipangi. "Challenges and Opportunities in Implementing Green Data Centers in Indonesia Toward Sustainable Digital Infrastructure." *Jurnal Penelitian Pendidikan IPA* 11, no. 6 (2025): 104–18.
Tache, Cristina Elena Popa. "Between Human Rights and the Digital Economy." *Pandectele Romane*, 2022, 65.
Taidong, Zhou, and Xue Qi. "The Digital Silk Road and Southeast Asian Countries." *The Fourth Industrial Revolution and the Future of Work: Implications for Asian Development Cooperation. Ed. by Anthea Mulakala. Sejong-Si: KDI School of Public Policy and Management*, 2020, 132–64.
Tan, Haoli. "Study on Chinese Cross-Border e-Commerce Payments from a" Double Cycle" Standpoint." *Journal of Computing and Electronic Information Management* 16, no. 2 (2025): 46–50.
Tan, Veltrice. "Belt and Road Initiative: The Interplay between Corruption, Plea-Bargaining and Civil Alternative Dispute Resolution." *Journal of Financial Crime* 30, no. 3 (2023): 603–17.
Tan, Ziwen, and Channing Zhang. "China's PIPL and DSL: Is China Following the EU's Approach to Data Protection?" *Journal of Data Protection & Privacy* 5, no. 1 (2021): 7–25.
Tang, Chunqiang, and Rozaini Rosli. "Internet Technology in Legal Economics and Policy: Strategic Enterprise Innovations in the US-China Trade Relationship." *China and WTO Review* 10, no. 1 (2024): 28–45.
Tang, Hairong. "Research on Investment Protection Mechanisms within the International Legal Framework of the Belt and Road Initiative." *Science of Law Journal* 3 (2024): 147–51.

Tay, Lee-Ying, Hen-Toong Tai, and Gek-Siang Tan. "Digital Financial Inclusion: A Gateway to Sustainable Development." *Heliyon* 8, no. 6 (2022).

Taylor, Monique. "The Party-Led Internet Economy." In *China's Digital Authoritarianism: A Governance Perspective*. Springer, 2022.

Taylor, Richard D. "'Data Localization': The Internet in the Balance." *Telecommunications Policy* 44, no. 8 (2020): 102003.

Tayo, Omolara, Randall Thompson, and Elizabeth Thompson. "Impact of the Digital Divide on Computer Use and Internet Access on the Poor in Nigeria." *Journal of Education and Learning* 5, no. 1 (2016): 1–6.

Telukdarie, Arnesh, and Aviksha Mungar. "The Impact of Digital Financial Technology on Accelerating Financial Inclusion in Developing Economies." *Procedia Computer Science* 217 (2023): 670–78.

Timilsina, Govinda R. "Financing Climate Change Adaptation: International Initiatives." *Sustainability* 13, no. 12 (2021): 6515.

Tinmaz, Hasan, Mina Fanea-Ivanovici, and Hasnan Baber. "A Snapshot of Digital Literacy." *Library Hi Tech News* 40, no. 1 (2023): 20–23.

Torrisi, Rachele. *China's New Personal Information Protection Law (PIPL): Implications for Companies and Human Resources Management*. 2023.

Tranos, Emmanouil. *The Geography of the Internet: Cities, Regions and Internet Infrastructure in Europe*. Edward Elgar Publishing, 2013.

Triolo, Paul, Kevin Allison, Clarise Brown, and Kelsey Broderick. "The Digital Silk Road: Expanding China's Digital Footprint." *Eurasia Group* 8 (2020): 1–13.

Tripathi, Gyan Prakash. *Geopolitics of AI Standardisation and Its Impact on Fundamental Rights*. 2025.

Tritto, Angela, Yujia He, and Victoria Amanda Junaedi. "Governing the Gold Rush into Emerging Markets: A Case Study of Indonesia's Regulatory Responses to the Expansion of Chinese-Backed Online P2P Lending." *Financial Innovation* 6, no. 1 (2020): 51.

Trivedi, Mansi, and Jitendra Kumar Gautam. "Transforming Cross Border Trade with the Advancement of Digital Platform: An Analysis." *Journal of International Economics* 16, no. 1 (2025): 33–44.

Trivedi, Mansi, and Jitendra Kumar Gautam. "Transforming Cross Border Trade with the Advancement of Digital Platform: An Analysis." *Journal of International Economics* 16, no. 1 (2025): 33–44.

Tullis, Christopher. "Public Key Infrastructure: Implementing High-Trust Electronic Signatures." *World Bank Digital Transformation White Paper Series*, 2024.

Tullis, Christopher, Nay Constantine, and Adam Cooper. "Electronic Signatures: Enabling Trusted Digital Transformation." *World Bank Digital Transformation White Paper Series*, 2024.

Turgel, Irina, Larisa Bozhko, and Elizaveta Ulyanova. "'Smart City' concept in Digital Economics: Practice of Russia and Kazakhstan." *International Journal of Economic Policy in Emerging Economies* 16, nos. 2–4 (2022): 139–57.

Twum, Angelina Kissiwaa, Jijian Zhang, Xuhui Ding, and Joana Cobbinah. "Advancing Renewable Energy Strategies towards Sustainable Development Goal 13: Insights from Belt and Road Initiative (BRI) Countries." *Environment, Development and Sustainability*, 2024, 1–32.

Udeagha, Maxwell Chukwudi, and Edwin Muchapondwa. "Striving for the United Nations (UN) Sustainable Development Goals (SDGs) in BRICS Economies: The Role of Green Finance, Fintech, and Natural Resource Rent." *Sustainable Development* 31, no. 5 (2023): 3657–72.

Udoh, Victoria, and David Ademola Olajide. "Data Protection in Nigeria: A Review of the Nigerian Data Protection Regulation 2019 and the Need for Nigeria to Sign the African Convention on Data Protection." *Available at SSRN 3766819*, 2021.

Ugarte, Ricardo E., and Stephanie Wu. "International Arbitration in China: 2023 in Review." *Journal of International Arbitration* 41, no. 5 (2024).

Ullah, Maseeh, Muhammad Abbas Jehan, and Muhammad Haris. "Towards a Digital Silk Road: The Role of China's Digital Trade Provisions in Shaping Global Economic Corridor." *Journal for Current Sign* 3, no. 2 (2025): 365–78.

Veitch, Scott. "Duty Free." In *Law, Obligation, Community*. Routledge, 2018.

Venkateswaran, PK. "Dispute Resolution Mechanisms in International Trade Law: A Comparative Analysis." *Anusandhanvallari*, 2025, 1255–63.

Verri, Barbara. "The Chinese Frontiers of Data Protection: The Personal Information Protection Law (PIPL)." In *Quo Vadis, Sovereignty? New Conceptual and Regulatory Boundaries in the Age of Digital China*. Springer, 2023.

Veselovsky, Mikhail Yakovlevich, Tatiana Vitalievna Pogodina, Raisa Vasilyevna Ilyukhina, Tatyana Anatolyevna Sigunova, and Nina Fedorovna Kuzovleva. "Financial and Economic Mechanisms of Promoting Innovative Activity in the Context of the Digital Economy Formation." *Entrepreneurship and Sustainability Issues* 5, no. 3 (2018): 672–81.

Vines, David. "The BRI and RCEP: Ensuring Cooperation in the Liberalisation of Trade in Asia." *Economic and Political Studies* 6, no. 3 (2018): 338–48.

Vinnyk, Oksana M., Dmytro V. Zadykhaylo, Olena M. Honcharenko, Olga V. Shapovalova, and Nino B. Patsuriia. "Economic and Legal Policy of the State in the Field of Digital Economy." *International Journal of Criminology and Sociology* 10, no. 1 (2021): 383–92.

Vladisavljev, Stefan. *China's' Digital Silk Road'Enters the Western Balkans*. Association for International Affairs, 2021.

Voss, W. Gregory. "Cross-Border Data Flows, the GDPR, and Data Governance." *Wash. Int'l LJ* 29 (2019): 485.

Wachter, Sandra. "Limitations and Loopholes in the EU AI Act and AI Liability Directives: What This Means for the European Union, the United States, and Beyond." *Yale JL & Tech.* 26 (2023): 671.

Waincymer, Jeffrey. *Procedure and Evidence in International Arbitration*. 2012.

Walton, Nigel. "Digital Platforms as Entrepreneurial Ecosystems and Drivers of Born-Global SMEs in Emerging Economies." In *International Entrepreneurship in Emerging Markets*. Routledge, 2022.

Walz, Axel, and Kay Firth-Butterfield. "Implementing Ethics into Artificial Intelligence: A Contribution, from a Legal Perspective, to the Development of an AI Governance Regime." *Duke L. & Tech. Rev.* 18 (2019): 176.

Wang, Christoph Nedopil. "China Belt and Road Initiative (BRI) Investment Report 2021." *Green BRI Center, International Institute of Green Finance (IIGF)* 9, no. 5 (2022).

Wang, Faye Fangfei. *Law of Electronic Commercial Transactions: Contemporary Issues in the EU, US and China*. Routledge, 2014.

Wang, Guansu, Zhihong Huang, Dalin Li, and Jinyan Liao. "Analysis of ASEAN Water Resource Policies in the Context of Belt and Road Initiative: A Perspective on Sustainable Development Goal 6 (SDG6)." 2023, 119–37.

Wang, Heng. "China's Approach to the Belt and Road Initiative: Scope, Character and Sustainability." *Journal of International Economic Law* 22, no. 1 (2019): 29–55.

Wang, Hongying. "The New Development Bank and the Asian Infrastructure Investment Bank: China's Ambiguous Approach to Global Financial Governance." *Development and Change* 50, no. 1 (2019): 221–44.

Wang, Michael, Paul Childerhouse, and Ahmad Abareshi. "Global Logistics and Supply Chain Integration in the Digital Era: A Focus on China's Belt and Road Initiative." *Journal of International Logistics and Trade* 22, no. 2 (2024): 58–79.

Wang, Ruirui, Md Qamruzzaman, and Salma Karim. "Unveiling the Power of Education, Political Stability and ICT in Shaping Technological Innovation in BRI Nations." *Heliyon* 10, no. 9 (2024).

Wang, Shumin, Qianyu Li, and Muhammad Bilawal Khaskheli. "Management Economic Systems and Governance to Reduce Potential Risks in Digital Silk Road Investments: Legal Cooperation between Hainan Free Trade Port and Ethiopia." *Systems* 12, no. 8 (2024): 305.

Wang, Wei, and Lin Li. "Digital Payment, Money Market Fund and Investment Behavior." *Pacific-Basin Finance Journal* 85 (2024): 102348.

Wang, Wenfang, Xinrui Gao, and Linman Zheng. "Can E-CNY Pilot Policy Promote Green Innovation? Empirical Analysis Based on Data from Chinese Cities." *Energy & Environment*, 2026, 0958305X261431129.

Wang, Yebin, Huiyu Gao, and Haijun Wang. "The Digital Silk Road and Trade Growth–A Quasi-Natural Experiment Based on Silk Road E-Commerce." *Research in International Business and Finance* 67 (2024): 102140.

Wang, Yidan, and Yidan Wang. *Education in a Changing World: Flexibility, Skills, and Employability*. Vol. 69104. World Bank Washington, 2012.

Wei, Chunyang, and Qinjie Shen. "Strengthening ASEAN-Guangxi Trade Relations: Enhancing Regional Integration and Industrial Collaboration." *American Journal of Business Science Philosophy*, 2025, 150–68.

Wei, Houkai, Meng Nian, and Le Li. "China's Strategies and Policies for Regional Development during the Period of the 14th Five-Year Plan." *Chinese Journal of Urban and Environmental Studies* 8, no. 02 (2020): 2050008.

Wei, Zeng. "China's Innovative Dispute Resolution under the" Belt and Road" Initiative." *Public Health Policy and Laws Journal* 10, no. 1 (2024): 153–68.

Weidemaier, W. Mark C. "Sovereign Immunity and Sovereign Debt." *U. Ill. L. Rev.*, 2014, 67.

Wentao, Wang. "Modern Digital Technology in China's Insurance Industry." *Вестник Томского Государственного Университета. Экономика*, no. 55 (2021): 148–65.

Williams, Robert D. *International Law with Chinese Characteristics: Beijing and the" Rules-Based" Global Order*. Brookings Institution, 2020.

Winter, Tim. "Geocultural Power and the Digital Silk Roads." *Environment and Planning D: Society and Space* 40, no. 5 (2022): 923–40.

Wirjo, Andre, Vásquez Callo Müller, María del Carmen, Divya Sangaraju, Lui Jiquan Crystal, and Shawn Siah. "Assessment of Capacity Building Needs to Support WTO Negotiation on Trade Related Aspects of E-Commerce." In *Assessment of Capacity Building Needs to Support WTO Negotiation on Trade Related Aspects of E-Commerce*. Singapore: Asia-Pacific Economic Cooperation Secretariat, 2020.

Wolff, Josephine, and Nicole Atallah. "Early GDPR Penalties: Analysis of Implementation and Fines through May 2020." *Journal of Information Policy* 11 (2021): 63–103.

Wu, Terry, and Doren Chadee. "Comprehensive and Progressive Agreement for Trans-Pacific Partnership (CPTPP): Implications for the Asia-Pacific Region." In *International Business in the New Asia-Pacific: Strategies, Opportunities and Threats*. Springer, 2022.

Wu, Xiaoping, and Muhammad Bilawal Khaskheli. "Systems Thinking of Marine Policies in Promoting Environmental Law, Sustainability, and Digital Technologies: Social Challenges in Belt and Road Initiative Countries." *Systems* 12, no. 10 (2024): 400.

Wu, Xiaoping, and Muhammad Bilawal Khaskheli. "Systems Thinking of Marine Policies in Promoting Environmental Law, Sustainability, and Digital Technologies: Social Challenges in Belt and Road Initiative Countries." *Systems* 12, no. 10 (2024): 400.

Xiaobin, Wang, Fuxi Wu, Majed Alharthi, Syed Muhammad Faraz Raza, and Olayan Albalawi. "Natural Resources, Trade and Fintech in the Era of Digitalization: A Study of Economies Involved in Belt and Road Initiative." *Resources Policy* 93 (2024): 105082.

Xiaoyu, WANG. "High-Quality Development in China-Arab Digital Economy Cooperation: Opportunities, Challenges and Prospect." *International Relations* 12, no. 4 (2024): 147–55.

Xing, Lirong, Chuanxiang Cao, and Ehsan Elahi. "Advancing Coupling Coordination: Bridging China's Digital Economy and Green Agriculture for Sustainable Rural Development." *Information Technology for Development* 31, no. 4 (2025): 1017–38.

Xiong, Ping, and Roman Tomasic. "Soft Law, State-Owned Enterprises and Dispute Resolution on PRC's Belt and Road-towards an Emerging Legal Order." *Hong Kong LJ* 49 (2019): 1025.

Xu, Jiaqi, Shengxiang She, and Wen Liu. "Role of Digitalization in Environment, Social and Governance, and Sustainability: Review-Based Study for Implications." *Frontiers in Psychology* 13 (2022): 961057.

Xu, Zhao, Muhammad Adeel Afzal, Jamil Afzal, and Md Rasidul Islam. "China-Pakistan Cultural Exchanges and Cooperation under Belt & Road Initiative." *Siazga Research Journal* 2, no. 3 (2023): 186–91.

Xu, Zhao, Maria Qayum, Jamil Afzal, and Muhammad Aslam. "Availability and Access to Livelihood Capital Assets for Development of Sustainable Livelihood Strategies of Fishermen: A Case Study of Manchar Lake Pakistan." *Heliyon* 9, no. 12 (2023).

Yadav, Vikrant Sopan, and Abhijeet Dhere. "AI Agents and Legal Intricacies: A Comprehensive Literature Review." 2025, 28–45.

Yang, Jun. "An Overview of the Chinese 'Personal Information Protection Law.'" *Pin Code* 10, no. 1 (2022): 8–13.

Yang, Lijuan. "Effects of ISO Technical Standards on China's Digital Exports." *Applied Economics Letters*, 2025, 1–6.

Yang, Yue. *Digital Economy and the Sustainable Development of ASEAN and China*. Vol. 9. World Scientific, 2022.

Yanney, Anita Ama Sakumaa. "Cross-Border Financial Regulation and Its Influence on Multinational Business Operations, Tax Structures and Investment Flows." *World Journal of Advanced Research and Reviews* 26, no. 3 (2025): 597–620.

Yanyan, Cao, and Nabeel Mahdi Althabhawi. "China's Online Dispute Resolution Mechanism for Cross-Border E-Commerce: Challenges and Solutions." *Pakistan Journal of Life & Social Sciences* 22, no. 2 (2024).

Yean, Tham Siew. "Development of E-Commerce in Malaysia." *E-Commerce, Competition & ASEAN Economic Integration*, 2019, 169–92.

Yi-Chen, Zhang. "China's Personal Information Protection Law (PIPL) 2021: An Analysis." *Modern Jurisprudence* 3, no. 3 (2025).

You, Chuanman, and Qingxiu Bu. "Transformative Digital Economy, Responsive Regulatory Innovation and Contingent Network Effects: The Anatomy of E-Commerce Law in China." *European Business Law Review* 31, no. 4 (2020).

Yu, Jianping, Shoukat Iqbal Khattak, and Manzoor Ahmad. "Enhancing Sustainable Development through Digital Economy and Natural Resource Management in One Belt One Road Countries." *Technology in Society* 81 (2025): 102812.

Yun, Heylyung. "China's Data Sovereignty and Security: Implications for Global Digital Borders and Governance." *Chinese Political Science Review* 10, no. 2 (2025): 178–203.

Zadi, Kashif Imran, Usman Hameed, and Sunbal Islam Chaudhary. "China International Commercial Court (CICC) in the Context of Commercial Disputes under Belt and Road Initiative: Organizational Structure, Rules and Jurisdiction." *Pakistan Languages and Humanities Review* 5, no. 2 (2021): 601–12.

Zakharova, Kseniia. "Competitive Strategies in Sustainable Development Ecosystems: Challenges and Opportunities." *Economics, Finance and Management Review*, no. 2 (22) (2025): 16–28.

Zeng, Li, and Wee-Yeap Lau. "The Digital Yuan in the Shadow of Dollar Hegemony: Rethinking Asia's Financial Autonomy amid US-China Tensions." *Asia and the Global Economy* 5, no. 2 (2025): 100126.

Zenglein, Max J., and Anna Holzmann. "Evolving Made in China 2025." *MERICS Papers on China* 8 (2019): 78.

Zhang, Chuhan, and Xiuting Li. "Unveiling the Technological Dynamics of Banking Systems: A Network Analysis of Chinese and Global Banking Innovation." *Systems* 13, no. 5 (2025): 323.

Zhang, Chunling, and Yumei Xu. "Institutional Innovation Essence and Knowledge Innovation Goal of Intellectual Property Law in the Big Data Era." *Journal of Innovation & Knowledge* 8, no. 4 (2023): 100417.

Zhang, Gongtao, and MN Ravishankar. "Exploring Vendor Capabilities in the Cloud Environment: A Case Study of Alibaba Cloud Computing." *Information & Management* 56, no. 3 (2019): 343–55.

Zhang, Jiangang. "The Development Strategy and Practice Path of Chinese Industrial Modernization from the Perspective of Technological Revolution." *China Political Economy* 8, no. 1 (2025): 45–62.

Zhang, Jinzhu, Wenqi Zhao, Baodong Cheng, et al. "The Impact of Digital Economy on the Economic Growth and the Development Strategies in the Post-COVID-19 Era: Evidence from Countries along the 'Belt and Road.'" *Frontiers in Public Health* 10 (2022): 856142.

Zhang, Kun-min, and Zong-guo Wen. "Review and Challenges of Policies of Environmental Protection and Sustainable Development in China." *Journal of Environmental Management* 88, no. 4 (2008): 1249–61.

Zhang, Xiaoyan, Jinbao Li, Dong Xiang, and Andrew C. Worthington. "Digitalization, Financial Inclusion, and Small and Medium-Sized Enterprise Financing: Evidence from China." *Economic Modelling* 126 (2023): 106410.

Zhang, Yaolin. "Developing Cross-Border Blockchain Financial Transactions under the Belt and Road Initiative." *The Chinese Journal of Comparative Law* 8, no. 1 (2020): 143–76.

Zhang, Yizhi, and Muhammad Bilawal Khaskheli. "The Role of Digital Technologies in Advancing Sustainable Economic Development into Intersections of Policy, Law, Environmental Economics, and a Comparative Study of China, the EU, and the USA." *Sustainability* 17, no. 19 (2025): 8666.

Zhang, Yuwen. "From Weixin to WeChat: Analysing the Expansion Strategies of a Chinese Social Media Platform." In *Digital Platforms and the Global South*. Routledge, 2023.

Zhao, Bo, and Yang Feng. "Mapping the Development of China's Data Protection Law: Major Actors, Core Values, and Shifting Power Relations." *Computer Law & Security Review* 40 (2021): 105498.

Zhao, Huirong. "China and Belarus' High-Quality Collaboration in the Belt and Road Initiative: Achievements, Challenges, and Prospects." *Chinese Journal of Slavic Studies*, 2025.

Zhao, Sainan, Yichao Zhang, Huma Iftikhar, Atta Ullah, Jie Mao, and Tiantian Wang. "Dynamic Influence of Digital and Technological Advancement on Sustainable Economic Growth in Belt and Road Initiative (BRI) Countries." *Sustainability* 14, no. 23 (2022): 15782.

Zhao, Xiaoyin, Xi Meng, and Bingxin Wang. "Advancing Railway Systems with Next-Generation 5G Connectivity." 2024, 357–62.

Zhao, Yun, and Hui Chen. "Enhancing Access to Digital Justice: Digital Governance of Dispute Resolution and Dispute Prevention in Online Commercial Activities." *Journal of International Dispute Settlement* 15, no. 2 (2024): 273–304.

Zheng, Jie. *Online Resolution of E-Commerce Disputes*. Springer, 2020.

Zheng, Weidi. "Digital Vines: Mapping China's Network of Global Platform Ecosystems." *Information, Communication & Society* 28, no. 14 (2025): 2563–79.

Zhixie, Rong, Wang Jie, and She Zhendan. "Impact of the Digital Economy on Technical Regulations and Standardization in the Context of the Belt and Road Initiative." *Роль Технического Регулирования и Стандартизации в Эпоху Цифровой Экономики.—Екатеринбург, 2023*, 2023, 444–52.

Zhong, Ma, Majid Ali, Khan Faqir, et al. "China Pakistan Economic Corridor Digital Transformation." *Frontiers in Psychology* 13 (2022): 887848.

Zhou, Morgana Mo, Zhiyan Qu, Jinhan Wan, Bo Wen, Yaxing Yao, and Zhicong Lu. "Understanding Chinese Internet Users' Perceptions of, and Online Platforms' Compliance with, the Personal Information Protection Law (PIPL)." *Proceedings of the ACM on Human-Computer Interaction* 8, no. CSCW1 (2024): 1–26.

Zhu, Lijun. "The Influence of Digital Transformation on Chinese Firms' Outward Foreign Direct Investment." *Finance Research Letters* 72 (2025): 106567.

Zhu, Xiaoxiao. *The Architecture of the Belt and Road Initiative-Feasibility Study on Sustainable Development of Free Trade Zone Made by BRI*. 2022.

Zhu, Yuan. *Bridging the Gap: Strategies and Roles of Chinese Fintech Entrepreneurs and Startups in Sub-Sahara African Markets*. 2025.

Zinovieva, Vera, Mikhail Shchelokov, and Evgeny Litvinovsky. "Legal Issues of Protection of Personal Data: Cases of Transport Data Leaks." *Transportation Research Procedia* 68 (2023): 461–67.

Zreik, Mohamad. "The Belt and Road Initiative: Vision, Objectives, and Complexities." In *Qatar's Role in China's Belt and Road Initiative: Bridging Two Economic Titans*. Springer, 2025.

Zuo, Liwen, and Yuheng Ren. "How Renewable Energy Consumption and Digitalization Contribute to Environmental Sustainability: Evidence from One Belt One Road Countries." *Journal of Environmental Management* 380 (2025): 124379.

Ли, Жун, and Екатерина Геннадьевна Господарик. "Platform Economy Development in SCO Countries: Current Status, Regional Differences, and Key Drivers." *Веснік Брэсцкага Ўніверсітэта. Серыя 2. Гісторыя. Эканоміка. Права*, no. 2 (2025): 90–96.

Сембаева, ЖС. "Emerging Green and Digital Sustainable Markets in Central Asia: A Comparative Analysis of Kazakhstan and Uzbekistan Within China's Bri Framework." *Известия. Серия: Международные Отношения и Регионоведение* 61, no. 3 (2025).

이지은. *Study on Legal Consideration of E-Contracts in International Digital Trade*. 2023.

MIX
Papier aus verantwortungsvollen Quellen
Paper from responsible sources
FSC® C105338

If you have any concerns about our products,
you can contact us on
ProductSafety@springernature.com

In case Publisher is established outside the EU,
the EU authorized representative is:
Springer Nature Customer Service Center GmbH
Europaplatz 3, 69115 Heidelberg, Germany

Printed by Libri Plureos GmbH
in Hamburg, Germany